To the memory of my father Gad Alon
and of Dorit Markovich

THE MAKING OF JORDAN

Tribes, Colonialism and the Modern State

Yoav Alon

I.B. TAURIS

LONDON · NEW YORK

Published in 2007 by I.B.Tauris & Co Ltd
6 Salem Road, London W2 4BU
175 Fifth Avenue, New York NY 10010
www.ibtauris.com

In the United States of America and Canada distributed by Palgrave Macmillan
a division of St. Martin's Press, 175 Fifth Avenue, New York NY 10010

Library of Modern Middle East Studies 61

ISBN 978 1 84511 138 0

A full CIP record for this book is available from the British Library
A full CIP record is available from the Library of Congress

Library of Congress Catalog Card Number: available

Printed and bound in India by Replika Press Pvt. Ltd
From camera-ready copy supplied by the author

CONTENTS

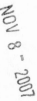

PREFACE

In May 1998, only a few weeks into my first research trip in Jordan, I was summoned to the office of a high-ranking official in the Ministry of the Interior, overlooking al-Dakhiliyya Square in Amman. Having received a copy of the draft of my MA thesis on shaykh Mithqal al-Fayiz of the Bani Sakhr tribes and himself being the son of another prominent shaykh from the days of the mandate who appeared in my thesis, he invited me to discuss several points. What began as a friendly meeting, strictly adhering to the customs of the famous Jordanian hospitality, turned into something completely different. I gradually realised that I was trapped. The shaykh's son objected to several points concerning his father. In particular, he objected to my description of his relations with shaykh Mithqal and the impression that Mithqal was more powerful and influential than his father. This impression was the result of a long quotation from an intelligence report written in the early 1930s.

As the atmosphere got more and more tense, my host suddenly threw another unexpected element into the debate. He rose from his chair behind his desk, grabbed a newspaper from his briefcase and opened it. To my sheer amazement and creeping fear I now learned that on that very morning, and without my prior knowledge, the Jordanian newspaper *Al-Aswaq* had published the first article of a three-part series reviewing my thesis. The headline, spread over an entire broadsheet page, read: "Mithqal bin Fayiz in an MA Thesis of a Researcher from Oxford." Before I was able to digest what I had just discovered, the official expressed his fear that what he saw as a disgrace for his father's historical name and reputation would be made public with the appearance of the remaining two parts of the review. By now outraged and exasperated, he raised his voice and threatened to sue me for libel. The issue here went beyond the writing of history. I realised that my host's good name and that of his entire family and tribe in the present were at stake.

What followed was something of an anticlimax. In retrospect, it also resembled the way conflicts had been solved in Jordan for generations, a subject that features prominently in this book. I explained to my host that my writing was solely based on the historical records at my disposal, that what he had read was still a draft, and that I had never intended to publish it. I promised to ask the author of the review to make sure that he would not mention the sensitive historical episode in the remaining publications. I also offered to add the family's version to my thesis in its submitted form. For his part, my host invited me to a dinner party in his house, during which, he promised, he would provide me with historical documents and introduce me to elders from his tribe who had known his father. This meeting was intended to correct my understanding and help me better appreciate his father's greatness. This compromise suited both sides and we parted in a friendly manner. My relief though was surely the greater. He did keep his word and the party took place, but unfortunately I missed it since I was out of the country.

On leaving the Ministry of the Interior I rushed to buy the newspaper and immediately read the article. I called the author and begged him not to jeopardise my research by causing an uproar. He assured me that he had never had any intention of doing so. I was still very tense and worried about the prospects of my work in Jordan. To test my nerves and push them to their limits, that day also corresponded with Israel's 50th anniversary and the more or less simultaneous commemoration of the Palestinian *Nakba*. I could feel the tension in the air, or perhaps I just imagined it. Fortunately, I had prearranged to spend the weekend with my British archaeologist friends digging in Pella (Tabqat Fahl) in the Jordan Valley. As I was leaving Amman on the bus to the Valley, I could not resist the feeling that I was running away, seeking temporary refuge in a different *dira* (tribal territory), fleeing angry tribesmen as had happened so often in the history of the region and its tribes. That night in Pella we sat on the roof of the archaeologists' building. As we watched the fireworks over Bet Sh^can (Bisan) celebrating Israel's independence, I reflected on the day's events.

I began to realise the complexities of writing on Jordan's tribes. Not unlike Andrew Shryock and his interlocutors' experience while trying to compose the history of the Balqa' tribes, I realised that I might have got myself caught in an explosive maze of conflicting versions, sensitivities and rivalries between tribes and shaykhs. What is more, although these narratives are rooted in history, they are very much alive and relevant to the present. I also finally understood the frequent reaction I got from many Jordanians when I told them about my research subject. They remarked that it was a very difficult topic to write about. The paucity of tribal histories, the difficulties faced by the historian of the ^cAdwan featured in Shryock's book, and the controversy that accompanies each publication on tribal affairs by Dr. Ahmad ^cUwaydi al-^cAbbadi (the main protagonist of Shryock's book and the most prolific scholar on the subject), all corroborate this impression.

This lengthy recounting of my personal experience, or baptism of fire (as it were) into the subject of the book is meant by way of a clarification of one or two points I wish to make, not least for the Jordanian readership. My intention with this book was to write the history of Jordan during the formative years of the Emirate under British mandate, and to explore the unique way in which the territory's tribes were integrated into the modern state structure. As such it is not a tribal history *per se*. Unlike books written in Jordan on specific tribes, or on all of them, this work is not a genealogical study (*Ansab*). While studying the tribes I was interested in their response to the establishment of the Emirate of Transjordan, their role in state-building and the ways in which they were affected by it. My understanding is derived from the historical records I managed to trace, as well as the theoretical literature, anthropological and otherwise. I am aware that I did not manage to write about all the Jordanian tribes and their shaykhs, and missed out many aspects of their history which were less relevant for my study. Perhaps some readers will feel their families and tribes have been left out altogether, or did not get the attention they deserve. I nonetheless hope that they will appreciate my efforts to study this 'difficult' topic. I also hope that they will take my word that my historical pursuits are derived from a purely scholarly interest. My ultimate satisfaction would derive from local responses that asserted that a scholar rooted in a foreign (although neighbouring) culture managed to make sense of Jordanian tribal culture and history.

* * *

In pursuing the project many individuals and institutions have given me assistance and I owe them an immense debt of gratitude. The book originates from a doctoral thesis written in Oxford. Eugene Rogan was a critical and demanding supervisor and at the same time supportive and encouraging. His unique knowledge of Jordanian history made his criticism extremely constructive. I am grateful to Judith Brown, for both her help in facilitating funding and for helping me to see Jordan within the wider context of British colonialism (which was absent from my original intent). Paul Dresch and Ahmed Al-Shahi's rigorous class on the anthropology of the Middle East opened a new world for me and enriched my understanding of the region.

The Middle East Centre at St Antony's College, Oxford, has provided me with an academic home during my time of study and remains so today. Its well known strength in 'Jordanian studies' made it the perfect place for thinking, researching and writing about the subject of this book. I learned a lot from the expertise of Philip Robins and Avi Shlaim, as well as from Derek Hopwood and Nadim Shehadi. James Onley has been a friend and colleague, with whose work my own field of interest partly overlaps. I owe particular thanks to Clare Brown, the archivist of the Private Papers Collection, who was both a friend and a guide to the British officials' writings. The current archivist Debbie Usher has been extremely helpful, as were Diane Ring and Mastan Ebtehaj. I owe much to Elizabeth Anderson for her friendship and sense of humour.

Prior to Oxford I enjoyed excellent teaching from the faculty of the Department of Middle Eastern and African History at Tel Aviv University. I have returned to the department as a lecturer and continued to benefit from this stimulating environment while working on this book. In particular I would like to mention Israel Gershoni, Ehud Toledano, Mottie Tamarkin and David Menashri. Prof Menashri and Yekutiel Gershoni facilitated my post-doc fellowship and guided me in my early years in the department, making the transformation from student to teacher smoother. Joseph Kostiner, who introduced me to the fascinating world of tribal societies in the Middle East, and Asher Susser, a leading authority on Jordan, have consistently read my work, offering excellent comments that have undoubtedly improved my writing. I cherish their support and friendship. I am grateful to Eyal Zisser, the department chair, for assisting the financing of the book's editing as well as for Anat Grosspaise and Anat

Gross. Also in Israel, Amatzia Baram has been a source of inspiration and constant encouragement. His fascinating studies on tribalism in Iraq are a source for envy.

Several bodies helped to finance my studies at Oxford and my research in the Middle East. I am grateful to the Sherman Foundation (UK), the Avi Fellowship (Switzerland) and the Anglo-Jewish Association for generously supporting my study. I was fortunate to receive an ORS award from the British government. The Beit Fund in the Faculty of Modern History financed my fieldwork in Jordan and awarded me the Robert Herbert Memorial Prize for colonial history. I would like to thank the former Warden of St Antony's College, Sir Marrack Goulding, for awarding me a grant from the Israeli Students Fund.

Several individuals read earlier versions of the work, or parts thereof, and offered valuable comments. I would like to thank Saᶜd Abu Diyya, Tancred Bradshow, Toby Dodge, Khalid Fahmy, Michael Fischbach, Asima Ghazi-Bouillon, Jan Goldberg, Joseph Kostiner, Norman Lewis, Wm. Roger Louis, Nasser Mirza, Niall Ó Murchú, Amos Nadan, Michael Reimer, Philip Robins, Relli Shechter, Avi Shlaim, Andrew Shryock, Asher Susser, Kathryn Tidrick and Mary Wilson. I have learned a lot from my discussions and correspondence with Norman Lewis and Andrew Shryock and I am grateful for both of them for their time and willingness to share their vast knowledge on tribal Jordan with me. I also thank the three anonymous readers of the original manuscript for their most helpful suggestions. Ursula Wokoek has been my most critical reader and a friend.

I was always amazed by the willingness of many Jordanians to engage with my project, to offer help, friendship and generous hospitality. I would mention but a few. HRH Prince Hasan bin Talal and HRH Princess Basma took a sympathetic interest in my project and offered me assistance. At the University of Jordan I am indebted to the director and members of staff of the Centre for Strategic Studies, the Centre for Documentation and Manuscripts, and the library. At the National Library I was fortunate to have been welcomed by the Deputy Director, Muhammad Yunis al-ᶜAbbadi. Abu Samer, being a historian and a tribesman himself, took great interest in my research and offered much help. I also enjoyed the help and friendship of many other members of staff. I would also like to thank the staff of ACOR, the British Institute for Archaeology and History and the German Protestant Institute.

In Israel I would like to thank the members of staff at the Israeli State Archives, the Hagana Archives, the National Library, the Dayan Centre and the Central Zionist Archives, Yoram Mayorek and Ilana Oz in particular. I also enjoyed working at the National Archives in London, the Imperial War Museum and the Bodleian Library in Oxford.

I was fortunate to enjoy the friendship, affection and support of many friends. In their different ways they all contributed to this project: Ma'mun ᶜAbd al-Qadir, Eva Achladi, ᶜAziz and Muhammad ᶜAjarma, Manos Antoninis, Idan Barir, Eitan Bar-Yosef, Yuval Dagan, Assaf David, Yaron Deckel, Asima Ghazi-Bouillon, Dima Gladkov, Dania Greenberg, Harel Horev, Clive Jones, Michael Jungreis, Romi Kaplan, Taekyoon Kim, the Kuznitzki family, Matteo Legrenzi, Efrat Lev, Limor Lidsky, Tilman Ludke, Nadia Masid, Salim Marᶜi, the Mileikowsky family, Khaled

Muhammad, Shany&Shany Payes-Kaminer, the Pick family, the Rabfogel family, Ayelet Rosen, Sioned Rowlands, Shlomit Sarfatti, Anya Shternshis, Batia Sigal, the Tamarkin family, Idit Toledano, Emma Westney, Peter Wien, Stacey and Vikash Yadav and Avital Zalmanovitch. Four close friends in particular deserve mention for reading earlier drafts of this work, sharpening the prose, and helping me to develop my ideas. Their input forms a large part of this book. For their time, care and patience I am indebted to Markus Bouillon, Gordon Peake, Kevin Rosser and Noga Tal. Guy Tourlamain carefully and sympathetically edited the manuscript, pushing me to clarify some of my arguments, challenging others, and making this work more readable that it might otherwise have been. I.B. Tauris' commission editor, Abigail Fielding-Smith, made the sometimes strenuous process of publication much more agreeable. I am grateful for her for supporting the project as well as for her patience and encouragement. Orna Zafrir-Reuven carefully and patiently drew the maps. I also thank Adi Hasid for formatting the manuscript and preparing it for publication, as well as Ayelet Rosen and Nimrod Ram who laboured on the index. The last drafts of the book were written in Café Sukar in Tel Aviv. I am grateful to the staff of the café, and especially to the lovely Sharon and Shlomit, for making my hard work enjoyable.

Finally, I want to acknowledge my gratitude and love for two families. Since I first embarked on this project I have been privileged to enjoy the unlimited generosity and devotion of Jean and Ken Marks. I am well aware that I will never be able to repay the immense debt I owe them. My mother, Liora Alon's support for me in the last few years knew no limits. I also owe a great debt for the support and love of my brother Uri and his wife Liat, and my sister Hilla. Finally, my late father, Gad, sowed the seeds of my academic undertaking. Although we lost him many years ago, his intellectual and personal legacy remains a prime influence on me and is manifested in many ways, most of which I am probably not even aware of. It is in commemoration of my father and of my late great friend Dorit Markovich that I dedicate this book.

MAPS

Map 1: Transjordan

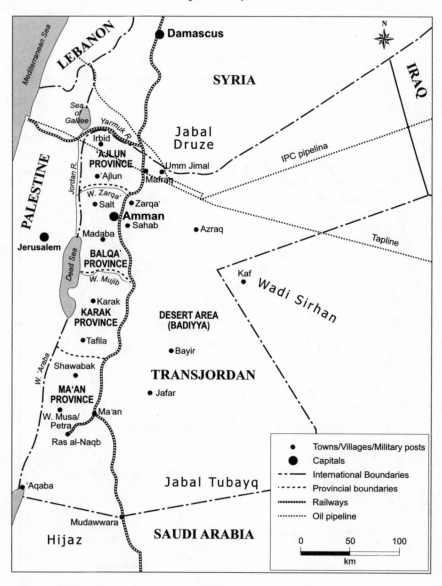

A Note on the Tribal Maps

These maps represent an attempt to give a general idea of the locations of the tribes during the time of the Emirate. They were drawn from a variety of sources, often conflicting, and are provided here only to guide the readers and allow them to follow the different names of tribal groupings, their shifting alliances and their approximate regions. As far as nomadic tribes are concerned, the locations on the map indicate their summer camps. As with many 'things tribal,' areas of influence are fuzzy, changing according to the existing balance of power among neighbouring tribal groups, the climatic conditions, the season or the intervention of state authorities. In the desert, tribal areas often overlap rather than fit within bounded confines.

Map 2: Tribes and Districts in the ʿAjlun Province

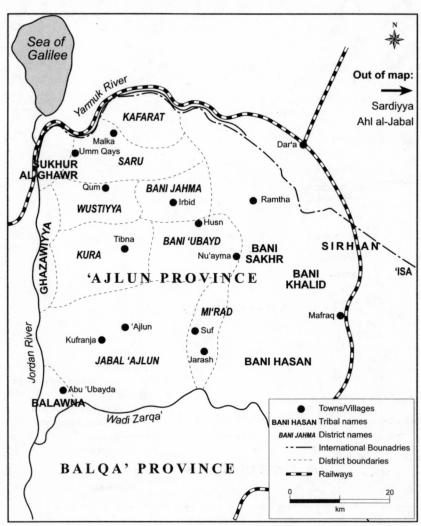

Map 3: Tribes in the Balqa', Karak and Maʿan Provinces

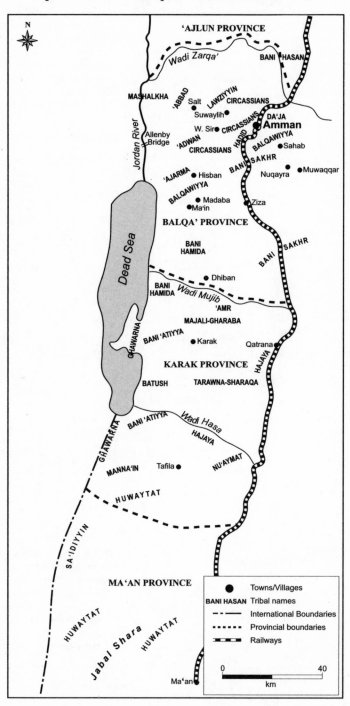

INTRODUCTION:
THE STUDY OF STATE, TRIBE AND
COLONIAL RULE IN JORDAN

Tribes and the Hashemite Kingdom of Jordan

Eighty five years after its establishment as a separate, and later independent, polity, the Hashemite Kingdom of Jordan still attracts relatively little scholarly attention compared to neighbouring countries. Although recently there has been growing interest in the country, the history of its formative years under the British mandate and especially the social history of this period are still underdeveloped.

It is this striking paucity in scholarly writings that makes Jordan susceptible to miscomprehension. Thus, when discussing Jordan, it is common for commentators and sometimes even scholars to describe the political and social structure of the Kingdom using a familiar set of clichés. One is the division between Bedouin and Palestinian citizens. Another is the assertion that the Bedouin tribes are loyal supporters of the ruling Hashemite family. The notion that tribal loyalty can be taken for granted, that Bedouin or tribespeople are natural supporters of the Hashemite regime, is too simplistic. Loyalty is a difficult concept to measure and an unscientific means to explain political behaviour. Yet, there is a grain of truth in these intuitive assumptions, as tribes did and still do form the regime's backbone of support. But contrary to conventional wisdom, there is nothing intrinsic to the Jordanian Bedouin that makes them loyal to the monarchy and there is nothing inherently 'tribal' or 'Bedouin' in such political behaviour.

Rather than a natural inclination, the support lent by tribes to the ruling family must be seen as the result of a specific historical process of state-building during the formative years of the British mandate. It allowed for the integration of the tribes into the modern state and their acceptance of the political order. In the course of this process, tribal people developed a clear stake in the survival of the Jordanian state. Uniquely, this process of integration was achieved with a relatively low level of violence or coercion. It also allowed tribes to carve out a political role for themselves within the framework of the modern state. The Jordanian case therefore stands in marked contrast to the experiences of state-formation in other parts of the Middle East, where

1

the common result was the coercive subjugation of the tribes accompanied by their marginalisation in society. The success of the state-building project has been one of the main reasons for the stability and resilience of the Jordanian state and Hashemite regime. Nevertheless, the origin of the relationship between the tribes and the state has not yet been satisfactorily explored. It forms the subject of the present book.

Tribalism has been a central theme in the development of Jordan. Unlike the other countries of the Fertile Crescent, based on urban elites and cultures, the Hashemite Kingdom explicitly incorporated tribalism into the political order and built on it for its own legitimacy and survival from the outset. Jordan's founding myth goes back to the 1916 Arab Revolt of a coalition of tribes led by the Hashemite family against the rule of the Ottoman Empire. The late monarch, King Husayn bin Talal, took pains to stress his descent from the Quraysh, the tribe of the Prophet Muhammad. Symbolic of the importance of tribalism in the national imagination is the Arab Legion with its Bedouin-like uniform. Moreover, up to the present tribal identities, although significantly modified since the days of the mandate, continue to play a major role in the Kingdom's political, social and cultural life. Recent studies have argued that tribalism is an integral part of the Jordanian national identity and remains a central issue in contemporary Jordan.[1]

To understand the centrality of tribes and their contribution to Jordan's present stability it is necessary to explore the roots of this phenomenon in the state's formative years, namely the mandate period and the reign of Emir (later King) Abdullah bin Husayn. This study offers a historical account of this process from the end of the Ottoman rule in Transjordan in 1918 to the end of the British mandate in 1946. It analyses the structure of the British mandate and the process of tribal integration into the state-in-formation, showing how the creation of a modern state affected the tribes and how they, in turn, contributed to the state's consolidation and influenced its nature.

This line of investigation explains the success of the integration process in Jordan by tracing the unique way in which the state developed. It argues that while gradually consolidating its power, the central government allowed tribal groupings to retain a significant degree of autonomy in their internal affairs. The laissez-faire nature of British rule in Transjordan, which was limited in scope and less intrusive than other colonial regimes in the Middle East, favoured a considerable degree of independent local development. Moreover, tribes themselves and especially their leaders were invited by state authorities to play a role in the process of state-formation. In this way tribes and shaykhs remained formidable actors on the Transjordanian political scene, and were able to exert considerable leverage vis-à-vis state authorities. As a result, tribes were gradually subsumed into the state and the transition from the imperial legacy of the Ottomans to the era of a modern territorial state took place more slowly and with fewer disruptions than elsewhere. On the eve of independence, Transjordan had already acquired many of the traits of a modern nation-state (although notably without a 'nation') while retaining many aspects of the tribal polity that existed before. The outcome of the state-building process is best characterised in terms of a hybrid between a modern state and a tribal confederacy. The foundations laid during the mandate period are one of the keys to understanding the state's resilience and its ability to face the challenges of the post-independence years.

Against all Odds: Artificiality versus Resilience

This book tells the story of a modern state directed and inspired by the British emerging in a tribal, and largely nomadic, society, seen by many as the epitome of tradition. One could be forgiven for assuming that this combination was doomed from the start. On the one hand, Britain imposed a colonial system to safeguard its imperial interests as it attempted to lay the foundations of a modern state. This new polity was modelled on Western principles that had evolved in European thinking since the seventeenth century. In broad terms, this political philosophy envisioned a strong and centralised state enjoying a monopoly on the use of force, and the ability to dictate the rules of the game within clearly demarcated borders. It also cherished some liberal values such as forms of participation and representation in the political process. On the other hand, this British design was applied to an antique society which enjoyed an established culture that had effectively moderated social and political behaviour even before the emergence of Islam in Arabia. Society was organised according to real or mythical kinship lines, and daily life adhered to tribal notions and customs. Among these cherished notions, personal as well as group autonomy was one of the most sought-after ideals. Although never static but rather evolving, this society nevertheless kept what anthropologists term a particular 'state of mind.'[2]

Jordan's origins lie in this improbable combination of foreign and colonial regime together with indigenous Arab tribal society, a combination that common sense suggests would be the recipe for a miserable failure. It also created a problematic image for the Kingdom. Jordan is commonly perceived as an artificial colonial creation. According to this perception, Jordan is mainly an arid piece of land left over after the carving out of Palestine, Syria, Lebanon and Iraq. This 'desert kingdom,' a camping area for sparse nomadic tribes, 'truculent' in their nature, was created to satisfy the personal ambition of an Arab prince who was left after World War One without a territory to rule. At present many of the Kingdom's adversaries use this narrative of its creation to question its *raison d'être*. Jordan's original inhabitants, mainly tribespeople, are dismissed as a minority which clings to the monarchy in order to preserve its privileged position within the state. By suggesting that Jordan is or should become Palestine (or part thereof) both Palestinian nationalists as well as right-wing Zionists unwittingly share an opinion which ironically resembles the old Zionist view of Palestine as "a land without a people for a people without a land."

Although much exaggerated and subjective as a narrative, it is true that "the raw material of statehood," in the words of Philip Robins, was unpromising by objective criteria such as the existence of a power centre, economic surplus to sustain state institutions, defined 'natural' boundaries, previous historical existence as a political unit or a unifying ideology.[3] Nonetheless, Jordan proved a great success in many ways. First, Jordan was one of Britain's most successful colonial projects in the Middle East and elsewhere. Second, state authorities managed to integrate the tribes into the structures of the modern state and turned them into loyal citizens who fully

participated in its political processes. Time and time again tribesmen responded to
the call to defend their king and country. Third, Jordan as a political entity has
enjoyed a remarkable stability and continuity. Despite predictions to the contrary and
successive crises between 1948 and 1971, the Kingdom has survived and its regime
proved to be strong and resilient. Moreover, King Abdullah I not only succeeded in
founding a new state but also established a dynasty which has now been ruling the
country for four generations. In an era in which effective monarchies are seen as a
distant echo of the past, this is without a doubt a remarkable achievement.

Only through a close examination of the different components of the process by
which Jordan was created does it become possible to explain the puzzles presented
here. Thus, one line of inquiry in this present study focuses on the British colonial
administrators, the tribes and Emir Abdullah. The second focus of this book concerns
the outcome of the encounter between these three protagonists, and examines the
development and nature of the emerging state. Some introductory observations will
help set the scene for the interplay between forms of colonial rule, tribalism and
processes of state-formation.

State, Tribe and Mandate

The British mandate in Jordan exemplifies a new era in European involvement in the
Third World which might be termed 'late colonialism.'[4] By the time Britain found
itself responsible for this territory, the political atmosphere both at home and in the
international arena in the aftermath of World War One had become less favourable
to foreign domination in other countries. The moral conviction of Europe's right
to rule indigenous peoples -- so prominent in the nineteenth century -- was now
lacking or evaporating in some circles of the British ruling classes. This was especially
true in the Middle East, after the Allies fought shoulder to shoulder with the Arabs
during the Arab Revolt against the Ottoman Empire. This shared experience, as well
as a sense of moral debt to the Arabs never to be fully fulfilled seemed to dictate a
different relationship between the superpower and the local populations: a form of
government which resembled a kind of partnership rather than sheer domination.
The mandate system sanctioned by the League of Nations resulted from the new
outlook in international affairs. It was seen and designed to be a more progressive,
enlightened, modern and human form of government than traditional forms of
imperialism. It held the promise that an 'advanced' power would keep a younger
nation in temporary custody and train it for independence.[5]

In Transjordan, as elsewhere, the new system's beginning corresponded to the
new philosophy. However, it quickly became clear that the mandate merely gave a
more honourable dressing to an essentially familiar form of foreign rule. Perhaps as
a result of the new circumstances, Britain was slow to develop an appetite for ruling
Transjordan. In fact Britain was only reluctantly drawn to extend its possessions
across the Jordan River. British interests were vague and undefined and several
branches of the British government held different opinions. Persistent pressure from
the government of Palestine, headed by High Commissioner Herbert Samuel, to
incorporate the territory into Palestine was balanced by the objections of the Ministry

of War and a cautious attitude in the Foreign Office.[6] This slow beginning, as well as the changing attitudes towards colonialism, caused British policy in the country to be hesitant and noncommittal for the first few years. Ironically, in many ways this fact explains the success of British rule. Since the British were slow in devising a clear vision for the development of the country, they tended to be less intrusive in the first years and allowed for Arab rule and local political participation. In later years, when British attitudes changed and an interventionist rule was imposed, Britain still allowed for a measure of local autonomy for the tribes in particular. However, as with earlier, more ambitious and aggressive forms of colonialism, late colonialism proved that old habits die hard. Britain clung to its formal rule as late as 1946, long after Iraq and Egypt gained independence (and also after Lebanon and Syria gained independence from France). Even with independence Jordan continued to be part of Britain's informal empire until General John Glubb (Glubb Pasha) was deposed as the commander of the Arab Legion in March 1956.[7]

Notwithstanding some similarities with other foreign-governed areas in the region, British and French alike, Transjordan represents a unique example of British imperial rule; in Transjordan the colonial system worked effectively. British rule did not face any major challenge in the form of an all-out rebellion as it did in Iraq, Egypt and Palestine. It was also a system that required low investment in terms of finance, manpower and military presence. In fact, the British in Jordan implemented the ideal vision -- rarely achieved elsewhere -- of 'Empire on the cheap.' Thus, mandatory Transjordan highlights some of the strengths of the British colonial system.

Britain benefited from the service of officials who served for long periods in Transjordan and grew to know the country and its population well. This was particularly true with regard to the tribes, of which the two commanders of the Arab Legion, Frederick Peake and John Glubb, had expert knowledge. A remarkable degree of stability was also achieved at the most senior administrative level after 1924. Henry Cox acted as the British Representative for the next fifteen years. Alec Kirkbride, who replaced him, served in Transjordan intermittently between 1920 and 1951. These four men shared an intimate knowledge of the country and its people and were familiar with the dominant tribal culture. Thus, their individual as well as collective understanding was important for devising policies and implementing them. Thanks to these skilled and experienced officials Britain ruled Jordan relatively smoothly and peacefully. It was often the lack of long service and experience among administrators that made ruling indigenous populations extremely difficult elsewhere.

Accumulated local knowledge allowed the British to make the most of their philosophy of indirect imperial rule. Rather than a systematic method of control, this attitude meant no more than some basic and general guidelines. It prescribed a government that based itself as much as possible on traditional modes of leadership and political culture. Colonial administrators were expected to seek out willing collaborators, activate existing institutions and respect local customs, thus leaving society intact. The rational behind this policy was its economy; it was designed to guarantee cheap government with a small British staff and limited military backup and financial expense.[8] It was also a way to base colonial rule on elements which seemed more convenient to the British, excluding educated natives suspected of anti-colonial nationalism.[9]

In Transjordan British officials developed this policy into a fine art, especially in the 1930s. In this respect, the highly rich and sophisticated tribal legal system provided ready-made mechanisms to ensure law and order. These were effectively utilised by the British once they grew to know them and appreciate their merits. This practice stands in marked contrast to the experience of many modern colonial regimes which sought to unify, standardise and therefore simplify complex customary local practices, thereby making them 'legible' to state officials and more governable from the centre. As James Scott shows, it was this dismissal of local knowledge that so often failed ambitious colonial projects and provoked resistance among rural societies.[10]

As for local elements, tribal shaykhs emerged as a collaborative elite with which the British could share power. Conveniently, they were not opposed by literate local elements since they hardly existed in the country. During the 1920s and most of the 1930s the shaykhs still stood outside the orbit of Arab nationalism and were therefore uncontaminated in British eyes. They were willing to collaborate with the British, as long as their interests and those of their tribes were respected. In addition, moderation, leniency, negotiation and mediation -- all values that characterised tribal processes of conflict resolution -- were adopted by British officials. They soon also discovered the merits of their main partner, Emir Abdullah. With his moral standing, his understanding of local society and long experience as a tribal leader, Abdullah could help them govern, at least to some extent, even the most unruly tribes roaming the deserts. The close relations he cultivated with the tribal chiefs proved an effective way of maintaining at least a minimal sense of law and order in the country and a measure of cooperation with the government. In this way Britain ruled the tribes, and therefore Transjordan, until at least the end of the 1920s. Even later, when the British authorities took a direct interest in ruling the desert and consolidated their power elsewhere, Abdullah's contribution to the exercise of state authority was invaluable.

All in all British rule in Transjordan was very different from other colonial settings, provoking much less opposition. An inclination for non-confrontational policies, subtle intervention, low visibility of their rule and a preference for operating more often than not behind the scenes through the good offices of the Emir allowed for a more agreeable colonial rule from the point of view of the colonised than elsewhere. It also resulted in more subtle forms of local resistance. Finally, it generated a more acceptable British legacy in Jordan. Thus, long after independence British rule is viewed ambivalently. Jordanians are no different from other Middle Easterners in condemning the evils of colonialism and imperialism. However, the British mandate is not necessarily perceived as the ultimate sin and is not blamed for all the shortcomings of the state, as in many other former colonies. Moreover, even after independence, Britain has managed to maintain a special position in this country.[11] In the post-colonial era the two countries have managed to reformulate their relations from domination and dependency to an alliance. Even today, when the USA has replaced Britain as the main supporter of the Kingdom, the relations between the two political elites are close and attest to mutual respect.

A final word concerning tribes, tribalism and the modern state in the Middle East is in order. Far from being an anachronism, tribalism has demonstrated impressive resilience. For decades tribalism was thought of as a dying phenomenon retreating before the sweeping forces of modernity while trying to delay their positive progress. The post-colonial nation-state was expected to erode tribal forms of identity and social and political organisation. Contrary to these predictions, tribes have not only survived modernity and statehood but in some ways also enjoyed a revival. In Jordan, as well as several other Middle Eastern and Central Asian countries, tribal values and social organisation have proved to be the allies of the modern state, not its rivals. This is true not only for the formative period but to a certain extent even in the present. This becomes particularly apparent whenever a new government is formed or when elections to the parliament or local councils take place. In such instances tribal affiliation forms a crucial criterion for nomination and often determines voting patterns. Political influence aside, tribal values continue to dominate Jordanian society and culture. For example, a special tribal law code was recognised as an official law for regulating the life of certain tribes as late as 1976. Even with its formal abolition, tribal law continues to be practiced, side by side with the civil code and with the tacit agreement and even encouragement of the government and the palace.

Moreover, in Jordan in particular, but in other states as well, tribes became the partners of state founders, whether local or foreign, and played an active part in the process of state-formation. In fact, tribes in Jordan as well as in Saudi Arabia, the Gulf states, Yemen and even in Saddam Hussein's Iraq,[12] rather than disappearing, became the building blocks of the modern state. In this way they help safeguard the state and the ruling regimes. Moreover, with the intensification of modernising processes, tribes have acquired a new role for themselves. In the modern states of the Middle East central governments gradually increased their capability and determination to regulate society. Faced with the intrusive, impersonal, abstract state structures and its new institutions, the often alienated citizen needed mediating services as well as a sense of familiarity. These needs could be attained only within the tribal community. In this way tribes play a crucial role in cushioning and smoothing out processes of rapid modernisation. By doing so, they help to maintain a sense of close and intimate community (*gemeinschaft*) -- frequently lost in modernised societies (*gesellschaft*) -- and prevent or at least postpone social unrest. These new functions have been beneficial for governments and have therefore been encouraged by them. Consequently, tribes, though very different from the social organisation they were only several decades ago, have proved their importance and relevance for a large number of people in today's Middle East.

State and Tribe: Methodology

This book draws upon recent works on tribal societies in the modern Middle East undergoing processes of state-formation, as well as the more general scholarship on state-society relations. In recent years a new body of scholarship challenges many common assumptions regarding state-tribe relations. It suggests new definitions for the notions of 'state' and 'tribe' and introduces better tools for analysing tribal societies in modern states under formation.[13]

This approach transcends the dichotomy between state and tribe and emphasises a more dynamic interaction. It shows that tribes react in many different ways to the creation of a centralised state and maintain different degrees of autonomy and subordination. For their part, state authorities can pursue a variety of policies towards tribes. They may attempt to destroy them, to change the traditional way of life, or to dismiss their values as irrelevant to the requirements of modernity or statehood. More often than not, however, governments co-operate with tribes, share power with them, co-opt their leaders and even incorporate tribal values into the ethos of the state.[14] Philip Khoury and Joseph Kostiner suggest that "tribes are just as likely to resist states by acting as antistates as they are to coexist with them."[15] In a similar vein, Nazih Ayubi argues that "tribe and state complement rather than contradict each other" and asserts that many tribes have acquired a stake in the survival of their state.[16] In his work on tribes in Iran and Afghanistan Richard Tapper demonstrates that "tribes and states have created and maintained each other as a single system, though one of inherent instability."[17]

Scholars have failed to agree on a generic definition of a tribe. Consequently, a new tendency prefers a more limited and modest definition to one which is broad and all-encompassing. Tapper, defining the term to fit his analysis of the tribespeople on the Iranian frontier and translating the indigenous term, suggests the tribe is a "localised group in which kinship is the dominant idiom of organisation, and whose members consider themselves culturally distinct (in terms of customs, dialect or language, and origins)."[18] For the Arab Middle East a more satisfying definition would be a group of people distinguished from other groups by notions of shared descent, whether real or imagined. This latter definition best conforms to local conceptions of tribes in Arabia.

It should be noted that tribe and state are not static notions but change over time, partly due to their interface with each other. The state's nature changes according to the ability or aspirations of the central government to rule over society and to enforce its policies. The concept of 'stateness,' which was coined by J.P. Nettl and developed by others, depicts the changing nature of the state's strength over time, space and certain segments of the population in terms of the government's ability to rule, to enforce the law, and accommodate pluralism, social mobility and political representation. Therefore, states accommodate tribes in varying degrees of social integration and political participation depending on their level of 'stateness.' Tribes, too, change over time and play different roles within the state structures. Thus it can be said that "tribe and state... form a dialectical symbiosis: they mingle and sustain each other; each part changes owing to the other's influence; and sometimes they seek to destroy one another."[19]

Indeed, the compatibility rather than contradiction between state and tribe have been demonstrated in those studies that examine the way in which rulers in the Gulf and in Yemen dealt with their tribes. This was achieved by consociational arrangements whereby both inducement and enforcement were utilised to build up tribal alliances that led to the emergence of the contemporary states. The specific tools in this carrot-and-stick approach included financial rewards and penalties, inter-familial and inter-tribal marriages, renewed recognition for certain remote tribal branches, or forced emigration of opponent groups or individuals. However, as Khaldun al-Naqib shows, these policies brought about another result: instead of being a mechanism for national integration, the link between the tribe and the state only deepened patron-client relations and strengthened the incentive to identify with a tribal group since social promotion became contingent upon finding a distinguished patron. Loyalty to the state remains weak as tribes transform themselves into pressure groups, lobbying for special benefits and defending particular interests.[20] In this way tribes survive the forces of modernisation that were thought to erode tribal identities. The interaction described for Arabia resembles mandatory Transjordan, and persists, in part, to the present day. Unlike the Gulf examples, however, in contemporary Jordan tribalism did not prevent the emergence of nationalism.

These developments in the literature dealing with tribes and states coincide with renewed theoretical interest in the nature of the state and its relations with society, both in general and within a specifically Middle Eastern context. Joel Migdal shows how in the Third World the fragmented structure of society affects state capability and to a large extent determines the character of the state. This in turn reinforces the fragmentation of society. His recommendation to examine the often neglected role played by local strongmen is particularly relevant to Transjordan, whose tribal shaykhs have been largely neglected by the literature.[21] Migdal's work adheres to the dominant approach in political science, which treats the state as a political actor distinct from society. Recently, however, scholars such as Timothy Mitchell, Roger Owen and Sami Zubaida have criticised the notion of the state as a unified and autonomous political actor that can be clearly distinguished from society. They prefer to see the state as a 'political field'-- a term coined by Zubaida -- in which many different actors compete for resources and influence rather than attempt to overthrow the existing political order, and replace it with one of their own making.[22]

This study adopts this critique of the statist approach. The state is not treated as a political actor, but rather as a framework within which a political struggle for influence and resources takes place. The state is also seen as the outcome of the state-building process, influenced by the nature and strength of society. For their part, tribes and their leaders are examined not necessarily as expressions of atavism, but rather as constituencies within the state structure. They competed with each other while trying to exert concessions and benefits from the central government. At the same time, they jealously guarded their autonomy. If the state is to be understood as a framework or arena for political contest, a 'political field,' rather than an actor, it is easier to understand why tribes can co-operate with this political arrangement. Acts of resistance -- as occurred in many tribal societies, including Transjordan throughout the mandate period -- can be understood in light of this principle not as an attempt to overthrow the state, but to influence it and compete for resources from the central government.

Another aspect of the theoretical background that informs the present analysis is the model of chieftaincy (or chiefdom).[23] This concept provides a useful way of looking at the complexities in state-tribe relations, by focusing on the level of tribal confederacy, and examining its leaders' relations with central states. The concept of chieftaincy is modelled on the big tribal confederacies in Arabia and Iran. It also draws on the writing of the fourteenth century Arab historian Ibn Khaldun. A chieftaincy is an intermediate political structure between tribe and state, which incorporates some features of both. It is a power-sharing partnership which involves pastoral nomads, semi-sedentary tribesmen, and urban dwellers. The common action of this organisation is initiated and supervised by the chief, whose status and role is a vital characteristic of the chieftaincy. He must combine moral authority over his fellow tribesmen with the ability to deliver benefits and services to his followers. The historical chieftaincies were relatively short-lived entities. They lacked strong and institutionalised central authority, clearly defined boundaries, and a common value system. Examples of such confederacies in Arabia include the first two Wahhabi states and the third up to World War One, the Hashemite alliance during the Arab Revolt or the Rashidi Emirate at the beginning of the twentieth century. Two examples from Iran are the Shahsevan and Qashqa'i. It is true that in Transjordan tribal confederacies represented much smaller and weaker political units and never developed the same level of institutionalisation as the more powerful and 'classical' confederacies. Nevertheless, they resembled them in their organisational structure and political behaviour and are best analysed as chieftaincies.

Apart from the conceptual tools outlined above, a close historical study of state-society relations also requires accessing a wide range of sources and necessitates a departure from the exclusive reliance on British official correspondence. Therefore, this study makes use of new sources not previously utilised in the study of domestic politics in Jordan: records of the Transjordanian government and the Arab Legion, local press, oral testimonies, tribal histories as well as files of the various Zionist agencies, are used to complement the official British view. By using a wide range of sources and applying insights from the literature, this study attempts to examine and interpret local actors from their own standpoint, rather than merely from a state-centred and external view, as is commonly the case.

Structure of the Book

The two-odd years that preceded the establishment of the Emirate provide a good introduction to the social forces operating on the scene prior to the initiation of the state-formation process. By closely examining the politics and dynamics typical of tribal society, Chapter One challenges the common historical wisdom that dismisses this period as a short interlude of anarchy and chaos. Rather, it was a period of intense mobilisation of tribal alliances. They became a formidable challenge to any future central government and thus had a long-standing impact on the nature of the development of Transjordan as a state. This period also saw the first, unsuccessful British attempt to rule the country.

The British failure in ruling the country paved the way for the establishment of the Emirate as a partnership between the British and Abdullah bin Husayn in 1921. During the first three years of its existence several power centres clashed over the nature of the new political entity, and in particular its attitude towards the tribes. The core of Chapter Two considers this confrontation, which came to a head in the summer of 1924 and was finally resolved by a British take-over of the administration. Thereafter, the British imposed a governing framework that, although frequently contested and modified, remained the basic guideline for the development of the Emirate.

The second half of the 1920s saw a period of consolidation of state power in the limited settled zone as a change in British policy brought about increased momentum in state-formation. Chapter Three analyses this development and studies Abdullah's monopoly in dealing with the desert tribes. It emphasises that a shrewd reliance on the tribal structure of society and Abdullah's skilful handling of tribal politics were of fundamental importance to the establishment of centralised authority.

The intensification of raids on the Najdi borders in the last two years of the 1920s transformed British policy towards controlling the desert. From the early 1930s the central government consolidated its power vis-à-vis the nomadic tribes thanks to the work of Captain John Glubb and the Desert Patrol of the Arab Legion under his command. It was also facilitated by a simultaneous economic crisis, which decreased the nomads' resilience and resistance. Chapter Four portrays the change in British desert policy and attempts to give a comprehensive account of Glubb's work beyond his military tactics. More importantly, the chapter highlights Glubb's enormous effect on tribal society throughout his service.

By the late 1930s the central government had expanded its functions, tightened its control over the population, and engaged in many spheres of life that had been previously exclusive to the tribe. However, central power was not absolute and tribesmen continued to exert power and influence government policies. Chapter Five examines these developments and shows that by the end of the mandate the Emirate had already obtained many characteristics of a modern state. At the same time however, Transjordan kept many of its tribal features and tribes continued to be important and formidable actors on the Transjordanian political scene.

The eve of independence in 1946 offers a suitable moment to assess the overall processes of state-formation and tribal integration over two and a half decades. The Conclusion provides an attempt to assess the limited nature of the British mandate, the nature of the evolving state, and the lasting legacies of the mandate period. In doing so, it offers an overview of Jordanian history from independence until today and identifies persistent characteristics that were established during the mandate. It is this historical continuity that explains much of the resilience of the Hashemite regime.

CHAPTER ONE:
BETWEEN TWO EMPIRES:
TRANSJORDAN ON THE EVE
OF ABDULLAH'S ARRIVAL

The administrative situation in my country before my arrival quite resembled *anarchy*, namely tribal feuding and a degree of weakness and incoherence of the local governments such that most of the famous leaders were not able to travel from their tribal areas to the surrounding areas.[1]

A golden period arrived for the greedy and warlike Bedouin shaykhs of Trans-Jordania. A hundred hands full of gold and promises are stretched out to them, attempting to win their sympathy. The shaykhs accept all offers... They, for their part, are ready to serve, are ready to fight and invade wherever there is a good booty in view.[2]

On the eve of the establishment of the Transjordanian Emirate in 1921, almost the entire country's population was organised along tribal lines and adhered to tribal values and customs. The country reverted to a local order similar to that which had prevailed prior to the extension of direct Ottoman rule in the last third of the nineteenth century. The tribe or tribal confederacy determined practically every aspect of people's lives, forming in most cases their principal frame of reference. The forging of political alliances, control over land and water, seasonal migration, the provision of personal security, conflict resolution and marriage arrangements all took place either within the tribal system or in accordance with its conventions. By the time Abdullah bin Husayn arrived in the country in November 1920, powerful tribes had become the country's effective rulers. Having been consolidating their position with the support of outside powers for several years, they now posed a challenge to the establishment of a centralised state. As a result, the two-odd years preceding Abdullah's arrival and assumption of power in Transjordan had a considerable effect on the establishment and development of modern Jordan.

This brief period is all too often dismissed as an interregnum between two eras of Transjordanian statehood, the first under the Ottomans, the second under British imperial rule. But the importance of the Faysali government, which succeeded the country's erstwhile Ottoman rulers, or of the British-supported local governments, forerunners of the Emirate, cannot be so easily overlooked. To begin with, when the Emirate of Transjordan finally came into being as an Anglo-Hashemite partnership, it utilised institutions and personnel inherited from all three previous governments: the Ottoman, the Faysali and local governments. Moreover, perhaps more crucially, this period and these governments helped instil and validate the notion of a central authority among the local population. As a result, the majority of people no longer regarded the state as an alien concept, leaving only the details of the exact relationship between the central government and society to be negotiated.[3] Finally, these years saw the first British attempts to establish some sort of control over the country. They were outsiders who lacked sufficient knowledge of local society. As such, the British misinterpreted many of the country's indigenous traditions and customs, misread its political culture and order, and, as a result, badly misjudged the region's key political players' interests and motives. These misperceptions go a long way towards explaining why the British ultimately failed to rule Transjordan through the medium of local governments. This failure forced them to turn to an alternative form of indirect colonial rule, namely that of supporting a Hashemite prince. While previous accounts of the period, centring on the role played by the external powers, naturally tended to depict Transjordan as perceived by Whitehall or Government House, this chapter focuses on and reconstructs the indigenous local order, examining its political and administrative legacy on the eve of Abdullah's arrival in the country.

Transjordan's Integration into the Syrian State

In October 1918 at the end of World War One the Allied and Arab forces entered Damascus, where *sharif* Faysal bin Husayn established an Arab Administration as part of the Occupied Enemy Territory Administration-East, under the command of General Allenby. This administration extended its influence over Transjordan. The northern areas of the country were part of the Hawran district; while the area ranging from the Balqa' in the north to Tabuk in the south was under the command of the Arab Army in the region. To support the Arab government, small British and imperial garrisons were formed around the country.[4]

According to English literature on the Faysali period, as well as various Arabic texts, the Arab government's jurisdiction over Transjordan was negligible.[5] This was certainly the case during the last months of the government following the withdrawal of the British forces. Nevertheless, the first year of Faysal's rule proved a relative success. An integral part of Syria, the new regime could boast several achievements, not least in the field of state-building. From the beginning the Faysali regime did its utmost to return the country to normalcy. Retaining the Ottoman administrative structure, it activated defunct Ottoman institutions and infrastructure, and with the help of the gendarmerie and police force, began to run the country's various districts. It collected taxes, at least in the settled zone west of the Hijaz railway. It provided various basic services, albeit on a very small scale, including public security, health, education and relief. Thus, it instituted a health service in Ma'an, Tafila, Karak, Qatrana, Madaba, Amman, al-Salt and 'Ajlun. It repaired and extended communications systems destroyed during the war and installed additional telephone and telegraph lines. The railway line now ran from Madina to Damascus. The government also reconvened the courts. It opened schools in al-Salt, run by government appointed staff, changing the language of instruction from Turkish to Arabic. The government also implemented relief measures to assist locals severely affected by the war, with the British military command distributing free seeds and livestock.[6]

Seeking to benefit from their influence, the new regime promptly recognised various local leaders, while Faysal forged alliances with many of the country's tribal heads. Recognising their importance, he forgave even the shaykhs who supported the Ottomans rather than the Hashemites during the war. For their part, those shaykhs took advantage of the new regime's magnanimity to recover their positions within their constituencies. Hamad bin Jazi of the Huwaytat, Mithqal al-Fayiz of the Bani Sakhr, Rufayfan al-Majali, shaykh of the Majali and strongman of Karak, and 'Awda Qasus, leader of one of Karak's Christian tribes were among those who benefited from Faysal's policy of rapprochement.[7]

Faysal adopted the Ottoman wartime practise of granting subsidies and honorary titles in order to secure the leading shaykhs' allegiance. He recognised several shaykhs as paramount chiefs (*shaykh al-mashayikh*), a position accompanied by a handsome salary. Accordingly, 'Utwa al-Majali became *shaykh mashayikh* of Karak as did Sultan al-'Adwan in the Balqa'. The shaykhs were paid to assist officials sent from Damascus to run local government. In a further effort to gain their favour, Faysal lavished regal hospitality on tribal leaders. In his memoirs, the Karaki notable 'Awda Qasus recalls how when the Emir invited the notables of Karak to Damascus, he and Rufayfan al-Majali were asked to stay longer as Faysal's guests, all in all spending two and a half months in the capital.[8] Encouraging political participation was another way of integrating the Transjordanian population into the state. In the elections for the Syrian Congress, local leaders were elected to represent the various communities of Transjordan in accordance with Ottoman electoral law. Faysal's efforts paid off with many of Transjordan's major players proclaiming their loyalty to him.[9]

In order to consolidate the government and maintain law and order, Faysal and his officers mediated in disputes between rival tribes. The list of resolved disputes is impressively long, indicative of the regime's successful tribal policy. In November 1919, the government helped bring about the reconciliation of the Bani Sakhr and Bani Hasan tribes, which was afterwards celebrated at the Arab Club in Damascus. Peace between the inhabitants of Madaba and the Bani Sakhr and Balqawiyya meant that throughout 1919 the region enjoyed a measure of security. Similarly, relations were mended between the northern tribes of the Bani Sakhr and the town of Ramtha, as well as between several tribes in Karak.[10]

Until the end of 1919 most parties in the country seemed content with the new order. The nomads and semi-nomads enjoyed the benefits of the new administration, which proved to be no more than an extension of the tribal coalition of the Arab

Revolt, ruling with a light touch, and allowing them a high degree of autonomy. As Joseph Kostiner observed, during the 1916-1917 revolt the Hashemites had led a tribal confederacy of the sort that had for centuries been the prevalent form of government in Arabia. They forged alliances with the dominant tribes in the areas they sought to rule. They paid them large sums of money, expecting them, in return, to pledge their allegiance to the Arab alliance, join it and on occasion even fight for it. The relationship between the Hashemites and the tribes was a personal one, conducted through the shaykhs. But the tribes were neither fully integrated into the new entity nor were they required to reform their values or social structure in accordance with alliance norms nor give up their autonomy.[11] This political configuration continued well into the Faysali era. As far as the settled communities were concerned, they were grateful for the measure of security and resumption of public services. Given the long years of uncertainty and deterioration in public safety since the outbreak of the war, the new regime now offered them some much appreciated normality.

Hence, it is reasonable to assume that Faysal enjoyed a degree of local support. His administration certainly appeared preferable to the various alternatives on offer. With Britain occupying Palestine and French troops in the Lebanon, the Arab government stood, at the very least, for a form of local rule. This was an important factor, for, with the collapse of the Ottoman Empire, Arab nationalism had become the predominant ideology among the politically conscious.[12]

Faysal's Loss of Control and the Resurrection of Tribal Order

The government's early successes did not last long. Towards the end of 1919, storm clouds gathered over the Syrian state and time quickly ran out for the Arab government. Faysal failed to reach a settlement with Britain and France, which between them had agreed on a British withdrawal from Syria. By 1 December British forces had withdrawn and shortly afterwards Britain halved its financial support for the Arab government, which meant that Faysal could no longer subsidise the local leaders.[13] These developments, coupled with the Emir's long absence from the country while he was busy negotiating in Europe, were the main reasons behind the Arab administration's failure to control both Syria and Transjordan. With the government's influence in Transjordan and parts of Syria quickly evaporating, a vacuum emerged that was filled by local elite.[14]

The Arab administration's weakness together with the unsettled political future of Greater Syria prompted several forces -- the most active were Faysal's men and the French -- to compete for the shaykhs' favour. At first, many of the local leaders enrolled in the government's campaign to defend the independence of Syria, signing petitions, sending letters and attending rallies. Some even contemplated offering the government military support. According to British reports, Mithqal al-Fayiz wrote to Rufayfan al-Majali asking him to assist the independence movement. The same Mithqal was involved in attempts to attack British forces across the Jordan River with a tribal force that included the Balqa' confederacy led by Sultan al-ʿAdwan. The latter consistently refused appeals of this sort.[15] Nonetheless, many tribes repudiated Faysal's authority. The government's helplessness, foreign intervention, and the leading tribes' tendency to exploit weak regimes in order to extend their autonomy all combined to weaken the government. Its frantic announcement of forced conscription in January 1920 met fierce local defiance.

When asked by Faysal to meet him in Damascus, several shaykhs ignored the invitation; those who accepted defied his orders to mobilise their forces behind the government. Mithqal, Mashhur al-Fayiz, the paramount shaykh of the Bani Sakhr, Rufayfan, ʿAwda abu Taya from the Huwaytat and Sayil al-Shahwan, shaykh of the ʿAjarma, emerged as the regime's principal opponents, apparently, only after first securing French support. Allegedly, by handing over huge sums of money and distributing lavish gifts -- in February 1920, for example, Mithqal returned from a trip to Haifa in a French car and, it was said, a £1,000 richer -- the French encouraged the growing discord between the shaykhs and the government.[16]

By February 1920 the nomadic tribes had shaken off any residual sense of obligation to the government. Reporting on the situation, the commander of the Karak gendarmerie notified the district governor that: "The Bedouin from Huwaytat, Al-Salayta, Bani Sakhr and Shawbak defy government orders. Their assaults on telegraph wires and railway lines and on the directors of the rail stations have increased. In doing so they follow the steps of ʿAwda abu Taya who openly declares his disobedience to government orders and sees himself as the absolute ruler and conqueror of this country."[17] In an audacious act of impudence, the Bani ʿAtiyya captured one *sharif* ʿAli, releasing him only after being paid a handsome ransom.[18] Government authority was limited to a few towns and their immediate hinterlands, notably al-Salt and Amman. These towns' inhabitants, fearing the nomadic tribes and with no desire to fall under their control, still supported the government. In Karak Rufayfan al-Majali led the town independently of the government while nominally proclaiming his loyalty.[19] In the face of dwindling government control, most of the country descended into what has been described by contemporary observers as a state of lawless anarchy.

Facing an uncertain future, Transjordan now experienced a period of intensive mobilisation. Nomadic tribes, seeking to dominate the country's settled areas once again, began extracting protection moneys (*khawa*) from local villages and towns, as had been the custom before the Ottomans extended their rule into Transjordan. The stronger tribes strove to expand their tribal dominions (*dira*s), while the smaller ones and the settled communities looked to powerful allies to guarantee their safety. In the Balqaʾ this political reconfiguration took the form of the struggle for Madaba. Exploiting the government's impotency, the southern tribes of the Bani Sakhr (the Zaban, Mtirat and Haqish) tried to take over the town and rob its inhabitants. In response to the call for help, the Balqaʾ confederacy decided to defend it in order to prevent the Bani Sakhr from encroaching on their land, as Madaba marked the border between these two rival confederacies.[20] This was not the Bani Sakhr's only attempt to expand. Their northern tribes of Khuraysha and Jubur had ordered the people of Ramtha to pay *khawa* in return for their protection. In response, the Ramtha people allied themselves with the settled tribes of the Kura and Bani Jahma districts. Together they surprised and defeated the Bani Sakhr, who were supported by the

Ghazawiyya and Sukhur al-Ghawr tribes. In local memory, this battle is remembered as the end of the *khawa* system, freeing the peasants from nomad domination.[21]

To outside observers -- the British, the Zionists and even Abdullah as indicated in the opening quotation of this chapter -- these incidents appeared arbitrary, symptomatic of the endless feuds between the region's tribes. Indeed, on the face of it, it is hardly surprising that when describing local conditions many sources and scholarly writings invoke the word 'anarchy.' Rather than engaging in indiscriminate disputes, however, the tribes were busy redrawing the country's internal political boundaries, establishing new alliances or strengthening existing ones and repositioning themselves externally. This kind of inter-tribal politics and taking up of arms had not been seen in Transjordan since the extension of direct Ottoman rule in late 1860s in the northern and central districts of the country, and in the mid-1890s in the south. The notion of 'local order', proposed by Eugene Rogan to describe inter-tribal politics before the establishment of direct Ottoman rule, can, with some adjustments, also be applied to this transitional period. Composed of chieftaincies and tribes, it was marked by strong leadership, an organised relationship between the nomads and cultivators, and specific territorial divisions. It also boasted an economic and legal system as well as conflict resolution mechanisms. Never static, the balance of power between the rival chieftaincies was "frequently disrupted by territorial ambitions, competition for pasture, access to productive villages, or raids and feuds." Turbulent though it might be, "a functional chiefdom" nevertheless "provided security and a system of justice all defined in indigenous terms in return for taxation," and giving "all members of a chiefdom a common interest in the local order."[22]

In order to further understand the relative stability of the 'local order' it is important to recognise the role played by customary law in regulating social relations of Middle Eastern tribal communities and its ability to mitigate, contain and even prevent conflicts. As noted by the Jordanian jurist and anthropologist, Muhammad Abu Hassan, it was the failure to take the tribal legal system into account that misled both Western and Arab writers into portraying Arab tribal society as a warlike society subject to endless petty conflicts.[23] The effectiveness of tribal mechanisms in containing disputes can be attributed to a "complex system of special customs and regulatory procedures within each group..."[24] Hence, the concept of collective responsibility, extending either to the tribe as a whole or to the tribesman's extended family up to five generations removed (*khamsa*), offered all individuals a measure of protection. It is true that collective responsibility could potentially turn a conflict between two individuals into a war between two families or tribes. At the same time, however, the knowledge that one man's actions might drag the whole tribe into a bloody conflict usually served to restrain individuals. When a crime was committed the principle of collective responsibility often facilitated a quick settlement; even if the culprit absconded, his tribe was liable to pay compensation to the victim's family. Indeed, compensation in cash or kind, rather than punishment, was the tribes' chief means of settling disputes, hence the existence of elaborate protocols for compensation. Many elements of the customary law helped prevent the onset of a vicious circle of murder and revenge. Thus, third parties stood to gain much in terms of prestige if their intervention and mediation (*wasta*) led to the settlement of a dispute. In addition, there was a brief time period during which revenge was prohibited and agreement encouraged (*ʿatwa*). Finally, tribal law allowed for a place of refuge where the murderer and his family could take sanctuary until a settlement was brokered (*jalwa*). Various elements within the judicial system, such as the judges' pre-eminent position in society or the appointment of third party guarantors (*kafil*) on behalf of the culprit in order to ensure the fulfilment of the judge's ruling, helped guarantee the implementation of legal procedures.

Among the numerous legal conventions that ensured the safety of individual tribe members and regulated relations between the tribes were a number of measures pertaining to the safe movement of people outside their tribal territory (*dira*). These allowed people to pass through foreign territory if accompanied, usually after payment, by an escort (*rafiq*), who whilst serving as their guide was also obliged to protect them. The strict hospitality laws, with the host personally responsible for his guests' safety and welfare, served a similar purpose, as did the concept of the *dakhil*: a stranger who seeks and receives refuge in another tribe for fear of his life. Even raiding was highly regulated, as is apparent from the following intelligence report:

> ... raiding... seems rarely, if ever, to involve the displacement of one tribe by another. It is besides, restricted by a highly complicated system of usages of which the purpose seems to be to obtain some sort of security for life and property, by rendering the consequences of robbery, at least when accompanied by bloodshed, serious.[25]

However, if in the pre-Ottoman era the tribes were left largely to their own devices, this was no longer the case by the early twentieth century, when various external actors began taking an active part in the local political game. During World War One the Ottomans, the Sharifians, the British and the French were all busy courting the tribes, vying for their loyalty with promises of gold, grain and arms. The stronger nomadic tribes, in particular, gained military experience fighting for different masters, their leaders becoming more politically adept. It was also during this period that renowned warriors, such as ʿAwda abu Taya of the Huwaytat and Mithqal al-Fayiz of the Bani Sakhr built up and consolidated their position within their tribes.

In addition to the French involvement, at the end of the war the Turks, Zionists and Palestinians all began meddling in local politics. The Turks were busy fighting the French in northern Syria and continued some activity in Transjordan. The local Circassian population proved to be the Turks' most loyal supporters, but they also cultivated good relations with a few tribal shaykhs, principally Mithqal al-Fayiz.[26] The Zionists also had a stake in Transjordan. Their leadership was worried lest, owing to Faysal's increasingly feeble control, the tribes might be tempted to cross the Jordan River and attack Jewish settlements. Rumour also had it that the Palestinian Arabs were inciting the nomads to invade Palestine. In April 1920, Jewish officials arranged a meeting in Jericho between Chaim Weizmann, president of the World Zionist Organisation, and ten Transjordanian shaykhs. Leaving nothing to chance, the Jews offered the chiefs financial incentives, both to attend the meeting and sign an agreement ensuring the safety of the Jews of Palestine. In the event, rioting in Jerusalem prevented Weizmann from attending the meeting. Disappointed, the shaykhs returned home, albeit generously compensated for their time and expenses.[27]

The shaykhs' simultaneous dealings with rival forces earned them a reputation as shameless mercenaries and unscrupulous opportunists among contemporary observers. As one British officer remarked: "The Sheikhs of Trans-Jordania, almost without exception, are perfectly willing to take any amount of money from anybody and make all sorts of promises in return, and, if sufficient money were distributed, say, by the Chinese, they would sign a petition for a Chinese mandate."[28] But what was erroneously condemned as greediness provides a poor explanation for the shaykhs' behaviour. Rather, the shaykhs conformed to the structure and dynamics of tribal society and politics. A chieftaincy's leader had to guarantee a constant flow of resources to the members of his alliance. If he failed in this, or indeed in any other duty, there was every chance that a more able leader among his own tribe or family would challenge his leadership. One way of securing his position was to win the financial and political support of external forces. In the aftermath of the war the shaykhs took this principle one step further, seeking not only to augment but to diversify their sources of income as well. Moreover, by no longer being dependent on a single power, as had been the case during the Ottoman era, the shaykhs gained more independence and autonomy. Finally, given the country's unclear future they hedged their bets, maintaining good relations with all those who sought to play a role in the region. In an era of transition, with the old forms of politics giving way to renewed tribal domination and re-alignments, all of which required more resources, and with the future of the country still unknown, this strategy made a great deal of sense. It was rooted in political considerations rather than financial greed.

First British - Tribal Encounter on the Frontier of Empire

The collapse of Faysal's administration in July 1920, following the defeat of the Arab forces by the French in Maysalun, heightened the state of uncertainty in Transjordan. The period that followed was one of intense local political mobilisation and re-organisation, with the chieftaincies seeking to fill the vacuum left by the disintegrating Arab state. The British, in response, made their first attempt to control the country. However, reluctant to occupy and administer the territory directly, they hoped to maintain their influence indirectly by piloting the locals towards some form of self-government, under the guidance of a tiny British personnel. A few months later, having failed miserably in their task, the British adopted an alternative form of indirect colonial control, recognising the rule of Abdullah bin Husayn. The remainder of this chapter examines Britain's early experiences in Transjordan and follows the process of internal mobilisation in the country's various regions. It highlights the tension between the way the British perceived the interests and motives of the region's key actors and the reality on the ground. British overconfidence, ignorance and their gross misinterpretation of the indigenous culture feature prominently in the following analysis.

With the collapse of the Faysali government, the locus of political activity in the area moved to Jerusalem, with Britain, as the power responsible for Transjordan, now contemplating its next move. Its prime concern was to prevent the French in Syria from gaining control over the territories assigned to the British sphere of influence in the war-time agreements, which divided the Ottoman Fertile Crescent between the two powers. The British were also afraid lest unrest east of the Jordan River spill over into Palestine. It was a reasonable concern given that several months earlier, during the twilight of the Faysali regime, villagers from northern Transjordan led by shaykh Kayid al-Miflih al-ʿUbaydat, had raided Britain's military bases in Samakh and Bisan as well as several Jewish colonies before being stopped by British airplanes.[29] For their part, many shaykhs realised that Faysal's fall had produced a new situation on the ground, one in which the British were the key players. The shaykhs of the ʿAdwan, Rufayfan al-Majali and other notables from Karak, Hamad bin Jazi of the Huwaytat and representatives from al-Salt, all met or sent friendly messages to Herbert Samuel, the newly-arrived High Commissioner for Palestine. Some even went as far as to ask for a British administration in Transjordan.[30]

Encouraged by the shaykhs' overtly friendly attitude, and believing that it reflected the attitude of society as a whole, Samuel and his advisers concluded that a British occupation would be welcomed by all. Accordingly, the High Commissioner lobbied Whitehall relentlessly to occupy Transjordan and administer it as part of Palestine. Optimistic to the extreme, he predicted that only a small number of British troops would be needed to occupy and run the whole country. Noting that "Occupation [is] greatly desired by tribes so very small number of troops required," he suggested raising a gendarme force from the region's smaller tribes, insisting that he could "... administer [the] territory up the Hejaz railway through tribal organization supervised by two British District Governors and small staff."[31] Nor was this the only example of Samuel's overly confident and, as it turned out, unrealistic outlook. He was equally convinced that Transjordan could support itself simply by instituting an efficient tax collection system. He even went as far as to predict that once the administration's expenses were paid, a considerable surplus would remain sufficient to fund local development programmes such as schools and roads with the remainder going to Palestine.

Samuel's pressure notwithstanding, the Foreign Secretary, Lord Curzon, dismissed the idea of extending Britain's commitments in the Middle East any further. He certainly refused to sanction the use of troops to this end. It was a view shared by the Cabinet as a whole. Post-war austerity, the Iraqi revolt against the British, and Transjordan's strategic marginality combined to persuade the Cabinet not to extend Britain's involvement in the region. Accordingly, Curzon instructed Samuel to keep Transjordan "independent but with closest relation with Palestine." He did, however, authorise Samuel to dispatch four to five political officers to help the locals establish a government of their own as well as encourage trade with Palestine. But, Curzon emphasised, no British troops would be sent to the area nor would a British administration be set up.[32]

Believing that he had the population's unequivocal support, Samuel went to al-Salt in August 1920 to meet various local notables and obtain their consent for the proposed plan. At the meeting he explained that Britain sought to help them establish local governments and, to this end, offered them the assistance and guidance of British officers. Samuel further promised that Transjordan would not be placed under the Palestine administration's direct control and assured them that there was no intention of conscripting or disarming the locals. Samuel left the meeting "well pleased," convinced of "the success" of his mission. It was a feeling shared by the British officers who had attended the conference.[33] On the face of it there was much reason for this British buoyancy. Attendance at the meeting in al-Salt had been high; some 600 came, including a great many shaykhs and notables. Moreover, they had all, or so it seemed, agreed to Samuel's proposals. However, a closer look at those who had actually attended the conference sheds a different light on the affair and particularly on the question of the degree of local endorsement for Samuel's proposals. While those present at the meeting included Sultan al-ʿAdwan, Hamad bin Jazi and Rufayfan al-Majali, all the other important leaders, namely the chiefs of the Bani Sakhr who dominated central Transjordan failed to appear. Another notable absentee was ʿAwda abu Taya, at that time the dominant figure in the south, who was more influential than Hamad bin Jazi.[34]

Nor is it entirely clear how those present received Samuel's offer. According to some accounts they welcomed his plan, either because they were afraid that the alternative was a French occupation or because British presence still allowed for extensive autonomy.[35] Local accounts, however, suggest that they were puzzled by Samuel's scheme, doubting that in the current state of affairs self-government was indeed a feasible option.[36] And, while they were willing to give it at least a chance, it is still probably safe to assume that quite a few were disappointed with Britain's reluctance to extend its administration into Transjordan. Certainly widespread disappointment with the British plans was quick to surface. As one British intelligence report observed: "...there appears to be a distinct undercurrent of mingled dissatisfaction and mistrust of the policy of peaceful penetration at present being carried out."[37] An earlier report gives what appears to be a fairly accurate description of local dissatisfaction. It notes that the locals had expected the British to deliver practical results in the form of either military occupation or payment of regular subsidies to tribes in order to ensure the maintenance of order. But once the British failed to meet their expectations, people began complaining, asking: "What did he [the High Commissioner] do? He came, he went and left 3 shepheards [sic] behind."[38] Another report brought home the extent of local disillusionment: "British prestige in ES Salt [sic] Town very much depreciated. People have begun to realize that the British officials carry no authority - and therefore do not regard them any longer as likely to exercise any powers."[39]

Before turning to a closer examination of the way in which the British-supported local governments functioned, it remains to be explained why the British misread the local situation to such an extent as to render the arrangement proposed by Samuel at al-Salt unrealistic from the start. To begin with, there was a huge cultural gap between British officials and local tribal leaders. A recurrent theme in both the British officials' reports and personal letters was the local communities' sympathetic and gracious attitude towards them personally. And, hugely impressed by the Transjordanian notables' polite and friendly manner, the British in Palestine were quick to interpret their behaviour as unqualified support for the British administration. However, the Arab etiquette that demands perfect hospitality, respect for guests and extreme politeness, does not necessarily imply political agreement or support. The British, famous for their own tendency towards understatement, failed to recognise a similar trait among the tribesmen. These misunderstandings characterised the first few months of local government under British guidance. They also explain why the initial British reports were optimistic, taking great pride in the fact that the shaykhs agreed to all their suggestions and seemed to be co-operative. However, once they realised that their advice was being ignored and their orders disregarded, it began to dawn on them that, polite nodding apart, perhaps they had never secured an agreement at all.

Kathryn Tidrick's analysis of Britain's attitude towards administering the Arab world in the aftermath of World War One offers a useful conceptual framework for understanding Britain's misperceptions and behaviour during the early stages of its rule in Transjordan. She attempts to explain why the British were so confident in their ability to rule the Arabs with no more than a handful of British officers. According to Tidrick, Bedouin good manners had long appealed to the British ruling classes, who associated them with the concept of the English gentleman. This myth of the resemblance, and so affinity, between the English and Arabs had its roots in various travellers' accounts dating from the nineteenth century. Writers like John Burkhard, Richard Burton, Gifford Palgrave, Wilfrid Blunt and Charles Doughty promoted the image of the noble Arab who, they emphasised, unlike other Orientals, was a true gentleman.[40] Furthermore, this travel literature had another effect as it contributed to the belief that the British possessed a specialised knowledge of the Arab world, knowledge that could be easily translated into power. This well-established tradition of British expertise vis-à-vis the Arabs "came to be regarded as almost a racial characteristic: it was the nature of Englishmen to understand Arabs, and it was in the nature of Arabs to be understandable to Englishmen."[41]

It was this "common gentlemanliness" coupled with a belief in British special knowledge of Arabian society that gave rise to British overconfidence in their ability to rule Arabia. Thus, the British "felt they could rely on a native aristocracy with whom they felt so much at ease to co-operate with them once it had been established that it was in their interests to do so."[42] The ease British officials felt in the company of the Bedouin or tribal Arabs also arose, in part, from a sense that their lives were structured by a similar experience. Tidrick points to a resemblance between the desert way of life and the English public school, where most British officials who served in the Middle East were educated. Tidrick concludes that "the ease which Englishmen felt in the Bedouin company, combined with a tradition of English interest in Arabia, produced a feeling that the English presence in Arab lands had something quite natural and inevitable about it."[43]

Tidrick's all-encompassing theory should be treated with some caution. Certainly the alleged Anglo-Arab affinity did not apply to all British officials in the Middle East and her theory of the public school tends to essentialise the graduates, presenting them in their ideal-type form. However, the theory is useful in understanding Transjordan at this particular moment in time. Britain's complacency with regard to governing Transjordan and her officials' attitude towards the local shaykhs are better understood in light of this tradition. However, there were additional factors that need to be taken into account, complementing Tidrick's explanations, in order to fully explain British behaviour. The ease and satisfaction that the British felt in the company of Transjordanian notables were perhaps also due to the marked contrast between the shaykhs' friendly behaviour and the attitude of the Palestinian Arabs who were suspicious of the British and regarded them as collaborators with the Jews. This juxtaposition was further fed by a deep British cultural bias against the Palestinian population. As noted by Bernard Wasserstein, many British officials despised the Palestinian Arabs, regarding them as inferior to what they claimed were the genuine Arabs of the desert and the cultivated areas outside Palestine. While glorifying their neighbours as authentic and pure Arabs, they denounced the Palestinians as "degenerate 'levantines' of mixed race."[44]

In Transjordan, however, it soon became apparent that, regardless of what they believed, the British had a poor understanding of the country and its people. And it was their failure to grasp the realities of local society that largely accounts for the shortcomings of their rule. At this point it is important to note the diversity of local views regarding Britain's policy, something the British conspicuously neglected. Oblivious to the nuances of local politics, the British failed to realise that the shaykhs who had first approached them were not necessarily the dominant forces in the country. On the contrary, they were the weaker local notables. They approached the British precisely because they were either unable to curb the encroachment of their more powerful rivals or because they hoped to improve their position within their constituency. This was especially true of the townspeople and semi-settled tribesmen, who lacked an effective military force of their own. They dreaded the emergence of a power vacuum, which would give an overwhelming advantage to the nomadic tribes, who, in the main, did not seek British involvement. Moreover, these shaykhs were uncertain of their own position and needed to forge some kind of relationship with a higher authority. The British, responsible for Transjordan and stationed in large numbers just across the river, were in effect the only game in town. These shaykhs would welcome any government, as long as it allowed for some measure of autonomy. In this context it is worth noting that the British were welcome, if only to prevent a possible French occupation. Given France's heavy-handed behaviour in Syria, it was the last thing these locals wanted.

A combination of these factors convinced some segments of society to throw in their lot with the British. A prime example was al-Salt. It was Transjordan's largest town and because it had served as the main government centre for the preceding fifty years it enjoyed a high degree of security, thus developing a dependence on the presence of a governing power in the town. Other settled urban communities, including Amman, Madaba and Jarash, as well as various rural communities, though less dependent on the government than al-Salt, were no less afraid of the nomads. In

Karak, the Majali's relations with the Bani Hamida tribes had been strained for some time. The Majalis also had a long tradition of co-operating with external forces -- first the Ottomans, then Faysal and now the British -- to ensure their local standing. Indeed, they had already been in close touch with the British during the Faysali government.[45] The ʿAdwan's tense relations with their chief rivals, the Bani Sakhr, had further deteriorated over the question of who would control Madaba. Then there was the challenge posed by Mithqal al-Fayiz to the ʿAdwani's leadership of the Balqaʾ alliance. Inter-tribal politics might also explain why Hamad bin Jazi, leader of several strong nomadic tribes, was ready to co-operate with the British. During the war the Huwaytat had split, with some, under Hamad, electing to support the Ottomans, while others, under the leadership of his rival, ʿAwda abu Taya, chose to back the Arab Revolt. Of the two leaders, ʿAwda proved a better gambler, emerging as Faysal's principal ally during his campaign in Transjordan and subsequently the strongman in the south. It is likely that after the war Hamad tried to improve his position by forging an alliance with the British. Several minor Bani Sakhr chiefs also approached the British Representative in al-Salt for similar reasons. The region's major players, however, having no need of the British, stayed back.[46] These divisions in local society escaped the attention of most British observers, who laboured under the misapprehension that they managed to secure unanimous support.

It was the Intelligence Officer of the Beersheba district who tried to impress a completely different reading of the situation on the Palestine government, seriously questioning the feasibility of Samuel's scheme. Criticising the government's over-simplistic approach, he warned the Administration "not to be influenced too much by the blandishments of Sheikhs who represent the fellahin clustered round the towns rather than the unruly and truculent nomads comprising the tribes further out." Elaborating on the different interests of peasants and nomads as reflected in their attitudes towards the British administration, he exposed the fallacy of Britain's policy: "Our task with neither money nor troops, if I may be permitted to say it, will be an extremely onerous if not impossible one."[47] The British Representative in al-Salt expressed a similar view, pointing out that the nomadic tribes "are frankly looking for subsidy...If they do not get a subsidy, they are likely to become troublesome, *no matter how polite and pleased they may seem nor how many promises they may make to any of us whether here or in Jerusalem.*"[48]

False Start: Implementing the Local Governments

The brief period of local government exposed all Britain's misperceptions and miscalculations vis-à-vis Transjordan. Following the meeting at al-Salt, Britain despatched several officers to help set up three local governments: Major Somerset and Captain Monckton in ʿAjlun; Major Camp and Captain Alen Kirkbride in al-Salt with Captain Dunbar Brunton sent to Amman; and Captain Alec Kirkbride in Karak. All six, holding purely advisory positions, were instructed to encourage the inhabitants to form local councils, nominate paramount chiefs, collect taxes and uphold the existing gendarmerie. A few weeks later, the Foreign Office decided to send a seventh officer, Captain F. G. Peake, to take overall charge of the gendarmerie.

By then the British had introduced another feature to their local government scheme, establishing a local police force, known as the Reserve Force, under British command.[49] The following analysis of the three governments exposes the assorted social and political realities on the ground, which, in time, were to have a strong effect on the evolution of modern Jordan.

ᶜAjlun

ᶜAjlun was the most densely populated area in Transjordan. Three quarters of the population were villagers clustered in around 130 villages. The remainder were semi-nomadic tribes, the largest of which was the Bani Hasan confederacy. These tribes, which engaged in a combined pastoral and farming economy, lived in the southern part of ᶜAjlun around the Circassian town of Jarash and in lands further to the east. The north-eastern part of the region along the Hijaz railway line was the domain of the Khuraysha and Jubur tribes of the Bani Sakhr as well as of several small nomadic and semi-nomadic tribes, members of the Ahl al-Shimal confederacy under the Bani Sakhr, including the Sirhan, ᶜIsa and Bani Khalid. To the west, along the Jordan Valley (Ghawr), the Sukhur al-Ghawr, al-Ghazawiyya and al-Mashalkha roamed the two banks of the river. Nomads from the Hawran, such as the Sardiyya and Ahl al-Jabal also camped in ᶜAjlun for part of the year. The region's principal towns Irbid and Ramtha, with about 3,500 and 4,500 inhabitants respectively, were inhabited by local tribes, though Irbid was also home to an immigrant community of merchants from Syria and Palestine.[50]

The British failed to form a centralised local government in ᶜAjlun, as planned. The most they achieved were a number of separate localised 'governments,' reflecting the existing socio-political tribal order. Initially, impressed by the warm welcome he had received, Major Somerset was quick to write home that the shaykhs had all accepted Britain's terms and were busy setting up a local government in Irbid. But his rejoicings proved premature as only a few days later the shaykhs of Kura, Bani ᶜUbayd, Jabal ᶜAjlun and Jarash all demanded the establishment of their own government within their regions of influence. Somerset appreciated that he had little choice in the matter. Despite protests from the leaders of Ibrid, he therefore helped set up not one but four governments, at least on paper: one in Irbid under the leadership of ᶜAli Khulqi, a former senior administrator in the Faysali government, which confederated the northern districts; the Dayr Yusuf government led by the Shurayda family, following an agreement between the leaders of the Kura and Bani ᶜUbayd districts to form a united government; the southern government of Jabal ᶜAjlun under shaykh Rashid al-Khuzaᶜi of the Furayhat; and further south a government whose rule embraced the Circassian town Jarash, the Miᶜrad district under the al-Kayid family from the village of Suf as well as the Bani Hasan tribes to the east. In addition, following the border demarcation between France and Britain in January 1921, which led to incorporation of the district of Ramtha into Transjordan, Somerset appointed the son of the local leader Fawwaz al-Zuᶜbi as governor, and established a police post. But even this rather radical modification of the original plan did not last long with other shaykhs trying, with some success, to form governments of their own. For example, soon after the formation of the Ibrid government, the leader of the Wustiyya district, Naji al-ʿAzzam, with Somerset's reluctant consent, established an independent government.[51]

There are Jordanian historians who accuse Somerset of pursuing a policy of divide and rule, encouraging the establishment of several governments in order to ensure the country's dependence on the British.[52] However, far from reflecting British meddling, these governments were an outgrowth of local reality, namely the product of deep-seated local identities, which led to the re-emergence of local chieftaincies under strong leaders. These chiefs seeking to strengthen their position were intent upon mobilising their tribes and striking alliances, a local phenomenon characteristic of periods of uncertainty and weak government. It marked a return to the situation prior to the extension of Ottoman rule in Transjordan during the last third of the nineteenth century. Now, half a century later, tribal shaykhs, whose position had been undermined by the Ottoman government, took advantage of its absence to reinforce their leadership. In some cases, the same families that had dominated the area before the Ottoman advance re-emerged as local rulers, for example, the Shurayda of Kura and the Furayhat of Jabal ʿAjlun.[53] It is hardly surprising, therefore, that the various communities around ʿAjlun, having at long last recovered their independence, refused to recognise the Irbid government's authority and resented the town's leaders. This pattern, with each district, or group of villages forming a tribal unit and rejecting the authority of neighbouring, possibly rival, tribes, repeated itself during the first years of the Emirate and ultimately led to the Kura rebellion of 1921-1922. This division along tribal lines, in the words of Sulayman Musa, this "tribal spirit" (*al-ruh al-qabaliyya*),[54] was the principal reason why Somerset failed to establish a single unified government. In fact, rather than ameliorate this state of constant tribal competition, his actions served only to preserve it.

Having recovered from his initial set-back, Somerset reconciled himself to the new divisions. He drew some encouragement from the way the locals welcomed him, writing that "they are all very polite and say they will agree to what ever I decide," and adding that "everybody is very pleased to see me." Flattered by his cordial reception Somerset totally misconstrued local etiquette and was convinced that the locals' convivial hospitality was a statement of political support.[55] Less susceptible, Somerset's aide, Captain Monckton, offered a more plausible explanation of the shaykhs' affable behaviour. Sent to administer the southern part of the region, Monckton picked up on local culture and etiquette, writing that "it is the custom of the country *always* to *welcome* a *stranger*."[56]

Comparing Britain's leniency to France's brusque behaviour in nearby Hawran, and fearing French advancement southward, most locals were far from hostile to the British. They were also worried about the prospect of Zionist colonisation east of the river. But none of this meant that they embraced the Palestine government's policies in their entirety. Rather, the local leaders were bent on exploiting the British presence to consolidate their position, while enjoying a large measure of autonomy. Indeed, even Somerset soon confessed that "[t]he people here are tiresome, all wanting to be officials and have government in their own district," and admitted that "It is difficult to control them without troops...[and] The Government isn't functioning very much…" He also failed to persuade the shaykhs to collect taxes. In the absence of real power, the best he could do was to "engage in a propaganda campaign."[57]

If Somerset failed in his primary task of setting up an effective local government, he could, nevertheless chalk up a number of achievements to his name. He did manage to collect some taxes, especially after receiving support from Peake's Reserve Force whose soldiers enforced payment in Jarash in December 1920. With the consent of local leaders, Somerset appointed several officials, including a *qaimaqam*, treasurer and public prosecutor, to each mini-government, thereby providing the region with a skeleton administration, eventually utilised by the new Emirate. Towns such as Irbid and Jarash had the benefit of a small gendarme force. Finally, the local socio-political structure worked, fragmented though it may have been, for, as Somerset reported, the area was relatively quiet with the local shaykhs exercising their authority. Monckton remembered how all the "paramount sheikhs were excellent at keeping order, and this was no mean feat in an area where everyman [sic] carried a rifle."[58] This accomplishment was partly due to the support of the local farming population, who, in their desire for a quiet life and dreading the incursions of nomads from the east, supported the current political system.

Somerset's personality and singular gifts also, it seems, played a part in helping to establish at least the facade of government. Certainly that was how Monckton chose to remember things, when years later he attributed Somerset's success to his command of Arabic, vast local knowledge and strong character. According to Monckton, Somerset took great pains to learn the details of the various land disputes and memorise the names of all the shaykhs. He would regularly tour the country, befriending the Arabs and spending time in their company. Having studied local customs, he was always very careful to observe them.[59] Somerset's style as portrayed by Monckton resembled the image of British officers in India, South-East Asia and Africa. More than any of his colleagues in Transjordan, he embodied the image of the ideal British District Officer, who was expected, and indeed expected himself, to exercise authority single-handedly by strength of character, wisdom and courage. In doing so Somerset won the admiration and respect of his colleagues.[60]

Leaving Somerset's personal qualities aside, however, there is little doubt that like many of his counterparts throughout the colonial world, his qualified success owed much to the power of the Empire. It was the British troops across the river, rather than his personality or familiarity with the place and its inhabitants, that underpinned Somerset's authority. The local population was well aware that a massive British force was camped only a short distance away in Palestine, a point rammed home by the Royal Air Force's frequent flights over Transjordan. Monckton impressed on the locals that Jaffa was only an hour's flight away, a tactic employed also by Brunton in Amman and Kirkbride in Karak. British officers on the ground made full use of various other symbols of Empire, including the flag and uniforms, in order to buttress their authority. Monckton, for example, remarked that the British flag flying over his house in Jarash was sufficient to deter the nomads from raiding the town. He further reported that he had bought a big house in the village of ʿAjlun simply in order to enhance his standing among the locals. Big houses were a rarity and usually owned by local strongmen, the imposing stone house built by the head of the Shurayda family in Tibna (Kura) in the mid-nineteenth century being a case in point. In line with this policy of prestige, Monckton also considered opening a *madafa* (guest-house), since "the prestige to be derived from an 'open House' if properly conducted is of course enormous," but had to give up this plan due to lack of funds.[61] In sum, as Mary Wilson noted perceptively, "kindness, influence and propaganda were to be their [the British] means of authority."[62]

The Balqa'

The British effort to establish a local government in the Balqa' in central Transjordan was their most ambitious, but, as it turned out, ill-fated undertaking. There were several reasons why the British could expect the task of setting up a centralised government in the Balqa' to be a relatively easy and straightforward affair. First, the area was the home of mostly nomadic or semi-nomadic tribes with whom the British, somewhat conceitedly, presumed they could reach an understanding. Second, they had already established good relations with the Balqa' tribes. Third, they had invested a great deal, in terms of money, personnel and infrastructure, in the government of the Balqa', certainly more than anywhere else. Furthermore, once they realised their initial optimism notwithstanding, that they were unable to control the country, they established a local military force, under British command, to support the government. But, yet again, Britain's initial confidence proved misplaced. It was in the Balqa' that the British faced their greatest challenge, having to tackle several of the country's most powerful nomadic tribes. Still the government of the Balqa', more than any other, exhibited a high degree of continuity, utilising infrastructure left over from the days of the Arab Government.

The majority of the Balqa's population, mostly semi-settled, semi-nomadic and nomadic tribespeople, lived in encampments, leading, to varying degrees, a mobile life. Politically, they were divided into two powerful and rival tribal confederacies. The nomadic camel-herding Bani Sakhr, whose tribal domain reached the Syrian desert as far as Wadi Sirhan, controlled the eastern part of the region where their shaykhs owned large tracts of cultivated land. They were also a political force in Amman, which, at the time, was little more than a village numbering about 5,000 inhabitants, the majority Circassians and Syrian merchants, who had immigrated to Transjordan in the late nineteenth century. The Bani Sakhr's rivals, the ʿAdwan, led the semi-settled Balqa' alliance which controlled the fertile western part of the Balqa' up to the banks of the Jordan River. This confederacy included the many small tribes known as the Balqawiyya as well as the ʿAjarma and Daʿja tribes. The Bani Hasan, a large group of tribes in the north-eastern Balqa', and the northern Bani Hamida were also part of the alliance. Despite their location in the heart of the Balqa' region, on the hill slopes overlooking the Jordan River, the semi-settled ʿAbbad tribes were not part of the local alliance but instead maintained cordial relations with the Bani Sakhr. Al-Salt, the country's largest town with about 12,000 inhabitants, and its associated tribes, managed to maintain its independence from the two rival chieftaincies.[63]

The ʿAdwani shaykhs proved enthusiastic supporters of the British regime. In August 1920, they provided Samuel with an armed escort as he made his way to the meeting at al-Salt. Sultan al-ʿAdwan, paramount chief of the Balqaʾ, was one of the two shaykhs (the other was Rufayfan al-Majali) who dominated the meeting and orchestrated the positive response to Samuelʼs proposals, at least in British eyes.[64] A few days later according to British reports Sultan and his son Majid "reiterated their expressions of friendship and wish to help the British," expressing their impatience "at the long delay in making a definite start with the new regime."[65] The ʿAdwan together with their Balqaʾ alliance took an active part in local government, where Majid represented the latter alongside notables from al-Salt, Amman and Madaba. Yet these gestures of good will notwithstanding, it soon became clear that support for the British did not necessarily mean that the ʿAdwan were willing to submit to government authority. The local governmentʼs influence was limited to al-Salt and its surrounding villages, while the Balqaʾ tribes continued to enjoy complete autonomy. Like other areas of Transjordan this period saw the re-emergence of the ʿAdwan chieftaincy as an independent political entity after years of subordination to the Ottoman state. The ʿAdwanis had been the lords of the western Balqaʾ until the late 1860s, but were forced to surrender much of their autonomy and power to the Ottomans. Making the best of things, the tribes, exploiting the Ottoman land registration ordinance, shifted from a pastoral to a farming economy adopting a semi-settled rather than nomadic life. In the process, the ʿAdwan shaykhs accumulated vast tracts of land and became big landowners. However, though they acquired great riches, they also lost their mobility and with it a measure of their military power. Against this background, the decision of the ʿAdwan to support the British seems to derive from their need to fall back on an external power. British support could potentially prevent the Bani Sakhr from encroaching on their territory, to maintain their leadership of the Balqaʾ tribes and protect their vast economic enterprises.

The Bani Sakhr took the opposite approach. Confident in their strength and vitality, they felt no need to rush to the support of the British, pursuing a more independent, occasionally confrontational line instead. Hence, in August 1920 their representatives failed to show up at al-Salt. The Bani Sakhr, however, did keep several lines of communication with the British open. Accordingly, the brother of Mithqal al-Fayiz, one of the two leading shaykhs of the confederacy, called on the British officer in Jericho and when Major Camp, the British Representative in al-Salt, sent the Bani Sakhrʼs shaykhs telegrams, they replied in a friendly manner. But, when the British tried to extend their influence from al-Salt to Amman, Mithqal was quick to dispatch a series of "menacing telegrams" to the effect that the designated British Representative, Captain Dunbar Brunton, was a *persona non grata*.[66]

What followed was a power struggle between Brunton and the Bani Sakhr shaykhs led by Mithqal. When Brunton established a military force to support the local government and defend the settled populations from the nomads, Mithqal responded by mobilising the tribes in the area and, in an attempt to consolidate his own power, forming a new alliance under his leadership. Reassured by his surprisingly warm reception in Amman, Brunton was convinced that he could adhere to the traditional imperial policy of co-opting and ruling through the local elite. He thus suggested appointing Mithqal as the president of a Tribal Council and the official paramount chief of the Bani Sakhr, Mashhur al-Fayiz, as the governor of Jiza, giving both "tribal autonomy as far as possible." But Brunton's plans came to nothing as Mithqal remained aloof and refused to meet him. To Brunton's intense frustration, as is clear from his reports to his superiors, despite being the representative of a powerful empire he lacked the military means to control Mithqal, who emerged as the strong man on the ground.[67]

Quick to realise that without adequate military support he could not successfully challenge the Bani Sakhr, Brunton concentrated on building up the local Reserve Force. The Reserve Force was a compromise product of the decision not to send British troops to Transjordan and the impossibility of exercising authority in the region without military backup. It became the nucleus of the Arab Legion, and was one of the local government's more important legacies to the future Emirate. Brunton recruited to the force ex-soldiers of the Ottoman and Arab armies who were wandering the streets of Amman, as well as Circassians. The latter seemed perfect for the job. Before the war they had served in an Ottoman force commanded by their leader, Mirza Wasfi, whose duty it was to control the nomadic tribes harassing the settled zone's inhabitants.[68]

The Reserve Force's baptism of fire took place in the village of Sahab and proved to be a turning point in the balance of power between the Bani Sakhr and the British-supported local government. The story of the affair as told by Uriel Dann focused on the British performance, overlooking, like the majority of scholarly accounts, the part played by the locals in the unfolding of events. The villagers of Sahab, south-east of Amman, were proving troublesome. Constantly defying government orders, they also refused to pay taxes, expelling the tax collectors, and stealing several telegraph poles to boot. Although the Reserve Force was as yet unprepared for action, Brunton decided to use it both to teach the villagers a lesson and as an example to the rest of the region. But the Force's first attempt to subdue the village failed. Commanded by Brunton's deputy, ʿArif al-Hasan, and supported by gendarmes from al-Salt, it suffered a humiliating defeat at the hands of the locals. The next day Brunton himself arrived on the scene with reinforcements and dispatched an ultimatum to the village to surrender. According to Dann -- who presumably based his account on Brunton's testimony given many years later -- a brief battle took place following which the village headmen surrendered so that "the Reserve Force had come out of its first action with flying colours."[69]

There is, however, no evidence of any exchange of fire and according to Brunton's own report at the time, the surrender was the result of the mediation efforts of several shaykhs. Brunton and his deputy advertised their determination to attack the village, a propaganda strategy commonly used by the British throughout Transjordan, and employed here to good effect. ʿArif al-Hasan went one better and informed the shaykhs that he had asked for aerial support. Having instilled a fear of the Empire into the locals, Brunton then asked the shaykhs to decide whether they were friends or foes of the local government. Unwilling to face the wrath of the British Empire, the shaykhs were quick to act, with Haditha al-Khuraysha, shaykh of the Khuraysha tribe of the Bani Sakhr and Minwar bin Hadid, shaykh of the Hadid, persuading the villagers to accept Brunton's terms. In his account of the events Brunton acknowledged the shaykhs' part in ending the affair, remarking that Haditha, in particular, "deserves the greatest credit for the way in which he acted as intermediary." He went on to describe the shaykh as "sensible and reliable… is not wealthy but never begs like others and is generous to a degree. His manners are quiet and he has a great personal charm. One might term him the only real gentleman among the sheikhs of this region."[70] Haditha clearly embodied the stereotypical Bedouin gentleman so admired by the British. It is worth noting that Britons serving in Transjordan in later years often remarked on his virtues.

Although not decisive, the demonstration of power had its effect, or at least this was Brunton's impression. He reported that the tribesmen now respected the government. Indeed, upon his return from Sahab, Brunton at last found the formidable Mithqal waiting for him in Amman. Henceforth, lukewarm though his attitude might be, Mithqal kept in touch with the British and the Reserve Force, choosing not to confront them directly.[71]

But, while Brunton tried to reach some kind of *modus vivendi* with Mithqal, the latter was more concerned with improving and consolidating his position within his chieftaincy, perhaps as a precautionary measure vis-à-vis the British. Mithqal provoked a rift in the rival Balqa' alliance to form what was seen by Brunton as a "block of Bedouin" which represented a threat to the order he was trying to establish. The ʿAjarma, Bani Hamida and ʿAbbad were among the communities which now recognised Mithqal's leadership, forming the most prominent force in the Balqa'.[72]

By now Brunton displayed a better understanding of what was going on, but this new realisation together with strong local opposition brought about a deeper sense of frustration. He withdrew with his force to al-Salt and, soon after, resigned and left the country for good. A short while before his departure he had been assigned to work under Peake, inspector of the police force and now commander of the Reserve Force. But Peake fared no better than Brunton. Mithqal, seeking to prove that he was a force to be reckoned with, imprisoned the British officer. However, having made his point, Mithqal, being realistic and careful not to put his power to the test against the Empire, released Peake after only 24 hours.[73]

Karak

Of all Transjordan's local governments, it was the one in Karak that actually attempted to establish a form of central government.[74] In light of the region's exceptional degree of coherence this government, in principle at least, had a greater chance of success. Karak had a strong local identity, shared by all the region's tribes. Furthermore, according to custom Karaki tribes did not raid each other. The town of Karak was the region's focal point and dominated the entire area from the Dead Sea Ghawr in the west to the plateau to the east. Karak enjoyed cordial relations with the nomadic tribes of the Bani ʿAtiyya to the south and west of the town, though its relations with the semi-nomadic Bani Hamida in the north were strained. The balance of power between the two local tribal alliances, the *Gharaba*, under the Majali and the *Sharaqa* under the Tarawna made for a reasonable degree of co-operation, competition and suspicion notwithstanding.

Unlike the lands to the north, Karak did not witness the re-emergence of local forces, mostly because these had never disappeared in the first place. Whereas the Ottomans had managed to curb the autonomy of the local lords in the settled areas of ʿAjlun and the Balqaʾ, their success in incorporating Karak into the Ottoman state was at best partial, and was achieved through partnership with and not the displacement of local leaders.[75] This long-established, experienced and recognised leadership was well placed to assume the responsibilities of government. Certainly the region's new Council reflected local political reality, with the British Representative Alec Kirkbride confirming that the elections to the Council had been a straightforward affair owing to the elected shaykhs' indisputable claim to membership. The existence of a pool of capable veteran administrators, members of the region's prominent Christian tribes who were part of the *Gharaba* alliance, also worked in the government's favour.[76]

On top of all this, the British had also formed a special relationship with the area's leaders, which continued even after their withdrawal from Transjordan in late 1919. Immediately following the al-Salt meeting, in which Rufayfan had played an important role in securing local support, Samuel invited the Karaki shaykhs to Jerusalem as his guests. The atmosphere of good will on the part of both sides worked to the advantage of the British-supported government. In light of the above it was hardly surprising that the newly elected Council started on the right footing, with great enthusiasm designating itself the "National Government of Moab." Upon its appointment the Council instantly dissolved the Faysali government and dismissed officials from outside the region. It was, however, careful to preserve a measure of continuity by re-appointing local officials. The Council also elected Rufayfan to the post of *mutasarrif*, although this represented little more than official recognition of his political primacy. Another initiative adapted the law to the existing state of affairs by adding some local customs to the Ottoman and Faysali laws. The government also issued official stamps boasting its emblem. The entire budget of the government was £1,000, derived from a concession to exploit local minerals sold to a naïve British entrepreneur. The government used this money to pay its officials' salaries, and those of 50 gendarmes.

As long as the local balance of power remained intact, the Council was able to maintain some measure of control. This was qualified however, since no taxes were collected, as the shaykhs refused to pay them, and the southern town of Tafila soon began to run itself autonomously. But even the limited authority of the government collapsed when a local dispute shook the balance of power in Karak. This conflict rendered any centralised government co-ordination impossible, and the Karak administration, now a government in name only, became as ineffective as the rest. With no external, neutral, higher authority such as the Ottoman or Faysal's governments to turn to, reconciliation between the warring factions proved difficult if not impossible. Although some settlement was reached, it did not clear the atmosphere. Tension continued and became a pretext for an even more severe clash between the two alliances in the first months of Abdullah's Emirate.[77]

Operating independently and in isolation from his superiors in Jerusalem -- the telegraph lines in Karak were out of order -- Kirkbride's position proved particularly precarious. All he had to fall back on were propaganda and the politics of prestige and, like his colleagues, he sought to impress the locals by periodic flights of British planes. Quick to recognise the inadequacy of the British scheme, he chose to make the best of things, treating the whole affair with cheerful disdain. He spent his time riding, sightseeing and shooting, as well as touring the area and establishing personal relations with the inhabitants. Summing up his experience in his memoirs, Kirkbride quoted one of the Council members, saying that "it was fun."[78]

Ma'an Area

The British did not even try to control the area south of Tafila, nominally part of the Hijaz Government. However, the state of affairs in that region, which became part of the Emirate in 1925, closely resembled that of the rest of Transjordan in terms of tribal mobilisation. This vast area was mostly desert land, with only a few small permanent settlements, Wadi Musa, Shawbak, Ma'an and 'Aqaba, situated where water was available. Nomadic tribes, including the Bani 'Atiyya, Hajaya and Sa'idiyyin roamed the region, which was dominated by the Huwaytat tribes. The Huwaytat was a confederacy of several tribes, whose domain stretched from the southern desert to the town of Tafila in the north. Traditionally the Huwaytat combined camel herding with some farming, mainly in the fertile lands of Jabal Shara west of Ma'an. However, in the years leading to the war two of their most gifted leaders, 'Abtan bin Jazi and 'Awda abu Taya united the tribes and diverted their energy into raiding, which soon became the Huwaytat's main source of income. United and powerful, the Huwaytat raided deep into Arabian lands, greatly increasing the number of camels in their possession. Pastoralism led to nomadism and as a result the Huwaytat soon neglected their cultivated lands.

A few years prior to the outbreak of the war the Huwaytat split following the murder of 'Abtan and the revenge killing of a member of Abu Taya family. During the war one division of the Huwaytat, led by the Abu Taya, allied themselves with the Arab Revolt in return for large sums of money. By contrast, their rivals, the Ibn Jazi, elicited considerable sums of money from the Ottomans, who were hoping to secure their support. As a result, by the end of the war the Huwaytat not only possessed a great many camels but huge sums of money as well. According to a British report, by the end of the war the Abu Taya family had £50,000 in gold and the tribes owned 20,000 camels. Hamad bin Jazi was thought to still have war money as late as 1931 and was considered one of the richest shaykhs in Transjordan. Whereas by the end of the war most of the Huwaytat led a wholly nomadic way of life, some of their tribes such as the Nu'aymat and Mara'iyya were semi-nomadic. They combined farming in Jabal Shara with raising sheep, camel herding and raiding, all within limited range. Clearly the Huwaytat were at the peak of their power in the aftermath of the war. Although still divided, they continued to raid Najdi tribes who were too weak to retaliate. The town of Ma'an fell under the control of 'Awda abu Taya who jailed the local governor, occupied the government house and turned it into his headquarters. His rival, Hamad bin Jazi became the lord of Rashadiyya just north of the town.[79]

Conclusion

The British quickly realised that it was impossible to govern Transjordan with a system of local governments supported by a minuscule British contingent. Officers on the ground were constantly asking the government of Palestine to despatch British forces, with Samuel supporting their demand in his communications to London. The French were also putting pressure on Britain, demanding more rigorous efforts to prevent raids to the Hawran and to check Syrian exiles who took refuge in Transjordan. They threatened to take unilateral action, implying the possibility of an invasion southwards.[80] The arrival of Abdullah bin Husayn at Ma'an in November 1920 threatened to undermine Britain's nominal control of the country even further, and brought the experiment in local government to an end. Exchanging one form of indirect rule for another, that of the Hashemite Emirate, the new British venture proved a success. It was Abdullah who would rule the country with British aid and supervision for the next three decades.

The first few years of British-Transjordanian relations were a time of mutual adjustment, which continued, to a degree, even after the establishment of the Emirate. During this period both sides got to know each other, assessing one another's weaknesses and strengths, as well as determination. The tribes realised that Britain had a firm stake in the country and was willing to defend its interests, if necessary, by force. The British discovered that the more powerful tribes were a force to be reckoned with and that some aspects of their autonomy should be respected. No less importantly, they also finally conceded that as outsiders they had difficulty in understanding and handling the tribes. The early 1920s were thus formative years in British-Transjordanian relations. Indeed, as will be seen in the next chapter, even the first few years of the Emirate were beset by troubled relations between Britain, the local inhabitants and Abdullah. Only towards the middle of the decade did the British and the locals finally manage to establish a *modus vivendi*.

There were two contradictory features of the interregnum period, encompassing both the Faysali government and the British-supported local governments, which had a crucial effect on the evolution of modern Jordan. First, though failing to maintain an effective administration, these two political frameworks did uphold various government institutions, most of which they had inherited from the Ottomans. They ran a skeleton administration complete with local bureaucrats, tax collectors, courts and a police force, all of which meant that Abdullah's government did not have to start from scratch. This institutional configuration became the nucleus of the young Emirate. Second, the years 1918-1921 witnessed the mobilisation of Transjordanian society, which manifested itself in a return to arms, an increase in the shaykhs' financial and military power, and the resurrection of tribal chieftaincies, which now controlled the whole of the country. As a result, the fledgling Emirate was faced with the formidable challenge of dealing with several well-organised tribal alliances, all armed to the teeth, with extensive military experience and able leadership. The following chapters focus on the one hand on the process of state-formation and on the other hand on its effects on Transjordan's tribal society.

CHAPTER TWO:
'BEDU AMIR' OR CONSTITUTIONAL
MONARCH? THE STRUGGLE FOR THE
NATURE OF THE EMIRATE, 1921-1924

After the disorderly performance of the local governments the British tried another tack. Their new approach preserved the concept of indirect rule, but instead of it being devolved upon local units, it was vested in one ruler, Abdullah bin Husayn, who initially took on the responsibility for a six-month trial period. The arrangement, through which he was the ruler of Transjordan under the aegis of the British Mandate in Palestine, was eventually made permanent and would culminate in the establishment of the Hashemite Kingdom of Jordan. An on-going experiment, the first three years of joint British-Hashemite rule were crucial to the future of the state. The initial lack of a clear British blue-print for the development of the new political entity and the different agendas of the various political actors gave rise to a fierce struggle as to its nature and orientation. This struggle has been presented too often as a clash of personalities between Abdullah and the British officials. A discussion limited to this narrow perspective runs the risk of ignoring the heart of the matter. What was at stake were not personal configurations but more significant disagreements on the way the country should evolve.[1]

Several power centres within Transjordan competed with one another, pushing and pulling in different directions. The various components of the state-in-the-making brought their own expectations, agendas and practical methods for implementing them. Abdullah saw Transjordan as his temporary headquarters and a springboard for the recovery of the rest of Syria. In the meantime, he was interested in establishing his rule by securing the support of the tribes, in a chieftaincy-like coalition that was an extension of the tribal alliance that existed during the Arab Revolt. His nationalist allies, Syrian and Palestinian veterans of the Faysali state, shared his ambition of returning to Damascus. Indeed their determination to do so was greater than Abdullah's and they attempted to use Transjordan as a launch pad for anti-French military activity. By occupying most government posts they were also in a position to implement their vision of a modern, orderly and strong government.

This precept was informed by their experience as Ottoman officers and officials. The British officials in Amman and Jerusalem, by contrast, did not have a clear vision for the future of the country. Nevertheless, they had an ambitious plan in mind for the daily running of the administration and tried to promote the notion of a constitutional state characterised by central institutions, the rule of law and accountable government. On the receiving end, the local population was divided in their expectations. On the whole, their experience of statehood stemmed from the Ottoman legacy. The settled population sought a return to the Ottoman principles of lenient taxation in return for law and order in the settled zone, coupled with a degree of local autonomy. Strong tribes, mainly nomadic ones, preferred a weaker and less intrusive government and the preservation of their tribal autonomy.

The different actors contested several issues regarding the evolution and functioning of the state: the relationship with the mandatory power; the system of government, with related questions such as the status and authority of the Emir and the extent of bureaucratic influence within the institutional framework of the state. Finally, the debate revolved around the government's relations with and the extent of control over the tribes, both nomadic and settled. In fact, the attitude towards ruling the tribes represented one of the greatest bones of contention between all the actors.

Uneasy relations and periodical crises threatened to disrupt the whole arrangement. They culminated in the summer of 1924 in the most severe confrontation of the mandate period between the British government and Abdullah. After this time the British imposed a governing framework, which although frequently contested, challenged and consequently modified, remained the basic guideline for the development of the Emirate until its independence in 1946. During these years, several patterns of state-formation and state-society relations emerged that characterised and determined the development of the state.

During this early period of statehood, initial steps towards state-formation -- albeit hesitant and limited in scope -- also allowed the central government to partially subjugate the settled tribes. However, the administration was still weak and tribal chieftaincies were allowed to operate within the newly created and rudimentary state structure and enjoyed benefits from co-operating with it. As far as the nomadic and semi-nomadic tribes were concerned, the creation of a state had only a minimal effect on them. They benefited from the existence of weak and limited government and continued to enjoy complete autonomy in the desert, which composed 80% of the country, for another decade. Here, state authority manifested itself only through the personal influence of Abdullah.

Abdullah's Arrival in Transjordan

In November 1920 *sharif* Abdullah bin Husayn, the second son of *sharif* Husayn of Mecca and one of the leaders of the Arab Revolt, had advanced from the Hijaz to Ma'an ostensibly to attack the French in Syria. In the following four months he established relations with the local leaders. His presence and the activity of his agents threatened to undermine even the minimal British control based on local governments.

In a manner reminiscent of the Hashemite strategy during the Arab Revolt of building tribal alliances before their advancing, Abdullah secured the support of the two main confederacies that controlled the area stretching on both sides of the Hijaz railway from Maʿan to Amman. ʿAwda abu Taya, the leading Huwaytat shaykh emerged as one of his first supporters and even contributed £3,000 for the *sharif*'s use.[2] After achieving peace among the Huwaytat, an important tribal practice which carries with it political capital, Abdullah managed to register the support of ʿAwda's rival, Hamad bin Jazi.[3] In Amman, the shaykhs of the Bani Sakhr were united in their support of Abdullah, further undermining the British hold on the town.[4]

Maintaining the support of these two chieftaincies was no small achievement, since Abdullah did not possess the wherewithal to pay the shaykhs, the strategy employed by the Hashemites in the past. Uncertainty regarding the future of Transjordan, fear of British occupation and Jewish penetration and strained relations with the British Representatives can partly explain why these shaykhs found a suitable ally in Abdullah. The gravity of the Hashemites in Arabian politics in the aftermath of the war and their mantle as Islamic leaders, recognised descendents of the Prophet, probably strengthened Abdullah's appeal. Abdullah's own political experience and skills in tribal politics certainly also played a role. At the same time, however, many local leaders stayed aloof, at least for the time being. Some, like most of the leaders of Karak and the ʿAdwani shaykhs, maintained their loyalty to the British while others preferred not to commit. ʿAli Khulqi and other leaders in ʿAjlun ignored calls to join the Hashemite cause and continued to operate within the framework of the local governments until Abdullah's entrance into Amman in March 1921.[5]

Abdullah's agitation undermined what was left of the weak position of the Balqa' and Karak governments. *Sharif* ʿAli bin Husayn al-Harithi of Abdullah's entourage busily organised support for his master in Amman and al-Salt. Consequently the Bani Sakhr pursued a more confrontational line towards the British and the tribes in the al-Salt area stopped paying taxes. In Karak, the *Mutasarrif* Rufayfan al-Majali found himself in a difficult position and left the town for Jerusalem. With the help of Faysal, the British managed to persuade Abdullah to restrain his supporters lest he jeopardise Faysal's negotiations in Europe. For the time being Abdullah waited in Maʿan and the tension temporarily abated, but a more secure solution had to be found.[6]

The convening of the Cairo conference in March 1921 provided the opportunity to find a better settlement for Transjordan. This gathering followed the creation of a Middle East Department within the Colonial Office responsible for Palestine, Transjordan, Iraq and Aden, and the appointment of the new Colonial Secretary, Winston Churchill, who presided over the conference. But just before the conference's opening, Abdullah decided to abandon his position as an interested bystander and took a gamble by challenging the British and moving north. This step proved to be a success, and his entrance to Amman on 2 March drove the final nails into the local governments' coffins and made Abdullah a factor the British decision-makers had to reckon with. The ʿAjlun region -- hitherto not much affected by the Hashemite moves -- swayed towards the *sharif*. Monckton's successor in Jabal ʿAjlun failed to prevent a deputation of shaykhs from going to Amman to meet Abdullah.

In Qatrana, on his way to Amman, Abdullah received pledges of loyalty from the shaykhs of Karak and Tafila.[7] The delegates to the Cairo conference were thus faced with a *fait accompli*. Initially, the Palestine government had come up with a proposal to occupy the territory, to which end Somerset and Peake submitted a military plan. However, Abdullah's advance to Amman rendered this original design void. Churchill favoured reaching an arrangement with Abdullah rather than confronting him. The conference adjourned without a decisive decision regarding Transjordan. Churchill cabled London asking for the permission of the Cabinet to conquer Transjordan and to set out to Jerusalem to meet Abdullah. He hoped to arrive at an amicable solution and that Abdullah would consent to leave the country voluntarily, making way for direct British administration.

The fate of the territory was determined in Jerusalem. Churchill revised his position and acquiesced to Abdullah's presence in Transjordan. Both men came to an agreement according to which the British government supported Abdullah's administration financially and militarily for a trial period of six months. Abdullah was also to receive a monthly subsidy of £5,000 and was given a British official to advise him. British policy at this time was limited in its objectives. Churchill hoped that with British assistance Abdullah would keep Transjordan quiet, thus securing Palestine and preventing anti-French activity on the Syrian border, which could have embarrassed the British government. By supporting Abdullah, Churchill also wanted to maintain and strengthen the Sharifian policy.[8] As the final status of the country had yet to be determined, it was impossible to set more elaborate guidelines for the development of the region. Yet Churchill's decision paved the way for the independent development of Transjordan under Hashemite rule. Thus, Jordan's creation is commonly viewed as little more than a strategy to serve British interests.[9] However, it is more correct to understand it as the evolution of a separate and unified political entity as a result of both British imperial interests and the moves taken by Abdullah in conjunction with important segments of local society.

Early Days: Building Tribal Alliances

Abdullah accepted Churchill's offer and returned to Amman to organise his new rule. He dissolved the local governments formed by the British and established three administrative provinces (*liwa*): ʿAjlun, Balqaʾ and Karak. On 11 April 1921 he formed his first government. The newly appointed central administration was mainly staffed by Arab nationalist exiles. The first government was composed of four Syrians, a Palestinian, a Hijazi and only one native Transjordanian. The British offered financial assistance, administrative guidance and military support from Palestine upon request and maintained a watchful position. The sole organised and effective military force at hand was a Hijazi household army of some 200 men under Hashemite command. Peake's Reserve Force was still under construction and dysfunctional.

For his part, Abdullah took only little interest in the daily administration of his government, leaving it to the discretion of the officials. Instead, he immersed himself in tribal politics and was kept busy securing support for his rule by making enormous efforts to satisfy and forge personal ties with the tribal shaykhs. In particular, Abdullah was careful to establish and maintain alliances with the strong nomadic tribes. For that purpose he removed them from the authority of the central government, and tribal affairs were governed either personally by him or by the Department of Tribal Administration headed by his cousin and confidant Emir Shakir bin Zayd. The result was the emergence of two almost separate systems of government. Nomadic or semi-nomadic tribes were under Abdullah's personal rule and enjoyed the persistence of chieftaincy-like patterns of ruling. The settled population was controlled by the Arab government along modern lines. This separation quickly proved inadequate, generating tension between the new regime and the population. This tribal policy also became a bone of contention among the different elements of the regime and in particular led to a conflict between Abdullah and his British critics.

Abdullah's need to win tribal support was manifold. For his own survival he was dependent on the strong tribes who held physical control over the country. He also needed to make good his pledge to rule Transjordan in a manner that would protect the eastern border of Palestine from raids. Therefore it was imperative for his political survival to succeed where the British had failed and to establish some sort of control over the nomads. This strategy made sense in a polity like Transjordan: a small population numbering around 200,000, organised mainly along tribal lines, which had not yet undergone processes of rapid urbanisation and industrialisation. By securing the support and co-operation of only a few dozen notables, Abdullah managed to achieve a degree of control over the population as a whole. In this regard an estimated census of the population, prepared by the Department of Tribal Administration in 1922, is most revealing. The document is broken down into locality or tribe. Next to each and every village, town or tribe it indicates the names of the shaykhs.[10] A related, although different, reason for Abdullah's tribal strategy was a consequence of the small military force placed at his disposal. The British refusal to allow Abdullah to raise an army of a several thousand men, supposedly with the aim of liberating Syria from the French, forced Abdullah to rely on the military power of the tribes. This was necessary in order both to assert his control over the country and to defend it from external threats like the Wahhabi attacks on local tribes since 1922.

For their part, the concept of a state was not new to the tribal chiefs and they were not inherently opposed to it, as common wisdom has suggested. The late Ottoman era proved that the tribes were amenable to state patronage.[11] Providing the new administration allowed the shaykhs a degree of autonomy, and the room to exercise their leadership over their fellow tribespeople, they would co-operate with it.

Abdullah's policy was an immediate success and the British swiftly voiced their approval. Colonel T. E. Lawrence, Churchill's advisor, sent a very positive account from Amman of Abdullah's first days in power. He reported that Abdullah and his lieutenants were busy settling tribal and family disputes, commenting that "[w]ith tribal elements of eastern part Abdullah's position is very strong." To British satisfaction, Abdullah appealed to the tribes to keep law and order on the borders with Palestine and Syria, and even began to collect taxes. Lawrence's sole recommendation was to concur with Abdullah's request for airplanes and armoured cars. Samuel also commented that Abdullah's personal influence was "a great asset." He recommended giving Abdullah generous financial support for hospitality and gift-giving, which would in turn reduce expenditure on a defence force.[12] Subsequent reports written by Albert Abramson, the first British Representative in Amman, and others credited Abdullah and members of his retinue with preventing large scale raids. They attributed this success to his prestige among the tribes as well as to his use of his household army.[13]

Abdullah's building of a tribal coalition was modelled on a typical Arabian chieftaincy. The British financial assistance together with support from his father and money borrowed from rich Transjordanian merchants allowed him to cement his relationships with tribal shaykhs. Regular payment of subsidies to shaykhs was a common means employed by successive rulers in Arabia for centuries in order to secure allegiance or at least their good behaviour. However, due to his limited resources, Abdullah was not able to pay regular subsidies to shaykhs and it seems that in most cases the payments were only occasional. Only in the case of shaykh Nuri Shaʿlan of the Ruwalla tribes is there evidence for the payment of a regular subsidy (until 1926).[14] Instead, Abdullah lavished other privileges on the most important leaders. He offered presents ranging from headgear to cars, transferred plots of state land to private owners and exempted or reduced the tax burden for certain tribes.[15] The Emir offered his new supporters public recognition and respect. He granted them honorary titles, invited them to public ceremonies, and allowed them to escort him on his many tours of the country to the extent that several of them become an integral part of his entourage. He often generously entertained them in his camp or, more importantly, honoured them by visiting their homes.[16] The chiefs enjoyed free access to the Emir, who acted on their behalf in government affairs, often bypassing and overruling government orders.

Apart from being a skilful and experienced tribal politician, Abdullah was able to draw upon a certain *savoir faire* in dealing with tribesmen. Abdullah, who spent most of his life in two of the most important urban centres of the Middle East, Mecca and Istanbul, was schooled in the culture of the desert and behaved in Transjordan like a 'Bedouin' shaykh in his dress, good manners and political style. When he was not in his camp in Marka, just outside Amman, he would tour the length and breadth of the country, holding court in the traditional tribal style. He even joined his shaykhs in outdoor games to the astonishment of the British and Arab officials.[17] A good illustration for the 'Bedouin' impression created by Abdullah can be found in the memoirs of Mendel Cohen, a Jewish carpenter who worked at Abdullah's palace between 1938-1948. Even he, who spoke fluent Arabic and knew the area well, begins his description of the Emir as follows:

> Abdullah was a *natural Bedouin*. With all the royal palaces, he [still] felt comfortable sitting in a tent. Even after the construction of the palace with its different rooms and wings he would prefer to spend the summer nights inside the tent that was pitched near the palace...As a *natural Bedouin* he respected and was fond of his horses, more than the fancy and expensive cars he had... he

would describe and praise the tent in detail...sometimes he received important guests in his tent...he would sit crossed-legged.[18]

Moreover, Abdullah's personal and direct style of ruling allowed him to take full advantage of his remarkable inter-personal skills. A variety of sources -- British, Arab (both pro and anti-Hashemite) and Zionist -- seem to agree that Abdullah was gifted with the ability to gain the affection of the people he met.[19]

In addition to securing the shaykhs' allegiance, Abdullah encouraged their participation in the building and strengthening of his rule, and consequently of the Emirate.[20] The reliance on the chiefs was a function of the government's weakness in this early period. In addition to the military handicap, the infrastructure the Emirate inherited from previous governments was lacking or needed time to be re-activated. Therefore, Abdullah was careful to act with the shaykhs and entrusted them with administrative tasks, thus recognising their leadership of their tribes. He re-appointed Rufayfan al-Majali as *mutasarrif* in Karak and sent a committee of shaykhs headed by Shakir to settle a dispute among the Bani Hamida. Mashhur al-Fayiz, the paramount shaykh of the Bani Sakhr, went to retrieve some cattle stolen by the Mtirat tribe of the Bani Sakhr. ʿAwda Qasus, the leader of a Christian Karaki tribe, recounts in his memoirs how Abdullah sent him to resolve conflicts involving Christian communities in Madaba and the village of Maʿin. Shaykhs were held responsible for breaches of the law on behalf of their tribesmen and were asked to produce the guilty men.[21] In light of this practice, Abdullah's decision to present several important shaykhs with cars can be understood not only as a way to secure their loyalty, but also as a practical way to maintain speedy communication with them and facilitate their work.

This policy did not prove to be very successful. Rufayfan could not restore law and order in Karak, which did not come under government control before the Reserve Force was ready for operation in the spring of 1922. Mashhur was shot at and killed in the Mtirat camp. Mithqal, now the new paramount shaykh of the Bani Sakhr, pursued the murderers who took refuge with the Bani Hamida tribesmen. He, too, was faced with opposition and three of his nephews were killed. This resulted in a blood feud between the Bani Sakhr and the Bani Hamida and the violence escalated. Following this incident, Abdullah urged the British to supply him with planes and armoured cars, which they duly did.[22] Abdullah's request for military support clearly indicated that reliance on shaykhs was not a real alternative for establishing central authority backed by substantial military force.

Conflict with Settled Tribes

Abdullah's attempts to appease the tribes, and especially his reliance on and therefore preferential treatment of the nomads inevitably discriminated against other segments of the population. In Madaba Abdullah was called on to solve a land dispute between the Christian Abu Jabir family of al-Salt and Mithqal al-Fayiz. Although the former produced the title deeds and initially satisfied Abdullah that the land belonged to them, Mithqal managed to influence Abdullah, causing him to delay before deciding that the matter should be referred to the courts. Meanwhile Mithqal maintained the land in his possession and farmed it profitably.[23] Abdullah showed the same leniency towards the nomads when he dealt with the lingering conflict between the Zaban tribe of the Bani Sakhr and the inhabitants of Madaba. Although he accepted the right of the latter over the disputed land, he advised them to pay £500 as compensation to the shaykhs of the Zaban.[24] In another case that involved nomads and settlers Abdullah found it difficult to persuade shaykh Haditha al-Khuraysha of the Bani Sakhr to return 2,500 sheep stolen from the villagers of al-Husn.[25]

These cases, however, did not necessarily indicate a natural bias of Abdullah towards the nomads as claimed by the British Representative whose reports of these incidents were later reflected in some of the scholarly writing.[26] Abdullah's policy was simply a result of his dependency on tribal goodwill. Even if he had wished to, he could not have forced the strong tribes to accept government orders. He had to negotiate with them in order to persuade them to accept his or his government's wishes whilst maintaining their support.

Settled or semi-settled tribes not only saw their position compromised vis-à-vis their nomadic rivals, but also suffered from the harsh attitude of the government. Whereas the new administration was sensitive to the needs of some tribes, mainly the nomadic and semi-nomadic tribes, it failed to take into account the sensitivities as well as the power of the settled ones. These were under the jurisdiction of the new administration, which was composed of newcomers to the territory. Several factors impeded their ability to govern Transjordan. As outsiders, they lacked local knowledge and could not predict the local response to their initiatives. They were further detached from the population by their different background. As urbanite, educated, modern and nationalist Arabs they did not understand the political culture of the tribal population in a periphery like Transjordan. Therefore, they did not and could not respect the local quest for autonomy. Rather they adhered to modern precepts of good government, which included such notions as intrusive government control, orderly payment of taxes, and equality of citizens before the law. Moreover, the aspiration to restore independence to Syria shared especially by the hard-core nationalists, members of the *Istiqlal* party, meant that they were orientated towards achieving their ultimate goal rather than concerned with the welfare of the locals.[27] Whereas Abdullah intervened on behalf of the nomads to smooth out differences with government officials, he allowed his officials a free hand in administering the settled tribes. Their miscalculated and unchecked policy inevitably brought about an open clash between some settled communities and the new regime. It was therefore Abdullah's neglect of the settled tribes -- and not his benevolence towards the nomads -- that was his main domestic political failing in this period.

Strained relations between the government and the settled population characterised the first years of the Emirate and culminated in the Balqa' revolt of 1923. The first conflict, however, happened only one month after the government was formed. The Kura affair epitomises the impossible situation of state-formation in the early years of the Emirate. A feeble government failed to subjugate tribal society, which was organised, heavily armed and could be quickly mobilised by its leadership to protect its vital interests. The Kura incident also demonstrates the incompetence of the system governing the settled population under the 'Syrian' administration and can be seen as the forerunner of the Balqa' rebellion. A close analysis of the case discloses the different attitudes to state-formation.

The newly-appointed *Mutasarrif* of ʿAjlun, Amin Tamimi from Nablus, provoked fierce opposition in the Kura district when he tried to resume the collection of taxes in late April.[28] The villagers of Rahaba refused to pay, claiming that they had already paid the previous local government. The gendarmes who escorted the tax men tried to confiscate some property. They encountered opposition from the villagers and one of them was killed. Tamimi reacted with excessive clumsiness, sending a military force to the heart of the hilly Kura region. The force suffered a humiliating defeat. After 15-20 soldiers had been killed and others wounded, it gave itself in and its members were stripped of their arms and horses and then released.

As described in the previous chapter, the Kura area had enjoyed complete autonomy under the leadership of Kulayb al-Shurayda since the collapse of Ottoman rule in the country. Even during the height of their rule, the Ottomans were careful to respect al-Shurayda's unique tribal leadership position. In contrast, Tamimi bypassed al-Shurayda, ignoring the military force under his command on the one hand and the lack of a strong government force on the other. 150 members of the Reserve Force faced hundreds of armed tribesmen -- one thousand men according to the testimony of Kulayb's son, ʿAbdullah. In that way, a local incident soon turned into open defiance of the government. Consequently, immediately south of the Kura district, in Jabal ʿAjlun, the local strongman, shaykh Rashid al-Khuzaʿi, shut down the government house in an attempt to take advantage of the situation to assert his own position of leadership and autonomy. In the ensuing negotiations, al-Shurayda insisted that he had not rebelled against the rule of the Emir or the British but only refused to be governed from Irbid, ʿAjlun's administrative centre. Instead he requested direct government from Amman. He also offered to return the arms and horses and to send a deputation to Abdullah. It was a manifestation of the same sense of localism that only a few months earlier had led to the rejection of Irbid as an acceptable seat of the local government.

Responses to the crisis from different centres of power indicated the conflicting approaches towards state-formation and tribal control. These differences emerged as early as May 1921 and were contested during the first years of the Emirate. Tribal policy was a cause for disagreement between Abdullah and successive governments as well as between himself and the British authorities. It was frequently the case that whereas Abdullah was acting on behalf of the tribes, the government, with British support, put pressure on him to limit their autonomy and special rights. In this first test, however -- uncharacteristically -- it was the British Representative in Irbid and Abramson in Amman who called for a moderate reaction, recognising the limitations of the government. They did so however with great reluctance. In the aftermath of the affair, Abramson had to admit that the settlement arrived at was far from ideal but the only one possible under conditions of weak government. In marked contrast, the government, Abdullah and his court demanded firm action in order to punish the villagers. As the crisis lingered, Abdullah changed his position. He was persuaded to seek out an amicable settlement based on tribal practices such as reaching a compromise through the mediation of shaykhs and allotting compensation instead of inflicting punishment. The ministers continued to press for a firm line to be taken against the rebels.

Finally, a settlement based on customary law was reached when Abdullah toured ᶜAjlun. He received al-Shurayda, who declared his loyalty, and appointed a court composed of two officials and two shaykhs (Majid al-ᶜAdwan and Rufayfan al-Majali) who formulated an arrangement. The Kura people returned the arms and horses in addition to pledging to pay blood-money for the dead men and horses. The government also reasserted its authority in the Jabal ᶜAjlun district when its forces re-took the government house. The *Mutasarrif* was relieved from his post and returned to Palestine.

The bold action of the government in this affair provoked shaykhs from both settled and nomadic tribes to undertake measures to check the government. While trying to reorganise the Reserve Force, which had entirely disintegrated following the defeat in Kura, Peake faced strong opposition from shaykhs whose intimidation prevented potential recruits from joining the force. So successful were these shaykhs that Peake had to enlist 250 men from Palestine and Sudan. Only after the establishment of a nucleus unit did local recruits join in, and the foreigners were discharged.[29] No doubt the shaykhs tried to prevent the creation of a repressive state instrument that might affect their autonomy.

Although far from coherent or united, tribal shaykhs emerged as opposition to the government and as a local force that played an important role in the development of Transjordan in the following years. They resented the foreign Arabs who had assumed power. Mithqal, Rufayfan and several other tribal leaders met in Amman to discuss the problem. As a result, they demanded that Abdullah check these officials, threatening otherwise to use force to remove them.[30] Wilson speculates that this move was created by the British, who encouraged the shaykhs to oppose the Syrians. Her argument, however, is (as she admits) based only on circumstantial evidence.[31] On the contrary, it seems that the tension between local leaders and Arab nationalists who had assumed government positions became a major feature of Transjordanian politics throughout the 1920s and, although to a lesser degree, the 1930s, and was reflected in British, Arab and Zionist sources. It was a result of the officials' different cultural background, their lack of interest in the affairs of Transjordan *per se* and the fact that they occupied government positions which by definition threatened the autonomy of the locals. Even if the British did provoke the shaykhs to oppose the nationalists, they merely capitalised on an existing social and political reality, but did not invent it.[32]

British Frustration with the Prevalence of the Local Order

The implications of the Kura incident for the efforts to strengthen the government were devastating, at least temporarily. The humiliating defeat and heavy casualties brought about the disintegration of the whole Reserve Force and the Emirate was left without a central armed force apart from the small household army. The regime drew the right lesson and did not try to challenge the local order before the new

Reserve Force was fully recruited and operational in early 1922. Despite the amicable settlement with al-Shurayda, the government's presence in ʿAjlun and indeed in most of the country was only symbolic. In fact, effective government control was limited to the Amman-Salt area. In a private letter, Peake revealed that he was "living a peaceful life hardly ever going outside Amman, as it is no use listening for the 101st time to all the same old complaints."[33] The British reported that public security was bad and that the settled population remained exposed to the hostile nomads.[34] Tax collection was minimal and was extracted only from the weakest communities in the towns and the surrounding villages or from the Christians in Karak and the Ghawarna on the shore of the Dead Sea. Somewhat ironically, despite the defeat in Kura, the British were less concerned with the lack of government in the northern part of the country. Here, local tribal order continued to operate efficiently as it did before the establishment of the Emirate. The British reported that the area was quiet because each shaykh ran the area under his domination.[35]

While tolerating the tribal arrangement in the north, Abramson was vocal with regard to the Bani Sakhr in the centre of the territory. Looking for something on which to blame what was, from a British point of view, an intolerable situation, the Bani Sakhr tribes were singled out and bore the brunt of Abramson's criticism. He pointed to their anti-government attitude, accusing them of "nearly all the lawlessness that occurred of late..." He concluded that: "The problem of introducing public order into the whole of Trans-Jordania and asserting the authority of the Government would be best solved if an example could be made of the Bani Sakhr."[36] His recommendations echoed that of Brunton a few months earlier and would be repeated by most British officials until they were finally implemented in the early 1940s.

In fact, the new administration failed to change much of the local order which emerged in the aftermath of the war. To British eyes, this must have been an indication of their failure to find an appropriate arrangement for Transjordan. Indeed, early British optimism gave way to disillusion and severe criticism that focused on Abdullah's performance. This occurred as soon as the British realised that Abdullah's influence among the tribes did not guarantee the smooth running of the country in terms of public security, the payment of taxes and general "proper administration." They were particularly annoyed with the privileges given to the nomadic tribes and the insufficient control over them. They were also critical of Abdullah's reluctance to check his ministers' anti-French activity.

In essence, British criticism of Abdullah reflected a clash between two opposed political precepts. Abdullah ruled over a tribal alliance not so different from other tribal chieftaincies in Arabia. The British, although they did not have a clear political path mapped out for the future of Transjordan, did envisage a modern administration working along Western lines. These two visions of state-formation proved to be a bone of contention between Abdullah and the British, especially during the early years. It led to the British ultimatum in 1924 and persisted to a lesser degree throughout the mandate years.

It took Abramson only a few months to realise that Abdullah's regime was very different from that envisioned by the British. He complained about what he dubbed the 'Hijazi' system of government, namely Abdullah's partiality, disregard for the law, and unwillingness or inability to bring the nomads under government control. Abramson saw Abdullah as the obstacle to the desired development of the country and pessimistically forecast that as long as he remained in power,

> ...it will be almost impossible to bring the Bedu to respect and obey the Government, pay taxes and tithe and keep the peace if an Emir is in the head of affairs. Being a Bedu himself, his inclination is to settle all Government and other matters in Bedu fashion, and this would be fatal in Trans-Jordan...[37]

The British Representative's diagnosis that the rule of "Bedu Amir" was the root cause of Transjordan's problem led him to call for his deposition.

Frustration with Abdullah was shared by virtually all British officials concerned with Transjordan, both there and in Palestine. Many critics pointed out his ineffectiveness as an administrator. The Civil Secretary of the Palestine government reported that "His Highness' participation in the affairs of the Administration is a somewhat languid one." He partly attributed this behaviour to Abdullah's "temperamental disinclination to great exertion of any kind." Somerset, by that time serving as the British Representative in Karak, remarked that "[o]f course the show is going to be perfectly hopeless. Abdalla is quite affable and so on but he has very little administrative ability..." and later that "Abdulla is a very pleasant fellow, intelligent ... with an attractive manner, but hopelessly lazy..."[38] Abdullah's alleged laziness drew British criticism also because it was translated into giving a free hand to the nationalist circles, whom they suspected of anti-French activity.

Wilson suggests that 'laziness' and 'languidity' were cultivated by Abdullah as a deliberate strategy. By taking little interest in the administration he could both distance himself from the British criticism of nationalist activities of government officials and avoid carrying out inconvenient British demands without appearing too defiant.[39] It seems more likely that Abdullah was genuinely disinterested in matters of administration, which he left to his ministers. In fact, this disinterest persisted throughout his reign even when in later years he developed better relations with the British and his government was purged of nationalists. For Abdullah it was more important to concentrate his efforts on building and securing his tribal coalition. Sitting with the shaykhs in a tent for long hours, drinking coffee, eating festive meals and chatting in order to cultivate their friendship and goodwill obviously appeared idle in British eyes. But for Abdullah it was imperative for securing his rule. In later years, when British officials acquired deeper knowledge of the political culture of the country, they came to understand and appreciate Abdullah's style and even supported it. Words like 'lazy' and 'languid' no longer appeared in their reports.

Fresh Start: Crystallisation of State Power in the Settled Zone

Facing the mounting outcry from Jerusalem and Amman, Churchill sent Lawrence to Amman, and asked him to recommend a course of action. Lawrence reported that the situation was less severe than had been portrayed in the reports. He identified the lack of a strong military force as the cause of the incompetent administration and predicted that when it was fully recruited, trained and equipped, the renewed Reserve Force would help the government assert its authority. Lawrence also criticised the languid support of the Palestine government for the administration in Transjordan. Churchill accepted Lawrence's view and allowed for a new start for the Emirate. As Uriel Dann commented, Lawrence gave Abdullah "another breathing space, after Abdullah had been all but written off in London."[40] However, this phase in the development of Transjordan also proved inadequate. Although it brought about the strengthening of the state apparatus it also had two undesired side-effects: First, the assertion of excessive state authority in the settled zone provoked general dissatisfaction and ultimately led to a rebellion. Second, it created high demands on the budget and triggered a financial crisis that threatened to paralyse the administration.

Lawrence stayed in Amman two months, replacing Abramson who returned to Palestine, and acting as the British Representative until St John Philby took over in December 1921. From early 1922 until the autumn of 1923 the country enjoyed a period of stability during which the central administration succeeded in asserting its authority over the settled population. A change of personalities, resulting in more sympathetic British Representatives, Abdullah's recognition of his precarious situation, and an improved attitude of the Palestine government towards the independent administration of the country, contributed to the stabilisation of Transjordan and the subjugation of the settled tribes to the government's authority. More importantly, the resurrection of the Reserve Force, later renamed the Arab Legion, allowed for this success.

In February 1922 Peake led his forces to Karak and placed it under military control. The British reported that the occupation of Karak was welcomed by the weary population, which for more than a year had suffered from a spate of tribal feuds, and since the end of 1921 from a violent confrontation between the two alliances, the *Sharaqa* and *Gharaba*. There was also a simmering external feud between the Majali and the Bani Hamida. Immediately after the occupation of the town, a new non-Karaki *mutasarrif* was appointed. Law and order was restored and taxes collected. The military operation was complemented by the resolution of the outstanding conflicts between the rival parties in the town according to customary law. A committee of shaykhs appointed by Abdullah's delegate, *sharif* ᶜAli al-Harithi, determined the blood-money owed and peace was achieved. Abdullah likewise reconciled the Bani Hamida and the Majali tribes. A party of the Bani Hamida was caught red-handed on their way to raid the Majalis. To the annoyance of Philby, Abdullah released them and soon after convened the shaykhs of the two parties and arbitrated a settlement.[41] Once again tribal conflict resolution proved effective. Tafila received similar treatment at the end of the year, thus bringing the south of the country under the rule of the government and achieving a satisfactory degree of law and order.[42] The situation in Karak at the beginning of 1922 was a good example of a tribal system that at times reaches an impasse due to a severe blood feud and rivalry, which only an external authority, like a state, can untangle. In such circumstances, government intervention, therefore, is welcomed by the tribespeople.

Also, in the summer of 1922, the government felt confident enough to assert its power in the hitherto unruly ʿAjlun province and especially in the Kura district. The Reserve Force was not sufficiently strong for this task due to the inaccessible nature of the Kura hills, and the government asked for RAF support. Hundreds of bombs were thrown on three villages in Kura before Kulayb al-Shurayda fled the area. He took refuge with shaykh Haditha al-Khuraysha of the Bani Sakhr and sought the mediation of his host in tendering his submission to Abdullah. Kulayb, his sons and several followers were sentenced to death but Abdullah commuted their punishment to prison sentences and less than a year later granted them amnesty.[43] Upon his release, Kulayb was allowed to resume his shaykhly duties. His prominent personal position and that of his family was now recognised and utilised by the government. Kulayb acted on behalf of the government and in later years his son, ʿAbdullah, represented the Kura inhabitants in both the Legislative Council and the cabinet. The rehabilitation of dissident tribal leaders became a recurring practice in Transjordanian (and later Jordanian) politics. Abdullah himself articulated this policy in a speech he gave in 1924. Referring to the Kura affair and to its positive resolution, he described the rehabilitated Kulayb as a "loyal servant of the government."[44]

Thus, in the summer of 1922, the government managed to gain the submission of the settled and semi-settled tribes. Peake and Philby reported on the satisfactory collection of taxes and good public order.[45] Maʿan Abu Nowar asserts that, as early as August 1922, Abdullah could already point to several achievements in the process of state-building. His government maintained law and order, improved tax-collection, opened new schools and clinics, built roads, established telegraph and post office services and created *shaʿri* and civil courts.[46] These still modest achievements were more a reactivation of the old Ottoman infrastructure than complete innovations. What was less a matter of continuity was the rapid recruitment of foreign personnel to fill an expanding administration. Qasus explained the temporary transfer of the capital to al-Salt at the end of 1922 by the need to accommodate government departments and officials with their families, which was above the capacity of the small town of Amman.[47] Abu Nowar finds that by July 1923, the administration consisted of eleven departments.[48] In September of that year, the assistant British Representative estimated that the current administration was 500% more costly than the Ottoman administration just before the war.[49] This development inevitably resulted in growing demands on the budget as well as more intrusive administration.

Against the background of enhanced government control, Abdullah found his role in the new administration as a mediator between a foreign and centralising government and the local population. For assuming this position he received frequent praise from Philby. This was especially true since at the head of administration stood Rida Rikabi, an able ex-Ottoman administrator, who enjoyed the full confidence of the British but was at times uncompromising and unrealistic in his quest for a strong government vis-à-vis the nomads. According to Philby, Abdullah was "taking no part in the actual administration of the country but on occasion intervening with considerable acumen and effect to smoothe [sic] over difficulties and differences of opinion arising between the Government and the people."[50] With Philby's approval, Abdullah limited his rule over the settled population, allowing himself to be "wisely guided by the advice of his Ministers."[51] It suited Philby's own vision of the development of Transjordan as a constitutional monarchy. For him, Abdullah was at his best when he limited himself to dealing with the nomadic tribes and keeping them at bay while the government was too weak to carry out this task itself. For this purpose Philby was willing to turn a blind eye to Abdullah's preferential treatment of the nomads. Later on, when Abdullah 'exceeded' this mandate and obstructed the evolution of the constitutional monarchy Philby had in mind, the latter withdrew his approval, and a severe conflict arose.

Indeed, Abdullah's close relations with the shaykhs, especially the nomadic ones, were an important element in achieving the stability of the Emirate. Despite an enhanced level of 'stateness,' Abdullah allowed several of the chieftaincies to operate within the state. Alongside the Bani Sakhr, the Majali and the Huwaytat were the prime beneficiaries of this policy, which in turn helped to keep the peace. As the assistant British Representative wrote: "…in the absence of strong military forces, the Emir's presence, his sympathies and his largesse have been a potent factor in keeping the Badu in order."[52]

The following descriptions illustrate the persistence of the two southern chieftaincies under Rufayfan al-Majali and Hamad bin Jazi. An Arab Legion company arrived at a village near Karak and refused the hospitality offered by the local tribesmen. Since this was a blatant violation of local custom, the villagers did not feel obliged to guarantee the welfare of the soldiers and stole several horses. The next morning the company's commander arrested a villager as well as the shaykh of the village, both from the Majali, against Rufayfan's strong protest. The following day Abdullah himself arrived in Karak, released the prisoners and dismissed the officer in command. To illustrate the situation in the town following the resolution of this incident Philby quoted an officer who remarked grudgingly: "the Government at Karak is in the hands of the Majali but the Amir's Government counts for nought."[53] Similarly, the government fended off British pressures to increase taxes on landowners in the Karak province.[54]

Further south the Huwaytat maintained its hegemony over the townspeople of Tafila and the surrounding villages. The British suspected that the government refrained from interfering in a long-standing blood feud between the ʿAwran tribe of Tafila and the nomadic Mannaʿin because the latter were under the powerful patronage of shaykh Hamad bin Jazi of the Huwaytat. The Huwaytat themselves launched recurring raids against the villages of Dana and Busayra, demanding hospitality from their inhabitants. Hamad, with Abdullah's help, took over the village of Rashadiyya, which was legally owned by the villagers of these two localities.[55]

Thus, even when the government asserted its power within the limit of the settled zone, it could not affect the autonomy of the main tribal confederacies. On the contrary, these strong and therefore favoured forces enjoyed the support of Abdullah, who guarded their interests. They enjoyed light taxation, immunity from the Arab Legion and from the civil legal system and continued to administer their own affairs.

External Threat and the Role of the Tribes

While the country enjoyed internal stability during 1922-1923, a new external threat loomed in the south-east. The Wahhabi *Ikhwan* movement, King Ibn Saud's instrument of expansion, advanced northwards and westwards, and arrived at the un-demarcated borders of Transjordan in summer 1922. The *Ikhwan* were a cross-tribal striking force, whose religious zeal combined with the support of the King was too strong a military challenge for the Arabian tribes. The Wahhabi menace generated a convergence of interests between the nomadic tribes and the Transjordanian government, and for the first time since its establishment, the latter was in a more balanced position vis-à-vis these tribes. On the one hand, the Reserve Force was too small and too weak to fulfil the conventional role of a national army, that of defending the borders. It was merely a police force, collecting taxes and maintaining law and order within a limited territory. The government therefore had to rely on military support from the tribes. On the other hand, the nomads were no match for the *Ikhwan* and needed and demanded the help of the government and the support it could enlist from Britain. This was the background to a period of intensive co-operation between the central government and several tribes, most notably the Bani Sakhr and the Huwaytat, as well as the 'non-Transjordanian' Ruwalla. The Bani Sakhr were particularly concerned because the Wahhabis threatened to occupy Wadi Sirhan, their winter grazing area. In a quasi-feudal manner Abdullah was able to mobilise the tribes to prevent the expansion of Saudi influence. This development was very positive in terms of state-formation, marking the first stage of the integration of these tribes into the state. However, Abdullah's heavy reliance on the nomads resulted in a worsening of his already strained relations with the settled tribes, especially the Balqa' alliance, the traditional rival of the Bani Sakhr. This development culminated in the Balqa' revolt of September 1923.

In August 1922 a Wahhabi force attacked two Bani Sakhr villages, only 12 miles south of Amman. In a two-day battle the Sukhur assisted by the Hadid tribes defeated the raiders. The reinforcement requested from the British arrived only after the aggressors had already begun to flee.[56] In August 1924, a heavier attack was launched against Transjordan. 3,000-4,000 Wahhabi camelmen raided several villages of the Bani Sakhr and others in the Balqa' on the way to Amman. This time the British played a more active role. With RAF planes and armoured cars the Wahhabis were defeated. Despite the tribes' heavy losses -- about 130 people, mostly sharecroppers, were killed or wounded -- the British praised themselves for "this prompt and energetic action of the Royal Air Force" and claimed that their good performance "averted a serious menace to the peace of Transjordan and the safety of its capital."[57] Whereas British reports emphasised the role of the RAF, Jordanian contemporaries told a different story. According to the latter, the *Ikhwan* were engaged by tribesmen from many tribes including the ʿAdwan, ʿAjarma, ʿAbbad and the Bani Hasan. The government's announcement corroborated this version, praising the Balqawiyya, Bani Hamida, and ʿAjarma tribes, as well as the Circassian leader and warrior Mirza Wasfi, for their participation beside the Bani Sakhr in repulsing the attack.[58]

Because the Bani Sakhr were the prime target of the Wahhabi threats and attacks and since they dominated the area surrounding the capital Amman, it can be argued that they constituted the country's *de facto* armed forces during the early 1920s. Their paramount shaykh, Mithqal al-Fayiz, was instrumental in various initiatives pursued by Abdullah during this period with the goal of raising a force to deter the Wahhabis. In July 1923 Abdullah and Mithqal organised a military demonstration against the Saudis. The beginning was promising as large contingents of tribesmen under Shakir arrived at Kaf, where no Wahhabi presence could be found. However, after a short stay and due to the lack of the financial sources needed to maintain them, "the Amir's Bedouin Army had ...vanished into thin air."[59] An Arab Legion post in Kaf aided by a hundred men of the Huwaytat under their shaykh Hamad bin Jazi was the only practical result of Abdullah's attempts to prevent the Wahhabi advance towards his country. At the time of the second Wahhabi attack, the post comprised 15 soldiers and 40 Bani Sakhr warriors.[60]

In these early years of his reign Abdullah was dependant on the military support of the Bani Sakhr and therefore the favouritism Mithqal enjoyed is understandable. The dependency was acknowledged by the acting British Representative, Bertram Thomas, who illustrated the situation by likening it to a feudal system:

Against the Wahhabi menace therefore the Amir has had resource[sic] to a species of feudalism and the Bani Sakhr is under fealty an armed force of the Amir sworn to resist Wahhabi incursions in return for which their taxes have been remitted...and the lands of Ziza village have been given as "fief" to Shaikh Mithqal.[61]

The Balqa' Revolt

Abdullah's heavy reliance on the nomadic tribes, the Bani Sakhr in particular, resulted in a worsening of the already strained relations between him and the more settled tribes, especially the Balqa' alliance. The ʿAdwan and their allies found themselves weakened vis-à-vis both the government and their traditional rivals for hegemony in the region, the Bani Sakhr. Both the undermined leadership position of shaykh Sultan al-ʿAdwan and pressures on him from within his alliance to act prompted him to launch a revolt. It was one of the most formative events in state-tribe relations and seems to have demonstrated to the tribes the limits of their ability to challenge the central government. The Balqa' revolt was the last time that a tribal chieftaincy launched an armed struggle to preserve tribal autonomy. It was the swan song of a bygone era in Transjordan.

The crisis of August-September 1923 was the culmination of two different tendencies. Firstly, the strengthening of the central government during 1922-1923 allowed it to curtail the autonomy of the settled or semi-settled tribes by better policing and controlling their areas to the point of repression. Most significant in this regard was the issue of excessive taxation. Tax collectors backed by the military forced villagers to pay not only current taxes but also demanded uncollected dues for the years 1918-1920 before the establishment of the Emirate. Hence the frequent, but inadequate, reference in the literature to tribal jealousy and unequal and excessive taxation as the revolt's causes.[62]

The problem was accentuated by the second tendency: the heavy reliance of the government on the Bani Sakhr in light of the Wahhabi menace, and the favouritism showed to them for that reason. Their exemption from taxation on their vast cultivated land in the eastern Balqa' -- an incentive to keep their loyalty and military support -- increased the need of the government to tax other communities and triggered resentment and jealousy. It is perhaps no coincidence that the eruption of the crisis occurred only a few weeks after the expedition of the "Bedouin army" to Kaf, which marked the peak of the military co-operation between the Bani Sakhr and the government. The Bani Sakhr's unique position within the Emirate and in particular Mithqal's close connections with Abdullah threatened to change the *status quo* in the Balqa' at the expense of the ʿAdwan and their shaykhs.

The crisis was sparked in late August 1923 when the ʿAdwan and ʿAjarma refused hospitality to the camels of the Bani Sakhr at the wells of Hisban, well within the Balqa' alliance's *dira*. This conflict ran against the background of Bani Sakhr attempts to encroach upon the ʿAdwan and especially the ʿAjarma land in the area. In an attempt to prevent a war between the opponents, the Emir sent a military force to Umm al-ʿAmad, Mithqal's headquarters. However, this measure was seen by Sultan as an interference in Mithqal's favour and a further disregard for his leadership position in the Balqa' since any aggrandisement of Mithqal was bound to be at Sultan's expense. Sultan, probably pushed by the ʿAjarma shaykh, Sayil al-Shahwan, was now provoked to mobilise his chieftaincy to fight back in order to assert his leadership among his own people. The heavy tax burden and the general dislike for the Arab government made his natural allies responsive. He secured the support of member tribes of the Balqa' alliance from the Bani Hasan tribes in the northern Balqa' to the Bani Hamida and the Haddadin of Maʿin in the south. Although not formally part of the Balqa' alliance, the notables of al-Salt as well as Circassian leaders also lent their support.

To show his discontent and to put pressure on Abdullah, Sultan led hundreds of tribesmen on horseback to Abdullah's camp in Marka, via the centre of Amman, in an impressive and provocative demonstration of power. By this time he was also supported by a small group of young and educated Transjordanians, whose embrace of Sultan's demands elevated his movement from a localised tribal affair to a general popular protest against the foreign Arab government, an outcry for a complete reform of the Emirate. As well as reducing the tax burden and distributing it equally across the population, Sultan's demands included the expulsion from government of members of the *Istiqlal* and their replacement with native Transjordanians, as well as cuts in the salaries of government officials and the establishment of a representative assembly. Initially, Abdullah took a conciliatory approach, promising to study the shaykh's complaints and to pay a visit to him at his camp. Immediately afterwards, the government tendered its resignation, and a new government was formed in an attempt to appease the opposition movement. Sultan thus successfully brought home the public discontent to Abdullah and the government.

Abdullah, however, had second thoughts about this conciliatory approach, advised by his new government that it would be received as a sign of weakness. Having promised to pay a personal visit to Sultan's camp, his failure to keep the appointment left Sultan without much choice. To make matters worse, the government arrested and later deported to the Hijaz several of the educated natives associated with Sultan such as ᶜAwda Qasus from Karak, Mustafa Wahbi al-Tall from Irbid and Shams al-Din Shami, a leading Circassian from Suwaylih. This act must have been interpreted by Sultan as the first move to curtail his movement. The British position during the crisis was another key factor in Sultan's deliberations. Sultan's documented communications with Philby, as well as the accusations levelled against the latter by some of his colleagues for mishandling the situation, indicate that Sultan believed that the British forces would not intervene.[63]

Sultan rallied military support among the Balqa' but failed to secure a consensus among the many different elements of his chieftaincy. It was one thing to demonstrate discontent in Amman and another to defy the regime so bluntly. Consequently, his alliance disintegrated quickly. His difficulties in mobilising his alliance and maintaining its cohesion were typical problems faced by many tribal chiefs in the region and derived from the loose and sometimes *ad hoc* nature of tribal chieftaincies. To a large extent this outcome was a result of Abdullah's success in dissuading some of Sultan's allies from joining the rebellion. Several shaykhs from the Ghunaymat, al-Azayda and al-Shubaykat tribes came to Abdullah to swear allegiance. The Daᶜja, some of the Bani Hamida, most of the Bani Hasan and the people of al-Salt also refused to join the rebellion. Sultan's nearest agnates (the Saᶜud lineage) and even his son ᶜAffash, were said to oppose him. The Hadid tribes went as far as crossing the lines, supporting the regime in the ensuing fighting. Additionally, Abdullah was busy mobilising his loyal troops. Shakir and ᶜAli al-Harithi rallied support among the tribes in Karak and Madaba respectively and Abdullah sent messages to the shaykhs of the country casting doubt on Sultan's good name and character and requesting their help. The Bani Sakhr were alerted, and the Arab Legion was called to gather in Amman.

Matters came to a head on 15 September when about 300 horsemen and 500 warriors on foot marched from Hisban-Naᶜur towards Amman. They occupied Suwaylih and its police station, cut telegraph and telephone lines and blocked traffic on the Jerusalem-Amman road. The next morning, the Arab Legion, supported by two RAF armoured cars and shaykh Minwar al-Hadid and a few of his men defeated them in Jubayha in a surprisingly short one-hour battle, after which Sultan and his sons fled to Jabal Druze.

The suppression of the revolt and the disintegration of the alliance followed immediately after the battle. The Arab Legion pursued the rebels and carried out arrests in the Hisban area. In the Bani Hamida encampment several shaykhs were arrested. The Bani Sakhr took advantage of the defeat of the ᶜAdwan and ᶜAjarma to loot their encampments. More surprising still, they were joined by the Balqawiyya of Madaba. This was a striking indication of the disintegration of the alliance and the loose bonds between its different elements. Musa suggests that the revolt marks the "beginning of the end of [the Balqa'] alliance" and that gradually, the bond that had tied the members together loosened with the process of modernisation. He also suggests that the role of the paramount shaykh became more spiritual, based on cultural traditions. Musa's argument goes far in explaining the situation of the Balqa' alliance thereafter. Certainly it lost its might and ceased to function as a military alliance, leaving the task of providing security to state agencies. The tribes proved to be no match for the government, which could now assert its authority more easily. Indeed, in the immediate aftermath of the revolt, the British reported with satisfaction that the Balqa' tribes were paying taxes and that the military demonstration enhanced the government's prestige.[64]

However, as will be demonstrated in the course of this study, it was a policy of Abdullah and the government to uphold the status of chiefs and to maintain their patronage over their constituencies in order to achieve better control over the population. A few months after the revolt, *sharif* Husayn bin ʿAli, who visited Amman and temporarily replaced his son, Abdullah, as the highest authority in the country, granted amnesty to the ʿAdwani shaykhs. They returned to the Balqa' and made peace with Abdullah (in very much the same fashion as the Shurayda family had done after the Kura affair) and with the Bani Sakhr.[65] This reconciliation marked the beginning of enhanced co-operation between Abdullah and Sultan's family. In later years, Majid, who inherited the position of paramount shaykh after his father's death in 1934, became one of Abdullah's close allies. The same was true for the ʿAjarma rebels. Fadil, the son of shaykh Sayil who was killed during the revolt, inherited his father's shaykhdom and was recognised by the government as the tribes' representative. Shaykh Salim abu Ghunaym remained leader of the Ghunaymat after spending six months in prison.[66] Thus, the government created a new role for the chiefs and maintained their privileged status while gradually limiting their autonomy. In the case of the ʿAdwani shaykhs, their immense wealth was another factor that helped them to keep their chieftaincy together. Long after their defeat in 1923, they continued to perform the traditional tasks of tribal leaders such as charity-giving and hospitality, which in turn enhanced their special position. There are also some indications that their economic power gave them some leverage vis-à-vis Abdullah, whose scarce resources forced him to depend on wealthy notables. By hosting big feasts on behalf of Abdullah, they could partly relieve him of this costly task.[67]

Yet, the Balqa' revolt cannot be seen as a complete failure from the participating tribes' point of view. Despite their military defeat, the government took their grievances into account. For one, it remitted the outstanding tax arrears for the years 1918-1920. In addition, Abdullah seems to have paid more attention to the Balqa' chiefs thereafter, and even the Bani Sakhr were persuaded to give up some of their privileges. Soon after the end of the revolt, Mithqal al-Fayiz, accompanied by an Arab Legion unit, tried, albeit unsuccessfully, to collect taxes from the Mtirat tribe of the Bani Sakhr. They were opposed and shot at, and the Mtirat fled into the desert beyond the reach of the government, exactly as had happened two years earlier.

Notwithstanding this incident, the year 1923 saw the first collection of taxes from the Bani Sakhr tribes, including their shaykhs, although still on a small scale.[68]

Towards the Crisis of 1924

The Balqa' revolt coincided with and reinforced a change in British thinking towards administering the country. Officials in Amman and Jerusalem were unsympathetic towards the act of rebellion itself, but recognised the grievances of the settled population and realised that the current arrangement did not work.[69] Hence, a process of re-evaluation followed, culminating in a managed crisis in the summer of 1924. Just before the revolt and even more afterwards British officials expressed increased criticism of Abdullah and his ministers, as they had in 1921. This has often been described in terms of clashes of personalities and attributed to Philby and Abdullah's idiosyncrasies.[70] It is more fitting, however, to view this confrontation in the context of the debate between Abdullah and his British patrons on the nature of the evolving state. Philby was instrumental in this process because he initiated it and because he was Abdullah's main critic. Yet, his success in bringing home his criticism both to Jerusalem and London was due to the fact that he struck a cord with his colleagues and superiors. By addressing the sensitivities of British colonial officials in substantive questions to do with financial management, rule of law and accountability he managed to turn the official position against Abdullah. In that way what began as a quarrel between Philby and Abdullah was elevated to an open confrontation over the future of Transjordan. The fact that the crisis continued and reached its peak well after Philby left Transjordan further underlines the point.

Official but qualified recognition of Transjordan as a separate entity and of Abdullah as its ruler by the British in May 1923 gave Philby the opportunity to realise his vision: the establishment of a constitutional regime was ascribed in the wording of the declaration.[71] However, neither Abdullah nor his ministers were interested in sharing power with an elected assembly and they declined to move in that direction. Philby became obsessed with the idea of an assembly and was frustrated not only because Abdullah dragged his feet over the issue but also because he failed to secure support for his position from both his colleagues and superiors.[72] Finally, a quarrel over the preservation of an old basilica caused a fallout between Abdullah and Philby, which ultimately led to the replacement of the British Representative.

In the meantime, having failed to achieve a constitutional regime, Philby opened other fronts against Abdullah. He launched a campaign against the Emir, which revolved around issues pertinent to the nature of the current regime. Abdullah's favouritism towards the nomads was one of Philby's strongest weapons, especially against the background of the Balqa' revolt. Philby was now airing old stories to smear Abdullah's reputation, ignoring the fact that at the time he had not said anything and probably even approved Abdullah's policy. He complained about Abdullah cultivating tribal shaykhs by giving them presents, plots of land and more importantly, by exempting them from payment of taxes.[73] He reported that Abdullah deliberately delayed the dispatch of tax collectors to the encampment of the Bani Sakhr, thus allowing the latter the time to migrate eastwards and avoid the payment.

Some reports juxtaposed the subdued settled population, which was impoverished under the burden of heavy taxes, with the nomads who appeared to be above the law.[74] Along with the Bani Sakhr, the Huwaytat and their dependent tribes were also condemned as law breakers.

An entirely new element of criticism focused on what Philby and others described as Abdullah's "extravagant" way of life, referring to the money taken from the Treasury to finance the big parties and gifts given to the shaykhs. Abdullah was accused of exceeding his civil list, disregarding the budget and treating public money as his own purse. Samuel took a more moderate stance than Philby and showed more understanding for Abdullah's behaviour. He acknowledged that the Emir did not spend the money on himself, but instead that the money was spent on "doles" to shaykhs to ensure their loyalty and good behaviour. However, he also believed that these expenses were beyond the capacity of the Emirate and that it was necessary "to bring all the Amir's expenditure…on the general budget" in order to check his spending.[75]

Abdullah was also accused of undermining the authority of the Arab Legion and the legal system by protecting criminals, interfering with the courts and dismissing those members of the Legion who were accused of heavy-handedness towards the nomads. In May 1924, Peake produced a damning report, accusing Abdullah of being the main obstacle to the strengthening of the Arab Legion to the extent that "[t]he action of officers and men is paralyzed by that individual."[76]

There was much exaggeration in the British accusations against Abdullah, as Dann clearly demonstrates.[77] Nonetheless, these real or perceived failings of Abdullah continued to dominate British official correspondence even after the departure of Philby and the arrival in Amman of the new Representative in April 1924. Sir Henry Cox was an able and uncompromising administrator whose task was to check Abdullah's expenses and limit his authority. A British dictate reinstated the able administrator Rikabi as the prime minister in order to assist Cox in his mission. Imposing financial control on the government and Abdullah was their first priority, especially after the Treasury in Whitehall cut off the grant-in-aid without advance warning, a loss from the previous financial year of £90,000.

The new Representative faced the same problems as his predecessor and shared his views of Abdullah. This was especially true with regard to Abdullah's policy towards the nomads. Under Cox's aegis, the British showed signs of pursuing a more confrontational line with Abdullah and the nomads. They considered plans to force the Bani Sakhr to pay their taxes and contemplated employing the RAF for this mission. When Emir Shakir decided that the Bani Sakhr animals would be enumerated by his men and not the Arab Legion, Cox suspected this step was taken in order to lighten their tax liability. Indeed, Cox added Emir Shakir and his Department of Tribal Administration to Britain's bad books. In one of his first reports, he harshly criticised the Department, condemning in particular the employment of an individual whose function was to apply the customary practice of *bush'a* (an equivalent for the polygraph machine carried out by placing a burning iron under the tongue of the suspect in order to verify his oath). This paragraph provoked the appalled Secretary of State to dispatch to Abdullah a representation which demanded the cessation of this practice, described as "repugnant to the recognized principles of justice and humanity."[78]

In a comprehensive report from autumn 1923 that discussed the system of government and its performance,[79] the assistant British Representative, Bertram Thomas, put his finger on the crux of the debate, explaining it in terms of different attitudes towards building a state. Under the headline "Badawi Government and Constitutionalism," Thomas summed up the arguments of Abdullah's critics, whom he termed 'constitutionalists.' Although he explicitly referred to Abdullah's critics as hailing from the Arab press in Palestine and Syria, the *Istiqlal* party and the settled population in Transjordan, it is more likely that he had Philby in mind when writing the report. The critics, Thomas wrote, dubbed Abdullah's regime as "'Badawi' government" accusing him of "acting as though Trans-Jordan were part of the Hijaz or Hadhramant[sic]" rather than part of Palestine or Syria. They instead advocated a system that "would impose limitation on the Amir's power, strong and rigid administration based on law and uniformity and be antitribal in outlook." They further criticised "the Amir's persistent disrespect for Budgets, Law Court judgments and constitutional procedure, and his benign and preferential treatment of his Badu subjects." Thomas however justified this preferential treatment, writing that "however distasteful the thought to constitutionalists, the Bani Sakhr and Kerek chiefs constitute in a young and weak Arab state a kind of feudal baronage."

Thomas himself offered a different outlook and characterised Abdullah's way of governing more positively as a "benevolent autocracy, benevolent within the limits of the indigenous Badu elements." He pointed to the odd situation in Transjordan, which possessed a mixed system of government, or what he termed "a Syrian oligarchy superimposed by Hujazi [sic] absolutism." He diagnosed the problem of the current system in that mixture. First, Transjordan resembled neither the Hijaz nor Syria, but was in an intermediate developmental stage. Second, the "Syrian oligarchy" was considered by locals as not acting in the interests of Transjordan, and their occupation of the bureaucracy resulted in financial demands and therefore in the need for higher taxation. This odd hybrid of two different systems of government did not work, and according to Thomas, many people would have preferred a return to the Ottoman system. Put differently, the current arrangement was an awkward combination between two precepts of state. One, advanced by most of the British and the "Syrians," was that of a modern institutionalised state which adhered to Western concepts. The other, practised by Abdullah, was an Arabian chieftaincy. These two systems, simultaneously at work in the same territory, could not coexist, and triggered a crisis.

The tension was finally resolved when British impatience with Abdullah came to a head in the summer of 1924. In August, under instructions from London, Cox submitted an ultimatum to Abdullah to reform his administration and accept British supervision or to give up his throne. Abdullah had no alternative but to concede to a take-over of the administration and to a tight control over his own conduct. Cox reported that the most difficult condition for Abdullah to accept was the abolition of the Tribal Administration, a move designed to guarantee that "the Bedu be governed, like the rest of the people, by the Government." According to Cox, this was the case because Abdullah was both fond and afraid of Shakir. On the same day, Abdullah met a group of shaykhs, reportedly to ask for their continued support and loyalty.[80]

By issuing the ultimatum, Britain decided to reform the parameters of the arrangement that prevailed since the Abdullah-Churchill agreement of spring 1921. From that moment onwards Transjordan was to be ruled more directly with strict limits on Abdullah and his government's authority. Moreover, Britain forced its own vision of a state on Transjordan, namely a Western-like state with rule of law, efficient and economical central administration, and a certain degree of accountability. Four years later, another element was added - an elected Legislative Council.

Immediately after the renewed understanding between Abdullah and his patrons, the new reality was put to a test. Certain fugitives had been enjoying the protection of Mithqal al-Fayiz, who refused to turn them in. When a 250-strong force from the Arab Legion supported by armoured cars arrived at his village, Mithqal had no choice but to hand over the men. He then "ate humble pie" in Peake's office. Cox in a self-congratulatory manner concluded that "the Beni Sakhr have been brought into line."[81] This statement, however, would turn out to be premature, and these tribes continued to be seen by successive British officials as a cause for concern until the early 1940s.

Abdullah for his part tested the British determination to curtail him. Cox prevented him from interfering with government and court decisions, commenting that "[t]he Amir... is beginning to realise that he must behave in a constitutional manner."[82] Indeed, Abdullah found in Cox a tough and uncompromising rival, and uneasy relations ensued throughout Cox's long term in office. Abdullah's reference to Cox in his memoirs is telling of the extent of their disagreements. The man who administered the country for fifteen critical years earned only a brief mention. In a laconic manner, Cox is described as someone with *shakhsiyya idariyya*, a personality of an administrator.[83] Administration along British lines was antithetical to Abdullah's style of rule.

Conclusion

The British won the day and imposed the foundations for the development of the Emirate. The resolution of the conflict allowed for increased momentum in state-formation, although still limited to the settled zone of the country. However, British success was only partial and the struggle over the nature of the state continued, although the basic guidelines remained intact. The issue continued to be contested and struggles between Abdullah, the British officials and the cabinets remained a common feature throughout the mandate. Nomadic tribes enjoyed only limited government control as well as complete freedom in the desert until the early 1930s. Abdullah, although more restricted than ever, continued to favour shaykhs and strong tribes. In later years, Cox and successive high commissioners learned to appreciate Abdullah's policy and even supported him. In many aspects the chieftaincy-like politics persisted and contributed to the strengthening of the evolving state. Transjordan did not evolve according to the 'Syrian model' of a modern state, nor did it adopt the 'Hijaz model' of a tribal chieftaincy. Rather, it became what Toby Dodge has termed a 'hybrid state,' which combined and accommodated some traits of both.[84]

CHAPTER THREE:
THE MAKING OF A COLONIAL STATE, 1924-1930

The British ultimatum in August 1924 and its acceptance by Abdullah marked a new phase in the development of Transjordan. Hereafter the British changed their attitude towards administering the country and began to develop it slowly, restricted by an extremely tight budget. As Mary Wilson asserts, before that time little had been done to give substance to the handshake through which Churchill and Abdullah had created Transjordan. Afterwards, the creation of political institutions, the establishment of borders as well as the gradual internal migration to the capital Amman began to fill in the political and social structure of the country.[1] Several elements contributed to the relative success of state-formation during this period in particular, and throughout the mandate years in general. The reformed central administration and Arab Legion, together with the improvement of the country's infrastructure, created a framework for consolidating the government's power. In addition, shrewd reliance on the tribal structure of society and Abdullah's skilful handling of tribal politics were fundamentally important to the establishment of centralised authority.

The period of loose indirect rule that began with the introduction of the local governments four years earlier gave way to a British take-over of the administration and the military. The British, now at the helm of internal affairs, showed vigorous involvement and assertiveness in the daily running of the government, down to the smallest detail. At times Abdullah and his Arab government were reduced to the role of executors of British policy. From their newly acquired position of dominance the mandate authorities could impose British ideas of how a modern state should function. The result was the consolidation of state authority, albeit still confined to the narrow strip of the settled zone west of the Hijaz railway. At the same time, however, the relative weakness of the government and the small contingent of British personnel made it necessary to control the population indirectly via their local leaders, especially in the tribal areas outside the towns. Consequently, the chieftaincy continued to operate alongside the central government. Moreover, the nomadic tribes benefited from the existence of weak, limited government and continued to enjoy complete autonomy in the desert until the end of the decade. Notwithstanding some futile attempts by both the government and the British to achieve better control over the nomadic tribes, in the desert state authority manifested itself only indirectly through the personal influence of Abdullah and Shakir.

Reorganising the State: The Momentum of State-Formation

The main tools for creating a centralised state in the settled zone were two reformed institutions, the central administration and the Arab Legion. A central administrative system was created under the tight control and supervision of the British Representative, Colonel Henry Cox. As trained manpower was scarce in Transjordan, or so it was claimed, and the Syrian nationalists were undesired, from 1926 young Palestinians filled the ranks of the bureaucracy.[2] Of the few locals who were recruited, many were Christians.[3] Two Britons held posts as financial and legal advisors to ensure better control. The British take-over of the administration poses a methodological problem as it is hard to differentiate between British and Arab government's initiatives. Due to British hegemony one must assume that most government actions were at least approved, if not initiated, by the British officials in Amman.

Before examining the consolidation of government authority it is important to highlight one important feature of British rule in Transjordan. Throughout the mandate period (with the exception of the wartime in the early 1940s) British presence in the country was meagre. During the 1920s and 1930s British personnel numbered less then twenty, most of whom did not have direct contact with the population and were confined to working with the government's officials in Amman.[4] What at first sight might appear as British weakness paradoxically turned into one of the strengths of British colonial rule in Transjordan. The thin presence of British officials, and their limited contact with the locals in the daily business of government eased the coloniser-colonised tension which characterised many other colonial settings.

Indeed, the small size of British presence is even more striking when compared to other British (or French) colonies in the region. During the 1920s British personnel in Palestine numbered 400 officials. They were assisted by 3,000 locals, both Arab and Jewish.[5] British personnel in Egypt grew steadily since the time of occupation in 1882 and by 1904 reached 1,000 officials, making up 10% of Egypt's civil service. These figures reached a peak of 1,600 in 1919 and, after the revolution, decreased to about 575 officials during the 1920s and 1930s. This civil apparatus was supported by an army composed of a minimum of 5,000 British troops.[6] In the Sudan around 125 members of the elite Sudan Political Service were joined by several hundred "less-exalted Britons employed in high-level clerical, technical and military capacities." At the beginning of 1932 they numbered together 949 men and women.[7] The other colonial power in the Middle East, France, had even greater presence. According to Philip Khoury, in Syria "French administration was an oversized and expensive bureaucratic ship."[8] In the early 1920s the French High Commission had 350 staff members and the French army (*Armee du Levant*) was enormous, numbering 70,000 men and 1,000 French officers. During years of relative tranquillity these numbers substantially decreased but still remained high in comparison to Transjordan.[9] It is true that the Syrian population was ten times greater than that of Transjordan. However, the smallness of the British presence in Transjordan remains striking, even taking into account the relatively small size of the country and its population in comparison with Syria and the other colonies.

Against the background of limited resources and a very small personnel, the British set out to reform the administration. Cox and his right-hand man Rikabi, who served as prime minister until June 1926, had a European system of administration in mind. Immediately after Cox's arrival in Amman and the beginning of the reorganisation of the administration, Prime Minister Rikabi circulated several memoranda among government officials in an attempt to improve the functioning of the government. Rikabi required of his officials hard work, better performance, accountability and transparency. He issued clear regulations, demanded periodic reports on the activity of each department, even the times of daily arrival and departure of the clerks. He set time limits on the different provinces for replies to inquiries from the central administration according to their distance from Amman.[10] In their 1926 report to the League of Nations the British could write that "steady progress within the very limited financial resources of the local Government has been made in almost every branch of the administration."[11]

The tool for executing government orders was the Arab Legion, which from the end of 1923 brought the Reserve Force, the police and the gendarmerie together under the command of Lieutenant-Colonel Frederick Peake. It numbered almost 1,500 men in 1925. The Legion was deployed around the settled zone in many posts which were gradually better connected to Amman by modern means of communication (one anecdotal exception was the desert post in Azraq that used pigeon post). By 1924 the Legion was better funded and equipped and Peake had achieved complete control over the force as a result of several purges of nationalist officers and the dismissal of the Arab commanders of the police and gendarmerie, now integrated into the main force. These changes gave the Legion the coherence and effectiveness it previously lacked. The Legion, however, suffered a major setback in 1926. As a result of the establishment of the Trans Jordan Frontier Force (TJFF) to control the desert and inspect the nomadic tribes, the Legion was reduced to a small force of 855 men limited to policing tasks. Although the new force bore the name of, and was based in, Transjordan, it was essentially a force of the Palestine government under the control of the High Commissioner in Jerusalem and therefore did not directly contribute to the institutional strengthening of the Transjordanian state.[12]

Improvement of the infrastructure was essential for achieving better security. In 1925 the government continued the work started by the Ottomans to connect the main towns and villages with networks of roads, telegraph and telephone lines. Existing roads were repaired or improved, and new ones constructed. By the end of the decade these roads together with the telephone lines were sufficient to serve, at a minimum, British security interests, contributing to the maintenance of law and order. In 1926 the first telephone directory of Amman was published, and a regular postal service started operating. A train service running regularly on the Hijaz railway lines connected Amman to Maʿan, Haifa and Damascus.[13]

This period also saw the consolidation of Amman as the capital and focal point of the new polity. As with other aspects of state-formation in this period, the process was limited in terms of its pace and scale. Still, within a few years, Amman's population doubled. From a predominantly Circassian village of about 5,000 inhabitants in 1921 Amman grew to a town of 10,000 or more in the second half of the 1920s.[14] This development was a result of the choice of Amman as the new capital and centre for government presence and the influx of immigrants from Syria after the failure of the revolt against the French between 1925 and 1927. This population growth generated momentum in construction, and the streets of Amman were widened and new shops and houses constructed along them. In 1925, Abdullah's palace, Raghdan, was completed and by 1927 offices for Abdullah and the British Residency were built.[15]

Changing the scene on the ground by creating a capital, laying new roads, erecting government buildings and telephone and telegraph poles must also have had a symbolic effect. It was the visual manifestation of a central government which was slowly but steadily consolidating itself. The gunshot every noon from the Roman fortress overlooking Amman also contributed to an image of an imposing and powerful government in the late 1920s. Until this practice was abandoned in 1930 it was a reminder to the capital's inhabitants and visitors of the existence of centralised power.[16]

Efficient administration and effective military force allowed the government to assert a degree of control over the settled zone. By the mid-1920s the British could report on substantial improvement in security and control over the nomadic tribes as they roamed the settled zone during the summer period. Tax collection proceeded satisfactorily and even nomadic tribes like the Bani Sakhr and, since the incorporation of Maᶜan in 1925, the Huwaytat paid their share.[17] The central administration could now better enforce the law and execute court decisions. Even shaykhs, including those from the most prominent families, were no longer immune from legal action. A brother as well as several nephews of the paramount shaykh of the Bani Sakhr, Mithqal al-Fayiz, saw some of their property confiscated and offered for sale in an auction after they failed to pay their debts.[18] Mithqal himself was sentenced to a year in prison on account of theft of petrol. This sentence was later commuted by Abdullah to a fine after the shaykh fled to Najdi territory, from where he negotiated a settlement with the government.[19] Another important Bani Sakhr shaykh, Haditha al-Khuraysha, was also summoned to court after he was sued by one of Amman's merchants.[20] Occasionally, the government resorted to arresting shaykhs. Turki al-Haydar, the shaykh of the Zaban tribe of the Bani Sakhr, was arrested after a fight broke out between his people and the inhabitants of Madaba in 1929.[21] After a heated debate with the assistant governor of Maᶜan, the shaykh of the Huwaytat, Hamad bin Jazi, found himself under arrest on suspicion of directing his tribesmen to stir up trouble. The next day he was joined by sixteen members of his tribes, arrested for stealing from soldiers.[22]

However rosy the evidence of the government's success in asserting its authority, its achievements were still partial and were secured only after bargaining with, and granting concessions to, local strongmen, as the remainder of this chapter demonstrates.

State-Building in a Tribal Society

The success of the government in asserting its presence cannot be attributed solely to the limited steps in the direction of state-formation. The challenge was formidable, for the society in areas formally under the Emirate's control could resist state policies at will. Tribal society was organised along the lines of kinship and alliance, with its own leaders able, if necessary, to mobilise their fellow tribesmen into a powerful fighting force. This was especially true in the desert and the semi-settled areas in central and southern Transjordan. But even in the villages of the north, and among townspeople everywhere, tribal solidarity still played an important role and could result in collective action. Paradoxically, a crucial factor in the central administration's success was its ability to manipulate these tribal structures and norms of society to consolidate its power, turning many elements of these societal strengths to its own favour.

The government took advantage of three characteristics of society: the notion of tribal solidarity, the tribe as the basic unit of organisation and identity and the leadership role of the shaykhs. The tribe or tribal confederacy (or their sub-divisions as understood by the government) were recognised by the government as the basic administrative unit. This served purposes ranging from tax distribution, collection or exemption to the control of the spread of diseases or organising the elections to the Legislative Council. While structuring the administration, the government took features of tribal life into consideration in such a way that one can identify a close correspondence between the social structure and the administrative divisions. Three decisions taken in 1926 demonstrate this point. In the Madaba district the government set up an Arab Legion post and a *hakimiyya* (sub-district) in Dhiban because the area was a centre of many different tribes and therefore prone to disputes and conflicts. The government realised that it could combine the two separate *hakimiyya*s of ʿIraq and Ghawr al-Safi in the Karak province into one, so that the governor would spend the summer on the plateau and the winter in the depression south of the Dead Sea in accordance with tribal seasonal movements. It is safe to assume that this practice of 'mobile administration' was employed elsewhere in the rural zone due to the semi-settled nature of the population. A converse measure was taken in the Maʿan province where the government separated Shawbak from Wadi Musa. It was explained that the former locale served the surrounding tribes whose nature and customs differed from that of the inhabitants of Wadi Musa, probably referring to the settled nature of the latter.[23]

Tribal practices of conflict resolution were endorsed to achieve better public security. In this respect Abdullah's role was of crucial importance and he continued the policy he had pursued since entering the country in 1920. At the end of 1927 the acting British Representative reported that "the action taken by His Highness the Amir in settling the long standing blood feud between the Mannaʾin and the people of Tafileh has resulted in improved conditions in that district."[24] A year earlier

Abdullah brokered a peace accord between the long-time enemies the Bani Sakhr and the Huwaytat. In order also to encourage this custom in feuds at the village level, a peace settlement between two warring families or tribes would often bring about an early release of the prisoner, even in murder cases. A less successful means was the introduction of tribal courts following the abolition in 1924 of the Department of Tribal Administration under Shakir. This mechanism was a complete failure as customary law continued to be judged internally by tribal judges.[25]

The control system's main pillar was the enforcement of tribal collective responsibility. Aware of their limited ability to establish direct rule over every individual, the government and the British held the entire tribe or village responsible when a crime was committed and the culprit unknown. Major Jarvis' comments on how best to prevent raids by nomads on settled communities around Gaza and Beersheba provide some indication of British thinking on this matter. In his capacity as the governor of Sinai, Jarvis himself governed tribal populations and had intimate knowledge of Transjordan:

> There is only one method of dealing with this type of raiding, and that is recognition and enforcement of tribal responsibility. Punitive expeditions are too expensive to maintain and, moreover, are usually ineffective, whereas, if the Government are firm and hold the sheikh and other members of the tribe responsible in every way for the misdeeds of the few, raiding is nipped in the bud.[26]

By definition, this method depended on gaining or enforcing the co-operation of the shaykhs. The weakness of the newly established administration created a pressing need to use shaykhs for daily governance. The government delegated to them some of its authority; the only means to exert better control over the tribal population. Peter Gubser makes this point with regard to Karak, but it is also valid for the rest of Transjordan.[27] Most notably, as the government was unable to maintain law and order in tribal areas, it demanded that the shaykhs guarantee security in their area of influence themselves, to prevent crimes of all kinds, and to arrest or report on criminals or suspects.[28] The wording of a report in the official newspaper *Al-Sharq al-ʿArabi* is indicative of the government's reliance on the shaykhs. The report reads: "it was approved to extend the telephone line from Irbid to the village of Qum, the headquarters of Naji *Basha* al-ʿAzzam."[29] Al-ʿAzzam was the strongman of the Wustiyya district which functioned independently during the period of local governments. Although this is only a single piece of evidence, it seems likely that an effort was made to provide the most important leaders with modern means of communication in order to use their influence to control the population. As suggested in the previous chapter, the cars Abdullah gave to several shaykhs might have served the same purpose.

The centrality of the policies of collective responsibility and reliance on shaykhs was reflected in several laws and their implementation. The Protection of Cultivation Law was intended to protect farmers from tribes sending their herds to graze on cultivated land. The law allowed the governor to arbitrarily confiscate property from the invading tribe and even detain its members in order to coerce the tribe into paying the fine. Similarly, the Protection of the Telegraph Lines Law stipulated the shaykhs' responsibility to protect the lines in their vicinity. If they failed to do so and the culprit was unknown, a fine of £50-100 would be levied on the tribe. To guarantee this payment the local governor was instructed to confiscate any property of the tribe.[30] Occasionally, the government arrested shaykhs pending the payment of compensation or as a punishment. Once released, they were allowed to return to their tribes to resume their shaykhly duties.

It is clear that the shaykhs resented this forced responsibility. Their resentment was later echoed in the debates of the Legislative Council.[31] When the assistant Governor of Ma'an held Hamad bin Jazi of the Huwaytat responsible for a robbery in his area of influence at a time when the shaykh was in Amman, the angry Hamad asked the official rhetorically whether he (i.e. Hamad) had been receiving a salary for this purpose.[32] It is therefore unclear to what extent the shaykhs actually assisted the government to maintain law and order. Presumably such assistance was only partial. Occasionally, shaykhs co-operated with the government as in the case of a shaykh of the Bani 'Atiyya who helped to restore animals looted by members of his tribe. However, the abundance of fugitives reported in the pages of the Official Gazette suggests that tribal areas were still far from the reach of the government. The government's tendency during the 1930s to pass laws stipulating fines or even imprisonment of responsible shaykhs corroborates the impression that shaykhs were half-hearted in their collaboration.[33] It was therefore only partially successful in improving law and order in rural areas.

The system of using shaykhs to indirectly rule the population benefited those who collaborated. The government offered commissions to the shaykhs in exchange for their co-operation in collecting the animal tax from tribesmen. But the frequent changes in the commissions' rates reflected the difficulties in finding the right balance between the Treasury's need for greater income and the shaykhs' willingness to help. The original law from 1926 allotted the shaykhs 1% of the returns. In 1927 the commission was increased to a 25% cut for each camel, only to be reduced to 4% a year later and down to 1% again by 1929. This arrangement did not work and in 1932 the government raised the shaykhs' commission to 15%.[34] For several years the government paid the shaykhs of tribes roaming along the Amman-Baghdad route to guarantee the safety of the convoys.[35] The lucrative salary and special status associated with membership of the Legislative Council served as another incentive for the collaboration of the most powerful shaykhs.

Abdullah and the Shaykhs: The Preservation of the Chieftaincy System
The substantial reduction of Abdullah's civil list from 1924 and British control over the executive limited his ability to lavish special privileges on tribal shaykhs. However, Abdullah continued to play a crucial role in securing their co-operation and thus facilitated the state's rule in their areas of influence. This was particularly true in remote areas where the government position was precarious. Faced with growing state

power, the shaykhs willingly co-operated with Abdullah because he could guarantee their vital interests. In fact, co-operating with Abdullah secured the preservation of the chieftaincy system. The shaykhs of the Bani Sakhr, the Huwaytat and the Majalis of Karak were the main beneficiaries of this kind of politics, preserving their hegemony in their respective areas. Although the government established some presence in these remote regions its officials worked with the local leadership. Official recognition only increased the influence these fortunate shaykhs already yielded over their people, which they were also able to use to accumulate wealth. The British for their part tried, initially, to establish a direct link with shaykhs and notables, thus bypassing Abdullah. Gradually, however, they learned that Abdullah possessed greater influence over the shaykhs and tended to leave him to deal with them. Consequently, Abdullah rose in British estimation.

Although more restricted after 1924 Abdullah continued to exert his influence in favour of the shaykhs. Occasionally, he opposed Prime Minister Rikabi's demands for stricter control over the tribes, the nomadic ones in particular. Granting pardons was another important tool for Abdullah to show benevolence towards the shaykhs. ʿArif al-ʿArif, the Chief Secretary of the Transjordanian government during 1926-1929, wrote in his diary that in one year Abdullah pardoned 47 men, compared with only 9 pardons granted by the high commissioners in Palestine during seven years. He commented that as a result the criminals regarded the courts' sanctions with equanimity.[36]

The Bani Sakhr shaykhs enjoyed excellent relations with Abdullah. Mithqal al-Fayiz continued to be Abdullah's closest ally and perhaps even a personal friend. Partly due to this alliance he maintained the autonomy of his tribes and his personal fortune. Descriptions by Mithqal's visitors between 1925 and 1931 also demonstrate his special relationship with Abdullah. In 1925 the American traveller, W. B. Seabrook, witnessed a visit of the Emir to Mithqal's house during which both men were careful to project a sense of partnership: "The Amir's proposed visit to Mitkhal had nothing to do with politics, big or little. It was merely for friendship's sake and private business affairs of their own ...he and the powerful sheikh ... had been intimate friends and cronies for years."[37] As was the case during the early years of the decade, security remained an important field of co-operation between Abdullah and Mithqal. This was particularly true with regard to Transjordanian-Saudi relations and cross border raids. When called by the Emir to attend discussions with a Saudi delegation in 1929, Mithqal explained to a German guest that he was "Abdullah's Field Marshal."[38]

By allying himself with the Emirate and Abdullah, Mithqal gained many privileges and was able to strengthen his influence within his chieftaincy. He obtained a better position to supply the services that were expected from a tribal leader of his stature, like entertaining guests, providing financial assistance, judging, mediating, lobbying in high places and guaranteeing protection. He used his enormous wealth, private army and political connections to deliver these goods. Mithqal certainly benefited from the creation of the Emirate.[39]

Haditha al-Khuraysha also maintained close relations with Abdullah. According to the testimony of his son, he was Abdullah's link to the Syrian rebels during 1925-1927.[40] Abdullah, who aspired to obtain the Syrian throne, maintained a deep interest in Syrian politics but had to conceal his involvement from his British masters. The northern tribes of the Bani Sakhr headed by Haditha who roamed both sides of the border provided him with a convenient channel for his covert activities and support of the rebels.

Like the Bani Sakhr, the Majalis enjoyed close relations with Abdullah, and therefore the government. As Gubser shows, this special relationship, alongside the effective use of the military, brought about the end of raids and the establishment of the Emir's authority in Karak in 1922. According to Gubser, Abdullah "informally delegated some of his power and authority to Rafifan[sic] Pasha, instructing the local officials to work closely with him" and "Rafifan was able to help maintain a modicum of order at minimal expense..."[41] Apart from Rufayfan, other shaykhs enjoyed excellent relations with the government and acted on its behalf. They were also free to maintain their control, often quite despotic,[42] over dependent tribes in the area, the Ghawarna in particular.

In return for their good services the Majali shaykhs were generously rewarded. Rufayfan's brother, Dulaywan, served as the mayor of Karak from 1918 until his death in 1979. His nephew ʿUtwa, the paramount shaykh, received a salary enacted by law in recognition of his vital role as intermediary and his assistance to the government in keeping order. After ʿUtwa's death in 1937 his son inherited the post as well as the salary. In addition, several Majalis obtained government jobs well before other (non-Ottoman educated) Transjordanians were allowed to join the ranks of administration.[43] The Majalis and their allies were also over-represented among the students of the only high school in Transjordan, *Madrasat al-Salt al-Thanawiyya*. The school was opened in al-Salt in 1925 and admitted students from all around the country according to a quota system. It soon became the bedrock for the emerging Transjordanian elite.[44] Whereas Abdullah cultivated the Majalis' loyalty, he was also careful to maintain cordial relations with Husayn al-Tarawna, head of the rival tribal alliance in the area. Except for a short period from 1928 until the middle of the 1930s, when he led the nationalist opposition, al-Tarawna earned a monthly salary similar to the one he had received from the Ottomans.[45]

The way the government brought Maʿan under its rule in 1925 illustrates the importance of gaining the shaykhs' goodwill and Abdullah's invaluable contribution to achieving this. As a result of the fall of the Hashemite Kingdom of the Hijaz to Ibn Saud, the British urged Abdullah to occupy the former *vilayet* of Maʿan which also included the villages of ʿAqaba, Wadi Musa and Shawbak. Accompanied only by his entourage and one officer, Abdullah arrived in the town to explain the changing circumstances and take-over to the local governor and shaykhs of Maʿan and Wadi Musa. Abdullah secured their co-operation and arranged for the withdrawal of the Hijazi garrison. Only then did Arab Legion and RAF troops, as well as other officials, follow suit. Abdullah also met the two leading shaykhs of the Huwaytat, who pledged their loyalty. The acting British Representative credited Abdullah with the peaceful annexation of Maʿan.[46] Yet, outside the four localities, government presence was hardly felt; the vast southern desert continued to be dominated by the Huwaytat and its dependent tribes.

Abdullah scored another success when he kept Transjordan uninvolved during the Syrian revolt in 1925-1927, exerting influence over tribal leaders. Immediately after the outbreak of the revolt, the British tried to address the problem directly, Peake asking local notables in Irbid not to interfere. For the same purpose, the High Commissioner met fifty shaykhs in Amman.[47] But it was Abdullah who received the credit for keeping the country, on the whole, out of the revolt and sparing the British a diplomatic crisis with the French. The British authorities in Amman and Jerusalem began to realise his immense contribution to their relatively easy, cheap and peaceful control over the country.[48]

Abdullah's major success in his dealing with the tribes, at least from the British point of view, occurred during the Wailing Wall disturbances in Palestine in 1929. Transjordanian tribes had been organising themselves to cross the Jordan River, taking advantage of the instability to loot, without concern for the 'national' cause. But the Emir persuaded them to abandon this plan and the country generally remained quiet. Thus, the British were able to move most of the Imperial forces (TJFF and RAF) to Palestine. As a reward for this service, Abdullah was given a private estate in the Jordan Valley. It was this land that in 1933 was leased to the Jewish Agency. It made Abdullah a landowner and, as Sulayman Bashir demonstrated, in the 1930s land ownership became another important factor which bound him and the shaykhs by a common interest.[49]

Employing chiefs as mediators between the government and the tribesmen and minimal interference in the social structure of the tribes proved effective strategies. It was also beneficial for the shaykhs and their tribes. Mithqal al-Fayiz, Haditha al-Khuraysha, Rufayfan al-Majali, Hamad bin Jazi, Kulayb and ᶜAbdullah al-Shurayda, Sultan and Majid al-ᶜAdwan, Mahmud Krishan from Maᶜan and others all played a role in state-building, shaping its development. Since 1929 many of them sat on the Legislative Council, which further tied them to the state. They enjoyed a handsome salary, immunity during sessions, public recognition and a platform to express themselves. The electoral system itself preserved the chieftaincy system since it guaranteed the election of the most influential shaykhs from each province.

The arrangement for the election of the nomadic tribes' representatives provides the clearest manifestation of the preservation of the tribal order. The Election Law articulated and fixed what became an official (and sometimes quite arbitrary) distinction between tribes who were recognised as nomadic and those who were not. It reflected the prominence of the Bani Sakhr and the Huwaytat in their respective chieftaincies and safeguarded their representation in the Council, guaranteeing them each one seat. Thus, the nomads were divided into two categories, the northern and the southern Bedouin. The northern tribes were the Bani Sakhr, Sirhan, Bani Khalid, ᶜIsa and Salit; the southern Bedouin included the Huwaytat, Mannaᶜin, Hajaya (the Bani ᶜAtiyya were added later). They did not vote themselves like the rest of the population but were represented by their shaykhs. Abdullah's prerogative to appoint two ten-member committees of shaykhs -- one for the northern seat, the other for the southern -- to select a representative for each seat, and the fact that the selection took place at his palace allowed him almost complete control over the outcome.[50] This colonial division between nomadic and non-nomadic tribes became a strong factor in government policy after 1929 and has been interpreted as an instance of excluding the nomads from the Jordanian body politic.[51] However, the evidence suggests that it was at least as much a practical recognition of the prevailing social and political order. The creation of the two electoral districts reflected the ascendancy of the Bani Sakhr and Huwaytat in their respective confederations and was probably meant to keep them together for the sake of better administration and control. As for the voting mechanism, the explanation seems to be more simple. First, among the nomads the shaykh enjoyed the privilege of representing the tribe in its dealings with the government. Second, nomads could not be expected to participate in a formal election. At that time they were suspicious of the government's intentions and especially of any practice which necessitated formal registration, which would have been perceived as the first step towards conscription. Indeed, even among settled communities participation in the first election of 1929 was only partial and provoked public fear (see below).[52]

Modernity and Interference

Reliance on the shaykhs for the execution of many government practices added a modern dimension to the role of a shaykh and more then ever before blurred the boundaries between state and society. In fact, shaykhs became part of the state apparatus and fulfilled administrative chores, working closely with government officials. This practice characterised the Ottoman rule in Transjordan but was intensified under the mandate.

The shaykhs' links to the government occasionally created tension between their role as community leaders and their official status. In 1928 the Prime Minister notified the *mukhtars* that they were considered to be government officials and therefore forbidden to sign petitions of political nature. Later, the government prohibited village shaykhs from collecting the customary marriage fee.[53]

Modern methods of government added new functions to the role of shaykhs, to some of which they were receptive. They registered births and deaths and reported them periodically in a written form. Shaykhs of settled tribes were more likely to report accurately and regularly than nomadic ones. In 1927 the Department of Health asked the shaykhs to inspect their tribes for symptoms of cholera and to deliver a weekly report of their findings. According to the Department, "[t]he Mukhtars and Sheikhs have been and are continuing rendering those weekly certificates fairly regularly."[54] In order to sell animals in the market of Amman and to prevent theft, the seller had to purchase a certificate from his shaykh which identified the animal and spelled out its specifications.[55] When locust swarms appeared in the country between 1928 and 1930 the government ordered the shaykhs to notify its officials upon discovering the menace.[56] Shaykhs of tribes considered non-nomadic were asked to provide registrars with the names of the eligible voters among their men.[57]

Several of these regulations illustrate the government's tendency to interfere in society. It attempted to regulate practices which had previously been free from any governmental involvement. The government also sought to control the population and to increase its knowledge of it, which was hitherto private or confined to each tribe. British precepts of proper government motivated this policy. Sometimes, it entailed the introduction of completely unfamiliar and alien notions, inspired by Western culture. A government order to prevent shepherds in the ʿAjlun and Balqaʾ provinces from collecting and eating partridge eggs and inhabitants of the Ghawr from picking francolin eggs in order to protect the rare species of "these beautiful birds" was an extreme case in point.[58] The protection of the birds was probably not motivated by a love of nature but rather because shooting partridges was a popular pastime for many British officials. Also new were the measures to preserve archaeological sites. This tendency towards more regulation had an effect on even the most informal of institutions, Abdullah's court. Already in 1923 the palace decided to regulate the visiting hours of the Emir. Instead of an open door policy it set specific times for unannounced visits.[59]

The Limits of State Power

The state authorities did not always assess their abilities correctly and at times had to withdraw or amend their original initiatives in the face of opposition. Already in 1924 the government forbade carrying arms in towns. This task was particularly ambitious in a country in which almost every adult male carried weapons. Soon the government realised that it had to exempt from this prohibition tribesmen who resided outside the towns and only visited them, respecting their need and right to carry arms for their own protection. However, even this minimal control was difficult to enforce. In 1929 the Prime Minister issued an announcement drawing attention to the law and urging his officials to implement it.[60]

Conducting a census and preparing electoral registers were equally problematic. Initially, the government did not understand the sensitivity of these acts, which were publicly associated with forced conscription. Registration, conscription and disarmament meant compromising tribal autonomy, an autonomy the tribes refused to relinquish. The recent history of the country should have served as a pertinent lesson. At the peak of Ottoman rule personal registration had provoked the inhabitants of Karak and elsewhere to open revolt. Although its grip on the population by 1925 was far less firm than that of the Ottomans in 1910, the over-ambitious government began preparations for registration and the issuing of identification documents. It demanded that the shaykhs provide government officials with lists of their people and threatened to punish them for any they concealed. A year and a half later the government halted this procedure and never again attempted to conduct a census during the years of the mandate. The first census in Jordan was held in 1952.[61]

By 1928, while preparing the elections for the first Legislative Council, the government had already acquired enough experience to assess what was feasible. Voter registration was left to the discretion of the citizens; it was not compulsory. In order to encourage participation, a provision in the law recognised lists of names submitted by the shaykhs instead of individual registration. Notwithstanding this flexibility, at least in the first elections in 1929 the electorate represented only a very small segment of the population. Tribes like the Bani Hamida, Shawabka, ᶜAwazim and Ghunaymat in the Balqa' province and the entire population of the Maᶜan province refused to register altogether. Rumours about conscription and the flight of the inhabitants of Ramtha to the Hawran to avoid it, forced the government to issue public denials.[62] These first elections, however, were also politically contested and many boycotted them on nationalist grounds, protesting the limited independence granted by the Anglo-Transjordanian treaty of 1928. It is, therefore, difficult to establish the motivation behind the abstention from registration and voting. In any case, only intensive efforts by Abdullah to convince local leaders to participate in the elections, coupled with suppressive measures against opposition leaders, ensured the minimal number of voters needed for the election of the Legislative Council.[63]

By the end of the decade the government was still dependent on the goodwill of the shaykhs. It ruled through them, not instead of them, often delegating some of its responsibility for maintaining law and order, collecting taxes or settling disputes. The chieftaincy remained the main political unit and many aspects of tribal autonomy remained intact. The government's interference in internal affairs was minimal and many of its initiatives were never implemented. Therefore, these initiatives should be seen as no more than aspirations of the authorities, especially in remote areas. Gubser's description of politics in Karak between the wars is relevant to many other areas:

> ... the vast majority of minor problems and political affairs and most of the major ones remained solely within the traditional system. The power of the central government was exercised mostly, in this respect, to keep violence from rising to major proportions, disturbing the whole or a significant part of the society. Only gradually did its power seep down to minor affairs, and even in the contemporary period it does not encompass all of these.[64]

Provision of Services

From the mid-1920s the government also undertook another task of a modern state, that of providing services. As in other aspects of state-formation, a lack of financial resources meant that services were provided on a modest scale. In this realm, too, shaykhs played a major role. In their capacity as intermediaries and for administrative convenience, they became the main channel for distributing state resources. By fulfilling this function, the shaykhs enjoyed greater leverage vis-à-vis their own constituencies.

Establishing law and order and protecting the agricultural communities was the first priority of the government. This goal neatly corresponded with the self-portrayed colonial mission of the day which was fully articulated in Frederick Lugard's book, *Dual Mandate in Tropical Africa* (1922). According to the philosophy behind this mission, Britain had a dual duty to protect indigenous subjects and develop the economic resources of the colonies under its control. Apart from the moral obligation for the wellbeing of the population, it was hoped that improvement in security would encourage peasants to increase their cultivable land. This, in turn, would generate higher taxation, a major concern for British administrators everywhere. Prime Minister Rikabi articulated this policy when addressing shaykhs and notables after the incorporation of Ma'an and 'Aqaba into the Emirate in 1925. In his speech he said:

> There are millions of dunums in this province which lay fallow because their owners cannot seed them due to the conflict between the Bedouin and the settled population and the lack of security. We will seek to return the land to its owners after we solve the conflict justly. We will reconcile the desert and the city in a way that will benefit everyone without violating anyone's rights.[65]

The measures to prevent nomads from trespassing on cultivated land represented an attempt to protect and encourage cultivators. This was done by extracting money guarantees from their shaykhs and close inspection of the Arab Legion. Another method which also exposed the limits of the government and its reliance on local leaders was the government's order to the shaykhs to appoint local guards to watch over the fields and buildings in the villages and towns. On the whole, the government succeeded in protecting the settled communities. Attacks did occasionally occur but they were exceptional and handled firmly.[66]

Another way to encourage agriculture was to provide farmers who suffered crop failures with small loans from the Agricultural Bank, enabling them to purchase seeds. Typically, this issue was closely connected to security. Immediately following the outbreak of the Syrian revolt in the summer of 1925, the Transjordanian authorities applied to London for an additional allocation of £10,000. This sum was requested (but was apparently refused) for distribution among farmers along the frontier in order to ensure their "peaceful occupation" instead of getting involved with the rebels. In 1929 the government gave 20,000 kg of seeds to the impoverished Bani Hamida tribes after a succession of bad years. A year later the government distributed free seeds to several villages in the Tafila area as well as to nomadic tribes around Ma'an in order to encourage them to take up agriculture.[67]

The Health Department was particularly active and served large segments of society including the nomadic tribes, and its initiatives were generally welcomed by the population. From 1926 on, the Department offered vaccination against infectious diseases, eye drops for the treatment of trachoma, and free medical treatment in the newly-established government hospital in Amman and in regional dispensaries. Around 14,000 visits in the various government medical centres were recorded during 1926. Apparently, for many tribesmen and women the sight of medical officers conducting inspection or guidance tours in their villages or encampments was the only tangible sign of the state in those early days. At times however, the Department's staff failed to explain the new regulations to the locals and imposed fines in order to ensure compliance. This was the case with sanitation regulations, and only partial success was recorded in matters of hygiene in the villages. Health services provided shaykhs with another benefit they could distribute to their kin; the free eye drops they dispensed illustrate this point.[68]

Finally, the locals benefited from the improved infrastructure. Although only a by-product of measures to enhance security and government work, trains, roads and even telephone lines served the population.[69]

The State's Grip on the Desert and along the Borders

The gradual consolidation of government power was particularly difficult beyond the settled zone. Despite several over-ambitious attempts by the government to achieve control in the desert and along the borders, the desert remained, on the whole, the domain of the nomadic tribes. They continued to enjoy almost complete autonomy and government presence was limited to the personal influence of Abdullah and Shakir. At the same time, however, the government began to restrict movements across the borders. During the 1920s the division of *Bilad al-Sham* into several political units, sometimes hostile to each other, had just begun to affect the nomads. Its full repercussions were only felt in the early 1930s; by then, the respective governments had consolidated their control over the borders and limited tribal movements to some extent.

The Saudi Border

Geopolitical changes in northern Arabia in the middle of the decade made the desert area more important from a colonial point of view and prompted the authorities to try and expand their control into the desert. The fall of *sharif* Husayn's Kingdom of the Hijaz in 1925 to Ibn Saud and the incorporation of Ma'an and 'Aqaba into Transjordan resulted in closer proximity and a territorial dispute between the Hashemite Emirate and the expanding Saudis. Raids had been seen by successive governments in the region as internal tribal affairs which did not necessitate their interference. Suddenly they assumed the importance of an acute political problem that affected the international relations of the area and that of the British Empire. This was because Ibn Saud turned the issue into an instrument to undermine Abdullah. It can also be attributed to the organisational structure of the British government. The King's complaints about raids from Transjordan were received with sympathy at the Foreign Office, responsible for relations with Ibn Saud. The Foreign Office in turn put pressure on the Colonial Office, London's department responsible for Transjordan and a much weaker ministry since Churchill left the office of Secretary of State.

From 1925 the Transjordanian authorities attempted to control raiding, the result not only of pressures from London, but also the government's belief in its ability to tighten its hold over the nomadic tribes domestically. British policy towards the nomads was ambitious and comprehensive. In 1926 the High Commissioner Arthur Plumer articulated this policy by drawing a direct link between stopping the raids and the ultimate goal of increased settlement and cultivation. While he did not attach undue significance to seasonal raids, he nevertheless stated that: "our policy must be to encourage settlement on the land and gradual increase of cultivation and this cannot be achieved unless the settlers and cultivators have a sense of security for their lives and property."[70]

This policy was ambitious not only in its aims, but also in that British officials sought to interfere with what had previously been Abdullah's sole responsibility. At times he was bypassed altogether. This tactic, however, failed. As early as 1925, the British and the government took steps to prevent raids. For one, the British put pressure on Abdullah to order Hamad bin Jazi of the Huwaytat to return looted animals to the Zaban tribe of the Bani Sakhr. They were clearly annoyed with Abdullah's languid response as well as Hamad's ongoing raids. In the same year, the government announced its intention to convene the shaykhs of the various tribes in order to resolve their outstanding conflicts.[71] This initiative remained on paper and had to wait a year until Abdullah brokered peace between the Bani Sakhr and the Huwaytat.

The signing of the Hadda agreement marked a new phase in British attempts to interfere in nomadic affairs in order to keep the borders between their different protégé states in Arabia peaceful. Britain had been trying to draw borders between the Najd and its two mandates, Transjordan and Iraq, since 1923. In November 1925 the Hadda agreement was signed, settling the borders between Transjordan and Ibn Saud's kingdom. Abdullah was forced to give up the entire Wadi Sirhan, including its northern end, the oasis of Kaf, which was used as the winter grazing lands of the Bani Sakhr and Sirhan tribes. Ibn Saud gave up his demand for a territorial link to Syria. Sovereignty over ᶜAqaba and Maᶜan remained unresolved because the British failed to obtain the King's recognition of Transjordanian rule in this area. The agreement both created international obligations that had to be respected by the Transjordanian authorities and also provided them with a diplomatic mechanism to do so. Since the agreement over the border turned zones of influence into sovereign areas, and the new lines often violated tribal domains (*dira*), it gradually affected the free movement of tribes.[72]

At first however, the new borders had little effect on nomads. Borders, although drawn on maps, were not demarcated on the ground. Nomads did not know the actual border lines and were not always aware of crossing them. This is unsurprising given that even government officials demonstrated ignorance in such matters. In August 1929, the Minister of Justice asked the Prime Minister whether the Qurayyat al-Milh in the northern edge of Wadi Sirhan were under Transjordanian suzerainty. The government had ceded this area to Ibn Saud three years earlier. Moreover, the Hadda agreement was intended to ensure that the tribes would continue to enjoy their traditional grazing, habitation and ownership rights and would not be affected by the creation of sovereignty in the desert.[73]

Notwithstanding the wording of the agreement, the tribes were gradually affected following the consolidation of state power along the borders. The Bani Sakhr and Sirhan had to buy their way into Wadi Sirhan where Najdi officials forced them to pay the religious tax (*zakat*). The Huwaytat and Bani ᶜAtiyya also wintered across the border and were exposed to similar Najdi demands (These developments are discussed further in the next chapter). The problems faced by the ᶜUmran tribe of ᶜAqaba illustrate the effect of international borders on nomads. According to the Hadda agreement, the Transjordanian-Hijazi border passed only 2 miles south of ᶜAqaba, cutting across the tribe's *dira*. By the end of the decade, this tribe suffered economically from the introduction of the border and petitioned to be re-included in Transjordan. The Governor of ᶜAqaba and the *Mutasarrif* of Maᶜan urged their government to move the border further south, a distance of "a three-day march" from the town so that the international border would correspond to the "natural border of ᶜAqaba." Since the matter involved a revision of the delicate *status quo* with the Saudis, who in any case did not recognise ᶜAqaba as part of Transjordan, it was not pursued.[74]

Apart from defining the borders, the Hadda agreement stipulated the regulation of tribal movements in order to limit cross-border raids. In fact, it attached an entirely new meaning and significance to desert raids. By stating that "the Governments of Nejd and Trans-Jordan severally recognise that raiding by tribes settled in their territories into the territory of the other state is an aggression,"[75] cross-border raids were elevated from a local affair to a breach of international law which necessitated the interference of two states and an empire. The two governments undertook to inflict "severe punishment" on the perpetrators and to hold the shaykhs responsible.

To help the implementation of the agreement, the Transjordanian government created the new position of the Tribal Officer. The latter was entrusted with persuading the tribes to refrain from raiding. Additional tasks such as maintaining contacts with the shaykhs and encouraging the tribes to settle down indicate that the position represented an attempt to introduce tighter control over the nomads.[76]

At first, the British tried to employ the diplomatic arrangements inscribed in the Hadda agreement to secure peace among the tribes. One arrangement was the tribunal established to control raiding. The idea was to stop the cycle of raids and counter-raids by returning lost property via an arrangement that would take into account all claims. A restitution settlement was negotiated between the two parties with British mediation for almost five years, but with no outcome due to Saudi obstructions.[77]

As a diplomatic solution was still pending and raiding continued, the British resorted to military means. Since the middle of 1926 they made vigorous efforts to stop raiding both internally and externally. High Commissioner Plumer formed the Trans Jordan Frontier Force (TJFF) with the task of defending the eastern and southern borders of Transjordan against raids.[78] RAF planes and armoured cars ventured to penetrate the desert and demonstrate their power to the roaming tribes in their encampments as well as conducting reconnaissance. Cox remarked with satisfaction that the RAF "brought the fact of their presence and power home to the Bedouin more than has been the case before."[79] Following Saudi complaints, the High Commissioner contemplated a military operation against the Bani Sakhr and the Huwaytat in order to force them to return looted camels. To facilitate military movements between the Hijaz railway and the Iraqi border, the British embarked on building roads. Reporting on this enterprise in 1928, Cox explained that "[t]his area is now an open instead of a closed book and the work done had made the greatest influence in the maintenance of public security."[80]

By the end of the decade the Transjordanian authorities had acquired a certain capability to operate in desert terrain. As will be shown in the next chapter, they gradually penetrated the desert and were able to reach the nomads in their home domain. By 1929-1930 they were able to launch sporadic punitive activities, but failed to prevent raiding and their military forces proved especially unfit to protect their subjects from raids of Najdi tribes. It took a change in British policy before raids could be stopped altogether.

In the meantime, the British found in Abdullah a more effective means to calm the desert. In January 1927 the High Commissioner contemplated meeting the Huwaytat shaykhs to warn them that "they must be of good behaviour." Representative Cox persuaded him otherwise and suggested: "[t]he Amir has considerable influence over the bedu, and it is to our interest to assist him maintain that influence whilst causing him to exercise it for good."[81] Since the signing of the Hadda agreement Abdullah restrained the tribes from raiding Najd, asking them to wait for the conclusion of the negotiations on the disputed claims. Abdullah forbade raiding and organised a series of meetings with the shaykhs, to which Najdi representatives were invited but did not come. These actions marked a change in Abdullah's attitude towards desert raids. As Cox wrote, "[t]he Amir, who before the signing of the Hadda agreement had taken no active steps to prevent raiding into Nejdian territory, has since appreciated the seriousness of the situation..."[82] Moreover, raids had been previously seen as a legitimate activity, especially if they involved attacks on hostile Wahhabi tribes. The newspaper *Al-Sharq al-ʿArabi*, the Emirate's official mouthpiece, reported on such occurrences, praising the Transjordanian participants.[83]

Abdullah's efforts to pacify the desert culminated in May 1926 when he brokered a historic peace agreement between to the two main nomadic confederacies, the Bani Sakhr and the Huwaytat, who had been enemies for years. Perhaps it was British determination and the military pressure and threats they exerted on the tribes that allowed Abdullah to achieve this peace. An alternative or complementary explanation might have been a recent clash between Bani Sakhr and Huwaytat tribesmen, which resulted in the death of a Bani Sakhr shaykh. The agreement did not only provide a framework for stopping mutual raids but also included an undertaking to stop raiding altogether. By persuading the shaykhs to make peace, forget ancient claims, restore the loot from recent raids, put their faith in the Hadda tribunal and cease raiding into Najd, Abdullah made the British military contingency redundant. This came as a great relief to the British who had serious doubts about their ability to subdue the nomads.[84]

Abdullah succeeded in soliciting the co-operation of the tribes through their shaykhs. This success gained him the credit of the British. As far as the loot was concerned, immediately after the signing of the agreement between the two confederacies the British reported on the restoration of animals to the Ruwalla and to Najdi merchants. By the end of the year they reported that Transjordanian tribes had returned all stolen animals of undisputed claims from Najd. More significantly, for a year and a half following the agreement relative peace in the southern desert was kept. Internally, the two confederacies observed the peace almost fully, although they did not return all the loot, as was customary in such cases.[85] The government, therefore, empowered local governors to arrest those who refused to obey the terms of the agreement. Alternatively, in accordance with the accepted notion of collective responsibility, their relations up to five generations removed could be detained pending the return of the stolen goods. When a raid of Bani Sakhr tribesmen against the Huwaytat occurred three years later, the Emir, supported by the RAF, hurried to restore the peace and the animals were duly returned.[86]

By 1928 Cox had a complete change of heart regarding Abdullah. The fierce rivalry and criticism from his early days as British Representative gave way to an appreciation of Abdullah's style of rule and the merits of his policy. Cox and other British officials came to the conclusion that nobody was better qualified to handle the tribes than he and his cousin Shakir. In May he wrote that "experience have [sic] shown that it is the Amir who can best manage Beduin affairs with the assistance of his cousin the Amir Shaker." Only a few years earlier the same Cox accused Abdullah of being pro-Bedouin. The British also came to appreciate that the Emir's so called extravagance was his way of showing generosity and good hospitality, which was expected from an Arab tribal ruler and a means to gain the support of the shaykhs. Cox, who came to Transjordan to exert control over the Emir's expenditure, now lobbied for an increase of Abdullah's civil list. He explained that in order to keep in close touch with the Bedouin, Abdullah needed to entertain Bedouin chiefs in Amman and to visit them in their camps, "a procedure which costs a considerable amount of money but which is quite unavoidable."[87] Cox further admitted that Abdullah did not spend the money on himself but led a rather humble life, so much so that Cox reported that he himself had to support Abdullah's wives:

I don't deny that the Amir is inclined to be careless with money but he does not spend it on himself, it all goes on things which he considers are required by his subjects from one in his position. This is so much the case that I was obliged to put in his budget provision for a salary for each of his wives, and took the step at the request of the ladies themselves who were not getting enough to provide themselves with clothes.[88]

Not only did the British realise Abdullah's indispensable contribution to the security along the borders, but they also learned to appreciate local methods of conflict resolution. Recognising that the Hadda tribunal faced difficulties, the Palestine government -- after consulting Abdullah and Cox -- offered to appoint a British arbitrator instead. The latter was expected to determine claims by a method as close as possible to customary law. In addition, this proposal prescribed the participation of the litigants' shaykhs and guarantors and minimal interference of government representatives. Moreover, the arbitrator MacDonnell employed the familiar *bush'a* method of a burning iron placed on the tongue when he tried to verify oaths given by tribesmen.[89] Only a few years earlier this practice had provoked the outraged Secretary of State to demand that Abdullah stop its use.

Another change of heart, at least on the level of officials on the ground, occurred vis-à-vis the nomads. In the course of this process, the tribes gradually came to be seen by Cox, Peake, Lord Plumer and his successor Chancellor more as subjects or citizens, who deserved protection of their natural rights, and less as a problem. British reliance on Abdullah's influence on the nomadic tribes, their adoption of tribal methods to restore peace and their growing sympathy towards the nomads will be discussed further in the next chapter. These are also themes in the following discussion of the Syrian border.

Border Relations with Syria

While the Najdi frontier temporarily calmed down, the northern border remained a problem for the British and French authorities. Here, too, customary raids turned into a diplomatic crisis between two states and two colonial powers. The problem of the raids had two implications for state-building. First, it brought home the need to clearly delineate the frontier between Transjordan and Syria. Second, in dealing with external rivals, namely the French and the Syrian tribes, the Emirate's officials and its tribes shared another area in which their interests were compatible. This situation contributed to the integration of the tribes concerned into the state.

The first attempt to tighten control along the border followed the outbreak of the Syrian revolt in 1925 when the government tried to prevent any support to the rebels from Transjordan. RAF armoured cars were deployed at Azraq and Umm al-Jimal. The government forbade the crossing of the border after sunset and demanded that individuals who wished to cross should first report to the authorities.[90] Until then no such control had been attempted as the international border, still not finalised or demarcated, cut across grazing areas and village fields.

Cross-border raids concerned both governments. The British initially tried to stop raids by imposing a solution on the tribes, as they also did in the southern desert. In 1925 the British and French declared an armistice between the Bani Sakhr and the tribes of Jabal Druze. This imposed arrangement was duly ignored by the Sardiyya tribesmen who raided in Transjordan within days of the declaration. The French, preoccupied with the revolt, failed to respond to British suggestions.[91] It seems that the tribes themselves were also preoccupied with the revolt and raids decreased during 1926. Mithqal al-Fayiz and Haditha al-Khuraysha of the Bani Sakhr confided to the Syrian nationalist Dr. ʿAbd al-Rahman al-Shahbandar that the tribes did not raid that year lest they accidentally harmed the rebels.[92]

In the middle of 1927 raids were once again a cause of concern for Transjordanian and Syrian authorities. At this point the British tended to co-operate with rather than dictate to the tribes. They also showed better understanding of local realities. Tension rose as a result of a violent encounter between Syrian troops and Sardiyya tribesmen on the one hand and a party from the Bani Sakhr on the other, the latter suffering casualties in lives and property. By that time the British had mastered local methods of conflict resolution. They suggested the payment of blood-money for the killed tribesmen (among whom were a woman and a child) in order to settle the case amicably. Accordingly, Transjordanian and Syrian shaykhs concluded a settlement under the auspices of the two governments. They also undertook not to raid anymore.[93] This positive outcome was however jeopardised by a severe crisis that erupted towards the end of the year. In November French and Syrian troops crossed the un-demarcated border and drove off an Arab Legion NCO and several tribesmen who occupied an anti-cholera post in Umm al-Jimal. As the British noted, although the border had not been defined, a *de facto* arrangement based on the Sykes-Picot agreement had been in existence since 1920. Accordingly, Umm al-Jimal was well within Transjordan and was administered by its government.

The French move left the Emirate authorities and its tribes in the same boat. Peake asked the High Commissioner to send a representation to the French. He reported that their move "has had a very bad effect on the Beni Sakhr and Beni Hassan tribes and his Highness the Amir is, quite naturally, very angry at the violation of his boundaries."[94] With a clear manifestation of sympathy with the tribes and self-criticism towards Britain's inaction, officials in Palestine and Transjordan reported on extreme anger in Transjordan towards the French.[95] The crisis died down when the Sardiyya left Umm al-Jimal, having consumed most of the water to the annoyance of the Bani Sakhr, followed by a French withdrawal.[96] Raids across the Syrian border nonetheless continued.

Towards the close of the decade the British who served on the ground came full circle in their position towards the nomads. By 1928 Cox, Peake and to a certain extent Plumer showed sympathy for the nomads' needs and called for consideration of tribal migration and customary grazing rights when demarcating the frontier between the two countries. As had happened in the case of the Saudi border, London was less receptive to this reasoning, preferring imperial interests to local ones. While debating what the British position during the boundary negotiations should be, one of the reasons Cox gave for the line he suggested was to "enable the Transjordan northern Bedouin to roam over the country where they habitually graze for part of the year." Realising this position might be watered down by the High Commissioner or later by Whitehall, he stressed that "[i]n whatever manner the frontier line is drawn there should be an understanding that people shall have access to their usual watering places and grazing grounds," failing which "would be to cause intense discontent among the Transjordan Bedouin of the north."[97]

The border issue dragged on until it was finally settled in late 1931 and demarcated in 1932. Britain rejected French territorial demands within Transjordan and made only minor concessions. This was not so much for the sake of nomadic movement but rather to secure strategic needs such as the Baghdad-Haifa railway (never built) and the Iraq Petroleum Company pipeline. The agreement did however guarantee that tribes would continue to enjoy their traditional property, pasture, watering or cultivation rights across the border. It also facilitated their movement across the border with their animals and belongings without paying custom duties or any other taxes collected in the host country.[98]

Border Relations with Iraq, Palestine and Sinai

It was easier to attain peace on the borders with British-controlled Iraq, Palestine and Sinai. Informal relations between British officials facilitated easy understanding.

Sometimes, efficient lines of communication helped to police tribal movements.

In 1927 the Iraqi ᶜAmarat tribes entered Transjordan and raided the Huwaytat. The latter, in return, formed an alliance with the Bani Sakhr in order to counter-raid. While the TJFF was helpless, Abdullah and Shakir persuaded the tribes to accept a peaceful settlement. A tribal conference was convened in July 1927, and a settlement was agreed between the two parties under the auspices of their respective governments. The settlement resembled previous arrangements in two respects. Firstly, although it was based on custom, the chiefs promised to turn to their governments if attacked in the future, rather than counter-raid. Secondly, it was only partially implemented.[99]

Also in 1927 the governments of Palestine and Transjordan brought about a peace agreement between the Saqr and Ghazawiyya. These tribes roamed in the northern Jordan Valley on both banks of the river and regularly raided each other. Since raids continued, the two governments decided in 1929 to inflict fines on the two tribes and even threatened to arrest the shaykh if the tribe did not pay.[100]

Disputes which involved the Beersheba tribes were discussed in several meetings between representatives of the governments and the shaykhs. These meetings culminated in June 1930 when Transjordan signed an agreement with the government and shaykhs of Palestine resembling the one with Iraq. Similar methods were employed to settle claims between tribes from Transjordan and Sinai and cordial relations between Peake and Major Jarvis, the Governor of Sinai, facilitated a degree of control including the extradition of raiders and criminals.[101] Tribes such as the Huwaytat, Hajaya, Bani ᶜAtiyya, ᶜUmran and the Saᶜidiyyin continued to move uninterrupted between Transjordan, southern Palestine and the Sinai desert.

Conclusion

By the end of the decade central government was still weak and limited. Its policies were only partially implemented after negotiations and the granting of concessions to the tribes. Despite its weakness, it nonetheless succeeded in controlling the population. The country was stabilised, raids ceased in the settled zone, agricultural communities enjoyed a degree of security and the Treasury collected taxes. In a way, the government possessed a degree of control similar to that exercised by the Ottomans from the end of the nineteenth century. The authorities drew on Ottoman methods of governing tribal society and further developed them. Measures based on tribal identity, collective responsibility and shaykhly authority were either adopted from the Ottomans or freshly introduced during these years. They were later perfected when the state apparatus grew and the government could impose greater control. Thus, the 1920s laid the foundations for the central government and its relations with society, which was evident by the middle of the 1930s.

The success of the Emirate authorities in consolidating their rule lay in the combination of both traditional and modern systems of government. In this respect, a convenient division of labour had developed. Abdullah modelled relations with the tribes on the old chieftaincy system, seeking to gain the major tribes' loyalty and support, while allowing them to retain many aspects of their autonomy. Tribal chieftaincies were allowed to operate within the newly created state. Whilst preserving and utilising the tribal structure and ethos of society, the Emirate acquired modern traits, which were inspired by the mandatory authorities: the consolidation of borders, tax collection, growing power of the central authority and the accompanying tendency to interfere in societal matters as well as the provision of services. These nonetheless remained small beginnings at this stage, which came to fruition only in the mid-to-late-1930s.

By the decade's end most segments of the population had been affected by the establishment of the Emirate and had come into contact with state agencies. Settled tribes placed under the control of the Arab Legion paid taxes but also enjoyed better health services and sometimes assistance with their cultivation. In fact, their shaykhs acted as both local leaders and representatives of the government. Nomadic tribes had to respect law and order in the settled zone and towards the end of the decade witnessed the beginning of government presence on the fringes of the desert. The consolidation of several political entities in *Bilad al-Sham* and the strained relations between them forced tribes to fall back on the Amman government. In particular, the tribes sought protection from the Wahhabis in Arabia and the French in Syria. Gradually, government and tribal interests converged to allow better co-operation. The tribes developed a stake in the Emirate and the process of integration was well on its way.

Integration manifested itself less in the daily life of a tribesman or woman and more on the shaykhly level. Tribal leaders co-operated with Abdullah and Shakir, enjoyed their hospitality and became gradually involved in local and national politics. Amman became the focal point of these activities. In fact, this period saw the crystallisation of what Sami Zubaida terms the 'political field' of the nation state. As Zubaida emphasises, this political participation "does not necessarily imply solidarity or loyalty to the state, but a heightened consciousness of the national dimension of their livelihood and their relations to politics..." Shaykhs were "seeking to obtain power, influence and resources within the new political entities, using the language of nationality and of political ideologies to that end."[102]

Involvement in national politics and the use of the language of nationalism by the shaykhs who constituted the Emirate's elite will be discussed further in Chapter Five. This would be done in conjunction with a description of the next stage of state expansion and its impact on society. The next chapter, however, examines the extension of centralised authority into the desert and the subjugation of nomadic tribes to state rule.

CHAPTER FOUR:
COLONIALISM AS A FINE ART: GLUBB PASHA AND THE DESERT TRIBES, 1928-1936

The intensification of raids on the Najdi borders in the last two years of the 1920s brought about a change in British policy towards controlling the desert. Constant pressures from London on the authorities in Palestine and Transjordan resulted in the extension of direct British rule, achieved through the work of Captain John Glubb. By the middle of the 1930s this process was complete, and in many ways Glubb replaced Abdullah as the chief link between the tribes in the desert and the Emirate's authorities. Within only a few years the balance of power between the tribes and the central authority had been entirely transformed. The central administration finally managed to subjugate the tribesmen to its rule. The Emirate's control was extended into the desert, something the Ottoman government had never accomplished. This achievement has been attributed to Glubb and the Desert Patrol of the Arab Legion he commanded. But it was also facilitated by a simultaneous economic crisis which reduced the nomads' capacity for resistance. The tribes were weakened and desperate, and their need of assistance rendered them more amenable to the central government than they might otherwise have been. The nomads' economic plight was a result of violent raids from Najd, British attempts to stabilise the new borders, and successive years of drought and locust attacks. The tribal chieftaincy became dependant on the state, thus marking an important step in the integration of the tribes. This brought about major transformations in the life of the nomadic people and in tribal society in general.

Tribal War in the Desert

The raids on the Najd-Transjordan border resumed in 1928, after a year and a half of relative calm following the Hadda agreement and the peace between the Bani Sakhr and Huwaytat. Hostility between the Saudis and the Hashemites provided the background to the crisis. This antagonism dated back to 1916, when both ruling houses saw the other's expansion as a threat to their own influence in the peninsula.

More important still were internal developments within the Saudi state that reflected on Transjordan. By the mid-1920s Ibn Saud's policy of using the *Ikhwan*i tribes as his main instrument for territorial expansion proved to be a double-edged sword. Ibn Saud tried to develop his chieftaincy into a more centralised, territorially-defined modern state and accepted the British order in the region. This policy provoked the *Ikhwan*, who became the defenders of the old order. They wished to continue raiding and to preserve their autonomy and consequently they posed a powerful opposition to the King. By 1927 this disobedience turned into open rebellion. Large-scale raids into Iraq and Transjordan were the *Ikhwan*i way of subverting Ibn Saud's agreements with Britain and her Hashemite allies. Thus, in 1928 Transjordan became involved in the internal struggle in the Saudi state, which led to an unprecedented increase in the scale and violence of tribal raiding. The turning point came in February 1928 when an *Ikhwan*i force from the Ruwalla attacked with exceptional cruelty the Zaban tribe of the Bani Sakhr, killing the shaykh and dozens of men and abusing the women. This sort of warfare was unprecedented and unacceptable even in the rough desert life, and brought about a spate of raids across the border which lasted for the next four years.[1]

Abdullah and Shakir -- the exclusive authorities over nomadic affairs -- made enormous efforts to restrain the Zaban and other tribes from retaliating, asking them to await the return of the loot by Ibn Saud. Immediately after the raid they persuaded the tribes camping in the eastern desert to move away from the border. On several occasions Shakir succeeded in breaking up large concentrations of tribesmen preparing to counter-raid. When minor raids did occur, Abdullah secured a quick and full return of the looted animals. However, as Ibn Saud did not live up to his promise to return the loot from the Ruwalla, the Zaban became restive and reprisals were unpreventable. Abdullah approached the High Commissioner, pleading with the British government to make sure that Ibn Saud returned the loot, compensated the tribes for the dead and punished the raiders. He explained that he found himself in a difficult position as long as his tribes felt that justice had not been done. As time went by and no restitution was forthcoming, Abdullah warned the High Commissioner that authority over the tribes was slipping from his hands. Abdullah was right, and towards the end of the year the cycle of raids and counter-raids resumed, culminating in a raid carried out in Najd led by shaykh Tarad bin Fahd of the Zaban.[2]

Ibn Saud, at the time engaged in fighting against his rebels along the Kuwait-Iraq border, was quick to deny responsibility. Employing the same method that had already proved successful in dealing with the British in Iraq,[3] he blamed the Transjordanian authorities for the escalation of the raids and attempted to undermine Abdullah's position. His diplomacy, directed at the Foreign Office which was responsible for Arabia, bore fruit. British diplomats on the ground and in London showed sympathy towards the King's needs and accepted his claim that Transjordan was the guilty party. They disregarded the denials of the governments of Palestine and Transjordan via the Colonial Office, whose officials did not put their full weight behind their colleagues in the field. And because every massive *Ikhwan*i raid provoked many small-scale raids from Transjordanian tribesmen and subsequently frequent protests from the Najdi government, London got the impression that raids in Transjordan were endemic and that they needed to be treated from that side of the frontier.

In response to pressure from Whitehall, Cox and Abdullah arranged for a special investigation. In December 1928 Emir Shakir and Alec Kirkbride, then the Assistant Resident (Following the conclusion of the Anglo-Transjordanian treaty in 1928 the title 'Representative' was replaced with 'Resident'), visited the tribes involved in the raids. This was the first attempt ever made by the Transjordanian government to extend its authority into the desert area. As Kirkbride wrote, "The visit now reported is believed to be the first made into that part of the territory by Trans-Jordan officials."[4] It was certainly the first visit of its kind of a British official since Philby's adventures in the desert in the early 1920s. The investigation showed that the Saudi claims were exaggerated, often vague, and impossible to substantiate. The Transjordanian authorities stressed that in 21 cases they restored the loot to the Najdi owners while Ibn Saud refused to settle the much larger Transjordanian claim on behalf of the Zaban.[5]

The recognition of the injustice done to the tribes and the understanding showed for their actions notwithstanding, the Transjordanian authorities decided to punish the Zaban. This was another step towards penetrating the desert. Operating in its heart, 150 mile from Amman, Kirkbride remarked that:

> The operation has created a precedent and has demonstrated to the tribes, who have hitherto regarded themselves as immune from Government influence when East of the railway, that the Government with the assistance of the armed forces in the country are capable of tracing their camps, however far out they may be, and of inflicting any punishment they decide upon.[6]

The disciplining of the Zaban alongside the introduction of new military presence, such as the appointment of a RAF intelligence officer late in 1928, and the building of an Arab Legion post in desert area 20 miles east of Maʿan, served two purposes. First, the Transjordan authorities tried to demonstrate to their tribesmen, as well as to their superiors in London and the Najdi government, their determination to end raiding. Second, they hoped that their action would prompt a reciprocal move from Ibn Saud. Neither goal was achieved. Ibn Saud continued to obstruct the negotiations over a restitution settlement that had been stipulated in the Hadda agreement. This was possible because the Foreign Office was still reluctant to take a tougher line with him. Britain did not wish to make the King's situation even more difficult while he was fighting for political survival against the rebels in his own land. Consequently, raids continued even after the impressive demonstration of power. In March 1929 it was the turn of the Huwaytat to suffer a large raid of the Ruwalla from Najd. Their Nawasra tribe of the Tawayha suffered heavy losses amounting to 12 men killed and 200 camels and 300 sheep taken.[7]

Urged by the British and utilising their influence among the shaykhs, it largely fell on Abdullah and Shakir, at times assisted by the military, to prevent the raids. In May 1929 Shakir, with the help of a military escort and the leading shaykhs of the

Bani Sakhr and Huwaytat, Mithqal al-Fayiz and Hamad bin Jazi, broke up a group consisting of Zaban and Tawayha warriors on their way to recover their losses and to take revenge on the Najd. On several occasions, Abdullah asked for the intervention of the Imperial forces -- the RAF and the TJFF -- to enforce his will on the tribes and, upon receiving early warnings, to try and prevent raids from Najd.[8]

None of these measures bore fruit. The Transjordanian tribes suffered losses as the preventative action of the government made it difficult for them to counter-raid. Moreover, the small-scale raids, which for centuries had served as a means of livelihood as well as a way of life and a game with clear rules that limited the degree of violence, turned into a nasty war. The tribes could not match the new battle methods or the great numbers of the *Ikhwan*, who enjoyed the experience of a decade of conquest and operated more like an army than a raiding party. All the while the tribes from Najd continued to raid and escape the British forces. Abdullah was also affected and lost a great deal of influence over the shaykhs.

New Measures for Desert Control: A Change in British Policy

In response to mounting pressures from London to stop the persistent raids, the newly-appointed High Commissioner, Sir John Chancellor, introduced a new strategy which marked a change in British policy towards controlling the desert. Although still reluctant, the British had to interfere in the everyday control of the tribes. By combining military and administrative measures, they sought to prevent them from raiding into Najd.

Realising that Abdullah was losing control of the desert, the British decided to adopt a more active role. The corner stone of the new policy was *Lajnat al-Ishraf ʿala al-Badu*, the Tribal (or Bedouin) Control Board (TCB). It represented an attempt to prevent the tribes from carrying out raids, especially across the Najdi border. This device was inspired by a similar scheme proposed by Abdullah the year before.[9]

The TCB can be seen as the first attempt to institutionalise control over the nomadic tribes and also as a compromise which allowed for joint British-Hashemite regulation of the desert. Before its creation, nomadic affairs were controlled only informally and personally from the palace, without real involvement of British or other government officials. Whilst in most areas of government the British played the leading role and left Abdullah with limited authority, tribal politics were his exclusive remit. Abdullah insisted that this domain remain his and the British wanted to avoid direct confrontation over this issue. As the High Commissioner explained in his proposal for the new policy:

> His Highness attached great value to that responsibility and would oppose any arrangements which derogated from his authority over the tribes...with whom he (and he alone) is in close contact, and over whom neither the British Resident nor the Officer Commanding the Arab Legion exercise control.[10]

The commander of the RAF in Palestine and Transjordan further elaborated that Abdullah "would bitterly resent the removal of the chief item of real power which he possesses, and of his chief interest and preoccupation."[11] Trying not to undermine all of Abdullah's authority over the tribes and to avoid confrontation with him, the British devised the Board as a mechanism that would still allow his involvement, but deny him ultimate power and facilitate close supervision of his conduct. This was particularly important as they suspected Abdullah was influenced by his hatred of Ibn Saud.

The proposed Board was composed of Shakir as president together with the Commanding Officer of the Arab Legion and a shaykh nominated by Abdullah. The Board had the authority to deal with issues within the jurisdiction of the Tribal Courts, to control the nomads' movements and determine the locations in which they could camp, and to investigate any raids or breaches of the peace in which nomads were involved. The Board could also seize property and impose fines or prison sentences on raiders. Abdullah's hold on tribal affairs was secured by the need for him to confirm every sentence passed against a tribesman.[12] Ironically, the British, who in 1924 had dissolved the Department of Tribal Administration in order to curtail Shakir's involvement in tribal affairs, now created a platform that gave him a prominent and official role in the very same function; they pinned their hopes on exploiting his vast knowledge and reputation on nomadic affairs.

London's response to Chancellor's proposal was sceptical, and disagreement between the different departments hampered a quick decision. On the one hand, the cautious Foreign Office continued its bias towards Ibn Saud. It objected to one element in the proposal, the establishment of three Arab Legion desert posts along the border, after the construction of a desert post in Iraq during the previous year had provoked the King's fury. On the other hand, the Colonial Office and the Air Ministry, Whitehall's department with military responsibility for the Middle East, demonstrated impatience and even a hostile attitude towards Ibn Saud. The Air Ministry viewed the new arrangement as insufficient and predicted that it would not secure the end of the raids. The Ministry criticised the scheme on account of its undue reliance on Abdullah, whose sincerity was suspected and whose dependence on Imperial forces deemed too costly. The Air Ministry recommended greater measures of direct British control than those proposed by Chancellor and suggested establishing a permanent administration in the desert. In this context they referred the Colonial Office to the work of Captain John Glubb in Iraq, recommending a similar system of control in Transjordan.[13] It took more than a year to bring Glubb to Transjordan to do exactly that.

In the meantime the authorities in Amman established the TCB, which quickly became an instrument of unprecedented control and a tool to inflict severe punishment on raiders. Its most common action was to investigate raids and, on receiving sufficient evidence, to sentence raiders. Even the most powerful shaykhs were ordered to return loot, sentenced to pay fines and even to periods of imprisonment. In this way the Board implemented the principle of collective tribal and shaykhly responsibility which had become the backbone of state control in the settled zone. An Arab Legion document explaining the establishment and function of the Board reveals unequivocally that the Board would target shaykhs and employ severe measures against them. The acting Commanding Officer stated in his order that "[t]he object of the formation of this Board is one only; to stop all raiding in future, by severely punishing any Sheikhs who raid themselves or who allow or encourage their tribesmen to do so." He went on to explain that "Sheikhs known to be returning from raids or proceeding on them are in all cases to be arrested…No Warrant of arrest is necessary…" Probably out of respect for the shaykhs the order specified that their arrest must be carried out by the OC Districts in person. Similarly, in the first decision of the Board to imprison shaykhs, it was careful to emphasise that these shaykhs were considered political prisoners (*siyasiyyun*) and therefore should receive better treatment than ordinary criminals.[14]

The Board interfered in many aspects of nomadic life which the central administration had never attempted to regulate before. For one, it controlled the movement of tribes. The unprecedented move of the Bani ʿAtiyya away from the border necessitated a special meeting of the Board presided over by Abdullah himself. Similarly, in the spring of 1930 the Board forbade access to grazing grounds along the border in order to help the RAF to combat incoming raiders.[15]

The TCB also intervened with the social order of the Huwaytat in an attempt to achieve better control over these tribes by stratifying their leadership and enhancing the cohesion of the confederacy. The Huwaytat tribes were composed of two branches, one led by Hamad bin Jazi and the other by ʿAwda abu Taya and after his death in 1924, his son, Muhammad, then only 18 years of age. In a Board meeting in 1930 Abdullah declared Hamad bin Jazi the paramount shaykh of the whole confederacy. He also nominated shaykh Zaʿal bin Mutlaq as regent for the Tawayha branch on behalf of his cousin Muhammad bin ʿAwda abu Taya, presumably because Muhammad was too young to lead his people. Zaʿal was then made responsible to Hamad. This decision reflected the changing balance of power between the two groupings. ʿAwda, the most influential leader in the early 1920s, fell out with Abdullah and gravitated towards Ibn Saud. At the same time Hamad cultivated good relations with Abdullah. ʿAwda's death left Hamad the most prominent shaykh among the Huwaytat and his branch received preferable treatment from the Emirate's authorities. But the TCB's decision also had long-term implications as it institutionalised and therefore fixed the domination of Hamad and his family. This exercise in social engineering apparently worked. Hamad acceded to Abdullah's demand to send his nephew before the Board, which subsequently sentenced him to six months in prison for raiding. Similarly, Zaʿal delivered the desired goods, producing all wanted persons from the Tawayha.[16]

The TCB had an initial success in reducing raids carried out by local tribes and in restoring loot. A few months after the establishment of the new system of control, the Transjordanian authorities reported with satisfaction on excellent results. Kirkbride wrote that only small parties of the Bani ʿAtiyya were still raiding along the borders while the main tribes, such as the Bani Sakhr and Huwaytat, had ceased raiding altogether.[17] This impression was later confirmed by the commander of the RAF in Palestine and Transjordan, who wrote that the Board "has shown unexpectedly promising results. It had for a period controlled the Transjordan tribes very effectively…"[18] For his part, Chancellor had nothing but praise for Shakir's work. He commended his co-operation with Peake, his integrity and skills:

> On account of his intimate knowledge of Beduin law and customs and his great influence over the Beduin, Amir Shakir's services are of great value to the Trans-Jordan Government; and his decisions in tribal disputes are readily accepted and carried into effect by those concerned.[19]

The Board was also a success story in another respect. It quickly became a popular and influential mechanism for mediating disputes. Shakir's exceptional knowledge of tribal law and custom and his reputation as an honest judge earned him the respect of the litigants. The fact that the Board's proceedings were free of charge provided another incentive for tribespeople to seek its judgment. Against the background of dysfunctional tribal courts, the Board was flooded with cases. Many exceeded its jurisdiction, revolving around pedestrian disputes or submitted by settled tribesmen.[20] The Board's popularity is evidence of the vacuum created after the abolition of the Department of Tribal Administration in 1924 and the introduction of the inadequate alternative in the form of tribal courts. As stated before, tribal society requires neutral mechanisms for conflict resolution. Shakir's disinterested position and known impartiality therefore proved a satisfying arrangement for the tribespeople.

The Board's initial success notwithstanding, without reciprocal measures from Ibn Saud or more assertive British policy, raiding was bound to resume. In one of his reports Cox wrote that: "the tribes are now submitting with a degree of cheerfulness to a control the like of which the Ottoman Government never succeeded in imposing." Cox used an untypical flowery language and a bit of exaggeration in order to bring home to London his criticism of the current situation. While Transjordan was "fulfilling its obligations to its neighbours," he protested, it was "failing to fulfil them to its own subjects." Cox begged his superiors to provide the tribes with protection similar to that offered in Iraq. He predicted that the government would not be able to prevent the tribes from raiding indefinitely unless such measures were taken.[21]

Cox's and the earlier Air Ministry's predictions proved to be correct. By the beginning of 1930 the government had lost control of the nomads and raids resumed. Kostiner -- perhaps influenced by the Foreign Office correspondence which he studied -- clears Ibn Saud of responsibility, disassociating him from the raiders and only partially pointing the finger at his officials. He explains the persistence of raids as the result of some "problems inherent" to the frontier which were "particularly difficult to resolve."[22] But the resumption of raids must be attributed to Ibn Saud's policies. After he had finally suppressed the *Ikhwan* rebellion and re-established his authority in Najd, Ibn Saud sanctioned massive raids against the Huwaytat. These tribesmen suffered heavy casualties and lost thousands of camels and sheep. They had to flee from the desert and move westward into the settled area, losing more animals still during this flight. To compensate for their losses they raided local tribes.[23]

Increased raids prompted the Transjordanian authorities to adopt more repressive measures. They employed Imperial forces and tightened their hold over the TCB. In the spring of 1930 a mechanised company of the TJFF moved into the desert, but on the whole was helpless in gaining control. The RAF was also deployed in the desert and carried out reconnaissance flights along the border. In April 1930 it enforced the decision of the TCB to prevent the tribes from grazing near the border, threatening to fire at any party found in the area. The ban on grazing was lifted a few months later with the fall of the first rains. The damage had already been done, however, because this exclusion resulted in overgrazing and water shortage and therefore loss of flock. The Transjordanian tribes suffered further losses from uninterrupted raids from the Najdi tribes, to which they were prevented from responding. According to British investigations, the net losses of Transjordanian tribes by August 1930 were estimated at 3,662 camels, 5,270 sheep, 50 killed and £1,020 in other property.[24]

Having failed to deal with the crisis, the men on the spot became increasingly agitated. Abdullah lost a great deal of his authority over the shaykhs and was angry about the punishment of his tribes. Cox and Peake's relationship was badly affected due to their different opinions on solving the raiding problem and the strained conditions in which they were working. Cox's frustrations with the situation and the inability to convey the reality to London came to a head in August when he composed a strongly-worded dispatch. He declared that "everything that is possible to prevent raiding is now being done with the forces at our disposal." He emphasised that these measures were still inadequate and reiterated his request to appoint a British officer and to establish a desert unit. He attacked Ibn Saud, accusing him of trying to discredit Abdullah in the eyes of the British government, of alienating the local tribes and of seducing them to cross over to Najd. Hoping to strike a cord with the British sense of justice, Cox wrote:

> The Trans-Jordan tribes are labouring under a sense of the gravest injustice in that they have been punished and forced to return loot whilst none of the stuff looted from them has been returned. Every officer or official who has experience of Trans-Jordan shares this feeling and it is essential that it should be appreciated by the Secretary of State...I consider that it would be most unjust for Your Excellency to express any lack of confidence in the Amir or Shaker. They sympathise with their Bedu who are being so unjustly exploited and, understanding Ibn Saoud and his methods, hate him but I am convinced that they do not incite their Bedu to raid but, on the contrary, endeavour to restrain them.[25]

After further deliberations Chancellor sent another policy dispatch in June 1930, updating the one he had sent the previous year. Its approval in London heralded the arrival of Glubb and the establishment of desert administration. The scheme reflected what might be called the 'Glubb doctrine' that permeated the different branches of British officialdom both in the Middle East and London since the Air Ministry's recommendation a year earlier. The new elements in this proposal were the appointment of a British intelligence officer and the employment of local tribesmen to man the intelligence posts along the frontier. Chancellor reiterated the items of his earlier proposal which had not been approved so far, namely the establishment of three desert posts and his request for a Secret Service Fund worth £2,000 to pay shaykhs for their services and information. He also urged retaining the TCB. In an interdepartmental conference in August, Chancellor's proposal was approved and it was agreed to offer Glubb the new job.[26]

On the eve of Glubb's arrival in Transjordan the situation along the border could not have been worse. In September the Shararat launched a series of raids on the Huwaytat, stealing hundreds of camels. No action was taken by the Imperial forces. The raids occurred while shaykhs and officials from Najd and Transjordan gathered in Amman to present to the British arbitrator their respective claims for property and life lost during previous raids. When news of the Shararat raids reached Amman, Hamad bin Jazi lost his temper. An exchange of personal insults followed between him and the representative of the Najdi government that threatened to jeopardise the work of the arbitrator. It required all Abdullah's diplomacy to reconcile the parties, in order to allow the resumption of the arbitration. At the end of October three massive raids, reportedly sanctioned by the governor of Jawf with the authority of Ibn Saud himself, caused heavy casualties to the Huwaytat. The miserable failure of the British forces to intercept the raiding parties caused bitterness among the victims, who counter-raided in small parties despite all efforts to stop them. As Riccardo Bocco and Tariq Tell put it, "the prestige of the Amman government reached its nadir in the summer and autumn of 1930."[27] The good relations with the nomadic tribes so laboriously achieved by the central administration over a decade appeared to vanish. Glubb faced a formidable challenge in his task to regain influence for the government.

Economic Crisis

Before examining Glubb's activities and in order to place them in context, it is important to consider the tribes' predicament. Glubb, in achieving his mission, benefited from the destitution of the nomads during the 1930s because it reduced their ability to resist his policies. The weakened tribes, in need of assistance, were ready to change their attitude towards the government. They were, therefore, amenable to Glubb's initiatives, which offered them hope for a better future.

During the years 1929-1936 Transjordan suffered a severe economic crisis. The inhabitants' plight resulted from several factors which, while combined, proved devastating: regional politics, natural disasters and changes in the world and regional markets. Although many segments of society were affected, the nomadic population was particularly vulnerable and accordingly suffered most. By 1933, they were experiencing severe famine. Many died from hunger or diseases.

The first to experience the crisis were the Huwaytat who had suffered most from the Najdi raids. They were never compensated. The British official MacDonnell, who investigated the mutual claims of Transjordanian and Saudi tribes, questioned the reliability of his findings and the British persuaded both governments to agree to a mutual cancellation of all claims. Losses multiplied as the tribes lost their grazing areas, a result of fear of *Ikhwan* attacks and government restrictions. Immediately after his arrival Glubb studied the economic situation of the tribes. According to his investigations, in the formerly prosperous Darawsha tribe of the Huwaytat the average ownership decreased from 30 camels per tent in 1930 to only 2.5 following two Najdi raids, well below the minimum necessary for survival, assessed at 10-15 camels. Even the shaykh had been reduced to poverty, owning 12 camels as opposed to 200. According to Glubb, the Nawasra and other tribes of the Tawayha branch of the Huwaytat as well as parts of the Bani ʿAtiyya were in much the same condition. He also predicted that up to a third of the Huwaytat would face starvation within a year.[28]

Persistent droughts as well as another locust attack in 1932 reduced the grazing areas and brought about famine in the desert. Almost two years after his initial findings, Glubb reported that the Huwaytat were much reduced in numbers as the poorest died and others migrated to Palestine as casual labourers or beggars. London officials tended to dismiss Glubb's reports as exaggerations. An investigation carried out by the Assistant Resident, however, completely confirmed his findings. Writing in January 1933 after four successive bad years Glubb reported:

> Period of bad grazing and cycles of rainless years must have occurred in the past and indeed are indicated in various bedouin poems and traditions. No person alive, however, recollects such a series of droughts in the desert as have occurred in the last four years.[29]

Notwithstanding the exceptional climatic conditions, for Glubb, as well as for Cox, it was the failure of Imperial policy that brought about the nomad's predicament. Glubb claimed that there was nothing inevitable about their misfortune, as bad rain and grazing were not the primary causes of their impoverishment. Rather it was mainly due to the British failure to protect the tribesmen from the *Ikhwan* and their reluctance to force Ibn Saud to return the loot. Glubb pointed out that Saudi and Iraqi tribes had continued to prosper during these years.[30]

British-demarcated borders were another devastating factor for the nomads. The international boundaries in the desert were drawn with political rather than socio-economic criteria in mind, cutting across tribal *dira*s. This disregard for tribal needs limited the ability of the nomads to overcome hard climate conditions. Glubb made this point forcefully, writing: "The frontiers of Transjordan are so designed to cut across the tribal areas of the maximum number of nomadic tribes possible. ..."[31] The ceding of the Wadi Sirhan to Ibn Saud in the Hadda agreement was particularly harmful. Wadi Sirhan was an important grazing area for the Bani Sakhr, Sirhan and sometimes the Huwaytat, especially in years of bad rainfall in Transjordan. Although the agreement stipulated the preservation of their grazing rights and free access, the tribes suffered from hostile Saudi policies. Prior to the signing of the 1933 treaty of *bon voisinage* they endured persecution by Najdi officials and tribes, and even afterwards they continued to pay *zakat*. Upon returning in the spring they were taxed again by the Transjordanian government, paying more than they would have paid to the Ottoman government and five times the taxes paid by Saudi tribes. Furthermore, the Sirhan used to be the paramount tribe in the Wadi before its take-over by the

Saudis. In the aftermath, they were pushed northwards and westwards, with many of their people becoming semi-settled around Irbid. Now they spent only two months a year in Kaf and faced difficulties in collecting their share from the date gardens in the area. Apart from the Huwaytat, they were the poorest tribe in Transjordan during these years. Glubb so believed that it was essential that Wadi Sirhan be included within Transjordan that he devised a plan to recover this oasis should Ibn Saud lose his throne.[32]

The world economy also took its toll on the tribespeople. The camel trade lost much of its value after World War One, when the train and the car replaced the camel and the horse as means of transportation. Camels, as opposed to horses, were still valuable to the nomads, who could sell them to Egypt where their meat was consumed. Nonetheless, camel prices fell drastically as a result of the Great Depression, from £16-20 for a camel in the late 1920s to a mere £3-5 in 1932-1933. In order to maintain their income, tribesmen sold more camels than usual, thus contributing to the reduction of their herds.[33]

By 1932 the hitherto prosperous Bani Sakhr tribes had been hit by the crisis. Although they endured much less from the Najdi raids, they suffered from the drought, heavy taxation and the effects of the depression. In November Glubb reported that their flocks had been reduced to such an extent that many had too few animals to even move their tents.[34] Their vast land in the Balqa', which used to provide an income for their rich shaykhs since the latter third of the nineteenth century, did not prove as profitable in the second half of the 1920s. Moreover, surveys carried out in the early 1930s disclosed that much of the Bani Sakhr land was left fallow even before the drought years.[35] Persistent drought and crop failure cost the tribes their means of support. The Khuraysha tribe was the first to face famine in 1932. Afterwards they and other tribes of the Ka'abna branch of the Bani Sakhr resorted to wage labour in Palestine in order to survive.[36]

1933 marked the peak of the famine. The nomads lost thousands of sheep and camels. Many lost all their animals and were left with no means of support. Glubb estimated that the average income was reduced by half in that year. Hitherto rich shaykhs were no exception, and many were reduced to poverty. To mention but a few, Haditha al-Khuraysha and his large family had to survive on cheap barley, the kind used to feed cattle. Mithqal al-Fayiz, one of the richest men in the country in the mid-1920s and the largest landowner, fell into debt and the Bank put some of his land under a caveat to auction. By 1934 Muhammad abu Taya, the son of the famous 'Awda abu Taya, had only four camels in his possession and was kept alive by money he received from Glubb. Consequently, shaykhs could not help their fellow tribesmen by sharing their property with them, as custom demanded.[37]

Persistent destitution inevitably caused illness and death. As a result of under-nourishment tuberculosis broke out. Many died, including members of shaykhly families, amongst them the son of Mithqal al-Fayiz. An influenza epidemic also caused many deaths, exacerbated by the weakened physical condition of those on the verge of starvation. Even after some rain in the winter of 1934, a survey run by the medical officer of the Palestine government revealed that 84% of the Sirhan,

Huwaytat, and the Bani Sakhr suffered from malnutrition. The crisis lasted until 1936. Data provided by Glubb in its aftermath further reveals its magnitude: between 1932 and 1936 the livestock of the nomadic tribes fell by 70%.[38]

Pacifying the Desert: The Diplomatic Front

Against the background of persistent raids and worsening economic conditions Glubb was entrusted with the pacification of the desert. He had earned his reputation while dealing with the Iraqi tribes and was now expected to put an end to the raids and to help stabilise Transjordan's borders. The idea was to encourage the tribesmen to take part in their own defence against Najdi raiders, and to recruit them into the army. A mechanised unit manned by nomads, it was believed, would be able to penetrate the desert and prevent raids from both sides of the border.

Glubb arrived in Amman in November 1930. After being briefed by the local officials and examining the files at the disposal of the Arab Legion's Tribal Officer, he proceeded to assess the situation on the ground. His visit to the Huwaytat and his study of the history of raids produced a long memorandum in which he detailed the situation on the frontier. His report corroborated the position expressed by the Transjordanian authorities over the previous two years. In particular he gathered incriminating evidence of Ibn Saud's encouragement of raiding parties and his deliberate seduction of Transjordanian tribes to cross over and swear allegiance to him. Glubb also demonstrated the impoverishment of the Huwaytat. It was this destitution, Glubb explained, that necessitated continued raiding, in the hope of retrieving some of their losses. Glubb forcefully showed how Britain had failed to protect subjects living under its mandate. His main recommendations for immediate action were to force Ibn Saud to return the loot taken since August 1930 (the claims before that date were still under examination by MacDonnell) or alternatively to pay the Huwaytat £6,000 in compensation, which would alleviate their poverty and encourage them to stop raiding. Glubb warned that failure to tend to the Huwaytat's impoverishment would lead them to throw in their lot with the Saudi King.[39]

Glubb's memorandum was met with a sense of vindication by the authorities in Amman. Coming from the leading British authority on desert control and a close observer of Ibn Saud, it carried unchallenged credibility and it was hoped that it would carry the day in London. Peake praised Glubb, saying that his report was "a most masterly exposition of the true facts of the case and I agree with every word of it." Cox for his part wrote in his cover letter to Glubb's memorandum: "I trust that this frank statement [...] will bring home to Your Excellency and to His Majesty's Government the gravity of the well nigh intolerable situation which has arisen."[40]

Glubb achieved his first success towards gaining control over the desert. He managed to convince London of the situation on the ground and the need to stand up to Ibn Saud. His memorandum initiated a fresh series of discussions in Whitehall between the different departments and diplomatic activity vis-à-vis Ibn Saud. It resulted in a change in the position of the Foreign Office towards the King and its willingness to put pressure on him to return the loot.[41] On 28 February 1931 Sir Andrew Ryan, the British Minister in Jedda, delivered a strongly-worded message demanding the immediate return of 800 camels and co-operation with Glubb from his opposite number, ʿAbd al-ʿAziz bin Zayd. At the Air Ministry's insistence the message contained a threat that in case of non-co-operation the British government would consider recovering the loot unilaterally.[42] In a personal meeting Ryan impressed upon Ibn Saud the gravity of the situation and the British belief that the King himself had authorised the recent raids. The King, however, turned the tables on British policy when he rejected the demand to return the loot of the Huwaytat. Ryan recommended that the Foreign Office call him home for consultations; Whitehall had to decide on a response to the Saudi snub and assess the possibility of a crisis in Britain's relations with Ibn Saud.[43]

A fresh round of consultations resulted in a prolonged and sometimes heated debate in Whitehall. The different arms of the British government were again divided along lines similar to those that had emerged before Glubb's arrival in Transjordan. At one extreme, the Air Ministry took a militant line, suggesting an ultimatum be given to the King. His failure to meet the British terms would result in either the withdrawal of the British Minister from Jedda or the occupation of the oasis of Kaf. The India Government and India Office, on the other hand, wanted to prevent a crisis at all costs, claiming that it might further excite the Muslims in India. In between these extremes stood the Foreign Office, which was reluctant to risk an open break with the King, and the Colonial Office, whose position was most difficult. Its officials sympathised with the Air Ministry and the government of Transjordan but at the same time questioned the political practicality of military action, or even that of a severance of diplomatic relations.[44]

The deadlock in London resulted in an understanding between the Foreign and Colonial Offices to give the initiative to the local players, thus containing the issue at the local and tribal levels. London concentrated on arranging a meeting between Glubb and Ibn Zayd, "in the hope that somehow or other it may lead to a settlement."[45] London's strategy proved successful beyond all expectations, perhaps because it allowed a face-saving solution for Ibn Saud. It took a few more months and more obstructions and delays before Ibn Saud finally authorised Ibn Zayd to meet Glubb. Yet, their first meeting in June 1931 established amicable relations which resulted in co-operation in the control of the desert and the prevention of raids, as well as a partial return of the loot. The 'desert diplomacy' vis-à-vis Ibn Zayd and his successors in the capacity of frontier inspectors was a major pillar of Glubb's strategy. In his memoirs Glubb attributed this success to his personal skills.[46] More probably, it was Ibn Saud's realisation that Britain was determined to stop raiding that facilitated Saudi co-operation with Glubb.

Pacifying the Desert: Glubb and the Transjordanian Tribes, 1930-1932

While discussions were underway in London, Glubb started his mission. In December 1930 the RAF withdrew its units at his request, leaving Glubb sole responsibility for the desert. Information on Glubb's first two years in the desert is scarce and comes almost exclusively from his own published account. Despite this methodological handicap it is possible to draw a relatively reliable picture of the methods he employed to stop raiding. As will be shown, Glubb came as close as it gets to the classical image of the British colonial officer, single-handedly ruling indigenous people in frontier areas in the spirit of the philosophy of indirect rule. He also epitomised British fascination with nomadic people.

Glubb spent the winter in the different camps of the Huwaytat and managed to overcome their basic suspicion of the government within weeks. He persuaded them to stop raiding and organised their defence against the *Ikhwan*. In order to enlist their co-operation, Glubb dissociated himself from the Arab Legion. He therefore travelled without an escort. He also distributed money to shaykhs and ordinary tribesmen, relieving their material misery. His good Arabic and exceptional knowledge of nomadic life was another factor in his success. Finally, the arrival from Iraq of four of his former desert policemen and their recounting of his activities in Iraq against the *Ikhwan* enhanced his reputation. He later reported that it was his reputation more than anything else which helped him gain the co-operation of the Huwaytat and brought about the end of the raids.[47]

After gaining the Huwaytat's co-operation, Glubb began recruiting tribesmen to his new force, the Desert Patrol under the Arab Legion. This process was gradual and according to his testimony, a difficult one. He had to overcome their suspicions towards any central government and their hostility towards the government's forces, which had previously tried to prevent them from raiding in Najd and, from their perspective, persecuted them. Moreover, enlisting in a regular army was something of a revolution for the Huwaytat. The force was formed in February 1931 when 20 men enrolled and were trained by the Iraqi policemen. Glubb then moved to the Bani Sakhr area and several months later he had succeeded in enlisting 90 soldiers, the personnel quota approved for the new unit. Soon the demand to join outnumbered the available posts and Glubb was able to create a somewhat aristocratic force, giving priority to sons of shaykhs.

Glubb clearly benefited from the cordial relations already established between Abdullah and Shakir and the nomads. Glubb himself admitted this, at least as far as the Bani Sakhr tribesmen were concerned, writing that the task of their recruitment was easier since they camped near Amman, were in contact with the government and familiar with its policy. However, he mentioned only in passing the support he received from Shakir during his early days in the desert. In fact, it was Shakir who sent Glubb the first recruits who, together with Glubb's former Iraqi soldiers, formed the nucleus of the force even before the 20 Huwaytat men were persuaded to join.[48]

The Desert Patrol had great appeal for tribesmen. The warrior ethos was now manifested in the army. This was particularly true for sons of shaykhs, who had hitherto been groomed to lead raids and, with their prohibition, needed an alternative function. Glubb reported that he had not met disciplinary problems since the soldiers were highly motivated and enjoyed their service.[49] Economic considerations also contributed to the success in recruiting nomads. A soldier's monthly salary (£4.575 net) was enough to support several families during the famine of the 1930s.[50]

An important element in Glubb's success was his understanding of the region's topography and its relation to raids. Glubb discovered that Jabal Tubayq, a range of mountains along the frontier, served as the preferred route of raiders from both sides. Hitherto inaccessible to government forces, the occupation of the Tubayq in the spring of 1931 and the formation of a camel unit to control the area proved a key factor in stopping raids. Similarly, Glubb controlled raiding of the Ahl al-Jabal tribes along the Syrian frontier by penetrating the inaccessible lava belt. At the end of 1931 Glubb and his men constructed motor tracks, entered the area and surprised the raiders. Military presence and co-operation with the shaykhs reduced raids in the north to a minimum.[51]

By the middle of 1931 Glubb's unit was a force to be reckoned with. With £30,000 spent within the first year and a half of his work, Glubb created a small but effective force. By that time the Desert Patrol occupied three desert forts in Azraq, Mudawwara and Bayir, the latter two having been newly erected.[52] It was highly mobile as it possessed cars, camels and wireless and its soldiers used modern weapons. The RAF provided reinforcement upon request.

Already during 1931 cross-border raiding was reduced to a minimum. The majority of tribesmen abstained from raiding and *Ikhwani* attacks ceased altogether. The last raid occurred in July 1932. In his book Glubb rightly emphasised the unique method of ending raids. In comparison with other governments in Arabia which used heavy force and then faced recurrent tribal rebellions,

> In Trans-Jordan raiding, which had been practised for centuries, was abolished in a few months without inflicting a single casualty on the tribes and without putting a single tribesmen in prison. No subsequent attempt was ever made to revive it, even when the Government was deeply involved elsewhere in internal disturbances or in war.[53]

Beyond bringing the raids to a stop, Glubb had an enormous effect on tribal society throughout his long career. By the mid-1930s he achieved almost exclusive control over the desert, established law and order and paved the way for the central administration to finally expand into the desert. In the course of the 1930s Glubb acquired a special position for himself: that of chief mediator between the tribes and the government. In this capacity he also steered social and economic transformation. The remainder of this chapter examines Glubb's control methods and their effect on the tribesmen.

Glubb's Long Term Control Methods: Intimate Local Knowledge
Glubb's success in achieving control over the desert and the acceptance of his policies by tribesmen derived to a large extent from his ability to operate within the framework of nomadic society. He adopted its conventions and played according to similar rules, modifying them to suit his needs. Being cautious to avoid the pitfall of essentialism, it still might be suggested that tribal society offered ready-made mechanisms that guaranteed easier control if utilised by a central administration. A shrewd ruler could attempt to enlist the co-operation of shaykhs, taking advantage

of their influence over their fellow tribesmen. At the same time, he could operate methods of divide and rule because tribal leadership was fluid rather than fixed, a feature which encouraged constant rivalries among shaykhs. Moreover, the elaborate procedures prescribed by customary law provided accepted and effective methods to restore public order. Glubb's intimate knowledge of tribal life allowed him to take full advantage of these societal features. Indeed, Glubb followed Abdullah's principle of co-operating with, and co-opting, the shaykhs. He paid them special attention and involved them in his work. Glubb, like Abdullah, respected the existing social structure and used it to achieve his goals when dealing with tribespeople.

Subsidies for shaykhs would have been the obvious way to control the tribes, at least in the short term. This was the method used by many rulers when dealing with the nomads in Arabia. As mentioned, immediately upon his arrival Glubb distributed subsidies to the shaykhs to secure their collaboration. But he did not have the resources to maintain this policy and subsidies were the exception rather than the rule. They were only re-introduced in later years, during periods of crisis such as the Arab revolt in Palestine.[54]

Glubb used other more sophisticated and, in the long term, effective methods to co-opt the shaykhs. First and foremost was the recruitment of their sons to the Desert Patrol. This tied them to the government and prevented direct confrontation with their tribes. Glubb saw this strategy as an alternative to using force to control the nomads. His recruitment policy was put to the test and proved successful in 1936, when the Palestinians attempted to incite the tribesmen to join their revolt. Glubb reported that "most of the bedouin leaders now have sons in the desert police and are unwilling at the present stage at least, to incur government displeasure."[55]

Glubb worked closely with the chiefs in the daily policing of the desert and the settlement of disputes.[56] He took advantage of the shaykhs' traditional judicial role to enhance their co-operation with the government. The following paragraph from his assessment of the 1936 Tribal Control Laws reveals Glubb's understanding of the social system and the possibility of using it for his own ends. It also illuminates the problematic position of the shaykh in a modern state:

> The tribal shaikh forms something of a problem in the northern Arab countries. He is insufficiently educated to enable him to become an official in the present government, although he still exerts considerable influence in the tribes. He constitutes a danger, so long as he possesses influence with the people, but enjoys no share in the government. It is therefore important to associate the shaikhs with the government in every way possible. To employ these shaikhs to assist in the work of government and the administration of justice is the wisest of policies.[57]

Glubb was an ardent supporter of using customary instead of civil law, not only for nomads but also for settled tribesmen. Beyond the opportunity to employ the shaykhs by the government, the prominence of customary law in tribal society, its common acceptance as a regulating mechanism and its effectiveness (see Chapter One) could,

Glubb realised, strengthen control over tribesman. He observed the fundamental differences between Arab tribal law and European civil law, which rendered the immediate replacement of the former by the latter impossible. According to Glubb's analysis, tribal law was based on the absence of central authority and therefore the lack of punishment. It was solely concerned with compensation to the aggrieved party and contained elaborate procedures for the settlement of disputes. Since there was no central authority to protect the rights of that party, its family and tribe supported it in obtaining justice. By contrast, Glubb explained, European criminal code deals with the punishment of the offender, not with compensation to the victim. It would be impossible therefore to prevent tribesmen from pursuing their compensation even if the offender had been punished.

On the basis of these realisations, Glubb suggested preserving as far as possible the indigenous legal procedures, modifying them to suit modern conditions. In practice this meant the gradual introduction of the principle of state-inflicted punishment without the abolition of compensation.[58] In introducing modifications to the law, Glubb sought to use the moral authority of shaykhs, especially those like Hamad bin Jazi of the Huwaytat and Muhammad bin Zuhayr of the Bani Sakhr. In their capacity as *qadi* or *ra'y al-qilta* they enjoyed the prerogative of adjusting the law to new circumstances. Explaining the advantage of using the influence of shaykhs he wrote: "When it is proposed to change anything in local tribal custom or to add anything to it, the initiative should as far as possible, be arranged to come from the chiefs."[59]

The 1936 Bedouin Control Law and the Tribal Courts Law were the ultimate manifestation of Glubb's philosophy. From 1937 tribal courts, in which cases were tried exclusively by tribal chiefs, operated in every province and in the desert. By becoming recipients of a salary from the Treasury, shaykhs were further integrated into the state.[60] These new regulations introduced a legal procedure which resembled the traditional tribal system. In his assessment of the Laws, the Jordanian jurist and anthropologist Muhammad Abu Hassan wrote that "the law guaranteed the preservation of the legal Bedouin institution with its old ways by preserving the traditional Bedouin courts and allowed the Bedouin to pursue their customs in resolving their cases after it had introduced slight changes."[61] Thus, litigants were tried exclusively by recognised tribal judges chosen by the disputing parties themselves. Judges followed customary law and were also free to employ customary mechanisms of judgment such as *bush'a* or arbitration. They were even allowed to collect, on top of their salary, fees prescribed by tribal custom (*rizqa*).[62] The law, however, abolished the custom of handing over a girl from a murderer's family to be married to the closest relative of the murdered person as part of the blood-money agreement (*ghura*).[63] Five camels were given instead. Probably for the sake of efficiency, the period allowed for an appeal was limited.

Notwithstanding Abu Hassan's assessment, the Tribal Law represents a clear departure from tradition. Whereas the legal procedures were mostly kept intact, the framework within which they operated was completely transformed as state officials were drawn in to play an important role. It was the Arab Legion rather than the victim's party which was responsible for facilitating the judicial hearing as well as the execution of the verdict. In criminal cases, after compensation was determined by the judges, the governor could imprison the culprit for up to one year. Finally, the judges had to be chosen from a list approved by the government and the Emir.[64]

According to Glubb, the compromise between old ways and modern needs was largely accepted by the public. Justice done according to accepted values proved effective in maintaining law and order. Tribesmen co-operated with the authorities and criminals were brought to court. Within a year of the operation of the courts Glubb reported on "unqualified success" for the new system in the desert. Cox echoed Glubb, describing the success of the system in the settled areas as well. Two years later Glubb could provide statistics that proved the popularity of the courts all over the country and public confidence in them, which was manifested in the rarity of appeals.[65] The new system gained popularity among tribesmen because it addressed the major problem of the old one: the difficulty of executing the court's decisions. The new system allowed injured tribesmen to approach the nearest Arab Legion post to file a charge. If the court found their case justified, they were guaranteed that the army would enforce the payment of compensation. Yet, it is safe to assume that many cases continued to be heard by tribal judges without the involvement or knowledge of Glubb and other state officials.[66]

In following tribal practices while dealing with law-breakers in the desert, playing, as it were, the accepted rules of the game, Glubb himself showed leniency, preferring to deal with them according to local practice rather than inflict fines or imprisonment. He often followed the practice of *wisaqa*, confiscating property to guarantee a return of loot. Once the stolen items had been produced by the culprit, Glubb would release the seized property. A culprit who could produce a *Kafil* -- a guarantor to ensure the compliance and good behaviour of his protégé -- would usually avoid punishment.[67] Glubb and his men also showed customary hospitality to the desert men in an attempt to win their friendship and co-operation. Glubb even reported that he would use the *bush'a* system to verify oath since he "found the process of immense value when working as a magistrate."[68]

Finally, intimate local knowledge was instrumental in achieving law and order in a situation in which tribes could potentially raise hundreds of armed men, outnumbering the police forces at the government's disposal. This was done by exploiting the constant struggle for leadership among rival shaykhs. In Glubb's words, "[t]ribes outwardly united, are often torn by internal jealousies, which an experienced local officer can exploit." To take advantage of these internal divisions the police needed a thorough knowledge of the country, to be in constant touch with the leading personalities, and to understand their relations with one another and the day-to-day politics within the tribe. As Glubb wrote in a memorandum explaining the function of the Arab Legion:

> ...the whole country does not usually rebel as one block. One village or tribe is
> friendly, while the next is hostile, or even rival headmen in the same village may
> be on opposite sides. To handle such a situation successfully requires a lifelong

experience of local conditions, just as much or more than it requires military or tactical knowledge.[69]

Economic Assistance

Alongside the formation of the Desert Patrol and the achievement of gradual military control over the desert, Glubb attended to the economic difficulties of the tribes. His economic and welfare policies were important both to the immediate pacification of the desert and the eventual integration of the tribes into the modern state. Glubb's socio-economic policies have, however, attracted little scholarly interest.[70]

Glubb's approach was inspired by Sir Robert Sandeman's doctrine known as "human imperialism," which proved successful in pacifying tribesmen along the North West frontier of India (Afghanistan) from the late 1860s until the 1880s. Sandeman's principles were applied by Glubb to Transjordan: a humane and sympathetic approach towards the tribespeople's needs and provision of employment. As explained above, the policy placed special attention on the tribal shaykhs, relying on their assistance to control the desert as well as on the application of tribal law to as great a degree as possible.[71]

The vehicle for offering assistance and controlling the flow of services to the tribes was the Desert Patrol of the Arab Legion. As well as providing employment to its members, the Desert Patrol acted in many ways to help the nomads. The assignment of the unit to collect taxes upon Glubb's request further relieved tribespeople. Tax was more fairly distributed and the nomads no longer paid a share to government tax collectors and were not expected to bear the cost of their hospitality.[72] From time to time Glubb distributed clothes, flour or small sums of money to the most destitute people, mainly women and children from the Sirhan. Some even survived on leftovers found outside posts of the Desert Patrol.[73]

A further important source of income for the tribesmen were the relief works introduced in December 1932. In response to the reports on their destitution the British government gave a small grant of £2,000 to be used to employ needy nomads in road works. Glubb initially opposed the idea, but later admitted that he had been wrong when the project successfully saved many from starvation. He reported that many had to be turned away due to the lack of funds. Relief work continued to function as both an important contribution to the local economy and a cheap way to improve infrastructure on the periphery. In the winter of 1934/5 Glubb spent another £2,000 on building roads, benefiting the Huwaytat, Sirhan, Bani Sakhr, Ahl al-Jabal and ʿIsa. Relief came also from the Iraq Petroleum Company, which employed several hundred men to work on the construction of the pipeline and after the completion of the work maintained a 60-strong force to protect it.[74]

Urgent relief helped people to survive but could not solve the chronic problems of those who had lost all their property. Glubb was interested in finding ways to put them back on their feet and to improve the nomads' economy. From the mid-1930s Glubb introduced or supervised important and long-lasting initiatives in the realms of agriculture, education and health care. These developments and their enormous effect on the nomads will be discussed in the next chapter in the context of the expansion of the state's functions. Here it is sufficient to note that, beyond their humanitarian merit, Glubb saw these policies as another means to close the gap between the state and its tribes and to bring them, voluntarily, under government control. When lobbying for the introduction of health services in the desert and requesting the appointment of a medical officer, Glubb explained: "... a little simple doctoring is one of the readiness[sic] ways of winning the confidence of these rather distrustful persons and of bringing them into government."[75]

The motivations behind Glubb's 'human' policy and the question whether it was genuine or just shrewd, serving imperial goals of easier control, have concerned recent scholarship and are not easy to determine.[76] For Glubb, imperial interests and nomads' needs did not necessarily conflict with each other. Moreover, the impression one gets from reading Glubb's writing, both official and published, is that he was a 'Beduphile'. These assertions become more plausible if Glubb is examined as part of the British tradition (discussed in Chapter One) of an alleged affinity between Arab nomads and the British Empire.[77] In any case, whatever his motives, it is impossible to understand Glubb's enormous success in pacifying the tribes in particular, and in dealing with tribal affairs in general, without emphasising his sympathetic approach towards the nomads during a period of severe crisis. In the face of the terrible conditions in the first half of the 1930s, even the modest means in his possession were sufficient to help many survive this difficult period. The emergence of dependency and the welfare activity allowed for the expansion of state control over the nomadic tribes and facilitated their integration into its structure.

Glubb's Ascendancy at Abdullah's Expense

Glubb emerged as the chief mediator between the tribes and the government through his command of the Desert Patrol, his position as second in command of the Arab Legion, and his skills in dealing with the tribes. Naturally, his influence increased at Abdullah and Shakir's expense. In 1932 a struggle for influence in the desert erupted over the Ibn Rifada revolt. The British exploited the Hashemite role in the conspiracy as an excuse to remove the ultimate authority over the desert from Abdullah and Shakir and place it in the hands of Glubb. A rift between the two Emirs and Shakir's death in 1934 allowed Glubb to become the undisputed authority in the desert by the mid-1930s.

In the summer of 1932 the British foiled a conspiracy to provoke an anti-Saudi uprising in the Hijaz and ʿAsir. Behind the plans were members of the Hashemite family, the Egyptian ruling family and Hijazi notables. Their instrument was shaykh Hamid bin Rifada of the Billi tribe who led a 1,500 strong tribal force from Sinai and Transjordan to the Hijaz. Although the British did not manage to prove beyond doubt Abdullah and Shakir's complicity, they collected abundant circumstantial evidence against them.[78] The infuriated British authorities -- now speaking with one voice both in the Middle East and in London -- took advantage of the affair to challenge Abdullah and limit his authority over the nomadic tribes. The initiator of this move and its beneficiary was Glubb. He saw the Hashemite involvement in the revolt and their cover-up attempts by using the Tribal Control Board as undermining his own authority.

The root of the conflict was the Hashemite ambition to regain the Hijaz, clashing with Glubb's attempts to calm the border and create amicable relations with the Saudis. The power struggle between Glubb and Abdullah and Shakir assumed the form of a conflict over the handling of Bani ʿAtiyya tribesmen, who participated in the attempted revolt. These tribespeople bore the brunt of Glubb's irritation and paid dearly for their involvement in the affair. Contrary to his typical policy, this time he showed no mercy, imprisoning some tribesmen, exiling others and confiscating their animals. In response, Abdullah demanded the release of the shaykhs, the return of their seized animals, and a pledge to consult with him before taking further measures. Shakir, for his part, took advantage of Glubb's absence on leave to release the imprisoned raiders early, exempt them from the fine of the payment and return the camels seized by the government. Upon his return Glubb sent Cox a strongly-worded memorandum detailing Shakir's deeds. He observed that thanks to the special treatment from Shakir the tribesmen felt themselves immune from punishment. He also reported that Abdullah terrorised the Desert Patrol, enticing the Bani ʿAtiyya not to co-operate with the force, publicly attacking him and dubbing his Arab officers traitors. Glubb suspected that Abdullah saw the Bani ʿAtiyya as an instrument for further interference in the Hijaz if circumstances would allow. Therefore he recommended the unprecedented expulsion of the entire tribe from Transjordan, except one section which did not take part in the conspiracy. Cox embraced Glubb's suggestions, and asked the acting High Commissioner to order Abdullah to pass these resolutions through the TCB, "as a lesson to the tribe itself and also as a very necessary check to the Amir and Shaker."[79]

The British demand did not go down well with Abdullah. After receiving London's approval Cox met Abdullah and dictated the decisions that the Board should take. The appalled and astonished Emir first rejected the demand and even threatened to leave the country. Cox's unwavering position convinced him to accept the edict later that day. Cox reported that on the next day he found Abdullah very friendly and that the Emir expressed his "very real desire to conform to the policy of HMG [His Majesty's Government]." A sign of surrender was his request for British approval for his forthcoming trip to the desert.[80] Both men must have reflected on a similar event back in 1924 when Cox presented Abdullah with an ultimatum which the latter had no choice but to accept. In late November, after the Board had passed the required resolution, Glubb conducted the expulsion of the Bani ʿAtiyya. 110 tents representing around 700 men, women and children and a similar number of camels crossed the Najdi border. Those sections of the tribe allowed to remain in Transjordan, as well as some individuals who received special permission to stay, were not allowed to reside south of Tafila.[81]

Tension over influence in the desert characterised Abdullah and Glubb's relations for a while. In November Abdullah accompanied by shaykhs of the Bani Sakhr and Huwaytat conducted a camel-mounted expedition to the desert. Glubb offered an explanation for the visit: "His Highness's object in this visit was apparently to establish renewed contact with and personal prestige over the Bedouin tribes." The ill-feeling and rivalry between the Emir and Glubb was apparent when Abdullah refused to visit the Desert Patrol fort in Azraq, located only 2 miles from his camp.[82]

Glubb also used the Ibn Rifada affair to expand his legal authority in the desert at the Hashemites' expense. He requested exclusive responsibility for handling cross-border incidents involving the nomads. This would have entailed limited powers of punishment: a maximum of three months imprisonment or a £20 fine. Glubb's suggestion gained currency when the British realised that Shakir was using his authority over the TCB to assist the culprits in the revolt and also suspected him of obstructing justice by changing the verdicts after they have been signed.[83]

The British demand for an amendment of the 1929 Tribal Control Law in order to grant Glubb judicial power aroused first objections from Abdullah and then from the Legislative Council. Cox informed Peake that "[t]he question of amending the Beduin Control Law to give Glubb the desired exclusive jurisdiction is giving a certain amount of trouble."[84] It required the intervention of High Commissioner Arthur Wauchope to persuade Abdullah to pass the Law without modification. When the government placed the Law before the Council, councillors put up an exceptional fight. They rejected the original draft of the amendment, which read that the Commanding Officer of the Arab Legion, or his designated deputy, would possess ultimate authority, not subject to appeal in any case involving a cross-border raid. The Council rejected the notion of ultimate authority and the law was phrased in more moderate terms, stipulating that the authority of the officer derived from the Board.[85]

The wording of the law notwithstanding, Glubb gained what he wanted and could inflict punishment without Abdullah's approval.[86] The British authorities in Transjordan now felt confident in their ability to curtail Abdullah's power and prevent him from compromising British interests, especially with regard to Saudi Arabia. This was evident in the High Commissioner's reply to new guidelines from London. As a result of the Ibn Rifada affair the British government re-examined its policy in Arabia and came up with a policy paper, the outcome of a joint effort by the Foreign and Colonial Offices. For the first time Whitehall formulated a clear policy which explained how it could support both Ibn Saud and the Hashemites. This policy was presented in a letter from the Colonial Secretary to the High Commissioner, spelling out British aspirations to preserve the *status quo* and avoid choosing between the Arab rulers. In particular, and after commending the steps already taken by the local authorities, the High Commissioner was asked to recommend further means to prevent anti-Saudi activity in Transjordan and promote better relations between the two states. In reply, Wauchope referred to the amendment of the Tribal Control Law saying that it would "have the effect of reducing the Amir's control over the tribes, and thereby, it is hoped, of preventing the use of the tribes as weapons to annoy and irritate Ibn Saud." Although the Foreign Office was not entirely happy with this reply, the Colonial Secretary threw in his full weight behind Wauchope and refused to interfere with his policy vis-à-vis Abdullah.[87]

Britain's position in the desert was further enhanced by the rivalry between Abdullah and Shakir, which erupted in the middle of 1933 over the question of unity with Iraq and Abdullah's relations with the Jewish Agency. Shakir was in close touch with Arab nationalist circles in Transjordan, the *Istiqlali*s, who wanted to unite Iraq and Transjordan under the crown of King Faysal. The realisation of such a scheme would have been at Abdullah's expense. In order to prevent it, Abdullah tried to weaken his cousin's position and obstructed the work of the TCB. Shakir's exceptional knowledge of tribal law and custom earned him the respect of the nomads, which apparently alarmed Abdullah, who refused to sign the Board's rulings, thus preventing their execution. Faysal's death in September led the *Istiqlali*s to promote the leadership of Abdullah in the Arab world, which eased the tension, but only temporarily. Abdullah's appointment of a new government that was hostile to the *Istiqlal* party renewed the quarrel and the Board was subsequently paralysed. Glubb believed that Abdullah was looking for a way to remove Shakir from the Board, or even to abolish it altogether. He pointed out the irony that Abdullah, who had attached so much importance to the retention of the Board, was willing to do away with it.[88] What he failed to mention was that Abdullah was probably willing to sacrifice the Board because Glubb's position in the desert made it redundant.

It might be speculated that Shakir's involvement in nationalist politics was a direct result of his replacement by Glubb as the number one authority on tribal affairs. The loss of his main occupation since his arrival in Transjordan caused him to oscillate towards the *Istiqlali* politicians. They found him useful to counterbalance Abdullah, who by that time had demonstrated a willingness to co-operate with the Zionist movement in Palestine. Consequently, tribal affairs became intermingled with questions of high politics. At the height of the struggle Shakir passed a resolution through the Board against Mithqal al-Fayiz, who himself maintained close contact with the Jewish Agency and was the main opponent of the *Istiqlali*s. Shakir ordered a payment of blood-money and pressed the Arab Legion to enforce his decision although Abdullah had already pardoned Mithqal. Upon learning about the case, Abdullah overruled Shakir.[89]

With the Board paralysed, Glubb, acting on the spot, was free to make decisions. It is symbolic that in July 1933 the government agreed to change Glubb's official title from OC Desert Patrol to the more appropriate Commandant Desert Area. This formality accurately represented the change on the scene. It was Glubb who acquired almost exclusive authority in the desert, to such an extent that tribes had to acquire his permission before crossing the Saudi border in search of grazing grounds in the winter.

Abdullah's precarious position both externally vis-à-vis the British government and internally vis-à-vis Glubb on the one hand and Shakir on the other made him more co-operative with the British in desert affairs. In June 1933 he visited the desert forts as Glubb's guest. In another visit to the desert in August Abdullah spent several days next to Bayir fort. Moreover, he tended to dismiss complaints against the Desert Patrol, showing his support for the force. He also agreed to recognise Ibn Saud and to sign a treaty of *bon voisinage* with him, exercising moderation and flexibility during the negotiations. The agreement of July 1933 calmed the tense relations between the two governments and allowed for better co-operation along the desert frontier.[90]

Final consolidation of Glubb's power in the desert occurred following Shakir's death in December 1934, which was the final nail in the Board's coffin. Glubb was quick to note that the Board had ceased to exist since the TCB law mentioned Shakir by name as its president. He urged that "[h]asty measures to abolish or reconstitute" the Board should not be taken and instead suggested using the opportunity to reconsider the administration of tribal justice.[91] Glubb took his time until the vacuum created by Shakir's death enabled him to take over all issues of tribal law. Appointment of a new president was delayed, probably by British measures inspired by Glubb. An indication might be their poor excuse to the League of Nations that Shakir's rare knowledge of tribal law made it "impossible adequately to replace him…"[92]

Glubb's enhanced judicial powers were formalised in 1936 with the passing of the new Bedouin Control Law and Tribal Courts Law. As a result of the enactment of these laws Glubb became the ultimate authority in the desert. His powers were extended to allow him to inflict one year's imprisonment and £40 fine without the right to appeal. Abdullah's approval of the verdict was needed only if the punishment exceeded three months and £10 respectively. He also acquired the status of *mutasarrif* of the desert, which allowed him to add a year's imprisonment or a fine of up to £20 to a verdict given by the tribal judge. Glubb was proud of the fact that within three years of the introduction of the new law all 913 cases tried in the desert court were accepted by the parties without resort to appeal to the Tribal Court of Appeal in Amman, headed by Emir Nayif, Abdullah's younger son. Glubb explained that he himself acted as an appellate authority.[93]

Having established his position through the Desert Patrol and the removal of the Board, Glubb was most influential in gaining the submission of the tribes to the rule of the central government. The subjugation of the tribes manifested itself in many forms, the most obvious being the demise of raiding and the general improvement in law and order. Additionally, the high demand for army employment, well beyond the available posts, the success in collecting taxes from the nomads, and their positive responses to the state's initiatives can be regarded as indicators of this development.

Conclusion

The 1930s witnessed the end of the old order that had prevailed during Ottoman times and the first decade of the Emirate. The 1930s and the 1940s ushered in a new era, one in which the central government's dominance of the political, military and economic spheres of life paralleled the weakening of tribal society and its relegation to a position of dependence upon the government. A new structure took over many of the welfare and security functions previously carried out by the tribe and the chieftaincy.

These changes can be attributed in part to the tribes' own weaknesses. The nomads experienced extreme poverty. In this situation nomads were hardly in a position to mount open resistance. The weakened tribes' need for assistance brought about a change in their attitude towards the central government. Self-interest dictated their collaboration. By paying subsidies, preventing cross-border raids and providing employment in return for salaries, clothing and food, Glubb's policies helped the tribesmen survive this difficult period. His respect for many features of tribal life and his determination to preserve them, albeit with some modifications, facilitated the acceptance of his policies.

Glubb played a crucial role in this social revolution. Through his work the government established its control in the desert and succeeded in subjugating the nomadic tribes, who were forced to cease raiding and were gradually encapsulated by the super-structure of the state. Glubb's policies were one of the pillars of the successful integration of tribal society into the state. The process of submitting the desert tribes to the rule of the central government was unique in the Middle East in that the use of violence was minimal. Glubb testified that it cost the life of only three tribespeople. He did not, on the whole, apply harsh methods of punishment, and after three and a half years he could report that he had not sent even one man to prison. He rarely confiscated property for more than a short period of time.[94] It seems that the expulsion of the Bani ʿAtiyya was the exception to the rule.

In a recent study on the development of Jordanian national identity from a post-colonial and post-modern perspective, Joseph Massad portrays British tribal policies, particularly Glubb's, as especially repressive and as the main cause of the Bedouin's plight. By weakening the tribes through economic and military means, he argues, Glubb destroyed old tribal identities only to invent new ones which became the basis for Jordanian nationalism. Massad denounces Glubb's methods of control, ridicules his understanding of local society and his account of his own activity, and accuses him of oppressing the Bedouin. Massad goes on to portray Glubb as the initiator and executor of a social engineering project which 'debedouinized' the tribes, stripping them of their traditional attributes in order to clothe them in new ones created according to his own understanding of what a Bedouin was.[95]

Some of Massad's descriptions undoubtedly apply to Glubb's later years in Jordan, from independence until 1956, when the much enlarged Arab Legion under his command became the main tool for national socialisation. As an explanation for how and why events unfolded as they did in the mandate period, it seems premature. 'Debedouinization' was less a result of Glubb's designs than an effect of changed economic and political circumstances which weakened the nomads after World War One and particularly during the 1930s. Glubb steered some aspects of this process in his attempt to discipline soldiers and impose his control in the desert. He was, after all, a colonial officer, and there can be little doubt that his first loyalty was to the British government, not to the tribesmen. However, he also responded to these changes and tried to ease the nomads' transition to modernity. In fact, it was Glubb who stood up to his superiors, criticised British policy, and tried to help tribespeople through their difficult years, even if, in doing so, his ultimate objective was to bring them under his control. Not incidentally, Glubb was suspected by his colleagues and superiors of being too sympathetic towards the nomads, even to the degree of compromising British interests.[96] Indeed, Glubb played an important role, alongside

Abdullah, in ensuring that the nomads remained a privileged sector of Jordanian society, in marked contrast to their marginalisation in the surrounding countries.

Glubb's building of a desert administration was helped by an overall expansion in state capability during the 1930s and 1940s. This development, together with other manifestations of tribal integration, form the subject of the next chapter.

CHAPTER FIVE:
STATE CONSOLIDATION AND TRIBAL
PARTICIPATION, 1930-1946

The only truly modern, moral and up-to date way to prevent crime is to provide everyone with a lucrative and peaceful employment. Dig wells, make roads, develop cultivation, heal the sick, teach the children - be all things to all men - and the country is quiet and there is no crime!![1]

While the Desert Patrol under Glubb's command was busy administering the deserts, the overall process of state-formation had reached a point of critical mass by the mid-to-late-1930s. The central government expanded its functions and tightened its control over the population. Consequently the state apparatus assumed a deeper involvement in society and interfered in many spheres of life that had previously been the prerogative of the tribe. State agencies -- and no longer the tribes -- had become the prime controllers, regulators and providers in society. Security, economic relief, employment, healthcare provision, education, the regulation of land ownership, dispute resolution: functions that had been provided within the tribal structure only a few years earlier were now the responsibility of the central government.

There were three principal reasons for the manner in which the state expanded. First, it was the result of careful and deliberate long-term planning by British officials, as in the case of land reform. Second, initiatives to strengthen administrative capacities taken in the 1920s were now beginning to bear fruit. Third, and most importantly, the growth of state agencies and responsibilities was a product of economic and political necessity. The economic crisis of the early 1930s, Jewish attempts to colonise the country, the outbreak of the Palestine revolt and, finally, the outbreak of World War Two were the prime catalysts for the state's expansion.

Tribal reaction to the expanding state differed from tribe to tribe. Generally speaking, tribespeople resisted the centralisation of power that was undermining their autonomy, and regularly tested the government's determination to exercise its authority. Tribal resistance was often so strong that it required a change in policy implementation if not direction. Although the tribes were weakened and increasingly dependent on the government, central power was not absolute, as the continual negotiations and compromises needed in order to carry out many aspects of its policy made evident. State actors, whether the British, the government, or Abdullah, realised that it was wiser to continue their policy of co-operation with the tribes, via their shaykhs, than to confront them.

State expansion was not all bad news for the tribes however. They were receptive to the many initiatives that allowed them to benefit from state largesse. Moreover, state expansion increased the political participation of both shaykhs and rank-and-file tribesmen, giving them a stake in the emerging polity and thereby facilitating their integration. At the same time, however, political participation and growing self-government heightened -- sometimes latent -- tensions between tribes. The new institutions and their positions of power were seen by some of the population as unjust and despotic.

These developments inevitably transformed the lives of many tribespeople. Moreover, as the state expanded, tribes and tribal leaders lost many of their traditional functions. However, rather than becoming anachronistic, they successfully adapted to the new circumstances. While the Emirate had already acquired many characteristics of a modern state by the end of the mandate, it also kept many of its tribal traits and tribes continued to be important actors on the political scene.

This chapter examines the expansion of state capacity in five areas: the provision of economic relief, the expansion of the administration, the strengthening of the Arab Legion, land reform, and finally the provision of health care and education. While each category is examined individually, the last part of the chapter brings the different trends together, assessing their overall impact on society.

Provision of Relief and Development
Economic Crisis

Everyone -- nomadic and settled -- was affected by the economic crisis of the early 1930s. Farmers suffered from crop failures and a shortage of grazing due to droughts and locust attacks. Their predicament was compounded by the world depression, which led to a rise in the cost of living. Many farmers lost their ability to cultivate their land; lacking the money to buy seeds, they sold their ploughing animals. Farmers borrowed money from merchants and moneylenders in Transjordan and Palestine at exorbitant interest rates or, if more fortunate, received loans from the local Agricultural Bank. During discussions in the Legislative Council in 1931, Rufayfan al-Majali, the representative of Karak, claimed that due to their poverty only 40% and 25% of farmers in Karak and Tafila respectively still cultivated their land. He reported that in other parts of the south the situation was even worse, with no farmers in Maᶜan, Shawbak or Wadi Musa cultivating the land. The Council's Administrative Committee confirmed Rufayfan's claims. Naji al-ᶜAzzam from ᶜAjlun echoed Rufayfan, reporting on the accumulating debts among farmers in his region.[2]

Even harder hit were the semi-nomadic or semi-settled tribes of the Bani Hasan and Bani Hamida. For both communities -- undergoing the difficult process towards gradual sedentarisation and settlement -- the combination of bad climatic conditions, inferior land and lack of experience in cultivation was devastating. A British report stated that the poverty of the Bani Hasan derived partly from a series of bad crops and loss of livestock since the middle of the 1920s, and "partly by their own improvidence." It further described their methods of cultivation as "extremely primitive."[3] In 1934 the Bani Hasan, like the desert nomads, suffered from famine. In one year they lost 8,000 of their flock and, according to information received at the Jewish Agency, by February 1934 at least 94 persons had died of hunger.[4] The Bani Hamida also suffered from a succession of bad years and did not cultivate all of their land between Madaba and Karak. Some members of the southern branch of these tribes were reported to have already been reduced to poverty in the middle of the 1920s.[5]

Many segments of the population needed state assistance. Legislators as well as petitioners asked the government to relieve their predicament. In particular, they requested an amnesty on uncollected taxes from previous years and current taxes owed, accompanied by increased loans.[6]

Initial government help was insufficient. However, the persistence of the economic crisis, mounting public criticism, and especially Zionist attempts to take advantage of the situation to colonise Transjordan, brought the first change in British thinking. Since 1933 more assistance was offered, largely in the form of urgent relief. The British stepped up their support in 1936 following the outbreak of the Palestinian revolt. Economic relief was designed to keep the citizens content and make them less inclined to join the rebels. Finally, Transjordan's participation in the war effort after 1939 brought about economic prosperity. Although the mandatory authorities introduced some initiatives which addressed the long-term development of the country, they failed to tackle the basic problems of the economy and did not pave the way for its economic independence.

Early Relief Measures

The government was slow to respond to the public outcry. At the best of times it possessed only scarce resources and the world depression meant that the British Exchequer was more reluctant than ever to spend money in Transjordan. In the first three years of the crisis only sporadic assistance was given. The main help was in the form of tax postponement or exemption, writing off fines or increasing loans from the Agricultural Bank. For example, in 1932 London approved an exemption of past and present taxes amounting to £75,000. Due to the persistence of the crisis, this procedure became routine after the Treasury reluctantly accepted assurances from the high commissioners via the Colonial Office that these taxes were not collectable. During the second half of 1931 the Agricultural Bank provided £10,000 in loans and postponed the collection of £15,000. The government also introduced a public works programme. In the following years this would become the main tool for providing employment both in the desert and in the settled zone. The beginning was modest, with the government allocating £2,000 to lay a road between Tafila, Shawbak and Ma'an. Also in 1931 the government distributed 317 tons of dates and 156 tons of straw to help the poor in the south feed their starving animals. Rufayfan al-Majali reported to the Council that poverty was so bad that instead of giving the dates to their animals the people consumed them themselves.[7]

British Response to Zionist Pressure

The first change in British policy occurred in 1933 in response to Zionist pressures to allow Jewish immigration and settlement in Transjordan. The end of 1932 and the beginning of 1933 marked the heyday of the Zionist political campaign to change the British decision from 1922 to exclude Transjordan from the National Home promised in the Balfour Declaration. A group of landowning shaykhs and notables emerged who wished to see the opening of Transjordan to Jewish immigration and settlement. They offered to lease or sell their land to Jewish settlers in order to relieve their own economic predicament. To achieve this goal they operated as an interest group, countering the objections of the British and Transjordanian governments to the Jewish enterprise. Prominent members of this group included Mithqal al-Fayiz, Majid al-ᶜAdwan, Rufayfan al-Majali, Mitri Zurayqat (Karak) and Rashid al-Khuzaᶜi (Jabal ᶜAjlun). According to one estimate the group amounted to 100 merchants and shaykhs.[8] They were encouraged by Abdullah, who also negotiated with the Jews on his land. By the beginning of 1933 the Zionists had finalised two deals: an option for the lease of Abdullah's land in the Jordan Valley and a loan taken by Mithqal against the mortgage of his land in the village of Barazayn in the name of Zionist officials.[9]

The British government, already embroiled in an escalating conflict between Jews and Arabs in Palestine, feared the spreading of the conflict to the neighbouring territory and refused Zionist appeals. In their attempts to bring the British government to change its policy, the Zionists advanced two claims: firstly, that they had gained local support both from Abdullah and the landowners; and secondly, that Transjordan needed foreign capital and skilled labour, and only Jewish settlement could realise this goal and relieve the country from the deep crisis.

The British government was moved to act in response to the second Zionist argument. Cosmo Parkinson, the Assistant Under-Secretary of State for the Colonies, wrote in February 1933 to High Commissioner Wauchope, raising the issue of the poor economy:

> The Jews are saying a good deal nowadays about the stagnation of Trans-Jordan. They have their own reasons for that; but there is unfortunately a deal of truth in what they say and we were thinking about this long before Brodetsky and Arlosoroff [senior officials of the Jewish Agency] began to talk about it in connection with the recent move for the settlement of Jews in Trans-Jordan.

Parkinson further admitted that "Trans-Jordan is not coming on as one would wish in the case of a British mandated territory. We have of course kept the place going and spent quite a lot of money year by year, but that is not the same thing as developing the place." Although Parkinson accepted the thesis advanced by the

Zionists, he nevertheless suggested developing the country with British money, through an application to the Colonial Development Fund (CDF):

> You would probably agree that the real solution is to develop Trans-Jordan by Jewish enterprise and with Jewish capital, but for the present I leave that out of account because of the political situation and, if we are going to "do something" for Trans-Jordan, I should like to "do it now."[10]

Parkinson's letter initiated a policy change. Colonial officials in Amman, Jerusalem and London realised that "without development there was no prospect of Trans-Jordan becoming self-supporting." They hoped that with the help of the CDF they would be able to lead the country towards economic independence. The priority, they agreed, was to address the water and grazing shortage. They requested money for sinking water bores to assist the raising of flocks and herds.[11] Transjordan's application to the Fund in 1933 proved successful. The recommendations of a committee of three landowners and three government officials appointed by Abdullah laid the basis for further applications. In 1935 Transjordan successfully applied for money to extract water further east in the desert, again to enlarge grazing areas for the nomadic tribes. The £50,000 grant was also dedicated to purchasing seeds, the establishment of an agriculture experiment station, the expansion of the Land Department in order to speed up the land reform (see below) and the establishment of new department for development. A further £20,000 was approved for an irrigation scheme, but the failure of the government to regulate water rights, one of the conditions attached to the grant, prevented it from claiming the money.[12]

As well as grants from the CDF, the British government increased its direct relief to Transjordan from 1933. At the end of that year the British gave £38,000 in loans to buy seeds. It was the first cash injection given in response to the economic crisis. In 1934 as a result of the deterioration in the situation of the Bani Hasan and three villages in ʿAjlun (Nuʿayma, Sarih and Ramtha), the British government granted £8,000 for seed loans and road works. However, British interest in the welfare of the Transjordanians remained half-hearted -- this figure represented only half the sum requested by the High Commissioner, which in turn was a quarter of the original request made by the Resident in Amman. Other emergency measures to relieve the Bani Hasan included the employment of more then 1,000 men on public works. Others survived by receiving food rations from the charity money collected by the relief committee of the Arab Legion. The better part of a special allocation of £15,000 was dedicated to the employment of tribesmen in relief work (the Bani Hasan, Bani Hamida, Huwaytat, Bani Sakhr, Sirhan, Balqawiyya tribes, as well as tribesmen in the areas of Madaba, al-Salt, Jabal ʿAjlun, Kura and Irbid). Abdullah, too, tried to assist the tribesmen and approached his friends in the Jewish Agency, requesting them to supply work in the Dead Sea's Potash Company, where a few dozen tribesmen from al-Salt and its surroundings were employed in 1934.[13]

An increase in the number and volume of tax remissions, which became more general and comprehensive from 1933, was another aspect of enhanced relief. They resulted from close inspection of the crops by British officials and a sympathetic approach towards the farmers and their predicament. The Bani Hasan were exempted from most of their taxes in 1933-1934. In 1934 remission of taxes from the Bani Hamida amounted to at least 50% and in some of their villages up to 85%. Overall tax remission that year amounted to nearly £20,000.[14] The new policy paid dividends as the immediate relief helped the Bani Hasan to survive the height of the crisis until a good winter in 1935 allowed them to start repaying their debts. According to a newspaper report, by September they had already paid 80% of that year's tax.[15]

The Palestine Revolt

Only after the outbreak of the Palestinian rebellion in 1936 did the British government loosen its purse-strings and pour large amounts of money into relief, primarily to ensure that Transjordan remained peaceful. At the outbreak of the revolt the mandatory authorities found themselves in a precarious position. The revolt had an immediate effect on the population, which showed sympathy for the Palestinians in their struggle against the Jews and the British. The events across the Jordan River provoked growing opposition to the British, the Transjordanian government and sometimes even Abdullah himself. This was the result of both a growing national consciousness and an attempt to take advantage of a government in an insecure position.

Provision of employment and relief became an important tool for maintaining peace. In response to another exceptionally bad year with an almost complete crop failure and shortage of grazing in the country south of Madaba, the High Commissioner called for the provision of £6,000 for the relief of 3,000 families and the remission of 70% of the land taxes. His justification for the request was based more on political calculation than humanitarian concern.[16] The British government accepted his arguments and granted the money. A total of £19,000 was allocated to be spent on road works throughout the country.[17]

1936 saw also the return of the old system of subsidies to shaykhs. Alarmed by signs of support for the rebels among leading shaykhs, Glubb urged his superiors to allow him to distribute money in order to maintain their loyalty. Jerusalem and London agreed and granted Glubb as well as Abdullah money for this purpose (£1,050 and £1,590 respectively). A more significant source of funding for Abdullah was the Jewish Agency, whose generous contribution to the Emir was dispensed by Abdullah among tribal shaykhs.[18] The British -- as well as the Zionists -- attributed an improvement in public order towards the end of the year to the distribution of subsidies. In subsequent years Abdullah -- and occasionally Glubb -- continued to give handouts to shaykhs, his financial situation gradually improving due to British and Zionist assistance. In 1938 his civil list was increased by £1,000 to allow him to meet this financial need while the Palestinian revolt dragged on. During the late 1930s Abdullah became the main channel for the distribution of cash among shaykhs and notables.[19]

Despite their increased cash injections, British commitment to the development of Transjordan remained half-hearted. Following some recovery of the agriculture sector resulting from good rains in 1937/38, the British government cut the grant-in-aid from £63,000 in 1937/38 to £19,000 in 1938/39. The astonished authorities in Amman found it difficult to come to terms with this reduction. Resident Cox expressed his disappointment by referring to the inconsistency in the policy towards the financial independence of Transjordan.[20]

World War Two

World War Two brought economic prosperity to Transjordan, which took part in the British war effort from 1941. During the winter of that year between 5,000 and 6,000 tribesmen, nomads and peasants alike, worked for several months on road and railway construction in the south of the country, sharing £20,000 a month which was paid by the British military. In the north up to 8,000 labourers worked for the army, many of them from the Bani Hasan. Not only did tribesmen earn a salary but they were also fed by the army. A combination of robust demand for workers and a good agricultural year created a labour shortage in spring 1942. Many deserted the army works and returned to harvest their fields, and harvesters' wages reached a record of 400 mils a day.[21]

The large-scale war-time projects provided a revolutionary source of employment for tribesmen. The majority of the employees in the south undertook hard manual labour for the first time, as nomads despised manual jobs. Moreover, the British reported that this labour was drawn "from some of the wildest parts of Trans-Jordan." Nevertheless, the works continued smoothly, to the satisfaction of the British, who had anticipated difficulties. Indeed, there were some problems at the beginning, when the shaykhs found themselves with no specific function, as they refused to work alongside their tribesmen. The solution followed the established policy: minor shaykhs and sons of senior ones were employed as supervisors. They were expected to use their influence to prevent friction and to provide the requested quota of labourers from their respective tribes.[22]

The war also brought about a temporary revival of the traditional economy. For one, nomads rented out tents as accommodation for labourers in the military work camps. More lucrative income came from the camel trade, which revived as a result of the shortage of spare parts for motor vehicles. Smuggling was also very profitable and probably appealed to the nomads because it resembled their old raiding activities. Finally, in 1942 British army resources were given to Glubb "for the assistance of Trans-Jordan tribes."[23] Against the background of German advances in the Egyptian desert and serious doubts over the future of British rule in the Middle East, it was imperative to maintain the tribes' loyalty.

The nomads' gradual recovery following the economic crisis of the mid-1930s was further improved during World War Two. In 1938 the director of Public Health asserted that their nutrition had improved significantly in comparison to 1935, the last year of the drought. A medical survey among nomadic tribes carried out in 1940 confirmed these findings. Government employment and the diversification of their economy through land cultivation and the switch from camel to sheep herding (see below) markedly improved the tribes' standard of living. In the process, nomads were integrated more closely into the market economy. According to Norman Lewis, the Bani Sakhr sold wool, dairy-products and sheep for slaughter. In return, they bought more food than previously, including luxury items such as tea and sugar as well as fruit and vegetables.[24]

Employment in the Expanding Administration

The 1930s and 1940s saw a steady expansion of the administrative apparatus. In contrast to the first decade, the majority of government positions were manned by local Transjordanians rather than imported personnel. Government employment became an important source of income, especially against the background of severe economic crisis. More significantly, for the first time it involved local actors in state affairs, further knitting them into the framework of the state.

The process began with the inclusion in the cabinet of three local notables in October 1929. Until then only two locals served as ministers as token representatives (ᶜAli Khulqi from Irbid in the early 1920s and Adib Wahba from al-Salt in 1926-1929). The employment of non-natives had been a bone of contention between the government and the local elite since the establishment of the Emirate. One of the principal demands of the emerging national movement was to hand over government positions to "sons of the country." Probably in order to placate the vocal opposition and to co-opt its members, Prime Minister Hasan Khalid abu al-Huda nominated three members as ministers in 1929. Musa describes this move as "the first step towards the participation of representatives of the people in the administration of the country."[25] Indigenous representation remained no lower than three and sometimes increased to five in subsequent six-man cabinets until the end of the mandate. The ministers were not technocrats, but prominent tribal leaders from the settled zone, some of them paramount shaykhs or their sons. The brothers ᶜAwda and Hanna Qasus from Karak shared the position reserved for a Christian with Niqula Ghanma from Irbid. Muslim ministers included Adib al-Kayid (al-ᶜAwamla, al-Salt), Qasim al-Hindawi (Nuᶜayma village, ᶜAjlun), ᶜAbdullah al-Nimr al-Hamud (al-ᶜArabiyyat tribe of al-Akrad, al-Salt), Khalaf al-Tall (Irbid), ᶜAli al-Kayid (the shaykh of al-Miᶜrad district based in the village of Suf), ᶜAbd al-Mahdi al-Shamayla (Karak), ᶜAbdullah al-Kulayb al-Shurayda (Kura), ᶜAbd al-Rahman Rushaydat (Irbid). The rest of the positions went to the Circassians and merchants. The several-times minister Hashim Khayr represented the merchants but his political support came from his brother-in-law, Mithqal al-Fayiz, the paramount shaykh of the Bani Sakhr.

Apart from the 16 seats in the Legislative Council which entailed the handsome annual salary of £200,[26] and ministerial positions for local leaders, the government employed a growing number of Transjordanians in all ranks of the administration. Initially, a government decision in response to public pressure to remove foreign officials in order to make way for natives was only partly implemented.[27] Gradually, however, more locals found employment with the government.

An amendment to the Anglo-Transjordanian treaty in 1939 and the growing number of high school and even university graduates allowed for the expansion of the government and the replacement of officials seconded from Palestine. In August that year Prime Minister Tawfiq abu al-Huda formed a government that included five new ministries: defence, interior, finance, commerce and agriculture and transportation. The total number of government officials (including officers in the Arab Legion) increased from 683 in 1936 to 927 in 1939. By then 607 were from Transjordan.[28] By the early 1940s some of the local Transjordanians had risen to occupy senior positions in the administration such as local governors (*qaimaqam, mutasarrif*) and heads of department. Sound family background seemed to have been one of the main requirements for the most senior jobs. Thus in 1941 ᶜAbdullah Kulayb al-Shurayda became the *Mutasarrif* of Maᶜan and in 1943 ᶜAbd al-Majid al-ᶜAdwan, the son of Sultan, served as *Qaimaqam* in Jarash.[29]

As government positions became available they arose fierce competition between potential candidates. The Amman biweekly *Al-Urdunn* reported on great interest and speculation in politically-minded circles regarding the anticipated new appointments, the result of the 1939 amendment of the Treaty. At times competition for jobs took the form of opposition to foreign officials. One British report attributed the revival of the "Transjordan to the Transjordanians" movement in al-Salt in 1942 to the disappointment of candidates who failed to obtain government employment.[30]

Often rivalry over jobs reflected traditional power struggles among tribes. Moreover, the introduction of modern positions of power disturbed traditional social relations, especially in localities which were made up of several tribal or confessional groupings. As Michael Reimer shows, latent tension which so far had been contained by the traditional social equilibrium, achieved by "informal and collegial leadership" representing the different social groups, "had been overthrown by the autocratic ambitions of one man and some of his allies."[31] Thus, the elections for the Administrative Council of Karak in 1942 gave rise to "a series of brawls," obliging the Interior Minister to visit the town and calm the tension, and possibly also Abdullah's efforts to reconcile the rival parties.[32] In 1935 shaykhs and notables from Tafila petitioned the High Commissioner against Salih al-ᶜAwran. They claimed that the government was at pains to increase his influence by appointing him to the tribal court and intervening illegally to ensure his election both to the Legislative Council and the province's Administrative Council. The petitioners also complained that, alongside his salary as legislator and fees as a judge, for years he had enjoyed a monthly subsidy of £7.5 "not for any specific service he gives but merely in order to strengthen his influence." The signatures on the petition show that it reflected an old struggle between the two most prominent families in the town. Mustafa al-Muhaysan's signature appears at the upper left corner under the date, the position reserved for the most senior signatory. The other signatories were also members of the Kalalda tribe under his leadership or representatives of its allies from the Hilalat (Shubaylat).[33] As Reimer has shown, similar communal conflicts over the establishment of municipal administrations in the towns occurred throughout the country from at least the late 1920s.[34]

Abdullah was able to influence government appointments. The Organic Law of 1928 granted him the prerogative to approve each appointment and he often intervened at the request of notables who lobbied for a certain candidate. To check

Abdullah's interference and to reduce a frequent cause of friction between him and the Prime Minister, in 1941 he was compelled to issue a notice declaring that the Emir should not be asked to intervene in matters of appointments or promotions. Abdullah nonetheless continued to take an interest in such matters, leading to periodical crises between him and abu al-Huda that were only resolved by the British Resident.[35]

Abdullah also played a prominent role in the appointment of tribal judges following the reorganisation of the tribal courts in 1937, which also gave him important leverage vis-à-vis the shaykhs. A judge enjoyed prominent status in tribal society and Abdullah obtained control over this status symbol. Initial lists of judges were drawn for each province when the law came into effect. From the end of 1937 more shaykhs were constantly added to the list, not necessarily because of the growth in tribal claims but probably because they asked to be included.[36] A newspaper report from 1939 on the response to the appointment of the notable Muhammad *Basha* al-ʿIzab from al-Salt indicates the social status accorded by the nomination: "This royal benevolence has been received with exaltation and admiration. The *Basha*'s tribe rushed to send His Highness telegrams with their gratitude."[37]

Employment in the Expanding Arab Legion and Increased State Capacity

From the end of the 1930s, and especially during the early 1940s, the Arab Legion expanded dramatically, becoming the most important source of government employment. Recruitment of nomads to the small Desert Patrol had already had a positive effect on the desert economy in the early 1930s. The enlarged Arab Legion, however, offered a steady and comfortable income and other benefits to thousands of men, most of them nomads.

Enlargement of the armed forces and improvements in both vehicles and weapons resulted in a stronger position for the government and tighter control over the population. By 1939, or shortly thereafter, Transjordan acquired an important trait of the Weberian state, that of government monopoly over coercive power. Occasional resistance was dealt with easily. This was achieved not only because of the increase in the size of the Arab Legion, but also thanks to the expansion of its functions. The Legion undertook new responsibilities. These included protection, dispute resolution, land distribution, anti-locust campaigns and even laying roads from remote villages to the main markets. The Legion's military superiority together with the ability to provide these new services deepened the dependence of the tribes on the state apparatus and facilitated their integration.

Employment in the Arab Legion, 1936-1946

The expansion of the Arab Legion, like so many other policies, was not a long-term design but an immediate response to external pressures. Following the outbreak of the rebellion in Palestine, Glubb was authorised to recruit 65 men to the Desert Patrol as an emergency reserve force. The infiltration of Palestinian armed bands into Transjordan in 1938 forced a further increase in the military by 50 recruits. At the beginning of 1939 the desert units of the Legion numbered 300 men, double their original strength. Later in the year the British increased the Legion's reserve by several hundred recruits from nomadic tribes.[38] These increases reflected the British decision to rely on nomads not only for controlling the desert but also as a striking force, thus sidelining the main body of the Arab Legion which was based on settled manpower.

The Legion grew even more substantially during World War Two. 1942 saw the rapid expansion and reorganisation of the force (under the command of Glubb since 1939). By June it employed 86 officers and 3,644 other ranks. Its mobility improved and two desert mechanised regiments, each staffed by 600 men, formed its striking arm. A month later Glubb started recruiting another 600 men in order to establish a third regiment. The speedy enlargement of the Legion was possible because of high demand to join the army. In 1946 the Legion numbered 8,000 men, 6,000 of whom were in combat units and the rest serving as police and gendarmes.[39]

The expansion of the forces necessitated training new officers. Some were simply promoted from the ranks but the main avenue to becoming an officer was through the new rank of cadet. Secondary school graduates joined the army for a trial period and if successful were nominated as officers. Examining the names of cadets and young officers supports the conclusion that there was a conscious effort to recruit the sons of prominent shaykhs and other notables from the settled zone. It was a lesson learned from Glubb's application of this policy to the Desert Patrol, which proved successful in cementing loyalty and co-operation and thus achieving better control of the population. In a later testimony, however, Glubb claimed that these nominations were the result of political pressure exerted upon him. A few examples include the sons of Rufayfan al-Majali, Musa al-Maᶜayta, Kulayb al-Shurayda, Salih al-ᶜAwran, Mustafa al-Muhaysan and Minwar al-Hadid.[40]

1936-1939: Revolt in Palestine and Opposition in Transjordan

At the outbreak of the Palestine revolt the mandatory authorities in Transjordan found themselves in a precarious position vis-à-vis an agitated population. The TJFF, now deployed along the Jordan River, was sometimes required to reinforce the British forces in Palestine. This left the Arab Legion, whose size had not increased since the mid-1920s (apart from the Desert Patrol), with responsibility for the security of Transjordan.[41] During the years 1936-1939 British officials expressed their fear that the combination of economic distress and continued rebellion would undermine their control over the tribes.

Opposition escalated soon after the outbreak of the revolt. Attacks on telegraph and telephone lines, sabotage of the petrol pipeline, financial support for the rebels and arms smuggling, as well as demonstrations and conferences in support of the Palestinian cause were commonplace. The tribes who resided along the Jordan River were particularly supportive. In 1938-1939 tribesmen from ᶜAbbad, al-Salt and most notably the Sukhur al-Ghawr, who resided on both banks of the river, protected guerrilla bands and some even fought with them. Several tribal leaders offered active support to the Palestinians and risked a direct conflict with the government. Rashid al-Khuzaᶜi, the strongman of Jabal ᶜAjlun, had to seek temporary refuge in Syria because of his defiance of the government and Abdullah. Several shaykhs were suspected of nationalist activism.[42] Majid al-ʿAdwan is remembered locally for the provision of money, weapons and hospitality. According to one testimony, his house in Shuna in the Jordan Valley served as a base for arms smuggling to Palestine. Majid was also active in supporting the Syrian rebels. Notwithstanding this support, he was careful to avoid open conflict with the government. When in 1938 several Palestinians asked to use his territory as a base for anti-British activity, he refused and demanded their immediate departure.[43]

Nomadic tribes, hitherto thought to be immune from national ideology, showed increasing signs of sympathy for the Palestinians, alarming Transjordanian, British and Zionist officials. Both British and Zionist sources reported on intensive Palestinian efforts to persuade the tribes to join them -- attempts which in some cases seemed to be effective.[44] The Bani Sakhr particularly worried observers. Reacting to the economic crisis in Transjordan, members of the Kaʿabna branch sought employment in Palestine and were deeply affected by the confrontational events there.[45] Their shaykh, Haditha al-Khuraysha, who had already supported the Syrian rebels in the mid-1920s, also contributed to the Palestinian struggle. Moreover, Mithqal al-Fayiz, the paramount shaykh -- whose connection with the Zionists had meanwhile ground to a standstill -- was seen in British eyes as the most active tribal leader in Palestinian affairs. In June 1936 Mithqal organised a meeting of shaykhs in his village Umm al-ʿAmad to consider intervention in the affairs of Palestine. Glubb's report reflects his extreme alarm at this new development. The news of the conference, Glubb wrote, provoked excited rumours and there was a danger that such a gathering might lead to "violence which could have dragged the whole country into rebellion."[46]

The conference at Umm al-ʿAmad did not result in united action by the tribes, but it certainly had an impact. The belief that the government was experiencing difficulties gave rise to acts of defiance "in many small ways; a truculence of manner, a loudness of voice and a generally swashbuckling manner." Throughout 1937 Glubb reported on restlessness and insubordination among the different tribes of the confederacy.[47] Clearly, despite the success of the Arab Legion in controlling the tribes, this control was still precarious, and Glubb feared that in a crisis the government might lose its grip altogether. This indicates that Glubb had not yet achieved full control over the tribes. The process of state-building, although advanced in the mid-1930s, was far from complete.

To maintain control in times of political crisis and military weakness, the authorities had to resort to a combination of preventive methods. Distribution of subsidies, the provision of relief and employment and enhanced recruitment to the Desert Patrol were intended to secure the loyalty of the shaykhs and keep tribesmen employed and content. Occasionally, the government resorted to limiting the freedom of operation of local leaders to curtail opposition. Banishment and house arrests represented the main methods.[48]

However, the key to maintaining peace in Transjordan and preventing the spill-over of the revolt was Abdullah. The Emir was able to exert his influence on local leaders in order to vouch for the country's restraint, for which the British were grateful. In June 1936 High Commissioner Wauchope reported his satisfaction with the fact that Transjordan had remained calm in spite of strong anti-Zionist feeling. Wauchope gave the credit for this achievement to Abdullah, saying that "this fortunate state of affairs is largely if not entirely due to the Amir Abdullah, who has consistently thrown his weight against any form of political activity which might add to the troubles of Palestine and up to the present he has succeeded in keeping Trans-Jordan quiet."[49] The High Commissioner concurred with Cox's repeated assertions of Abdullah's service and good faith in the following months.[50]

Increased Military Strength and Border Control

Gradually, however, Transjordan gained increased military capacity. The first region to experience military control was the Jordan Valley. At the beginning of 1937 the government forbade carrying arms along the Jordan River without a license issued by the Legion, thus introducing the first serious attempt to control arms since the establishment of the Emirate. Arms control posed a formidable challenge for the government. As shown in Chapter Three it had failed to implement such measures before. New attempts to control arms were bound to provoke fierce opposition and probably a defeat for the government in the Legislative Council. Legislators were particularly suspicious of any increase in the authority and responsibilities of the Arab Legion. Only a year earlier they rebuffed the government's attempt to legislate immunity from legal claims for the Legion's officers. It was no coincidence therefore that the British waited until the end of the Legislative Council's session to enact the law. A provision in the Organic Law allowed the government to bypass the Council by empowering the Emir to enact ordinances outside the parliamentary sessions, which then required only retroactive approval by the Council.[51]

Shortly after the introduction of the new regulation in the Jordan Valley, the British reported that the licensing of arms was proceeding slowly because most of the inhabitants were suspicious of this measure. However, the Legion was able to enforce it, at least as far as the Ghazawiyya and Sukhur al-Ghawr tribes of the northern Valley were concerned. Furthermore, at the end of 1938 the Legion tightened its control over the Valley by deploying more forces and carrying out sporadic operations against these two tribes. As the British also suspected the Ghazawiyya tribes of supporting guerrilla bands, the Legion forced them to move their tents from the bank of the Jordan to the foothills. When the tribesmen defied the government and returned to their original camping area, the government banished one of their shaykhs, Amir Muhammad Salih, to Amman, before trying to remove their tents again and arresting several suspects. In addition it confiscated the licensed arms of the Sukhur, who were also removed from the river bank. Their shaykh was banished to ʿAqaba.[52]

The improvement in communications contributed significantly to the Arab Legion's operational capacity in Jabal ʿAjlun, where the topography was ideal for Palestinian armed bands or other fugitives to search for shelter. New roads were built in order to connect isolated villages, sometimes with the help of the locals. Indeed, they proved advantageous both to the villagers and the government. The villagers now received better services and enjoyed easier access to the markets, while the government was able to strengthen its hold on the country. During 1937 twenty more villages in Jabal ʿAjlun were connected by roads. In 1939 the Arab Legion cut 100km of tracks through the mountains for mechanised patrols in the Jabal ʿAjlun and along the Syrian border. The few villages left out of these works petitioned to be allowed to build tracks themselves. With the assistance of the soldiers, this work was done voluntarily. Glubb summed up the project by saying that: "the opening of these tracks has placed the government in a much stronger position in the Jebel Ajlun."[53]

Tighter border control from the middle of the 1930s also contributed to the overall submission of the population to the government. Although the governments in Arabia were careful not to stop cross-border pastoral movements, they did keep a watchful eye on tribal movements. Nomads were exempted from carrying passports but had to carry other written documents while crossing the frontiers to Iraq, Saudi Arabia and Syria. According to the agreement with the Syrian authorities, Transjordanian nationals searching for pastures in Syria were required to obtain a certificate from the custom officers before crossing the border. Possession of such a certificate would guarantee their exemption from paying taxes. Similarly, Huwaytat and Nuʿaymat camelmen, who carried pilgrims on the way to Mecca from Maʿan to Tabuk, were required to possess a certificate of identity issued by a Transjordanian official. Non-Transjordanian tribes were expected to do the same. Towards the end of the 1930s the government sought to monitor the movements of nomads coming from the surrounding countries. Realising that these nomads "did not know anything about passports and how to use them" they instead had to report to an Arab Legion post, where they received written permission to enter Transjordan.[54]

By the end of the 1930s the government achieved an impressive degree of control over its borders, especially with Palestine and Syria. Thus, the sharp increase in wages for harvesters in 1939 was explained as a result of restricted travel between Palestine, Syria and Transjordan. But even along desert frontiers the Arab Legion presence allowed close control. As mentioned in the previous chapter, nomads migrating to Saudi Arabia in search of pastures had to obtain Glubb's permission. The emergence of smuggling as an important economic occupation for nomads occurred only against the background of tightening control along the borders. The arrest of ʿAkif al-Fayiz on the Iraqi border in 1940, carrying secret correspondence between his father, Mithqal, and King Ibn Saud, further indicates the level and effectiveness of government control over border traffic.[55]

By the end of 1939 the British Resident was so confident of the ability of the enlarged Legion to deal with any malcontents, that he dismissed suggestions from certain shaykhs following the outbreak of the war that he should pay them subsidies in return for guaranteeing the peace.[56] Indeed, by that time the Legion was capable of carrying out large scale operations throughout the country. Between 1938 and 1943 a number of operations took place against certain tribes of the Huwaytat and the Bani Sakhr.

Nonetheless, Glubb still preferred to pursue a lenient approach. He would concentrate a large contingent of legionnaires and armoured cars, surprise the nomads at their camp, make several arrests and confiscate camels, which would be later returned to their owners.[57] Glubb explained the effectiveness of combining force and benevolence by saying that "such action is more eloquent than words to show the tribesman what the Government *can* do if it wants to. The seizure of his camel impresses the bedouin with the power of government, while their subsequent return convinces him of its benevolence. Thus a lesson in manners is administered which leaves no resentment."[58] Sometimes Glubb chose unique forms of punishment against misbehaving tribes. The Jubur tribe of the Bani Sakhr was forcibly moved from its traditional grazing area, given land in Nuqayra, south-east of Amman, and ordered to cultivate it (see below). The shaykh of the Zaban tribe of the same confederacy was ordered to feed 150 legionnaires who were dispatched to his camp.[59]

Glubb generally tried to avoid direct conflict with the tribes, preferring to enlist their co-operation to crushing them, as long as he could maintain the government's upper hand over the nomads. Even in times of conflict he was careful to respect shaykhly authority. Moreover, his sporadic operations did not develop into violent battles. According to Glubb, the fact that the Desert Patrol was made up of the tribesmen's relatives mitigated potential conflict.[60] The absorption of their best youths into the Desert Patrol, especially the sons of shaykhs who had hitherto fulfilled the role of raid leaders, added to the nomads' inability to resist the Legion.

The Legion was not only a coercive force, but also provided the tribes with new services. Increased rural security allowed for ecological innovations as semi-nomads and even peasants moved into the desert as far as Wadi Sirhan. The Bani Hamida were the first to move. By the late 1930s they were being joined by villagers. They enlarged their flocks and bought tents, which they took to the steppe or the desert in the winter or spring. Often the new arrivals and the nomads competed for land and water, with the Arab Legion mediating between them. The Desert Patrol was also instrumental in protecting grazing rights and even the property of the local tribes in their competition with non-Transjordanian tribes. Thus, it kept Saudi tribes out of Jabal Tubayq during the summer months. This was done in order to prevent them from consuming grass which should have been left for the Huwaytat who arrived there in the following autumn. When Syrian tribesmen looted camels from the Bani Sakhr near Azraq in 1941-- the first raid after many years of peace along this border -- legionnaires mounted on camels pursued the raiders into Syria and recovered the loot.[61]

Beyond the provision of security, the Legion also undertook 'civilian' tasks. When locusts descended on the desert in 1945, the desert mechanised regiments prevented the menace from spreading to the settled zone and to Palestine.[62] Fifteen years earlier, faced with a similar threat, the government had been forced to mobilise the population using the threat of fines. As will be shown, when nomadic tribes began settling and cultivating the land, it was the Arab Legion that distributed land and subsequently protected the rights of landowners.

Land Programme and the Expansion of Agriculture
The land programme represented both the most impressive and the most intrusive state initiative during the mandate. The reform allowed government authorities to assume the role of regulator and arbitrator in questions of land control, hitherto an internal matter for each tribal unit. As Michael Fischbach observes, the reform brought

about "the beginning of the end of corporate social control over landownership in Transjordan and the onset of the state's massive intervention in the minutest details of tenure."[63]

Land reform and the issues related to the use and control of the land best illustrate the main themes of this chapter, namely the central government's increased capacity and growing intervention in society during the 1930s and the changing functions of tribes and their shaykhs. As in other spheres, tribes and shaykhs did not lose their role. The final result of the land reform represented a collaboration and compromise between state officials and local actors. Indeed, as Fischbach also emphasises, the success of the reform lay in the fact that it was done with the co-operation of the cultivators and only after the British compromised their ambitious plans and lowered their expectations of what could be achieved. The following discussion is intended to complement Fischbach's account by elaborating on additional aspects related to land use among tribes, nomadic ones in particular.[64] It shows that from the mid-1930s the cultivation of land became an important source of income for many who were forced to limit their reliance on the pastoral economy. Government encouragement was instrumental in steering this process.

Land Programme

The land reform, introduced by the British in 1927, established a programme that continued into the 1950s. Its aim was twofold: to improve agricultural production and to increase revenue collection. To achieve these goals, the British overhauled the system of land tenure they inherited from the Ottomans, which was deemed inefficient. The programme was designed in accordance with the recommendations of Sir Ernest Dowson, a land reform expert who had completed a similar assignment in Palestine.

Between 1927-1933 surveyors carried out a fiscal survey, demarcating borders between villages and then dividing each village into parcels of land and estimating the value of each parcel for taxation purposes. The survey was carried out with local help. The Land Department instructed its surveyors to involve the landowners in the process and utilise local knowledge. For example, during demarcation of village boundaries the officers would draw on the expertise of the elders from the villages in question.

In order to make the tax system more efficient, the different Ottoman taxes were unified into a single land tax, to be levied equitably among individual cultivators. The British prepared a draft tax law in 1931 but faced harsh opposition from members of the Legislative Council. The big landowners represented in the Council wanted to prevent an increase of their tax liabilities and defeated the bill when it was first submitted. A great deal of negotiation and political manoeuvring was required from the government and the British Resident before the Council's approval was secured some two years after it was originally presented. The new bill contained a significant amendment. A new provision allowed individuals whose tax increased by 50% or more to pay it in instalments over five years. In addition, the tax increase throughout the country was limited to £10,000. In another British compromise shaykhs were invited to sit on committees whose task was to distribute the new land tax among members of the tribe. The British claimed that the committees abused their position and in any case dissolved them by the late 1930s. The new law was implemented gradually from September 1933, and by the end of 1935 it was applied throughout the country.

The most challenging aspect of the programme was the settlement of title. It was described by Fischbach as "the most significant and intrusive state policy ever carried out in Transjordan."[65] The Land Department officials demarcated and settled legal title over the land, and what affected the tribes most, partitioned commonly-held land, *musha'*. This land had been held under the responsibility of the shaykhs. They were the arbiters who decided who received what land and determined the shape of its annual redistribution. Shaykhly authority over this domain was now challenged.[66] However, to avoid strong opposition and to reduce time and costs, the Department decided to allow cultivators themselves to arrange their own partition scheme. At first land officials reluctantly accepted what they considered to be inadequate partitions. Later they were able to convince villagers to partition their land according to the official plan.

Partition of *musha'* land among the Bani Hasan tribes illustrates the partnership as well as the convergence of interests between the government and the tribes. The Bani Hasan suffered from endemic land disputes in the 1920s, often requiring a higher, neutral authority to settle them. At a meeting with the governor of Jarash in 1929 the shaykhs of the confederacy requested that the land be divided among their different tribes. Accordingly, a partial partition followed. Only in the late 1940s, however, did land officials return to the Bani Hasan to assign a specific land plot to each shareholder.[67]

Other tribes benefited from securing legal rights to their land, such as the ʿAdwan and Sukhur al-Ghawr who, after negotiation with the government, were allowed to register their land in the Jordan Valley. Tribesmen also enjoyed the increase in the value of their land and the opportunity to borrow money against their land or to sell it. Since title was now beyond dispute, making it a valuable asset, many landowners offered their land to merchants or moneylenders, especially in years of drought.

Fischbach concludes that the programme was generally popular among cultivators, but evidence suggests that the programme was better received in the north of the country. Even there, Fischbach himself stresses, some aspects of the programme, such as government's control over forests, were resented by tribesmen who continued to cut trees in defiance of the law.[68] Further south many segments of society objected to the reform and even obstructed its implementation. In the Balqa' province dissatisfied tribesmen from the Bani Hamida, ʿAjarma and Madaba tribes removed iron markers placed by the land surveyors. A land official complained about the lack of co-operation from the inhabitants of al-Salt during land settlement there. In the Legislative Council, two big landowners from Karak and the Balqa', Rufayfan al-Majali and Majid al-ʿAdwan, frustrated the government's attempt to regulate water distribution in the countryside -- a related aspect of the land programme -- for eight years. Only after their deaths in 1945 and 1946 respectively was the government able to pass the law.[69] Indeed, large landowners in the Balqa' or Karak objected to the programme since it increased their taxes and moreover came into effect during the years of the economic crisis when many of them fell into debt.[70] For that purpose a group of large landowners mobilised opposition to the tax law in the late 1930s and beginning of the 1940s, demanding a reduction in the tax burden.

These regional variations in accepting the programme can be easily understood in two contexts. Firstly, land in the ʿAjlun province was owned by small cultivators who certainly enjoyed the benefits of the reform. The social makeup of the region was also more favourable to such a scheme. Small tribes posed weaker opposition to the government. In contrast, in the central and southern regions large portions of the land were owned or controlled by powerful shaykhs, who did not want to part with their prerogatives and accept sharp increases in their tax burdens. The large nomadic or semi-nomadic tribes which dominated these regions were more suspicious towards government intervention in their affairs and could offer stronger resistance. Secondly, and equally important, the Ottoman state legacy was strongly felt in ʿAjlun, the first region to be incorporated under direct Ottoman control in the nineteenth century. This was particularly pertinent to land ownership. As Fischbach argues, "[b]y the turn of the twentieth century, ʿAjlun's population had grown accustomed to the intervention of the [Ottoman] authorities in land affairs." By then the Ottomans had registered the land and succeeded in an orderly collection of taxes. In contrast, as shown by Rogan, the Ottoman government never undertook systematic registration in the Balqa', let alone further south, and registration was left to the discretion of the tribesmen.[71] Rogan's thesis on the importance of the Ottoman legacy of statehood for the Emirate leads to the assumption that there was less opposition and suspicion in the north. This was thanks to the more significant legacy of statehood left by the Ottoman introduction of a modern state apparatus and practices in this part of the country. A report from 1935 on Maʿan and al-Tafila corroborates the assumption about the connection between the population's compliance and the period of time under central government. Stressing the administrative difficulties, the Administrative Inspector explained that the inhabitants "have not experienced [central] rule for long as the rest of the Emirate. This serious state of affairs in these primitive areas necessitates sending only the most skilful officials."[72]

Especially in the central and southern regions, the land programme did not nullify the tribal and shaykhly nature of landownership and shaykhs continued to play a major role as arbiters over land issues well into the middle of the century and beyond. As already mentioned, the Bani Hasan still owned land collectively in 1946. Land in Wadi Musa and Jabal Shara, both in the Maʿan province, was owned by tribal groups rather then individuals. Rufayfan al-Majali and Haditha al-Khuraysha divided their followers' land, while the latter owned Muwaqqar on behalf of his tribesmen. Only in 1947 was this land partly partitioned among the different lineages of the Khuraysha. Mithqal al-Fayiz remained the largest landowner in the country even after the reform.[73]

Indeed, the programme unwittingly worked in favour of the large landowning shaykhs. As Fischbach stresses, the land policies secured the pre-existing rights of the shaykhs. At the same time, however, they helped many to increase their already large possessions. The big landowning shaykhs had the resources to invest in their land. A handful employed motor-driven ploughs, thereby cultivating a sizeable amount of land. They also benefited from government assistance. When in 1939 the Agriculture Department distributed plants free of charge in Karak and Tafila, the main beneficiary was Rufayfan al-Majali who received 1,000 citrus plants. In 1934 Mithqal al-Fayiz was offered (but refused) £1,000 in loans and the guidance of the Department to develop his farm. And on the fringe of the desert Glubb gave preferential treatment to nomadic shaykhs turned cultivators (see below). So when land became a commodity and its prices increased, tribal shaykhs were able to purchase more land, some from impoverished villagers. For example, the British reported that Mithqal al-Fayiz had earned a lot of money from agriculture and was using it to purchase large amounts of land, some of it from members of his tribe or family. The shaykhs also enjoyed another aspect of the policy: the disposal of state land. For instance, three sons of shaykh Kulayb al-Shurayda bought state land in the Jordan Valley.[74] Thus, land reform reinforced the dominance of those among the tribal shaykhs who seized the opportunity and invested in agriculture.

Beyond Land Reform

Tribal ownership of land remained the main feature in the areas that were late to be incorporated into formal settlement. These lay in southern Transjordan, where settlement was completed only in 1952, and everywhere beyond the settled zone. In these areas it was Glubb and the shaykhs who played the dominant role in land control. Furthermore, with Glubb's encouragement nomads started to take up cultivation, thus diversifying their economy.

Independent of the land programme, but perhaps inspired by it, the mid-1930s saw an expansion of cultivation among nomadic tribes. Against a background of economic distress and beyond immediate relief measures, Glubb saw cultivation as the long-term solution for the ailing Bedouin economy. According to his understanding, the solution to the nomads' hardship was mixed agriculture, in which profits from cultivation would balance losses in the pastoral economy in years of bad grazing. There was an additional gain in cultivation, a political one. For the British it was another means to improve control over the nomads by giving them "a fixed stake in immovable property in the country, which will be not only an economic insurance but also a social anchorage."[75] It should be stressed, however, that in Transjordan sedentarisation of nomads was not compulsory but voluntary and occurred as a gradual process.

Glubb targeted the Bani Sakhr and the Huwaytat as the prime beneficiaries of his plan. In 1934 he first supplied them with the means to begin cultivation with a modest annual budget of around £1,000. The first to take up cultivation were 560 destitute families from the Huwaytat, who received only £1 each to buy seeds upon proving that they had begun to till their land in the vicinity of Maʿan. Here again Glubb applied his policy of preference to tribal chiefs, and recognised shaykhs were paid £5. A few years later the Department of Agriculture distributed for free 5,000 tree plants among the inhabitants of Ma'an and of Jabal Shara (the latter probably being Huwaytat).[76]

Agriculture became popular, especially among the shaykhs of the Huwaytat, since it helped to compensate for the loss of their traditional sources of income such as raids, payment of *khawa* and the breeding of horses and camels. The first to take up farming was their paramount shaykh, Hamad bin Jazi, who even owned a tractor. In the spring of 1935 the Minister for Administrative Inspection, Sa'id al-Mufti, reported satisfactorily on the responsiveness of the Huwaytat to cultivation, writing that the Ibn Jazi tribe tilled around 1,000 dunums of land.[77] Another shaykh, Za'al bin Mutlaq abu Taya, was described in 1935 as a "convert" to agriculture. By the end of the decade even Muhammad abu Taya, portrayed by Glubb as the only pure nomadic shaykh of the Huwaytat, cultivated his land.[78]

If farming was a novelty for most of the Huwaytat tribes, by contrast the Bani Sakhr shaykhs had been cultivating land since the nineteenth century. However, vast tracts of their land in the eastern Balqa' lay fallow because of the unfavourable climatic conditions and because land taxes made farming financially unviable. Moreover, some shaykhs sold, or, more commonly, mortgaged their land to merchants and moneylenders in the towns. In accordance with his policy of improving the welfare of the nomads, Glubb was interested in helping the Bani Sakhr return their land to full cultivation. He therefore requested an allocation of £1,000 to encourage them to cultivate these lands and to keep them in their possession. The reduced sum of £250 was allocated for this purpose in 1935. Glubb also encouraged the Bani Sakhr to extend cultivation into new land. With his help, shaykh Haditha al-Khuraysha cultivated the oasis of Azraq and members of the Zaban tribe (probably their shaykhs) tilled land east of the railway.[79]

By the end of the 1930s land had once again become an important source of wealth for the Bani Sakhr shaykhs, if not their main source. Farming was a major occupation in which shaykhs invested both time and money. A Jewish agent who spent six months at Mithqal al-Fayiz's village described the shaykh as a keen and industrious landowner, involved in every aspect of the farm's operations. Besides Mithqal, shaykhs Muhammad bin Zuhayr and 'Awwad al-Mur also employed motor-driven ploughs on their land.[80]

Smaller tribes such as the Sirhan and 'Isa also benefited from Glubb's encouragement. In the middle of the 1930s he assigned them land on the eastern fringes of the settled zone and partitioned it among their kin groups. Consistent with his policy, Glubb paid special attention to shaykhly families in his campaign to persuade the nomads to take up cultivation. In 1934 he initiated the partition of the land of the Sirhan tribe in Sama among its extended families. Similarly, Mijhim bin Madi, shaykh of the 'Isa tribe, received land near the Syrian border, built wells and cultivated it.[81]

After difficulties in the first years cultivation gained ground and became an important element within the economy of the nomadic tribes.[82] By 1938 the British were able to report that the transition to cultivation was so successful that "not only every tribe but also every section of every tribe in Trans-Jordan has been put into possession of a certain amount of cultivation."[83] The mechanised ploughs of some of the shaykhs also facilitated cultivation of hitherto virgin soil. By 1940 it looked as if the cultivated zone was stretched to its limit, at least in the central part of the country. That year 25 Circassian families from Turkey applied for permission to settle in the country and asked to be given land around Amman. In response to inquiries from the Prime Minister's office, the Director of the Land Department reported that there was no more cultivated land available because "the only Government land near Amman is on the border of the desert and with recent years of good rainfall all the felaheen and bedouin are beginning to cultivate these areas."[84]

Immigration of Foreign Tribes

So successful was the project that foreign tribes soon followed suit, requesting and receiving land for cultivation. Thus, the settlement policy resulted in the immigration of several tribes into Transjordan. As early as 1939 the Sardiyya tilled land in the north of the country. Although these tribespeople had enjoyed grazing rights in northern Transjordan, they were considered Syrian. The process of settlement and encouragement of cultivation by the government drew them into Transjordan and they became citizens of the Emirate. Other Syrian tribes who settled in Transjordan after receiving land from the government were tribes or smaller units from the Masaᶜid, ᶜAdhamat, Sharafat and Zabid tribes of the Ahl al-Jabal confederacy, who left the Hawran and the Laja and settled in Transjordan around the mid-1940s.[85]

The following story sheds some light on the dynamics behind Syrian tribes' immigration into Transjordan. It also serves to show the process of tribe-formation in connection with settlement on the land, as well as the practice of becoming a shaykh. In 1939 the Arab Legion investigated a request made through Haditha al-Khuraysha by a certain Tuwayrish bin Hamid to receive land in Transjordan. He claimed that he was a shaykh of a Transjordanian tribe of 100 tents under the Bani Sakhr and asked to be given the land of al-Baᶜij. During the course of investigation it became clear, however, that he had no followers of his own and had come from Syria a few years earlier and was working as a guard for the ᶜIsa tribe. He approached tribesmen from al-Sharᶜa tribe of the al-Muzawida, who had come from Syria in order to graze in Transjordan and were camping with the Khuraysha. Tuwayrish suggested they team up in order to receive land from Glubb. He also seems to have exploited the existence of a small al-Sharᶜa tribe under the Khuraysha, to which he claimed affiliation, giving added currency to his claim for land. The discovery of the fraud notwithstanding, the officer concerned referred the possibility of granting Tuwayrish and his collaborators a piece of land to Glubb. The documents in the archives do not reveal Glubb's decision but a book on Jordanian tribes published in 1997 sheds light on this affair and its consequences today. Under the category of the Ahl al-Jabal tribes the author mentions a tribe that originated from al-Muzawida tribe. It goes on to say that "they settled down in the northern Jordanian desert a long time ago after shaykh Tuwayrish, the forefather of al-Muzawida tribe, emigrated from Syria and took up residence in the region of al-Nahda and al-Baᶜij in the governorate of al-Mafraq."[86] Tuwayrish was successful both in acquiring the land and the shaykhdom.

At least one Palestinian tribe settled in Transjordan during the same period. The Zinati tribe of the Ghazawiyya sold their land in the Bisan Valley to the Jewish Agency in 1938 and their shaykh asked to be allowed to settle in Transjordan. This was done in 1944 to the chagrin of the other two tribes of the Ghazawiyya who lived in Transjordan.[87]

Land and Social Change

For some tribesmen taking up cultivation brought about a significant social change, as they overcame their traditional negative attitude towards manual work. Already by 1935 Glubb reported on "many" of the Huwaytat who were personally engaged in tilling their land.[88] Manual work was despised by nomadic people and the peasant, the *fallah*, was considered by nomads to be inferior to them. In fact, the term *fallah* was a derogatory one. It is therefore indicative of a change of attitude that a member of the Sirhan chose to refer to himself as *fallah* in a petition to Glubb.[89] Still many nomads continued to refrain from manual labour, preferring to employ waged labour or sharecroppers. For example, the Khuraysha employed labourers from the neighbouring village of Sahab and Circassians from Wadi Sir. They continued their nomadic way of life, tending to their herds.

In this context it must be stressed that cultivation did not bring about the end of nomadism, nor was this the motive behind this policy. Nomads camped near their cultivated land during the sowing season and left it for their winter grazing areas only to return for the harvest in the following spring. As Glubb made clear, nomads were expert in breeding livestock, for which they were required to pursue a mobile way of life. Cultivation was meant to support this source of income, not replace it.[90]

The government continued to support the pastoral economy. Money from the CDF financed the construction of watering holes in the desert to improve grazing.[91] Glubb encouraged nomads to improve water resources on their land. In 1938 a lot of work was done in the desert; wells were dug, old Roman cisterns cleaned and even two drilled wells equipped with water pumps installed, one for the Bani Sakhr and the other for the Huwaytat. Most of the work was done by the tribesmen themselves, who received money to buy the required material like cement and lime. The digging of the wells increased the value of the areas east of the railway, which became grazing grounds for sheep and attracted *fallahin* from the nearby villages. Glubb indicated with satisfaction that this project won the appreciation of the tribesmen. Government assistance to the pastoral economy also came in the form of the administration of grazing in times of bad rainfall. In 1936 the government allowed nomads from the south to feed their flocks in the forests in Jabal ʿAjlun and in 1941 the Transjordanian authorities applied to the Palestine government to allow 1,500 camels to graze in Samaria.[92]

The Arab Legion as Final Arbitrator

The move towards cultivation on the eastern edges of the settled zone led to almost endemic disputes between the different tribes as well as among themselves. Glubb and his officers were kept busy restoring peace and once again state authorities became the final arbiters. Whenever possible, shaykhs were asked to solve the disputes. At the same time, however, the neutral position of the Arab Legion limited the ability of a shaykh to usurp the rights of other members of his tribe. In 1939 the Arab Legion dealt with several complaints against the main shaykh of the Sirhan tribes, Hindi bin Kaᶜaybar. According to one complaint, Glubb encouraged shaykh Hindi to dig wells and cultivate in al-Mughayyar. The plaintiffs from the Haqil tribe claimed that they had invested money and hard labour in preparing this virgin soil for cultivation, but then Hindi and his kin sowed it. A few months later an Arab Legion officer made peace between them. The settlement of the Jubur in Nuqayra by Glubb aroused the anger of the neighbouring Khuraysha of Muwaqqar who accused the newcomers of usurping 10 wells and 4,000 dunum of their land. A solution was found when the two disputing shaykhs agreed to the arbitration of their paramount shaykh.[93] Sometimes alternative land was given to compensate the losing party. In 1939 a serious dispute erupted between two tribes of the Bani Hasan, the Khawalda under shaykh ᶜUlyan al-Husayn and the ᶜAmush under shaykh Marzuq al-Qulab, after the latter trespassed their land in al-Juba. In order to prevent the two parties from clashing the Arab Legion first stopped Marzuq from ploughing the land and later Glubb gave him an alternative settlement.[94]

Settlement and the expansion of cultivation gave rise to land disputes between Transjordanian tribesmen and subjects and governments across the borders, the Syrian in particular. Although the border was demarcated in 1932, property rights remained unsolved for many years to come. In 1936 the Transjordanian government declared that recent cultivation in the area adjacent to the border did not constitute rights of ownership. It also forbade further tending of this area until a joint Syrian-Transjordanian committee could determine ownership rights. While Transjordanian and Syrian officials came to an agreement in 1940 the matter was not closed and Druze and nomadic cultivators continued to contest each other's rights. In another agreement police officers from Transjordan, Palestine and Sinai together with shaykh ᶜAwda bin Najjad of the Huwaytat in 1944 partitioned the disputed cultivated land of Wadi ᶜAraba between the Saᶜidiyyin and the Ihyawat.[95]

The nomadic tribes had no monopoly on the expansion of cultivation during the 1930s and 1940s. The prevalence of law and order and government encouragement drove townspeople and villagers to the fringes of the desert. Here they found jealous nomads who refused to relinquish their large *dira* or had just received land for cultivation from Glubb. One of the main bones of contention between nomads and old-time settlers was the fertile land of Jabal Shara west of Maᶜan. The region had been disputed between the Huwaytat and the inhabitants of Maᶜan prior to the establishment of the Emirate. Already in 1925, with the incorporation of Maᶜan into Transjordan, the Prime Minister declared the government's intention to solve the dispute (see Chapter Three). Nothing was done, however, and strong opposition from the Huwaytat meant that the land was left fallow. The people of Maᶜan continued to lobby for years to be allowed to cultivate the area and from time to time did manage to farm some of it. With the move of the Huwaytat to cultivation they also had to face Glubb, who on one occasion evicted them in order to allow the Huwaytat to cultivate this land.[96] In the north, the villagers of al-Tayba challenged the new settlers from the Sirhan in Sama in a series of quarrels from 1937, which necessitated the intervention of the Arab Legion. In 1943 Glubb established a temporary post of the Legion in Sama. Its two officers together with shaykh Haditha al-Khuraysha spent twenty days there, during which they determined the boundaries between the parties.[97]

Change in Patterns of Ownership

The two simultaneous processes of expanding cultivation and government attempts to control land culminated in 1945 in a unique agreement between the different tribes of the Bani Sakhr under the auspices of Glubb.[98] In the agreement the Bani Sakhr agreed to partition among themselves the land east of the settled zone on the fringe of the desert. Previously this land was part of the general *dira* of the confederacy, but the expansion of cultivation required regulating its ownership. The boundaries between each tribe were determined according to natural landmarks or by milestones. In a move to encourage private ownership, the agreement prescribed the allocation of land within each tribe's area to those who did not own land. This was to be done "under the supervision of the government and by the shaykhs."

Although the agreement shifted land control from the confederacy level to that of each individual tribe and even initiated the process of private ownership,[99] the confederacy still played an important role. First, the area further east was declared to be communal land for the Bani Sakhr, dedicated to grazing. It was therefore forbidden to till this land without government approval. Secondly, every member of the Bani Sakhr continued to enjoy grazing and residual rights in any uncultivated land within the areas now owned by each tribe.

The Bani Sakhr agreement represents a watershed in the development of land ownership among these tribes. Until then land was owned by shaykhs alone. The 1945 agreement formalised ownership rights at the tribal level and opened the door to private ownership. It is not clear, however, to what extent and when land was partitioned among the landless members of the different tribes, but there is evidence that at least some landless families did receive land.[100] It needs to be emphasised that on the whole the Bani Sakhr still refrained from tilling the land themselves, preferring to hire labourers to do so, usually under sharecropping arrangements. The pastoral economy remained the main occupation of tribesmen. The agreement also marked a deeper involvement of the government in tribal life and established it as the final arbiter of land use. As with many other aspects, this was done with the acceptance and active involvement of the shaykhs.

The Provision of Health and Education

From the mid-1930s state agencies offered a new range of services to large segments of the population. Most notable were developments in the spheres of health and education. For the nomadic tribes what began as Glubb's personal initiatives in the desert became, after a few years, institutionalised as the state expanded.

Vartan Amadouny demonstrates the slow development of health services during the 1930s and 1940s. Gradually, government hospitals and clinics expanded their capacities, both in terms of numbers of patients who could receive medical treatment and the range and quality of services. However, government ability was still limited and the private sector played the dominant role in providing health care. As shown by Musa, government-employed doctors represented a minority of practicing doctors in the country and the Italian hospital in Amman remained, until 1939, the only institution carrying out operations. It alone possessed a laboratory and x-ray equipment. Only in the following year did the government finally open a hospital in Amman suitable for surgery and with its own laboratory, but even then complicated cases had to be sent to Palestine, Syria and Lebanon. As Amadouny emphasises, the most valuable work was achieved in the field of preventive medicine. In 1940 the Department of Health initiated works in Amman to improve the quality of the water supply to the town. A government report mentioned the participation in the project of the tribesmen residing in the area. In a complementary measure the Department distributed anti-Malaria medicines free of charge.[101]

Even more impressive, however, was the establishment of a Desert Mobile Medical Unit in 1937, the result of constant pressure on the government from Glubb. Until then the Department of Health undertook only sporadic initiatives in the desert, such as treating nomads who contracted typhus and inoculation against smallpox. For modern medical treatment, however, tribespeople either had to travel to the sedentary areas or they were sent abroad by Glubb. For example, in 1934 he sent three tribesmen -- one of them the son of ʿAwda abu Taya -- to receive treatment at his own expense for tuberculosis in Lebanon.[102] The government decided to establish the Desert Mobile Medical Unit in response to the alarmingly high levels of tuberculosis and malnutrition among the nomads discovered in a survey initiated by Glubb and conducted by the medical officer of the Palestine Government. The new unit operated mobile clinics that followed the movements of the tribes as they migrated and focused on the treatment of tuberculosis. In 1937 and 1938 10,661 and 14,672 attendances were registered respectively.[103] More progress was made in 1939 when Glubb allocated a number of buildings for the use of the Unit, replacing tents and improving sanitation.[104]

Veterinary services and inspection were also available from the late 1930s. Municipalities and areas near the capital seem to have received most of the services. In 1939 the government started to enforce a new regulation prohibiting camels walking through and kneeling down in the streets of the towns, which was designed to improve public hygiene. In the al-Salt area the cows of the Rahamna and Ziyadat tribes of the ʿAbbad suspected of contracting foot-and-mouth disease were put under inspection. Nomadic areas also enjoyed veterinary services. In 1940 the head of the veterinary services spent a month and a half touring the south, including the desert areas and especially among the Huwaytat and the Nuʿaymat, whose goats had contracted a lung disease.[105]

As with health, the creation of an education system in the desert was initiated by Glubb. He financed it from his own pocket for several years before the government found the financial resources to assume formal responsibility. Glubb proposed building schools in late 1932. He reported that the idea had not been his, but that he was responding to requests by several fathers to found a school for their sons. Glubb emphasised that he was not a great supporter of the idea, but new circumstances forced this development. He claimed that the nomads themselves realised that, faced with the spread of literacy among the settled population and the creation of new posts for the educated people, they would not be able to compete in the near future and would fall behind. Glubb saw education as a means of opening new job opportunities for the nomads, especially during the years of economic crisis. He warned that "to educate townspeople and fellaheen, but not bedouins, is merely to condemn the latter to increasing and perpetual poverty and insignificance."[106]

A select few among the nomads received some education even before Glubb's initiative. The Bani Sakhr shaykh, Mithqal al-Fayiz, was keen to give his sons modern schooling. He sent one of them, Nawwas, to the Quaker school at Rumana, Lebanon, where the boy learned English alongside Arabic. Another son, ᶜAkif, was sent by his father to acquire general education and agricultural training. In later years Mithqal employed an *Azhar* graduate to teach his children.[107] At least one shaykh of the Bani Sakhr, Zaᶜal Kniᶜan al-Fayiz, could read and write.[108]

Without waiting for funds from the government, Glubb started a school in Azraq in 1933, initially for 14 soldiers of the Desert Patrol. One of the first recruits to the Desert Patrol, interviewed by Abu Diyya and Mahdi, recounted that the soldiers were encouraged to learn as a precondition for future promotion. In December 1933 Glubb reported that 45 boys and 30 soldiers were learning reading, writing and arithmetic in three schools attached to the desert forts at Azraq, Bayir and Mudawwara. The school in Azraq occupied an unfurnished mud brick building; the Mudawwara 'school' was a tent.

The modest beginning proved successful and in October 1934 the Department of Education assumed responsibility for two schools and relieved Glubb of the need to pay the teachers. He still paid for the schools in Bayir and a new one in Rum. There were 66 boys studying in these special schools in 1936 . The *Annual Report* presented to the League of Nations highlighted the success of the project, stating: "the two schools erected on desert wells in 1934… continue to prosper. So intelligent are these Beduin boys that it is proposed to commence training a class of them as wireless operators." It was apparent that most of the pupils were sons of shaykhs, and the aim behind educating them was to find new occupations for those who had been principally desert warriors and led raids in the past. In 1937 the desert schools were also officially reorganised. In Jafar a school for the Huwaytat and the other southern tribes was established. The Bani Sakhr and the northern tribes alternately used a school in Muwaqqar and the permanent school in Azraq according to migration movements. From 1937 onwards some 40-60 students participated in the classes. As late as 1938 Glubb still maintained students at his own expense.[109]

Assessing the project fifteen years after its commencement Glubb claimed only partial success. Owing to their nomadic lifestyles, it was impossible for parents to camp near the school for more than two or three months a year. Only small numbers would attend school regularly, most of them orphans or sons of soldiers. In 1937 Glubb reported on the difficulties of maintaining a school for the Bani

Sakhr, as the tribes migrated to Wadi Sirhan over the winter. Similarly, the Education Ministry reported that in the winter of 1941 the school in Jafar was forced to close due to an insufficient number of students. Such difficulties limited the scope of the education to reading, writing and elementary arithmetic. Any boy who had mastered long division was considered a graduate and discharged from school. The project of educating boys and soldiers was successful in the sense that the schools supplied the next generation of recruits for the Desert Patrol. A few years after the initiation of the scheme the Arab Legion was able to benefit from it. In 1939 Glubb reported with satisfaction that all clerical and office work in the desert area as well as mechanical work, was done by "pure Bedouin jundis" and he anticipated that very shortly all wireless operators would be of the same group.[110]

Despite the impressive progress in the desert, the education system represented one of the least developed sectors in Transjordan. Between 1922 and 1924 the government put a special effort into developing the education facilities inherited from the Ottoman and Faysali states. However, after the British administrative take-over in 1924 education received a low priority and although the system had grown, it did so at an extremely slow pace. As with health, until the early 1930s the private schools, both Islamic schools (*katatib*) and missionary schools, had the lion's share of pupils.[111] In 1927 the government partly incorporated the *katatib* when it required their teachers to apply for a license and put them under government supervision. In fact the *kuttab* was the most common form of schooling from the late Ottoman period as the improvement in security encouraged teachers and *imams* from neighbouring countries to settle in Transjordan. This form of traditional education was available not only in the towns and villages but also in tribal encampments. Shaykh Ibrahim al-Rashid testified that he was a pupil in a *kuttab* in Abu ʿAlanda, which served children from his tribe, the Hanitiyyin (Balqawiyya). He added that some of the children left their families during their seasonal migration in order not to interrupt their learning. According to another former pupil, a Palestinian shaykh taught children around Marka between 1924 and 1944 and even married a girl of the Daʿja tribes. Glubb himself, together with his wife, sponsored and supervised a private school in Amman for poor children from central and southern Transjordan from 1941 onwards. According to a former ʿAbbadi pupil, the Glubbs provided them with the stationary, weekly allowance and even boarding facilities.[112]

The state system was late to follow suit. According to Abu Nowar, a significant expansion of this sector, aided by an increase in the budget, began only in 1935. Still, as Amadouny shows, these schools served largely the ʿAjlun and Balqaʾ provinces and provided only an elementary education for children up to the age of 11. Secondary education remained undeveloped until the end of the mandate; the whole country possessed only one full secondary school in al-Salt.[113]

The expansion of the education system in the second half of the 1930s also benefited the semi-nomadic tribes. At the end of 1935 *Al-Urdunn* reported that the government decided to establish three schools dedicated to specific tribes in the Balqaʾ: the Bani Hamida, Ghunaymat and ʿAjarma. In 1938 the government established schools for the Bani Hasan and the Bani Hamida. In the following year

Al-Jazira reported that the government decided to open a school for the Bani Hasan in Rahhab.[114] But this provision was not sufficient to educate all children. One or two schools for a large tribal confederacy like the Bani Hasan, with around 15,000 members, could not be more than a drop in the ocean.

It is likely that government neglect combined with an initial lack of public demand contributed to the late development of the education sector. The Minister of Education reported that until 1930 demand for education was insignificant and that schools had to resort to inflicting fines on parents who did not send their children to school. He pointed to a change a year later when 100 pupils registered in Amman but only half were accepted.[115] A change of attitude and popular demand for education was recorded in an *Al-Urdunn* article published in 1930 entitled "The Education Renaissance (*nahda*) in al-Karak." According to the article, the people of Karak demanded from the government their fair share in education. The Department of Education responded by opening a secondary school in 1928. This was so well-received that two years later 15 students from Karak were completing their secondary education in al-Salt and others in Jerusalem and elsewhere. The author was astonished that this renaissance had been taking place where people still lived in tents in the desert and expressed his hope that these young graduates would shortly lead their tribes into civilisation.[116] Glubb's report on the request from fathers to provide their sons with education and Mithqal al-Fayiz's insistence on formal education for his sons further suggest that ten years after the establishment of Transjordan a change in attitude towards the merits of education had occurred.

During the 1930s and 1940s demand exceeded the government schools' ability to accommodate pupils. In the academic years 1937/8 and 1938/9 around half of the applicants had to be rejected or deferred.[117] Although student numbers increased and many villages had a school, state officials expressed their uneasiness at the education sector's insufficiency. Abdullah expressed his anger in an interview in 1937 and the Minister of Education reported in 1943 that that system could not absorb some 6,000 additional students.[118]

Faced with poor education at home, pupils from wealthy families and the few recipients of scholarships received their education in Palestine or Syria. Some of them also obtained university degrees. In 1944 over one hundred students studied in Egyptian colleges or universities. A few of the very best graduates of al-Salt school were sent by the government to study at the two American universities in Beirut and Cairo or at Damascus University. Abu Nowar lists 27 students who obtained university degrees in the 1930s. Some of them became senior political figures in independent Jordan, including two Prime Ministers: Sulayman al-Nabulsi and Wasfi al-Tall.[119]

The spread of education had a substantial impact on the political and social life of the country. The increasing number of educated young men, combined with the enlargement of state bodies, within which the majority of them were absorbed, created a new avenue for social mobility. Consequently, a young educated elite emerged to challenge the shaykhly families. As Abu Nowar asserts, during the second half of the 1930s "a new generation of politically minded young Trans-Jordanians emerged as a direct result of the spread of education and political awareness."[120] Inspired by their teachers from Palestine, Syria and Lebanon, and impressed by events across the Jordan, secondary-school students led nationalist activity. During the Palestine revolt, the students of al-Salt high school were particularly vocal and caused persistent annoyance to the government and to Abdullah until it was decided to send all ninth and tenth-graders home. In Transjordan, as in Iraq, secondary schools became the bedrock of nationalist activity in the inter-war period.[121]

But the educated men's modern outlook and nationalist inclination did not lead to open opposition to the political establishment. Firstly, the group was very small and thus limited in its ability to bring about a radical change. Abu Nowar lists around 60 members of what he terms "intellectual elite" and suggests another 300 politically-minded teachers, professionals, civil servants and merchants who supported this elite.[122] Secondly, upon graduation from school or university, many took up positions in the administration or became officers in the Arab Legion. As the majority were absorbed into the state apparatus they tended to accept the basic precepts of the emerging state rather then challenge them. According to Abu Nowar, they satisfied themselves with "nagging" the government rather than rebelling against it. Indeed, although these circles continued to take part in nationalist activity and expressed opposition to the British, on the whole they were successfully co-opted into the Transjordanian 'political field.' In this respect, it seems that Abdullah's personality played an important role. Just as he felt comfortable sitting in a Bedouin tent with tribal shaykhs, he succeeded in embracing the young intellectuals and drawing them closer to him. Similar to his tribal *diwan*s, Abdullah held literary gatherings, where he easily led discussions on Arabic poetry, theology or Arab nationalism. In addition, the two Amman newspapers, *Al-Urdunn* and *Al-Jazira*, served as a platform for these intellectuals to publish their works and conduct literary debates with the active participation of the Emir, who would occasionally exchange verses of poetry with these young men.[123]

But this group did not confine itself to writing poems and soon became a political elite that could compete with and even challenge the old guard of tribal shaykhs and notables. According to Musa's analysis, this group formed the second generation of the Jordanian political elite after independence. Musa observes that the majority of these men, though hailing from tribal backgrounds, did not represent the shaykhly families but rather the middle ranks of their tribes.[124] According to Abu Nowar, their influence derived from a combination of factors: their education, tribal affiliation, wealth and position in the government. It seems that this final factor was the most important one. As the government increased its intervention in society, the civil service became increasingly important in allocating resources and controlling daily life. Tribal shaykhs had to go through senior civil servants to arrange their expanding affairs with the government.

The Effect of State-Formation on the Tribes
As the political, military and economic dominance of the state grew, tribal society was relegated to a position of dependence on the government. Moreover, tribes and more particularly the tribal confederacies, lost much of their *raison d'être* as many of their functions were gradually assumed by state agencies. Security, livelihood, conflict

resolution and even health and education now became available without recourse to the tribal framework. Tribes, however, did not disappear. On the contrary, tribal organisation, identity and ethos remained the main features of society. The persistence of tribal life and social structure, albeit in a modified way, resulted in part from policies undertaken by state authorities, which found it easier and cheaper to control society indirectly. This was achieved by keeping the tribe as the basic administrative unit and ruling it via recognised shaykhs, thus upholding and securing their special status. This was especially true in the desert but was even the practice in the settled zone where the government's position was more secure. The government ruled through the shaykhs, not in place of them, and continued to delegate responsibility for maintaining law and order, collecting taxes, settling disputes and distributing state largesse. Shaykhs thus remained the main link between the central government and the population, maintaining their relevance as important political actors even as the powers of the central government increased.

Changes in Social Organisation

As state agencies stepped up their intervention in social affairs and assumed many of the functions of security and welfare previously provided within the tribal unit, the institution of the chieftaincy increasingly became something of an anachronism. Growing struggles within the large two nomadic confederacies from the latter half of the 1930s indicate the loss of cohesion and a parallel shift towards smaller organisational units. These were the first symptoms of the break-up of the chieftaincy into tribes.

In the late 1930s the two nomadic confederacies, the Bani Sakhr and the Huwaytat, witnessed growing struggles between rival shaykhs. Competition for leadership had always featured prominently in tribal society. The establishment of a political alliance between Emir Abdullah and the confederacies, combined with state recognition of their leaders, had the effect of institutionalising the position of the two paramount shaykhs. Their leadership was secured against potential rivals in a way their predecessors could never have imagined. There is no evidence of a serious challenge to their leadership before the late 1930s. After that time, both Mithqal al-Fayiz and Hamad bin Jazi faced growing strains within their respective confederacies.

The power struggle among the Bani Sakhr erupted in 1937 when the shaykhs of the Zaban tribe gathered fully armed with their men in what was described as a demonstration against Mithqal. It took a strong force of the Desert Patrol to prevent a clash between the two parties. The issue at stake was a long-standing dispute over a piece of land, which came to a head because Mithqal involved the civil governor in a case which could have been settled internally by tribal custom.[125] Mithqal's authority was challenged on the basis that he was too closely identified with the government, thus compromising his people's interests and traditions. By this time, it seems, Mithqal's position in the confederacy increasingly relied on his connections with the government rather than his personal prestige and moral authority. The indifference of the Bani Sakhr to his brief arrest in 1941 after assaulting the Prime Minister is evidence of his decreased support. On this occasion only his immediate kin from the Fayiz tribe rallied around him.[126] Glubb's repeated observations on Mithqal's unpopularity and his limited influence in the desert further corroborate this point.[127]

Similar conflicts occurred among the Huwaytat, starting with the election in 1937 for the Legislative Council. Muhammad abu Taya, shaykh of the Tawayha, bid for the seat reserved for the Huwaytat by challenging Hamad bin Jazi, who had been elected to the previous three Councils. Hamad kept his seat in a close race, but tension among the shaykhs did not subside. Glubb reported that he "has never seen among the Trans-Jordan Bedouin such intense dissatisfaction as was evident after the 'election' five weeks ago. Several of the shaikhs seemed much nearer revolt as a result of the elections than they were during the Palestine rebellion in 1936."[128] In 1939 Abdullah brokered a peace between the two shaykhs and their respective branches of the confederacy, and a further attempt to mollify Muhammad was made a year later when Abdullah granted him the title *Pasha*.[129] However, these actions did not unify the Huwaytat as a confederacy. Rather, they were recognition of the importance of Muhammad abu Taya and the independence of the Tawayha from the Huwaytat. Moreover, Ahmad ʿUwaydi al-ʿAbbadi, who also identifies this trend among the Huwaytat, reports that in later years Hamad's parliamentary seat continued to be contested, albeit unsuccessfully, by Muhammad abu Taya and ʿAwda bin Najjad, shaykh of al-Sulaymaniyyin.[130]

To a large extent these rivalries reflected the weakening of the confederacy vis-à-vis the central government and the replacement of many of its functions by state agencies. With the enlargement of the Arab Legion the government was no longer dependent on the tribes as independent military forces, as it had been during the 1920s. Moreover, the loss of their best warriors and leaders to the Legion drained the chieftaincies of their power, and they could no longer mount an armed challenge. Another important reason for the weakening of the chieftaincies was the loss of their mobility as increasing numbers of tribesmen engaged in farming. Beyond its military weakness the chieftaincy was less relevant as a framework for collective security. Law and order in the desert and along the borders made the chieftaincy redundant as a guarantor of its members' personal security and rights.

The decline of the chieftaincy was accelerated by economic factors. The increased security of the countryside combined with the experience of the drought and the enlargement of the Arab Legion shifted tribesmen into new occupational pursuits. Having learnt their lesson from the difficult years of the 1930s, for many sheep-rearing took the place of camel-herding. The new conditions favoured the creation of larger flocks that could be built up more quickly than herds of camels. The tendency towards sheep-rearing and the development of water sources within the deserts also brought about a change in migration patterns. As camel herds shrank and water became available nearer to the settled zone, tribespeople had less need for access to large Arabian winter pastures. The Bani Sakhr, for example, resorted less and less to migrating to the Wadi Sirhan, confining themselves to the limited frontiers of Transjordan. These changing patterns of migration had a direct effect on the need for chieftaincies or even individual tribes to provide security. Herders were no longer required to move and camp in large groups as a precaution against raids. Families and small herding units moved freely to such grazing areas as they could find.[131] The availability of new sources of income further contributed to the decline of the chieftaincy as many tribesmen began to earn their livelihood independently of the tribal unit, working casually for the government in public works or permanently as soldiers.

The fragmentation of the tribal system was most evident among the nomads, who underwent the greatest social change, but settled tribes were not insulated. The disintegration of the Balqa' alliance has already been mentioned in Chapter Two. A change in organisation among tribespeople in al-Salt, which occurred in 1940, provides another example of this trend. Until that year al-ʿAnansa tribe had been in alliance with another tribe, al-Khalifat. With the increase in law and order this alliance was deemed redundant and the two tribes separated, each with its own *mukhtar*.[132]

The Changing Role of Shaykhs

In spite of creeping signs of the disintegration of the confederacies and growing attempts from within to challenge their position, shaykhs retained and even strengthened their ascendance within their tribes. Several factors accounted for their success. One was the continued importance of shaykhly status in tribal society. Another was the effectiveness of the shaykhs' own efforts to resist the encroachment of the government and to safeguard their influence and autonomy. The resilience of their position also owed much to a state policy, which preferred to control the population via recognised shaykhs, thereby upholding and even reinforcing their traditional status.

Beneath the surface of apparent stability, however, the nature of paramount shaykhs as well as shaykhs of individual tribes changed dramatically. Their legitimacy now derived less from the recognition of their moral authority by fellow tribesmen and more from their status as the exclusive representatives of their tribes vis-à-vis the central government. The expansion of government necessitated this change, requiring their intervention in the various government departments on behalf of their people. Glubb's comment on Mithqal in 1940 illustrates this point. He attributed Mithqal's newly accumulated wealth to his influence in the government, which allowed him to exact payment from litigants in return for settling cases in their favour.[133] Mithqal and other shaykhs were no longer leaders of independent and autonomous communities, but go-betweens for these communities and the state authorities. Shaykhs were thus increasingly entwined into the state structure and identified with its interests.

This new role brought about a change in the shaykhs' lifestyle and their relations with their fellow tribespeople as it required them to re-locate their centre of activity to the capital. Many rented or purchased houses in Amman and increasingly spent more time there than with their tribesmen. Mithqal al-Fayiz already owned a house in Amman in 1928 and by the mid-1930s was reported to be there more often than at his desert palace or in a tent among his people. Majid al-ʿAdwan owned a house in the capital from at least 1938.[134] Residence in Amman was also essential for members of the Legislative Council. From the seat of government the shaykhs could better represent the interests of their tribes. Here they were assisted by Abdullah, who granted them free access to his *diwan* and intervened with his ministers on their behalf.

Land became the shaykhs' main source of income and as such was an important factor binding them both to Abdullah, a landowner himself since the early 1930s, and the landowning merchants. During the early 1930s the large landowners emerged as an active political elite. Shared concern for land issues, their economic difficulties, their political support for the Emir and their attempts to fend off government interference cemented relations between the different members of this group and contributed to its coherence. They co-operated in the Legislative Council to press the government to offer aid to cultivators, reduce land taxes, limit the powers of the Arab Legion, and prevent government control over land rights. Many also promoted Jewish immigration into Transjordan.

In fact, the shaykhs were increasingly part of a form of 'politics of notables,' from which they had been excluded during Ottoman rule, when Transjordan languished on the periphery of the empire. With the establishment of a political centre in Amman, shaykhs operated within and spoke the language of the Transjordanian 'political field,' particularly when they were competing for newly-available state resources. The debate over the *baladiyyat* analysed by Reimer clearly illustrates this discursive development. Reimer shows how, in their attempt to persuade the government to establish or keep the municipal administration, notables quickly adopted the language of modernity, progress and even nationalism, which had circulated among government and urban elite circles outside Transjordan since the Ottoman reforms were launched in the mid nineteenth century. In doing so, their language and argumentation differed from that of the commoners. The latter viewed the *baladiyya* as a tool for the already prominent elements in society to increase their control over them to a degree of despotism.[135]

With their growing involvement in state activity, the shaykhs' position became increasingly ambivalent. On the one hand, they were closely integrated into the state, serving as state officials, performing tasks for state agencies and maintaining contact with Abdullah. Many became dependent on the central government for salaries, appointments as judges in tribal courts or benefits such as agricultural subsidies or handouts. On the other hand, the shaykhs were anxious to maintain a degree of autonomy and independence from the central government. But keeping the central government at arm's length proved all the more difficult given the extent of their collaboration with and dependence on it. The shaykhs sitting on the Legislative Council epitomised this problem. Their support was necessary for legislation allowing the government to pursue its programme, although they resented the loss of their autonomy and the government's tendency to interfere in their lives. While in most instances shaykhs approved the legislation, they nevertheless expressed frustration at their inability to place checks on the government.[136]

Shaykhs employed several strategies to overcome this dilemma and keep central authority at bay. Many cultivated good relations with foreign (and sometimes hostile) regional powers. By defying state authorities and playing off different actors against each other, the shaykhs could secure greater autonomy and influence. Foreign patrons served as negotiating tools against Abdullah or the government, thereby increasing the shaykhs' leverage vis-à-vis the state authorities. These contacts were also used as an insurance policy in case a severe conflict arose between them and the Transjordanian government.

The connections between shaykhs and the Jewish Agency partly served this purpose, representing another means to overcome their impoverishment during the early 1930s and to retain some independence of action. Members of this group openly defied the British Resident Henry Cox, the OC of the Arab Legion F. G. Peake and Glubb, all of whom fiercely opposed Jewish colonisation.[137] In 1934 the leader of this group, Mithqal al-Fayiz, turned down a British offer for a loan to relieve his financial difficulties. As Cox explained, Mithqal preferred to rely on the financial support he received from the Jews rather than submit his property to the control of the government.[138] In this way, he used his contacts with the Jewish Agency to protect his political autonomy and improve his financial situation without becoming too dependent on the government.

Support for Palestinian or Syrian rebels did not entail direct financial gain, though it enhanced the shaykhs' moral authority and could improve their bargaining power vis-à-vis the government. In a period that witnessed sweeping changes in the functions of the tribes, the shaykhs were obliged to redefine their role. A show of support for Arab nationalism and defiance of the British, the government, or even occasionally Abdullah, demonstrated the independent power of the shaykh. Opposition was also a way of reminding state authorities that they could not take the tribes' acquiescence for granted. The resumption of subsidies to shaykhs during the Palestinian revolt shows the effectiveness of this tactic.

Similarly, several shaykhs nurtured close relations with the Saudis. Muhammad abu Taya of the Huwaytat was the object of Saudi enticements in 1934. Glubb feared that the shaykh's extreme poverty might lead him to transfer allegiance to the Saudis and so supported him financially. In 1936 the Saudi governor of Jawf, close to the Transjordanian border, exerted pressure on the Huwaytat to immigrate to Saudi Arabia. Shaykh Zaᶜal bin Mutlaq abu Taya visited Jawf and was reported to have received a handsome sum of money from the governor as well as promises of regular salary and cultivable land in Saudi Arabia.[139] These promises seem never to have moved beyond the stage of negotiation.

Mithqal al-Fayiz turned the exploitation of his contacts with Ibn Saud into a fine art. He used these connections to enhance his position with the Emir, who was clearly annoyed by the association of his arch rival and his protégé. Good relations with the Saudi court were kept up through marital ties between Ibn Saud and Mithqal's kinsman Dahham bin Bakhit, who was a member of the King's household. When in 1937 Mithqal and Abdullah fell out with each other over the former's involvement in Palestine, Mithqal reacted by starting negotiations with the Saudi government to move into its territory.[140] In 1940 the Transjordanian authorities intercepted a secret correspondence between Mithqal and Ibn Saud. Glubb could not clearly establish the reason for Mithqal's contact with the King, but suspected that it was intended to provide him with leverage in relation to Abdullah.[141] When in subsequent years Mithqal was at loggerheads with the government and Abdullah, speculation was raised about his departure to Saudi Arabia. It seems that in 1943 he actually spent several months there until affairs calmed down. Another shaykh of the Bani Sakhr, Haditha al-Khuraysha, also went into temporary exile following his defiance of Abdullah and the British; he instructed his people who served in the Legion to abstain from suppressing Rashid ᶜAli's revolt in Baghdad in 1941.[142]

By striking a balance between collaboration and resistance, shaykhs were successful in preserving their special position of leadership. Commissioned by state authorities to act as go-betweens the government and their communities, granted official positions, titles, subsidies and assistance in cultivating their land, the tribal shaykhs managed to preserve their social status and privileged economic position in spite of the momentous changes happening around them. Many became rich in the late 1930s and in the 1940s when the economic situation improved. They consolidated their power by occasionally defying the central government or playing off different internal and external actors against each other. They continued to command respect and influence among their tribes and played an important political role at the national level. The shaykhly families who dominated the country in 1921 continued to be prominent throughout the mandate period. And when the end of the mandate coincided with a changing of the guard among some of the most senior tribal leaders, these families managed to keep the leadership positions within their immediate families. Thus, with Rufayfan al-Majali's death in 1945 his son Maᶜarik inherited his seat in the Legislative Council and the title of *Pasha*. A year later, following Majid al-ᶜAdwan's death, Abdullah conferred the title of the paramount shaykh of the Balqa' on his elder son, Hamud. Also in 1946 ᶜAkif al-Fayiz, who was by that time gradually replacing his ageing father in his public duties as paramount shaykh of the Bani Sakhr, was appointed by Abdullah to be the Head of Protocol for Tribes in the palace.[143] The shaykhs and their sons thus became an important part of the Transjordanian elite and developed a stake in the existence and survival of the Emirate.

Transjordan as a Tribal State

What is remarkable about the expansion of state capacity and its far reaching consequences for shaykhs and ordinary tribespeople is how smoothly the process proceeded. Two factors seem to have eased society's acceptance of the new situation and contributed to the tribespeople's successful integration into the state. Although towards the end of the mandate Transjordan had already acquired many traits of a modern state, many aspects of tribal life and culture survived. This was facilitated by a change in British attitudes towards ruling the country evident by the late 1930s. A classical colonial philosophy gave way to one more sympathetic to indigenous methods of politics and to increased local participation in administrative affairs.

Abdullah's conduct goes a long way towards explaining the persistence of a tribal ethos in Transjordan. A journalistic description of Abdullah from 1941 showed that he had changed his behaviour very little since arriving in Transjordan twenty years earlier: "Unlike his younger brother, the late King Feisal, The Emir has retained his Arab dress and his Arab way of life. He is also a typical Arab in his love of horses, and knows the pedigree of every brood mare belonging to his tribesmen."[144] Indeed, Abdullah continued to extol tribal culture and values, was careful to observe tradition and project the image of a tribal leader. He spent much time camping in the desert and exchanged gifts and tribal hospitality with his subjects when calling on tribal shaykhs or hosting them in his palace or winter camp. He also participated in popular pastimes such as horse races and shooting competitions. He even wrote a book on pedigree Arab horses.[145] This behaviour was not only in keeping with customs of sociability but also a deliberate political strategy. Abdullah maintained a chieftaincy-like political system based on close personal relations, an open-door policy, mediation (*wasta*) and, much to the chagrin of the government and the British, a show of leniency when possible. The increased responsibilities assumed by state agencies made his interventions ever more important for smoothing out differences between government officials and the population.

Beyond their place in Abdullah's political manoeuvrings, cultural traits like hospitality and mediation remained important symbols of shaykhly legitimacy. Indeed, shaykhs were all but expected to perform these tasks, for which they often gained the praise of the local newspapers. Majid al-ʿAdwan took it upon himself to cater for the tribesmen who came to Amman during the state visit of the Saudi Crown Prince in 1935. *Al-Urdunn* expressed its gratitude and admiration for Majid's ability to accommodate a seemingly endless number of guests.[146] On another occasion, the paper gave a detailed account of a party given by Mithqal al-Fayiz for the marriage of two of his sons. It was reported to be the biggest such party ever held and Mithqal's generosity was commended.[147]

Similarly, conflict resolution through respected mediators continued to be desired both by the government and the public. For example, the governor of Jabal ʿAjlun, together with local notables, restored the peace among members the al-Mu'mina tribe in the village of ʿIblin after a shooting incident. The local press continuously reported cases of successful reconciliation according to tribal tradition, such as between the different tribes of the Ghazawiyya, or two prominent families in al-Salt, or between the Bani Hamida and the inhabitants of Madaba.[148] *Al-Urdunn* even called on the *qaimaqam* of Madaba to reconcile the disputing al-Wundiyyin and al-Haddadin. Shaykhs who brokered disputes were commended by the press. Again, *Al-Urdunn* reported on the visit to Tafila of the mayor of Maʿan, shaykh Hamad al-Sharari, in order to solve conflicts among the town's different tribes, dubbing him "the big leader and peace maker." *Al-Jazira* reported on the arrival of Hamad bin Jazi, Rufayfan al-Majali and Haditha al-Khuraysha in Amman to settle a dispute between Mithqal al-Fayiz and ʿAdub al-Zaban.[149]

This persistence of tribal practices in politics and conflict resolution was facilitated by a change in British attitudes towards the administration of the country that also coincided with the retirement of an older generation of administrators. At the height of the state's expansion in 1939, both the British Resident Cox and Commander Peake retired, to be replaced by Alec Kirkbride and John Glubb. Cox and Peake were known for their paternal and bureaucratic attitude and tried to maintain tight control over Transjordan. In contrast, Kirkbride and Glubb took a much more relaxed attitude. They appreciated and respected local conditions more than their predecessors and took advantage of indigenous practices of government. This new approach also reflected greater sympathy for local people and their customs. A letter from High Commissioner Harold MacMichael to the Secretary of State on the eve of the negotiations to amend the Anglo-Jordanian treaty, written just before Kirkbride took office, articulated the change in attitude of British officials in Jerusalem and Amman. It also showed the enthusiastic support of the High Commissioner for a different approach. It was no coincidence that MacMichael was the only high commissioner who knew Arabic.

MacMichael started by criticising the general British tendency to impose Western models of government on the colonies with their emphasis on efficiency and bureaucratic procedures, and proceeded to question their suitability for the local culture and conditions. Instead he recommended keeping to Western notions of justice, order and financial probity while implementing "eastern" characteristics of more lenient government. To support his argument he even invoked the prescription for good government given by the fourteenth-century Arab historian Ibn Khaldun. Turning to the situation in Transjordan, the High Commissioner lamented the excessive financial controls placed on the Emir and his ministers, and suggested that the jurisdiction of the Tribal Court Law be widened to include tribes beyond the ones specified in the Law. Without making any specific recommendation, he called for some degree of "decentralisation, devolution" and relaxation of the "rigidity of bureaucracy." He further explained that his aim in putting forward these recommendations was "to check any tendency towards the idealisation of the bowler hat, on the ground that the 'Kaffiyeh' and the 'Agal' are better suited to this climate."[150]

The Anglo-Transjordanian treaty of 1939, which represented a step towards self-government, seems to have been one result of this new thinking. Other manifestations of this policy of laissez-faire included the increase in Abdullah's civil list from 1940, the decision to make him the proper channel for distributing subsidies to shaykhs, and even a more sympathetic approach towards the granting of pardons following the payment of blood-money and the restoration of peace between former antagonists.[151]

Conclusion

By the end of the mandate in 1946 the tribes were fully integrated into the state and played an indispensable role in it. Thousands of tribesmen served in the Arab Legion, while others owned and cultivated land, often with government help. They enjoyed healthcare and veterinary services and their sons and occasionally daughters were educated in state schools. Tribal shaykhs became officials of the state. Many were rich and influential, could mediate for their kin in government circles and remained the prime interface between the government and their fellow tribesmen. Shaykhs themselves belonged to a state elite cultivated and organised by Abdullah. Moreover, many aspects of tribal life continued to prevail and were respected, if not actively encouraged, by the government.

To a large extent, the persistence of the tribes as political actors was permitted by the mandatory authorities and Abdullah, in order to gain their acquiescence in a process they could not stop but could almost certainly disrupt. Tribes, though much less tribal confederacies, remained the most prominent form of social and political organisation. The legal system continued to be based on customary law. Almost every adult continued to carry a weapon. And the culture and ethos of the country was mainly tribal, embodied in no less a figure than Abdullah himself, who cultivated the image of a Bedouin *par excellence* and remained deeply engaged in tribal politics until the end of the mandate period. The long-term implications of this smooth integration of tribes and tribal culture form the subject of the concluding chapter.

CONCLUSION:
TOWARDS AN APPRAISAL OF THE
MANDATE'S LEGACY IN JORDAN

This book has explored the ways in which tribes were integrated into the state structure, tracing the development of the Transjordanian mandatory state. This line of inquiry offers several conclusions and points of comparison for the understanding of state-formation, colonialism and tribal societies in Jordan and elsewhere. It also helps explain later developments in Jordan, even up to the present day.

State, Tribe, and Mandate

One major conclusion of this study is that the process of state-formation in Transjordan need not be seen as a zero-sum interaction in which the central government gradually expanded its capability at the expense of the tribe's autonomy, identity and relevance as a political and social unit. On the contrary, tribes were active participants in the process of state-formation. They influenced its course and developed a clear stake in its success. For their part, state authorities constantly had to negotiate their policies with the tribes. They frequently had to modify these policies, or sometimes withdraw them altogether, in the face of opposition. Abundant examples demonstrate that shaykhs and their tribes exerted leverage vis-à-vis the central government. In this way, the relations between tribe and government represented a form of partnership, or even symbiosis. It was this negotiated relationship that allowed for the relatively smooth integration of tribes into the state structure.

This observation becomes even more significant when comparing state-tribe relations in Jordan with other newly-created Middle Eastern states. Such comparison reveals that Transjordan stood in marked contrast to the experiences of Iraq, Palestine, Syria and Saudi Arabia, where the common result was the coercive and violent subjugation of the tribes accompanied by their political, economic, and cultural marginalisation. In Jordan tribes were successfully integrated into the state. This was accomplished with a relatively low level of violence or coercion. It also allowed for a more gradual and less painful transition into the era of the modern nation state. This was particularly true for the nomads. As their traditional sources of income dried up after World War One, employment in the Arab Legion, the development

148

of cultivation on the fringe of the desert and the encouragement of the pastoral economy helped to offset their losses. In the process they acquired the means to enhance their social mobility and become an integral part of the national political field. The preservation, with modifications, of tribal codes and conventions, as well as the basic structure of the social order, further eased the transition.

The unique effect of the state-formation process on the tribes owed much to the nature of British rule in Transjordan. Contrary to the impression given by the British sources, and from much of the earlier literature written on the mandate period, Britain was not as powerful as it appeared. In looking at the lower level of politics and social hierarchy, and especially at tribal society and its leaders -- and in examining a broader range of the source material -- the limits of British control are all too apparent. This conclusion goes against the image of the colonial state as an all-powerful and intrusive body captured by the Hobbesian metaphor of the leviathan, which dominated colonial studies until recently. It also contradicts the more recent depiction of colonialism in much of the post-colonial literature, including that which examines the Middle East. This outlook often prefers to see colonialism as a totalising force seeping into and transforming every aspect of colonised societies. By exaggerating the role of the coloniser this approach, moreover, tends to depict local societies as docile and obedient, lacking agency to shape their lives. Timothy Mitchell's *Colonizing Egypt* and Joseph Massad's *Colonial Effects* come immediately to mind.[1]

Colonial rule in Transjordan was very different. During the first decade after the establishment of the Emirate the British failed to expand the control of the central government in Amman over much of the rural area. But even with the consolidation of state power starting in the mid-1930s, Britain's power was not absolute. British officials had to rely on Abdullah's acquiescence and were forced to placate rather than subdue their tribal opponents. They were unable to implement all their policies. The lack of efficient arms control, the avoidance of the census, the unwanted results of land policy and their defeats in the Legislative Council indicate that in ruling Transjordan the British did not always get their way and that local society was not changed unrecognisably. These observations corroborate the recent trend in British Imperial history to re-evaluate the strength of the colonial state. An up-to-date understanding stresses the weakness of the state, the limitations of its British rulers to enforce their policies, as well as significant historical continuities with the pre-colonial era.[2]

In the Jordanian case, perhaps paradoxically, it was this very weakness of the British that facilitated what was probably Britain's most successful state-building project in the Middle East. British rule was limited in its scope and ambition to bring about a transformation of local society. Britain's laissez-faire approach in Transjordan favoured more independent local development, allowing the tribes to be gradually enmeshed into the state through ties of mutual interest. In fact, in Jordan the colonial system worked. Unlike in its other possessions under direct responsibility, Britain's rule in Jordan did not face the major challenge of an all-out rebellion, such as those in Iraq, Egypt or Palestine (as well as Syria under French mandate). And, if compared with the protected Gulf shaykhdoms, in Jordan Britain achieved much more than a regional hegemony along a narrow coastal line where there was no real interference in internal affairs. In Jordan Britain established and moulded the modern state, which had an enormous effect on the entire population. Moreover, ruling the country required relatively low investment in finance, manpower and military presence.

Several factors existed in Transjordan, which were not always present elsewhere, and which allowed for less troubled relations between the coloniser and the colonised than in more typical colonial settings. In Transjordan Britain benefited from the service of skilled and experienced officials, whose accumulative local knowledge allowed them to make the most of their philosophy of indirect imperial rule. In Jordan the British also found two willing elements with which to share power: tribal shaykhs and Emir Abdullah. The shaykhs were willing to collaborate with the British, as long as their interests and those of their tribes were respected. In a society where tribal solidarities were still strong, they enjoyed considerable influence among their constituencies and could facilitate the government's rule. This situation was very different from the one in Iraq, where the British artificially tried to strengthen the shaykhs' control over their constituencies, at times reviving bygone tribal identities or inventing new ones altogether.[3] The main pillar of British rule in Transjordan, however, was Abdullah. Over time the British learned to appreciate the Emir, who became a loyal and co-operative ally. This was also due to his dependence on the British for his position; co-operation was therefore a pragmatic strategy for both sides. By his moral authority, his understanding of local society and long experience as a tribal leader, Abdullah helped them govern, to an extent, even the most unruly tribes roaming deep in the deserts. Britain thus ruled the tribes -- and therefore Transjordan -- via Abdullah at least until the end of the 1920s. Further factors also eased British rule in Jordan, distinguishing it from other colonial settings: a small and homogeneous population, the existence of a very small educated urban population (the sector of the population potentially most inclined towards anti-colonial nationalism), and a low level of economic development. All these characteristics contributed to the successful implementation of the British philosophy of indirect rule.

The new polity clearly benefited from the legacy of its imperial predecessor. The Ottomans left behind policies for dealing with tribal populations that were adopted by Abdullah and the British. Indeed, there were few differences between the Ottoman and British-Hashemite regimes, at least until the late 1920s. The main departure from the Ottoman era was the state penetration into the desert at the beginning of the 1930s and the thoroughness of the tribespeople's integration into the state. Still, many old features of state policy towards the tribes remained, such as encouragement for the nomads to settle and take up agriculture, minimum intervention in tribal life, and the policy of granting state recognition to tribal chiefs. Therefore the transition from Ottoman rule to the Hashemite state was marked by important continuities.

State-building should not be confused with nation-building, however. The outcome of this process in Transjordan was not the creation of a nation of Transjordanians.[4] Tribal, regional and religious affiliations remained the main idiom of self-definition. For the young and educated, Arab nationalism had much appeal but it overlay the 'traditional' identities rather than replaced them. In fact, very little attempt to create national consciousness was made by the local elite or the central government. The British were careful not to encourage nationalism, seeing it as the main threat to their position and that of their clients. For Abdullah, Transjordan was not a final destination but a base from which he hoped to extend his rule. He wished to be the king of Syria, and, as such, he had no interest in promoting a specifically Transjordanian nationalism. In the end he had to settle for Transjordan and parts of Palestine. Jordanian nationalism developed much later and in the context of the incorporation of the Palestinian population into the country (see below).

Abdullah's historical figure, as it emerges from this study, is considerably revised in comparison with much of the earlier literature. Although Abdullah's dependence on the British limited his room for manoeuvre, he still exerted significant influence over domestic affairs and on the development and shape of the Emirate. The British were dependent on his assistance to ensure local co-operation, especially in times of crisis. Shaykhs needed him in order to obtain state resources and to check government tendencies to encroach on their autonomy. In this way Abdullah enjoyed leverage both externally vis-à-vis his British patrons and internally vis-à-vis his subjects.

Indeed, Abdullah's position within Transjordan indicates that he had considerable influence on the outcome of the state-formation process. In fact, the mandate's end result was a reflection of the limits of British rule, the need to make concessions to Abdullah and conform to the dominant form of politics. British officials, Abdullah, the government as well as shaykhs and notables were engaged in constant pushing and pulling of the Emirate in different, and sometimes contradictory, directions. This had the effect of creating a new type of political structure -- what Toby Dodge terms a 'hybrid' state, combining both modern, Western-inspired aspects of government and many traditional features.[5] This gave a special character to Transjordan, more in keeping with the new states of Arabia than those of the Fertile Crescent.

Post-Independence Jordan

The pattern of state-tribe relations established during the mandate and the colonial legacy had crucial implications for Jordan. The mandate period laid solid foundations for the development of the Jordanian state and is one of the keys to understanding the state's resilience ever since. It created a broad base of support for the state in Jordanian society, something that was lacking in many Middle Eastern countries and other new states in the colonial world. By giving many tribesmen a clear stake in the existence of the state and the regime, the Emirate's authorities created staunch supporters who proved their loyalty in times of crisis and uncertainty when the regime seemed about to collapse and the state be undone. The mandate period also saw the building of institutions of state that proved capable of dealing with serious challenges after independence. By staffing the military and bureaucracy, content tribesman controlled the corridors of power and came to defend the regime against potential and actual rivals.

The 1948 Palestine war which broke out only two years after the granting of formal independence posed the first test to the new polity. The tribally-based Arab

Legion fought with bravery, military capability and discipline. Among Arab armies the Legion emerged as the most effective, delivering to Abdullah the sought-after West Bank. The Legion was joined by an estimated 1,200 volunteers from the tribes including the Bani Sakhr, Huwaytat, ʿAdwan and Hadid. As the Legion numbered only 4,500 fighting men this tribal contingent made a significant contribution to the Jordanian war effort.[6] All in all the Jordanian success in the war was a testimony of both the strength of the country and the close connection between the government and society.

Following the war, the incorporation of the Palestinians into Jordan as citizens opened a new era in the history of the country and presented new challenges. Overnight the country's population tripled. Around 450,000 original Transjordanians were joined by 900,000 Palestinians, half of them refugees. Although Abdullah tried to turn the newcomers into integral part of his kingdom by knitting the two populations into one, his successors were less committed to this utopian idea. As the 1950s progressed, control and partial integration rather than unity characterised relations between the two segments of society.[7] This control system, known as 'Jordanisation' of the West Bank, could only operate thanks to the unwavering commitment of the military, intelligence services, police, courts and other arms of the government -- all going back to the mandate period and largely staffed with the former Emirate's officials.

The incorporation of the Palestinians became all the more challenging with the rise of Gamal Abd al-Nasser to regional leadership and the emergence of pan-Arabism, of which the Palestinians where the staunchest supporters. The young King Husayn -- who ascended to the throne in 1953 following the assassination of King Abdullah in 1951 and the brief reign of King Talal -- seemed easy prey for Nasser. The Egyptian President attempted to usher in a new era in the Arab Middle East by eradicating all signs of Western imperialism. For many, Jordan epitomised just that. "The challenge of Arab radicalism," in the words of Uriel Dann, characterised King Husayn's reign until 1967. His first baptism of fire was Nasser's success in foiling Jordan's participation in the Baghdad Pact in 1955. Another notable concession the King made to the new mood in the Middle East was to sack Glubb as the commander of the Arab Legion in 1956. The surprisingly smooth transfer of power in the army indicated the strength of the state-building process. Ironically perhaps, Glubb managed to build a state army that could stomach even the humiliating redundancy of its allegedly legendary leader. The same army was also able to crush any opposition to the King's actions.[8]

Glubb's dismissal also marked the completion of Jordan's gradual release from British patronage. If Glubb's personal fate was abrupt and dramatic, the overall process of decolonisation was slow and incremental, going back to the Anglo-Jordanian Treaty of 1939 and the 1946 'independence.' By 1956 Jordan's political system was mature enough to face the challenges of independence more than in many other de-colonised countries. The British withdrawal did not therefore cause social upheaval or regime change as happened in many states. In Jordan Britain did apparently fulfil the requirement of the mandate to prepare a new state for independence.

For a brief moment though, the post-Glubb Arab Legion was a source for concern, as were armies in many former colonies. Some native Jordanians, affected and inspired by the changing *Zeitgeist* in the region, called the old political order into question. However, only a small group of politicians and senior officers actually challenged the monarchy. When they did so, most notably in the *coup d'etat* attempt in 1957, enough elements opposed them and remained loyal to the King that the regime survived. To a large extent, Husayn owed his success in surviving the *coup* to the role played by the Bani Sakhr, both in and outside the Legion. It was ʿAkif al-Fayiz, the son of the paramount shaykh, who alerted the King to the hostile organisation after he heard about it from Bani Sakhr soldiers. When the King faced the conspirators, he was supported by 2,000 Bani Sakhr members, who gathered in Amman at ʿAkif's call.[9] From then on the Legion remained loyal and stayed out of politics.

The Arab Legion's defeat in the 1967 war, which resulted in the loss of the West Bank, and the 1970-1971 civil war ushered in a new era in Jordan. The Jordanian attempt to integrate the Palestinians, and in the process weaken their particular sense of identity, failed with the rise of the assertive Palestinian movement led by the PLO and *Fatah* from the mid-1960s.[10] The regime responded by turning back to relying on its old of support base. Old patterns which characterised the Emirate days were now either reactivated or exposed. The regime rested on the Transjordan sectors of society, the tribes in particular, which were by now fully integrated into the state, co-opted and devoid of their former autonomy. As in the days of the Emirate, tribes are today seen as the legitimate building blocks of society. Moreover, tribal values and culture have been appropriated by the regime, which actively promotes them.

From Abdullah to Abdullah: Continuities in Jordanian Politics and Society

The Jordanian political system is a clear reflection of the Emirate days. The Kingdom's centre of gravity is a powerful monarch who alone can delegate authority. This prerogative was established with Abdullah I's power to nominate all posts, from officers in the Legion to government employees and tribal judges. Therefore, once the British had left there was nothing to balance the power of the King. The highest executive power, the government, is nominated by him, and therefore completely dependent on his support. Therefore real power rests in the King's court.

The other branch of government, the Parliament, resembles the Emirate's Legislative Council both in its makeup and the way it functions. After many years of suspension, parliamentary life was resumed with the by-election of 1984 and the general election in 1989. However, with its limited legislative powers, *Majlis al-Umma* serves mainly as a platform for public figures to express their views and offer some criticism of the government. It is also a means to co-opt powerful leaders. Like the old Legislative Council, and especially since the change of the Election Law in 1993, most present-day MPs are representatives of tribal constituencies, with special seats reserved for the 'Bedouin.' The weakness of the *Majlis* is a result of procedures which were determined by the British and Abdullah in order to limit the power of the old Legislative Council. For one, the parliamentarians' immunity is limited to the short period when the house is in session. Whereas former legislators were prevented from initiating new bills and could only approve or reject laws drafted by the government, MPs today do the same, even after the removal of legal barriers to independent legislation. It is the King who initiates the parliamentary session and adjourns it. He alone can dissolve the house and call a new election. Finally, a provision in the law allows the government to enact provisional laws outside the parliamentary sessions, which then require only retroactive approval by the *Majlis*. In many cases of controversial legislation the government chooses this convenient path despite heavy criticism by MPs and the public. This 'democratic' legacy might suggest that the lack of democracy in Jordan, and perhaps in other Arab states, does not necessarily derive from an essential Arab inability or unwillingness to absorb liberal political culture but is at least in part a result of the colonial past. 'Western' values imported by the British and French to the Middle East were markedly different from the ones they implemented in Europe. They were oppressive rather than liberal.

More important than the formal structure of power inherited from the mandate is the unofficial and unarticulated political system that directs the life of the Kingdom and which draws on many historical precedents. Since the days of Abdullah, the Hashemite family has been operating as an honest broker among tribes and prominent families. Hence what seems to be a strategic decision of the kings and heirs apparent not to marry into Jordanian tribal society in order not to lose their neutral stance among the different tribes. So far spouses were either members of the Hashemite family, foreigners, or Palestinians. Another indication is the sacred balance between regions and tribes each time a new government is formed or, more generally, in the appointment of senior administrative positions. In summary, the main domestic role of the monarch is to maintain the careful balance between the different tribes. So far this balancing act has proved remarkably successful.

The entire Jordanian system is built on the interplay between families -- many of them shaykhly families representing tribes. The importance of families had been identified by Andrew Shryock and Sally Howell, who suggest analysing Jordan's political system in terms of "house politics," namely "a mode of domination in which families (the royal one being only the most central and effective) serve as instrument and objects of power." The two scholars point to the origins and nature of this system: "...Abdullah and Hussein built a political system that corresponds to, addresses and depends on these houses in fundamental ways: as targets of incentive, punishment and reward; as site and methods of recruitment to public office; and as a means of exclusion from power."[11]

More needs to be said about two other principles of this political system: rotation and expectation. Rotation serves two purposes. It prevents the strengthening of one family or tribe to a degree that might threaten the Hashemite hegemony. It also allows many families to take part in government. The frequent reshuffling of the cabinet serves the latter purpose, to allow as many people as possible to share in ministerial positions. This method is built to a large extent on the notion of expectation. Even if at a specific moment in time a certain family is not represented in the power structure, it can resonantly expect that its position will improve in the next reshuffle. Thus it is the interest of no one to rock the boat.

However, the Jordanian power elite is small. A quick look at its members reveals remarkable continuity since the days of the mandate. A few dozen families -- many shaykhly tribal families -- which dominated Transjordan in 1946 still enjoy prominent status. Now the third generation holds power. The names Fayiz, Khuraysha, ʿAdwan, Majali, Tarawna, Shurayda, Tall, Jazi, Abu Taya and many others that frequently feature in the pages of this book represent the influential families today.

Indeed, the system of state resource allocation takes place according to tribal or familial lines. It is the tribe which serves as the main constituency for an aspirant politician. This partly explains the weakness of the party system in Jordan. If well-organised and united, the tribe, in its modern capacity as an interest group or lobby, can send one of its members to the parliament. Similarly, a senior administrative, academic or military position can guarantee an individual a leadership position among his tribe, even if he does not hail from one of the shaykhly families. The career of former MP Ahmad ʿUwaydi al-ʿAbbadi, so carefully portrayed by Shryock,[12] demonstrates this point. Once in power, the occupier of the position is expected to serve the best interests of his kin group. His effectiveness in performing this social duty -- commonly known as *wasta* -- then forms the main criterion for his fellow tribespeople for judging him. According to the predominant social norm, this figure would be expected to be easily accessible; he would be asked to help his constituency handle all sorts of bureaucratic matters, including lowering tax assessments, allocating licenses and commercial concessions, securing jobs or promotions and places or scholarships in universities. In fact, he functions as a modern shaykh.

Tribes not only play a major political role, but their values also shape much of Jordanian culture. For one, tribal practices of conflict resolution and customary law continue to operate, regulating social relations and informing legal procedures. The Tribal Control Laws of 1936 served as the legal basis for the Tribal Courts for forty years. In 1976 the Laws and the Courts were abolished, ostensibly to allow for the application of one law to all citizens. In practice, however, tribal law continues to regulate social relations in Jordan to this day. Moreover, state officials from the King down not only allow it but actively encourage and sometimes act as mediators in conflict resolution arrived at by tribal custom. Often, as in the mandate era, formal court hearings are accompanied by an agreement for compensation arrived at between the two families. Such successful resolution has the effect of encouraging the court to be lenient. Thus, tribal customary law remains an integral part of the Jordanian legal system.[13]

Tribal values also continue to be endorsed and utilised by the Hashemite monarchs and inform their conduct. Indeed, significant continuity can be detected in the monarch's style of rule since the days of Abdullah I. The Emir ruled Transjordan with many characteristics of a tribal chieftaincy. One of them was unmediated personal politics. Abdullah's long camping among the different tribes turned into King Husayn's famous *ziyara*s. During his long tours of the country, visiting the different tribal communities, he allowed every tribesman or woman to approach him and raise complaints, pleas for assistance, or just enjoy the opportunity to meet him in person.[14] Even today King Abdullah II spends much of his time visiting the country, addressing large gatherings of public leaders from the different sectors of society or meeting tribal leaders.[15]

Showing generosity and benevolence while dealing with political rivals is another important feature of the Hashemite style of rule, going back to the days of the mandate. It seems to be effective in dissipating antagonism against the regime. Abdullah made peace with the Shuryda and ʿAdwan shaykhs after they rebelled against him, with Husayn al-Tarawna who led the national opposition, and with Mithqal al-Fayiz and Haditha al-Khuraysha, with whom he periodically fell out. Similarly, King Husayn tended to forgive even his arch-rivals, made peace with them, rehabilitated their reputation and even brought them back into the power elite. ʿAbdullah al-Tall, ʿAli and Maʿan Abu Nowar and most recently Layth Shubaylat are some of the most prominent figures who enjoyed this practice adopted by the late King Husayn. It still remains to be seen whether the present monarch will pursue this policy.

Tribes and Jordanian Nationalism

Perhaps the most significant cultural legacy of the mandate is the manner in which it paved the way to the creation of a special kind of nationalism. This is unique in the sense that, as Linda Layne has shown, "tribes play such a dominant role in the symbolization of Jordan's national identity."[16] In fact, in modern Jordan, tribalism and nationalism are not contradictory phenomena. Rather, they inform and enhance one another, thus allowing the majority of the population hailing from a Transjordanian origin to identify with the state in an intimate way, which is rare in the new states of the Third World.

Since the early 1970s the regime has promoted a particular Jordanian nationalism. This occurred against the background of the demise of Pan-Arabism following the 1967 war and Nasser's death and as a result of the civil war. Calls from Israeli right-wing circles to turn Jordan into an alternative homeland for the Palestinians also prompted the regime to emphasise that Jordan was not Palestine, but instead had a unique identity. The emergence of Jordanian nationalism was facilitated by the spread of literacy from the 1970s, print culture being a precondition for the emergence of nationalism. Young educated tribesmen and women, products of the state schools and the universities, were amenable to the new concept of nationhood as promoted by the government. In constructing Jordanian identity, the regime drew heavily on the heritage of the Emirate days.

Arab nationalism, the Hashemite legitimacy to rule as descendants of the Prophet, King Husayn as the embodiment of Jordan and even the Nabatean heritage were invoked as components of the new identity alongside tribalism or 'Bedouinism.' Indeed, tribal values, as understood by the regime, have been incorporated into the creation of Jordanian nationalism. The regime tried to blend particular tribal solidarities into one unified identity based on the tribal heritage and affiliation of the majority of citizens of Transjordanian origin. In doing so it nationalised tribal identities.[17] The abolition of the tribal courts in 1976 served this purpose. It was designed to break down the official barrier between those tribes considered by the (colonial) law to be 'Bedouin' and the rest of the tribes. It was a way to create a general, unified, and hopefully unifying, tribal identity as part of the newly-constructed national identity.

This newly constructed identity was also coloured with 'Bedouin' values. As explained by Massad, "the Bedouin are seen as the carriers of Jordan's true and authentic culture and traditions."[18] Mostly for the external purpose of promoting tourism to the Kingdom, Jordan cultivated a 'Bedouin' image of itself, manifested in the uniform of the Desert Patrol and especially its red-chequered *kufiyya*, desert encampments in Wadi Rum and coffee paraphernalia. But, as Massad shows, this regime-sanctioned Bedounisation permeated into the popular culture through music, art performances and television programmes. To emphasise this identity people of urban origin went as far as adopting a 'Bedouin' accent. According to Massad, "Bedouinizing all Jordanians [was] a form of nationalizing them against the Palestinian national threat."[19] Indeed in today's Jordan many segments of the population would define themselves as Bedouin even though several decades ago their grandfathers would have viewed this as an insult.[20]

But the Bedouinisation and anti-Palestinian sentiments should not only be seen as top down processes or as a complete colonial invention as suggested by Massad. Layne and Shryock clearly demonstrate the gap between Jordanian nationalism as constructed by the regime and the way it has been absorbed and reformulated by Jordanians. As tribespeople were encouraged to imagine themselves as part of a nation their emergent 'imagined community'[21] was phrased in indigenous, genealogical terms, drawing on values that predated the colonial period. Whereas the government's rhetoric speaks of the big and united Jordanian family, regardless of origin, many citizens of tribal background came to ask who were the true Jordanians? Consequently, a significant branch of Jordanian nationalism excludes the Palestinian citizens of the country from the concept of the nation, as well as minorities like the Circassians and, at times, even the Hashemites. It thus defies the official line of national unity. Phrases like *Urdunni Urdunni* and *Ahl al-balad* (sons of the country) are frequently invoked to indicate 'authentic' origin. Similarly, the official Hashemite national narrative is often contested by a tribal one. Thus, as much as the regime nationalised tribal identities so triebspeople tribalised the nation.

Neither did the attempt to subsume the particular tribal identities into one single identity end in absolute success for the government. Literature on particular tribes' histories and geneologies from the 1980s, the spread of tribal *diwan*s throughout the country, the use of tribal names as family names, voting patterns and tribal solidarities which come to surface in times of need are some of the indications that tribespeople preserve their particular identities. Membership of a tribe forms a significant part of one's identity and a source of pride. Nevertheless, rather than undermining each other, the two notions of being a proud Jordanian and a proud member of a tribe complement and strengthen each other. The local, familiar, concrete and tangible tribal solidarity mediates the more abstract notion of an imagined national community.

The gap between the intended and actual result, its exclusivist nature, its tendency to alienate at least half of the population and its short existence notwithstanding, the fact remains that the new Jordanian nationalism is an important and visible cultural phenomenon. Jordanian nationalism is closely interrelated with the notion of tribalism; together they create a sense of intimacy between state and society, to a level which has been rarely achieved in other Middle Eastern and post-colonial states. Many Jordanians see Jordan as their home, they identify with it and object to any doubts regarding its *raison d'être*. Although at times they might criticise specific policies, fundamentally they support the regime that for years has benefited them. This convergence of interests between state and society, with its roots in the Emirate period, goes a long way towards explaining Jordan's remarkable stability. Compared with its modest beginnings in the early 1920s as a colonial creation, this is indeed a notable achievement.

GLOSSARY: TRIBES AND SHAYKHS

1. Tribes and Confederacies

The following lists the tribal groups which are mentioned in the book. As such, it is by no means a comprehensive list of tribes in Jordan. This list reflects the tribal situation at the time of the Emirate. Since then many changes have occurred in terms of tribal divisions, alignments and ways of life.

ʿAbbad – Large semi-settled[1] group of loosely-connected tribes, whose vast land stretched from the mountain slops west of al-Salt down to the Jordan Valley between the Zarqaʾ River and Wadi al-Shitta. Despite their location in the heart of the Balqaʾ, they were not part of the Balqaʾ alliance but instead enjoyed friendly relations with the Bani Sakhr. Their economy was based on crop farming and animal husbandry.

Adayat – One of the Balqawiyya tribes in the vicinity of Madaba.

ʿAdhamat – Semi-nomadic tribes of the Ahl al-Jabal confederacy. Originally from Syria but some immigrated to Transjordan in the 1940s after obtaining land from the government.

ʿAdwan – The leading tribes of the Balqaʾ alliance led by Sultan al-ʿAdwan and later his son, Majid. They conducted semi-settled life, owning much land on the shores of the Dead Sea and the Jordan River in the west to Suwaylih near Amman in the east. They were the dominant force in the Balqaʾ from the eighteenth century but later lost some of their land to the Bani Sakhr. With the Ottoman extension of direct rule to the Balqaʾ in the late 1860s and later the establishment of the Emirate, they lost some of their autonomy but remained powerful and rich tribes even after their failed revolt in 1923.

---

1   The classification of the tribespeople's way of life is far from exact and should not be seen in absolute terms but rather as a spectrum. One can speak of nomads, semi-nomads, semi-settled and settled, and even these categories are not precise, but often changed over time. Generally speaking, during the period under study there was slow and gradual tendency to limit nomadism and prefer more settled life. Moreover, sometimes the distinctions between people's ways of life was quite arbitrary, depending on how it served the government in its pursuit of different policies towards nomadic and settled tribes. This was the case with the Tribal Control Laws from 1929, which formalised what in the early days was only a very vague distinction.

Ahl al-Jabal – Confederacy of semi-nomadic tribes which included the ʿAdhamat, Masaʿid, Sharafat and Zabid. Their main territory was in Syria, but during the summer months they entered Transjordan, clashing with Transjordanian tribes over water and grazing. During the 1940s some of their members settled in northern Transjordan, east of the railway line along the Syrian border.

Ahl al-Shimal – Loose political alliance led by the Bani Sakhr and including the Sirhan, Bani Khalid and ʿIsa tribes.

ʿAjarma – Semi-settled tribes in the vicinity of Hisban-Madaba who combined cultivation of the land and animal husbandry. They are considered one of the oldest tribes in the Balqa' and were important member of the Balqa' alliance.

ʿArabiyyat – One of the largest tribes in al-Salt, leading the Akrad tribal alliance.

ʿAwamla – One of the largest tribes in al-Salt, leading the tribal alliance of *ʿAshaʾir al-Hara*.

ʿAwazim – One of the Balqawiyya tribes in the vicinity of Maʿin which was led by the Abu Wundi shaykhly family.

ʿAwran – One of the largest and most influential tribes of Tafila.

Azayda – One of the Balqawiyya tribes in the vicinity of Madaba.

The Balqa' alliance – Political alliance of mainly semi-settled tribes without genealogical ties, dominating the western part of the Balqa', as well as the south-eastern part of ʿAjlun and large parts of the Jordan Valley. Led by the ʿAdwan's shaykhly family they also included the ʿAjarma, Balqawiyya, Bani Hasan, the northern tribes of the Bani Hamida, Ghunaymat, Daʿja, Haddadin of Maʿin and several other tribes. Most of these tribes abandoned full nomadic life already in the late nineteenth century and became farmers. They registered land in the Ottoman *tapu*, taking advantage of the fertile land of the Balqa', its abundant water resources and good climate.

Balqawiyya[2] – Group of small semi-settled tribes in the Balqa', forming part of the Balqa' alliance: ʿAwazim (and their Wundiyyin), Azayda, Adayat, Hanitiyyin, Ghunaymat, Qarda, Qatarna, Raqqad, Shawabka (Amman), Shawabka (Madaba), and Shawakra. Their main sources of livelihood were the cultivation of the land and the herding of sheep and goats. Some raised camels.

Bani ʿAtiyya – Nomadic tribes summering in the vicinity of Karak and Tafila and wintering along the border with Saudi Arabia and beyond. Because they were involved in the futile Ibn Rifada Revolt in 1932 some of their tribes were expelled to Saudi Arabia in 1933. Politically they allied themselves with the tribes of Karak and maintained economic relations with them. Under the Emirate they were considered part of the 'Southern Bedouin' category for purposes of elections and the implementation of tribal law.

Bani Hamida – Confederacy of semi-nomadic tribes, roaming both banks of the Mujib gorge. The three northern tribes were involved in the politics of the Balqa' and were members of the Balqa' alliance. The southern tribes were involved in the politics of Karak. They began the process of gradual sedentarisation and abandoning

---

2   There is disagreement about the composition of this alliance. Some of the sources add tribes to the list provided here and omit others.

the pastoral economy in favour of farming late in comparison to other tribes in the Balqa'. Moreover, their land was less suitable for cultivation. Consequently, during the interwar years they suffered from harsh economic conditions and were often in need of government assistance.

Bani Hasan – Large confederacy of six semi-nomadic tribes, roaming in the south-east of ʿAjlun province around Jarash and north-east of the Balqa' and taking part in the Balqa' alliance. Once a prosperous confederacy they were reduced in numbers and lost much of their most fertile land in the Balqa' due to Ottoman policy in the late nineteenth century. Under the Emirate they continued the gradual and difficult process of sedentarisation, abandoning the pastoral economy in favour of farming. During the interwar years they suffered from harsh economic conditions and were often in need of government assistance.

Bani Khalid – Nomadic tribes roaming in the east of ʿAjlun province, north of Mafraq. They were part of the Ahl al-Shimal alliance and under the Emirate were considered part of the 'Northern Bedouin' category for purposes of elections and the implementation of tribal law.

Bani Sakhr – Powerful nomadic tribal confederacy led by the Fayiz shaykhly family and dominating central Transjordan. It was composed of three major branches, each comprising several tribes: Ghabin -- which includes among others the Fayiz and Mtirat -- Haqish, Zaban and Salit under the Tawqa and the Khuraysa (Khurshan) and Jubur under the Kaʿabna. A third branch was called Khadir. The Bani Sakhr were the major component of the Ahl al-Shimal alliance and under the Emirate were considered part of the 'Northern Bedouin' category for purposes of elections and the implementation of tribal law. Traditionally, their main rivals were the Sardiyya and Ahl al-Jabal in the north, the ʿAdwan and their allies in the Balqa', the Ruwalla in the east and the Huwaytat in the south. They maintained friendly relations with the ʿAbbad tribes. Before the establishment of the Emirate the main sources of income of these tribes derived from the traditional pastoral economy (raiding, *khawa* collection, herding camels and horses), as well as from the farms owned by their shaykhs since the end of the nineteenth century. After the founding of the state, their resources changed and diversified to include farming, herding sheep and goats and employment in the Arab Legion and public works.

Billi – Nomadic tribe from the Hijaz who launched a revolt in 1932 against Ibn Saud, instigated by Emir Abdullah.

Daʿja – Semi-settled tribes in the vicinity of Amman and member of the Balqa' alliance. Some of their land was taken by the Ottoman government and was given to the Circassians, for which they were compensated with land east of Amman. They combined cultivation of the land with the herding of sheep and goats.

Fayiz – One of the tribes of the Bani Sakhr from which the shaykhly family hailed. They roamed east of Amman and Madaba in the summer and Wadi Sirhan in the winter. Their shaykhs owned farms from which they derived much of their wealth.

Furayhat – The leading tribe in the Jabal ʿAjlun district, based in the village of Kufranja.

Gharaba – The western tribal alliance of Karak under the Majali and including the

Dhunaybat, Habashna, Maᶜayta, Madadha, Mahadin, Shamayla and the town's Christian tribes: ᶜAkasha, Haddadin, Halasa, Hijazin, Madanat, and Zurayqat.

Ghawarna – Settled tribes in the Dead Sea depression who are thought to originate from the Sudan. Because of their dark complexion they were viewed as socially inferior by other Karaki tribes, who treated them harshly.

Ghazawiyya – Semi-nomadic tribes roaming in the northern part of the Jordan Valley on both banks of the river. In the 1940s their Zinati tribe sold its land in Palestine and settled permanently in Transjordan.

Ghunaymat (Abu Ghanam) – One of the Balqawiyya tribes in the vicinity of Madaba.

Haddadin – Christian settled tribe from the town of Maᶜin south of Madaba, originally from Karak, and a member of the Balqa' alliance.

Hadid – Semi-nomadic tribes roaming in the vicinity of Amman. Originally they formed part of the Balqa' alliance but in the early 1920s left the alliance and took an independent stance, with close relations with their neighbours, the Bani Sakhr.

Hajaya – Nomadic and semi nomadic tribes. The former spent the summers around Tafila and Wadi al-Hasa. The latter confined themselves to life in the Karak province, breeding sheep and goats and cultivating the land. Their shaykh, Ghayth bin Hadaya, already owned and cultivated land near Karak in the early 1920s. Under the Emirate they were considered part of the 'Southern Bedouin' category for purposes of elections and the implementation of tribal law.

Hanitiyyin – One of the Balqawiyya tribes in the vicinity of Abu ᶜAlanda, east of Amman.

Haqish – One of the tribes of the Bani Sakhr, summering south-east of Madaba.

Hilalat (Shubaylat) – One of the tribes of Tafila.

Huwaytat – Powerful nomadic tribal confederacy which dominated southern Transjordan from Tafila to ᶜAqaba. It was composed of several branches, such as the Ibn Jazi, the Tawayha/Abu Taya and the Sulaymaniyyin and associated several other tribes such as the Maraᶜiyya, Nuᶜaymat and Saᶜidiyyin. Unlike most Transjordanian tribes who are said to have migrated from Arabia, the Huwaytat are thought of as the original inhabitants of their *dira*. Uniquely among the tribal confederacies, they claim to have originated from one ancestor. Under the Emirate they were considered the main tribes of the 'Southern Bedouin' category for purposes of elections and the implementation of tribal law. Just before World War One most of the confederacy abandoned its semi-nomadic way of life combining farming in Jabal Shara and pastoral economy and became one of the powerful and rich nomadic tribes in Arabia, deriving their income from raiding, *khawa* collection and herding camels and horses. Their Abu Taya branch played a crucial role during the Arab Revolt, fighting for the Hashemites and occupying the Ottoman fort of ᶜAqaba. Traditionally, their main rivals were the Bani Sakhr tribes but they made peace with them in 1926 under the influence of Emir Abdullah. After the founding of the state, their resources changed and diversified to include farming, herding sheep and goats and employment in the Arab Legion and public works. During this time the Ibn Jazi under the powerful leadership of shaykh Hamad bin Jazi ascended to become the most powerful component of the confederacy.

Ihyawat – Nomadic tribes roaming both sides of Wadi ʿAraba. During the period under study they were considered to be Palestinian tribes.

ʿIsa – Nomadic tribes roaming northeast of Mafraq, near the Syrian border. They were part of the Ahl al-Shimal alliance and under the Emirate were considered part of the 'Northern Bedouin' category for purposes of elections and the implementation of tribal law.

Jubur – One of the tribes of the Kaʿabna branch of the Bani Sakhr, summering in north-eastern ʿAjlun. They moved to Nuqayra, southeast of Amman, after Glubb forced them to cultivate its land.

Kalalda – One of the largest and most influential tribes of Tafila.

Khuraysha – One of the tribes of the Kaʿabna branch of the Bani Sakhr, summering south-east of Amman (Muwaqqar) and in eastern ʿAjlun and often crossing over into Syria.

Lawziyyin – Semi-settled tribe northeast of Amman (Jubayha) affiliated with the ʿAdwan.

Maʿayta – The largest tribe in Karak and an important member of the *Gharaba* alliance. They combined land cultivation and the herding of animals. Among the Karaki tribes they were considered the closest in their way of life to the nomadic tribes in the region.

Majali – The strongest tribe in Karak leading the *Gharaba* alliance. Its members spread in the town and north of it in several villages. They combined the cultivation of land and the herding of animals. Despite their 'urban' nature most of them resided in tents and led a mobile life that suited the different seasons.

Mannaʿin – Nomadic tribe roaming in the vicinity of Tafila and allied with the Huwaytat. Under the Emirate they were considered part of the 'Southern Bedouin' category for purposes of elections and the implementation of tribal law.

Maraʿiyya – Semi-nomadic tribe roaming and farming their land in Jabal Shara, west of Maʿan, and affiliated with the Huwaytat.

Masaʿid – Semi-nomadic tribes of the Ahl al-Jabal confederacy. Originally from Syria but some immigrated to Transjordan in the 1940s after obtaining land from the government.

Mashalkha – Semi-nomadic tribes roaming in the Jordan Valley, south of Wadi Zarqaʾ.

Mtirat – One of the tribes of the Bani Sakhr summering south of Madaba.

Muʾmina – Large tribe of settled farmers spread in several villages in the Jabal ʿAjlun district.

Nuʿaymat – Semi-nomadic tribe roaming in Jabal Shara, west of Maʿan, where they cultivated their land, as well as Wadi al-Hasa. They also raised sheep and goats and politically were affiliated with the Huwaytat.

Ruwalla – The largest nomadic tribal confederation in Arabia. Its tribes roamed the eastern parts of Transjordan during their seasonal migration from northern Najd to Syria and back. They were often at odds with Transjordanian tribes, especially when grazing and water for their large camel herds were short. After independence some of their tribes settled in Jordan becoming its citizens.

Saʿidiyyin – Nomadic tribes roaming in southern Transjordan on both sides of Wadi ʿAraba as well as Sinai. Under the Emirate they were considered part of the 'Southern Bedouin' category for purposes of elections and the implementation of tribal law.

Salayta (Salit) – One of the tribes of the Bani Sakhr, summering south of Madaba. Up to the 1920s they were considered by some of the sources to be an independent tribe (including the 1929 Bedouin Control Law).

Sardiyya – Semi-nomadic tribes whose main territory was in Syria but who entered Transjordan during the summer months, clashing with Transjordanian tribes over water and grazing. During the 1940s some of them settled in northern Transjordan east of the railway line along the Syrian border.

Sharafat – Semi-nomadic tribes of the Ahl al-Jabal confederacy. Originally from Syria but some immigrated to Transjordan in the 1940s after obtaining land from the government.

Sharaqa – The eastern tribal alliance of Karak under the Tarawna and including the ʿAdayla, Damur, Qatawna, Sarayra, and Suʿub.

Shararat – Tribespeople who uniquely did not possess their own *dira* but were affiliated with other tribes, roaming both sides of the Transjordanian-Najdi frontier and engaged in raids with Transjordanian tribes. They were considered to be Saudi subjects.

Sirhan – Nomadic tribes roaming in the east of ʿAjlun province in the summer and Wadi Sirhan in the winter, where they also owned date gardens. They were badly affected by the incorporation of the Wadi into Saudi territory in 1925 and had to limit their sojourn there. They were part of the Ahl al-Shimal alliance and under the Emirate were considered part of the 'Northern Bedouin' category for purposes of elections and the implementation of tribal law.

Shubaykat (Shawabka) – Two different tribes of the Balqawiyya, one in the vicinity of the village of Sahab, south-east of Amman; the other north of Madaba.

Shurayda – The leading tribe of the Kura district in the ʿAjlun province. Composed of settled farmers spread in several villages, such as Tibna and Kufr al-Ma'.

Sukhur al-Ghawr – Semi-nomadic tribes roaming in the most northern part of the Jordan Valley on both banks of the river.

Sulaymaniyyin – One of the tribes of the Huwaytat confederacy.

Tall (Tulul) – Prominent tribe in Irbid.

Tarawna – Semi-settled tribe and the leading component of the *Sharaqa* alliance in Karak. Spread in the town and several villages to the south-east of the town, their *dira* stretching up to Wadi al- in the south and the Hijaz railway in the east. They combined land cultivation and animal husbandry. Despite their 'urban' nature most of them resided in tents and led a mobile life suited to the different seasons.

Tawayha – One of the main branches of the Huwaytat confederacy under the leadership of ʿAwda and his son Muhammad abu Taya.

ʿUmran – Nomadic tribes roaming in the vicinity of ʿAqaba and northern Hijaz.

Zaban – One of the tribes of the Bani Sakhr summering east of Madaba.

Zabid – Semi-nomadic tribes of the Ahl al-Jabal confederacy. Originally from Syria but some immigrated to Transjordan in the 1940s after obtaining land from the government.

2. Shaykhs

The following is a list of the tribal affiliations and positions of the shaykhs who appear in the book.

al-ʿAdwan, Majid – Leader of the ʿAdwan tribes and the Balqaʾ alliance since his father Sultan's death in 1934 and until his own death in 1946.

al-ʿAdwan, Sultan – Leader of the ʿAdwan tribes and the Balqaʾ tribal alliance until his death in 1934.

al-ʿAwran, Salih – Head of the ʿAwran tribe and the most influential leader in Tafila.

al-ʿAzzam, Naji – Leader of the Wustiyya district in northern Transjordan who was based in the village of Qum.

bin Fahd, Tarad – Shaykh of the Zaban tribe of the Bani Sakhr and a leader of raids.

al-Fayiz, ʿAkif – Son and right-hand man of Mithqal al-Fayiz, paramount shaykh of the Bani Sakhr. Born in the early 1920s, he replaced his father as *shaykh mashayikh* in 1967 and in this capacity led the Bani Sakhr until his death in 1998. Beyond his shaykhly duties, he served in senior legislative and ministerial positions after Jordan's independence.

al-Fayiz, Dirdah al-Bakhit – Renowned military leader of the Bani Sakhr.

al-Fayiz, Mashhur – Paramount shaykh of the Bani Sakhr from 1917 until his death in 1921.

al-Fayiz, Mithqal – Prominent shaykh of the Bani Sakhr confederacy during World War One and their paramount shaykh from 1921 until his death in 1967.

al-Fayiz, Zaʿal Kniʿan – Shaykh of the Kniʿan lineage of the Fayiz tribe of the Bani Sakhr (who could write and read).

abu Ghunaym, Salim – Leader of the Ghunaymat tribes.

bin Hadaya, Ghayth – Leader of the Hajaya tribes.

bin Hadid, Minwar – Leader of the Hadid tribes.

al-Hamud, Nimr – Leader of the ʿArabiyyat tribe in al-Salt.

al-Hasan, Bashir (al-Ghazawi) – Leader of the Ghazawiyya tribes.

al-Haydar, Turki – Shaykh of the Zaban tribe of the Bani Sakhr.

al-Husayn, Muhammad – Leader of the ʿAwamla tribe in al-Salt.

al-Husayn, ʿUlyan – Shaykh of the Khawalda tribe of the Bani Hasan.

bin Jazi, ʿAbtan – Leader of the Jazi branch of the Huwaytat before World War One.

bin Jazi, Hamad – Leader of the Jazi branch of the Huwaytat and the recognised paramount shaykh of the entire Huwaytat from 1930 until his death in 1962.

bin Kaʿaybar, Hindi – Paramount shaykh of the Sirhan tribes.

al-Kayid, ʿAli – Leader of the al-Miʿrad district who was based in the village of Suf.

al-Khuraysha, Haditha – Leader of the Khuraysha tribe of the Bani Sakhr and the Kaʿabna branch of the confederacy.

al-Khuzaʿi, Rashid – Head of the Furayhat tribe and leader of the Jabal ʿAjlun district.

Krishan, Mahmud – Most influential leader in Maʿan and its representative on the third, fourth and fifth Legislative Councils from 1934 until 1947.

al-Maʿayta, Musa – Leader of the Maʿayta tribe in Karak.

bin Madi, Mijhim – Leader of the ʿIsa tribes.

al-Majali, Dulaywan – One of the leaders of the Majalis. Mayor of Karak from 1918 until his death in 1979. Brother of Rufayfan and renowned tribal judge.

al-Majali, Rufayfan – Leader of the *Gharaba* tribal alliance of Karak and of the Majali tribes until his death in 1945.

al-Majali, ʿUtwa – The recognised paramount shaykh of Karak from the days of the Faysali government until his death in 1937.

al-Muhaysan, Mustafa – Leader of the Kalalda tribe in Tafila.

al-Mur, ʿAwwad – Shaykh of the Haqish tribe of the Bani Sakhr.

bin Mutlaq, Zaʿal – Shaykh of the Tawayha of the Huwaytat who was nominated in 1930 as a temporary leader of the Tawayha branch.

bin Najjad, ʿAwda – Leader of the Sulaymaniyyin tribe of the Huwaytat.

Qasus, ʿAwda – Leader of the Halasa, a Karaki Christian tribe, a lawyer by profession and prominent politician and administrator.

al-Qulab, Marzuq – Shaykh of the ʿAmush tribe of the Bani Hasan.

bin Rifada, Hamid – Shaykh of the Billi tribe and leader of the failed revolt against Ibn Saud in 1932.

Salih, Muhammad – Shaykh of one of the Ghazawiyya tribes.

al-Shahwan, Fadil – Leader of the ʿAjarma tribes after his father Sayil's death in 1923.

al-Shahwan, Sayil – Leader of the ʿAjarma tribes until his death in 1923 during the Balqaʾ Revolt.

Shaʿlan, Nuri – Head of the Ruwalla tribal confederacy.

al-Shamayla, ʿAbd al-Mahdi – Leader of the Shamayla tribe in Karak.

al-Shurayda, ʿAbdullah Kulayb – Leader of the Kura district since his father Kulayb's death in 1941. Beyond his shaykhly duties he also held administrative, legislative and ministerial positions.

al-Shurayda, Kulayb – Leader of the Kura district until his death in 1941.

bin Srur, ʿAwda – Shaykh of the Masaʿid tribes.

al-Sudi, Sulayman – Leader of the Rusan tribe and the Saru district in the ʿAjlun province.

al-Tarawna, Husayn – Head of the *Sharaqa* tribal alliance of Karak and the Tarawna tribe. He also led the national opposition in the 1930s.

abu Taya, ʿAwda – Leader of the Tawayha branch of the Huwaytat until his death in 1924 and Emir Faysal's close ally during the Arab Revolt.

abu Taya, Muhammad – Shaykh of the Tawayha tribes of the Huwaytat from 1924, replacing his deceased father ʿAwda abu Taya.

al-ʿUbaydat, Kayid al-Miflih – Leader of the Kafarat district in northern Transjordan until he was killed in 1920 by British aeroplanes while leading a raid into Palestine.

al-Zaban, ʿAdub – Shaykh of the Zaban tribe of the Bani Sakhr (son of Tarad bin Fahd).

Zinati, Muhammad – Shaykh of the Zinati tribe of the Ghazawiyya who sold his land in Bisan (Palestine) and settled in Transjordan in the 1940s.

al-Zuʿbi, Fawwaz – Leader of the town of Ramtha.

bin Zuhayr, Muhammad – Shaykh of the Jubur tribe of the Bani Sakhr and the *qadi qilta* of the entire confederation.

NOTES

Introduction

1   Linda L. Layne, *Home and Homeland: The Dialogics of Tribal and National Identities in Jordan* (Princeton: Princeton University Press, 1994); Andrew Shryock, *Nationalism and the Genealogical Imagination: Oral History and Textual Authority in Tribal Jordan* (Berkeley: California University Press, 1997); Richard T. Antoun, "Civil Society, Tribal Process, and Change in Jordan: An Anthropological View," *International Journal of Middle East Studies* 32 (2000), pp. 441-463; Andrew Shryock and Sally Howell, "'Ever a Guest in our House': The Amir Abdullah, Shaykh Majid al-Adwan and the Practice of Jordanian House Politics, Remembered by Umm Sultan, the Widow of Majid," *International Journal of Middle East Studies* 33 (2001), pp. 247-269. For a different and in many ways contradictory approach see: Paul A. Jureidini and R. D. McLaurin, *Jordan: The Impact of Social Change on the Role of the Tribes* (NY: Praeger Press, 1984). Joseph A. Massad, *Colonial Effects: The Making of National Identity in Jordan* (NY: Columbia University Press, 2001) analyses tribalism from a critical post-colonial approach. See also the excellent study of politics in Karak: Peter Gubser, *Politics and Change in Al-Karak, Jordan* (London: Oxford University Press, 1973).

2   Philip S. Khoury and Joseph Kostiner, "Introduction: Tribes and the Complexities of State Formation in the Middle East," in idem (eds.), *Tribes and State Formation in the Middle East* (Los Angeles: I.B. Tauris, 1991), p. 7.

3   Philip Robins, *A History of Jordan* (Cambridge: Cambridge University Press, 2004), p. 15.

4   For elaboration of this concept in an African context see: Mahmood Mamdani, *Citizen and Subject: Contemporary Africa and the Legacy of Late Colonialism* (Princeton: Princeton University Press, 1996).

5   For a discussion of some of these ideas and their implementation in mandatory Iraq see: Toby Dodge, *Inventing Iraq: The Failure of Nation Building and a History Denied* (NY: Columbia University Press, 2003). The failure of state-formation in colonial Iraq represents the exact opposite of the Jordanian case.

6   Mary C. Wilson, *King Abdullah, Britain and the Making of Jordan* (Cambridge: Cambridge University Press, 1987) remains the standard work on mandatory Transjordan.

7   The persistence of British imperial drive worldwide, even after World War One, is one of the central themes in the much acclaimed P. J. Cain and A. G. Hopkins, *British Imperialism: Vol. II: Crisis and Deconstruction 1914-1990* (London: Longman, 1993).

8   Cain and Hopkins, *British Imperialism*, pp. 216-218; John W. Cell, "Colonial Rule," in Judith Brown and Wm. Roger Louis (eds.), *The Oxford History of the British Empire, Vol. IV: The Twentieth Century* (Oxford: Oxford University Press, 1999), pp. 237-243.

9   Mamdani, *Citizen and Subject*, pp. 72-77.

10 James C. Scott, *Seeing Like a State* (New Haven and London: Yale University Press, 1998).

11 Nigel J. Ashton, "'A "Special Relationship" Sometimes in Spite of Ourselves:' Britain and Jordan, 1957-1973," *The Journal of Imperial and Commonwealth History* 33 (2005), pp. 221-244.

12 Amatzia Baram, "Neo-Tribalism in Iraq: Saddam Hussein's Tribal Policies, 1991-6," *International Journal of Middle East Studies* 29 (1997), pp. 1-31.

13 Scholars such as Richard Antoun, Nazih Ayubi, Amatzia Baram, Steven Caton, Paul Dresch, Dale Eickelman, Philip Khoury, Fuad Khuri, Joseph Kostiner, Emanuel Marx, Khaldoun al-Naqib, Madawi Al Rasheed, Richard Tapper and Andrew Shryock.

14 Nazih N. Ayubi, *Over-stating the Arab State: Politics and Society in the Middle East* (London: I.B. Tauris, 1995), pp. 244, 51.

15 Khoury and Kostiner, "Introduction," p. 7.

16 Ayubi, *Over-stating*, pp. 244, 51.

17 Richard Tapper, "Introduction," in idem (ed.), *The Conflict of Tribe and State in Iran and Afghanistan* (London: Croom Helm, 1983), p. 8 cited in Khoury and Kostiner, "Introduction," p. 5; Ayubi, *Over-stating*, p. 125. See also Richard Tapper, *Frontier Nomads of Iran: A Political and Social History of the Shahsevan* (Cambridge: Cambridge University Press, 1997) and Dale F. Eickelman, *The Middle East and Central Asia: An Anthropological Approach*, 3rd edn. (Upper Saddle River (NJ): Prentice-Hall, 1998).

18 Tapper, "Introduction," p. 9 cited in Khoury and Kostiner, "Introduction," p. 5; Tapper, *Frontier Nomads*, p. 6.

19 Khoury and Kostiner, "Introduction," p. 7; Gabriel Ben-Dor, *State and Conflict in the Middle East* (Boulder: Westview Press, 1985), pp. 1-34; Kiren Aziz Chaudhry, *The Price of Wealth: Economies and Institutions in the Middle East* (Ithaca and London: Cornell University Press, 1997), p. 37.

20 Khaldun Hasan al-Naqib, *Al-Mujtamaʿ wal-Dawla fil-Khalij wal-Jazira al-ʿArabiyya* [Society and State in the Gulf and the Arabian Peninsular] (Beirut: 1987), pp. 171-174, cited in Ayubi, *Over-stating*, p. 241.

21 Joel S. Migdal, *Strong Societies and Weak States: State-Society Relations and State Capabilities in the Third World* (Princeton: Princeton University Press, 1988), pp. 28-32, 257.

22 Timothy Mitchell, "The Limits of the State: Beyond Statist Approaches and their Critics," *American Political Science Review* 85 (1991), pp. 77-96; Roger Owen, *State, Power and Politics in the Making of the Middle East* (London: Routledge, 1992), pp. 4-5; Sami Zubaida, *Islam, the People and the State*, 2nd edn. (London: I.B. Tauris, 1993), chapter 6.

23 As proposed in Khoury and Kostiner, "Introduction," pp. 8-11.

Chapter One

1   Abdullah bin al-Husayn, *Al-Athar al-Kamila lil-Malik ʿAbdullah bin al-Husayn* [The Complete Works of King Abdullah bin al-Husayn], 2nd edn. (Beirut: Al-Dar al-Muttahida lil-Nashr, 1979), p. 35. Emphasis added.

2   Trans-Jordania, 9 March 1920, Schneurson papers, Hagana Archive, Tel Aviv [Hereafter HA].

3   Eugene L. Rogan, *Frontiers of the State in the Late Ottoman Empire: Transjordan, 1850-1921* (Cambridge: Cambridge University Press, 1999), chapter 9; Abla Mohamed Amawi, "State and Class in Transjordan: A Study of State Autonomy" (Ph.D., Georgetown University, 1992), p. 165.

4   Rogan, *Frontiers*, pp. 242-245.

5 Uriel Dann, *Studies in the History of Transjordan, 1920-1949: The Making of a State* (Boulder: Westview Press, 1984), p. 18; P. J. Vatikiotis, *Politics and the Military in Jordan: A Study of the Arab Legion, 1921-1957* (London: Frank Cass, 1967), pp. 40-41, 57-58; Yoav Gelber, *Jewish-Transjordanian Relations, 1921-1948* (London: Frank Cass, 1997), pp. 9-10; Sulayman Musa, *Min Ta'rikhina al-Hadith* [From our Recent History] (Amman: Lajnat Ta'rikh al-Urdunn, 1994), p. 75.

6 Yusuf Salim al-Shuwayhat al-ᶜUzayzat, *Al-ᶜUzayzat fi Madaba* [The ᶜUzayzat in Madaba, n.d., n.p], pp. 125-126; Muhammad ᶜAbd al-Qadir Khrisat, *Al-Urdunniyyun wal-Qadaya al-Wataniyya wal-Qawmiyya* [The Jordanians and National and pan-Arab Issues] (Amman: Al-Jamiᶜa al-Urdunniyya, 1991), pp. 17-18; Muhammad ᶜAdnan al-Bakhit, "Mudhakkirat al-Duktur Jamil Fa'iq al-Tutanji" [Memoirs of Dr. Jamil Fa'iq al-Tutanji], *Dirasat al-ᶜUlum al-Tibbiyya* 12 (1985), p. 16; Musa, *Min Ta'rikhina*, p. 75; Muhammad ᶜAli al-Sawirki al-Kurdi, *Ta'rikh al-Salt wal-*Balqa' [The History of al-Salt and the Balqa'] (Amman: Dar ᶜAmmar, 1998), pp. 69-73.

7 Rogan, *Frontiers*, pp. 242-243; ᶜAwda Qasus, *Mudhakkirat* [Memoirs, unpublished typescript], pp. 132-133: Eliyahu Eilat, *Shivat Tsiyon ve-ᶜArav* [The Return to Zion and Arabia] (Tel Aviv: Dvir, 1971), pp. 127-128; *Al-ᶜAsima* (Damascus), 29 December 1919, cited in Khrisat, *Al-Urdunniyyun*, p. 15.

8 Qasus, *Mudhakkirat*, pp. 130-133; Gelber, *Jewish-Transjordanian*, pp. 9-10. On Ottoman policy: Rogan, *Frontiers*, pp. 227-228.

9 Khrisat, *Al-Urdunniyyun*, p. 18; Gelber, *Jewish-Transjordanian*, pp. 9-10; Camp, Summery of Jericho Political Information, 15 January 1920, RG-2/50a, Israel State Archives, Jerusalem [Hereafter ISA]; Munib al-Madi and Sulayman Musa, *Ta'rikh al-Urdunn fil-Qarn al-ᶜIshrin, 1900-1959* [The History of Jordan in the Twentieth Century, 1900-1959] 2nd edn. (Amman: Maktabat al-Muhtasib, 1988), pp. 85-88; Qasus, *Mudhakkirat*, p. 131.

10 Madi and Musa, *Ta'rikh*, p. 87; Khrisat, *Al-Urdunniyyun*, p. 24; Al-ᶜUzayzat, *Al-ᶜUzayzat*, pp. 125-126; Qasus, *Mudhakkirat*, pp. 132-133; *Al-ᶜAsima*, 17 February 1919, cited in al-Kurdi, *Ta'rikh al-Salt*, p. 73.

11 Joseph Kostiner, "The Hashemite 'Tribal Confederacy' of the Arab Revolt, 1916-1917," in E. Ingram (ed.), *National and International Politics in the Middle East: Essays in Honour of Elie Kedourie* (London: Frank Cass, 1986), pp. 134-140. Also: Joshua Teitelbaum, *The Rise and Fall of the Hashemite Kingdom of Arabia* (London: Hurst, 2001).

12 Ernest C. Dawn, *From Ottomanism to Arabism: Essays on the Origins of Arab Nationalism* (Urbana, IL: University of Illinois Press, 1978).

13 Qasus, *Mudhakkirat*, p. 130; Trans-Jordania, 2 February 1920, Schneurson papers, HA.

14 On the diplomatic dimension see: Aaron S. Klieman, *Foundations of British Policy in the Arab World: The Cairo Conference of 1921* (Baltimore and London: The Johns Hopkins Press, 1970), pp. 38-41; On the similar situation in inner Syria: James L. Gelvin: *Divided Loyalties: Nationalism and Mass Politics in Syria at the Close of Empire* (Berkeley: University of California Press, 1998), pp. 87-88.

15 Camp to GHQ, Cairo, Conditions at Kerak, 23 December 1919, News from Salt, 5 January 1920 and Summery of Jericho Political Information, 9 &15 January 1920, RG-2/50a ISA.

16 Rogan, *Frontiers*, pp. 243-244; Trans-Jordania, 2 February & 9 March 1920, Schneurson papers, HA; Mary C. Wilson, *King Abdullah, Britain and the Making of Jordan* (Cambridge: Cambridge University Press, 1987), pp. 44-45; Camp, 19 February 1920, RG-2/1 ISA, cited in ibid., p. 225.

17 Cited in Madi and Musa, *Ta'rikh*, p. 95.

18 Trans-Jordania, 9 March 1920, Schneurson papers, HA.

19 Rufayfan al-Majali to Nasib al-Bakri, 2 &16 May 1920, Jordan Collection, St Antony's College, Oxford.

20 Al-ʿUzayzat, *Al-ʿUzayzat*, pp. 116-118, 120, 127; Camp, News from Salt, 5 January 1920, RG-2/50a ISA.

21 Hind Abu al-Shaʿr, *Irbid wa-Jiwaruha, 1850-1928* [Irbid and its Surroundings, 1850-1928] (Amman: Jamiʿat Al al-Bayt, 1995), p. 158; Madi and Musa, *Taʾrikh*, p. 124; Interview with Dr. Fares Dhaher Al-Faiz, Amman, 4 July 1998.

22 Rogan, *Frontiers*, pp. 7-9.

23 Muhammad Abu Hassan, *Al-Qadaʾ al-ʿAshaʾiri fil-Urdunn* [Tribal Law in Jordan] (Amman: Al al-Bayt, n.d), pp. 23-24.

24 Ahmed Saleh Suleiman Owidi [al-ʿAbbadi], "Bedouin Justice in Jordan: The Customary Legal System of the Tribes and its Integration into the Framework of State Policy from 1921 onwards" (Ph.D., University of Cambridge, 1982), p. 40.

25 *A Handbook of Syria* (Geographical Section of the Naval Intelligence Division, Naval Staff, Admiralty, [1920?]), pp. 229-230. For an analysis of tribal customary law see: Abu Hassan, *Al-Qadaʾ al-ʿAshaʾiri*; Owidi, *Bedouin Justice*; ʿAwda Qasus, *Al-Qadaʾ al-Badawi* [Bedouin Law] (Amman: n.p., 1936).

26 Trans-Jordania, 9 March 1920, Schneurson papers, HA.

27 Gelber, *Jewish-Transjordanian*, p. 12. These shaykhs included Mithqal, Mashhur and Haditha al-Khurasyha of the Bani Sakhr, Rufayfan al-Majali and his principal rival for hegemony in Karak, Husayn al-Tarawna, Sayil al-Shahwan of the ʿAjarma tribes and an unnamed representative of the Huwaytat.

28 Camp to CID, OETA South, 19 February 1920, RG-2/50a ISA.

29 Wilson, *King Abdullah*, p. 45; Madi and Musa, *Taʾrikh*, pp. 91-92; Mahmud ʿUbaydat, *Al-Urdunn fil-Taʾrikh* [Jordan in History] (Tarablus (Lubnan): Manshurat Jadwa Bres, 1992), vol. I, pp. 314-315.

30 High Commissioner to Prodrome, 3 August 1920, Camp, Notes on Southern Part of Trans-Jordania, 27 July 1920 and Storrs to Samuel, 21 August 1920, RG-2/50a ISA.

31 Samuel to Prodrome, 7 August 1920, RG-2/50a ISA.

32 Dann, *Studies*, p. 18; Wilson, *King Abdullah*, p. 45.

33 Wilson, *King Abdullah*, p. 48; Monckton to his mother, 21 August 1920, Monckton papers, St Antony's College; Somerset to his father, 24 August 1920, Somerset papers, St Antony's College.

34 Wilson, *King Abdullah*, p. 226n; Dann, *Studies*, p. 28n. Abu Nowar's catalogue of the tribes and communities that failed to appear at the meeting is much larger but he fails to provide any evidence to back up his list, which includes the ʿAbbad, ʿAjarma, Hadid, Lawziyyin and Syrian merchants of Amman. Maʿan Abu Nowar, *The History of the Hashemite Kingdom of Jordan: Vol. I: The Creation and Development of Transjordan, 1920-29* (Oxford: Ithaca Press, 1989), p. 31.

35 Wilson, *King Abdullah*, p. 46; Dann, *Studies*, p. 19; Klieman, *Foundations*, p. 72.

36 Khrisat, *Al-Urdunniyyun*, p. 34; Khayr al-Din Zirikli, *ʿAman fi ʿAmman* [Two Years in Amman] (Cairo: Al-Matbaʿa al-ʿArabiyya, 1925), p. 40; Saʿid al-Mufti, "Saʿid al-Mufti Yatadhakkaru" [Saʿid al-Mufti Remembers], *Al-Dustur* (Amman), 3 March 1976; Abu Nowar, *The History*, p. 25.

37 GSI Beersheba, Intelligence Report no. 6, 13 September 1920, RG-2/51 ISA.

38 Director of General Public Security to High Commissioner, 30 August 1920, RG-2/50a ISA.

39 Director of General Public Security to Civil Secretary, 14 September 1920, RG-2/50a ISA.

40 Kathryn Tidrick, *Heart-beguiling Araby* (Cambridge: Cambridge University Press, 1981), pp. 1, 30-31.

41 Ibid., p. 208.

42 Ibid., p. 31.

43 Ibid., p. 211. For more on the public schools' long-lasting influence on their alumnae

see: Robert Heussler, *Yesterday's Rulers: The Making of the British Colonial Service* (Syracuse: Syracuse University Press, 1963), pp. 88-103. On the social background of British officials in the region: J. Morris, *Farewell the Trumpets: An Imperial Retreat* (Harmondsworth: Penguin, 1978), p. 264; Anthony Kirk-Greene, *Britain's Imperial Administrators, 1858-1966* (London: Macmillan Press, 2000), p. 16.

44 Bernard Wasserstein, *The British in Palestine: The Mandatory Government and the Arab-Jewish Conflict, 1917-1929* (London: Royal Historical Society, 1978), pp. 12-13.

45 Mustafa Hamarneh, "Social and Economic Transformation of Trans-Jordan, 1921-1946" (Ph.D., Georgetown University, 1985), pp. 107-108.

46 Camp to Civil Secretary, 13 August 1920, RG-2/50a ISA.

47 GSI Beersheba, Intelligence Report no. 6, 13 September 1920, RG-2/51 ISA.

48 Camp to Civil Secretary, 26 August 1920, RG-2/50a ISA. Emphasis added.

49 Dann, *Studies*, pp. 18-20.

50 Peake and Somerset, Observation on Dr. Weizmann's letter to the Secretary of State for the Colonies, 14 March 1921, Somerset papers; ʿUthman Qasim to Shakir bin Zayd, 23 August 1922 (courtesy of Sulayman Musa); Abu al-Shaʿr, *Irbid*, pp. 92-97.

51 Somerset to Father, 2 & 16 September 1920, 26 October 1920, 18 January 1921, Somerset papers; Somerset to High Commissioner, 11 September 1920, RG-2/50a ISA; Sulayman Musa, *Imarat Sharq al-Urdunn: Nasha'tuha wa-Tatawwuruha fi Rubʿ Qarn, 1921-1946* [The Emirate of Transjordan: Its Growth and Development in a Quarter of a Century, 1921-1946] (Amman: Lajnat Ta'rikh al-Urdunn, 1990), pp. 62-64.

52 Saʿd Abu Diyya, *Safahat Matwiyya min Ta'rikh al-Urdunn* [Folded Pages from the History of Jordan] ([Amman]: Dar Al-Bashir, 1998), p. 264; Sulayman Musa, *Wujuh wa-Malamih: Sura Shakhsiyya li-baʿd Rijal al-Siyasa wal-Qalam* [Prominent Personalities: Personal Portraits of some of the Men of Politics and the Pen] (Amman: Wizarat al-Thaqafa wal-Shabab, 1980), p. 26; Abu Nowar, *The History*, pp. 31, 58; Hamarneh, "Social and Economic," pp. 109-110. Abu Diyya and Hamarneh draw on Major C. S. Jarvis, *Arab Command: The Biography of Lieutenant Colonel F. W. Peake Pasha* (London: Hutchinson, 1942), p. 66.

53 Rogan, *Frontiers*, pp. 247-249; Michael Richard Fischbach, "State, Society and Land in ʿAjlun (Northern Transjordan), 1850-1950," (Ph.D., Georgetown University, 1992), p. 22; Salih Mustafa Yusuf al-Tall, *Mudhakkirat* [Memoirs, unpublished MS], pp. 16-17; Abu al-Shaʿr, *Irbid*, pp. 92-97. On the local chieftaincies in ʿAjlun during the nineteenth century see: Rogan, *Frontiers*, pp. 24-27; Michael Fischbach, *State, Society and Land in Jordan* (Leiden: Brill, 2000), pp. 10-17.

54 Musa, *Imara*, p. 63.

55 Somerset to Father, 9 & 16 September & 26 October 1920, Somerset papers.

56 Monckton to Mother, 28 February 1921, Monckton papers. Emphasis in the original.

57 Somerset to Mother, 24 September 1920, Somerset to Father, 1 October, 26 November & 14 December 1920, Somerset papers; Musa, *Wujuh*, p. 26.

58 Somerset to Mother, 24 September, 4 October & 14 November 1920; Somerset to Father, 14 December, 1920, Somerset papers; Monckton to Dann, 5 May 1968, Monckton papers.

59 Revised record of conversation between Monckton and Alsberg, September 1968, Monckton papers.

60 Kathryn Tidrick, *Empire and the English Character* (London: I.B. Tauris, 1990, 1992); Wm. Roger Louis, "Introduction," in Robin Winks (ed.) *The Oxford History of the British Empire, Vol. V: Historiography* (Oxford: Oxford University Press, 1999), pp. 21-23; P. J. Cain and A. G. Hopkins, *British Imperialism:* Vol. II: *Crisis and Deconstruction 1914-1990* (London: Longman, 1993), pp. 216-218, 233; John W. Cell, "Colonial Rule," in Judith Brown and Wm. Roger Louis (eds.), *The Oxford History of the British Empire, Vol. IV: The Twentieth Century* (Oxford: Oxford University Press, 1999), pp. 237-243.

61   Monckton to Dann, 10 February 1970, Monckton to Father, 18 & 29 December
     1920, Monckton to Mother, 10 October 1920, Monckton papers; Fischbach, "Land in
     ʿAjlun," p. 82; Rogan, *Frontiers*, pp. 40-41.
62   Wilson, *King Abdullah*, p. 45.
63   Jurj Farid Tarif Dawud, *Al-Salt wa-Jiwaruha, 1864-1921* [Al-Salt and its Surroundings,
     1864-1921] (Amman: Bank al-Aʿmal, 1994), pp. 238-239; Nawfan Raja al-Hamud
     al-Sawariyya, *ʿAmman wa-Jiwaruha khilal al-fatra 1864-1921* [Amman and its
     Surroundings, 1864-1921] (Amman: Bank al-Aʿmal, 1996), pp. 147-201; Rogan,
     Frontiers, pp. 27-28, 74-75, 86-87; Fischbach, *Land in Jordan*, pp. 14-15.
64   Monckton to Mother, 21 August 1920, Monckton papers.
65   Political Situation Report, 11 September 1920, Brunton papers, St Antony's College.
66   Monckton to District Governor, 23 August 1920, Monckton papers; Mithqal, Mashhur
     and Sayil to High Commissioner, 30 August 1920, RG-2/50a ISA.
67   Political Report, 14 October 1920, Brunton papers.
68   Dann, *Studies*, pp. 21-23; Muhammad Khayr Haghanduqa, *Mirza Basha Wasfi: Kitab
     Watha'iqi* [Mirza Pasha Wasfi: Documented Book] (Amman: Al-Jamʿiyya
     al-ʿIlmiyya al-Malakiyya, 1985), pp. 24, 31, 47-64.
69   Dann, *Studies*, p. 24.
70   Brunton, Political Report, 9 October 1920, Brunton papers.
71   Brunton, Political Reports 14 & 23 October 1920, Brunton papers.
72   Political Report, 23 October 1920, Brunton papers.
73   Autobiographical essay on Peake's activities in Trans-Jordan in the decade after 1918,
     pp. 12-14, Peake papers, Imperial War Museum; Jarvis, *Arab Command*, pp. 3-4;
     Zirikli, *ʿAman*, pp. 7-8.
74   Rogan, *Frontiers*, pp. 250-251.
75   Eugene L. Rogan, "Bringing the State Back: The Limits of Ottoman Rule in Jordan,
     1840-1910," in Eugene L. Rogan and Tariq Tell (eds.), *Village, Steppe and State: The
     Social Origins of Modern Jordan* (London: British Academic Press, 1994), p. 57; Rogan,
     Frontiers, p. 183.
76   Alec Seath Kirkbride, *A Crackle of Thorns* (London: John Murray, 1956), p. 21; On
     Karakian politics see: Peter Gubser, *Politics and Change in Al-Karak, Jordan* (London:
     Oxford University Press, 1973); On the correlation between tribal politics and local
     government: Musa, *Imara*, p. 64.
77   Qasus, *Mudhakkirat*, p. 139; Gubser, *Politics*, pp. 98-99.
78   Monckton to Dann, 10 February 1970, Monckton papers; Kirkbride, *A Crackle*,
     pp. 20-21, 28.
79   Zirikli, *ʿAman*, pp. 23-24; Eliyahu Epstein, "Be-Artsot Hamizrah" [In the Orient
     Countries], *Yarhon Ahdut ha-ʿAvoda* 13 (1931), p. 469; Major R. S. Y. Buller, "Report
     on the Winter Grazing Areas for Camels" enclosed in C. A. Shute to HQ RAF
     Palestine & Transjordan, 19 March 1931, Glubb papers, St Antony's College; Musa
     Imara, p. 65.
80   Klieman, *Foundations*, pp. 75-76, 206-207.

Chapter Two

1   For example: Mary C. Wilson, *King Abdullah, Britain and the Making of Jordan*
     (Cambridge: Cambridge University Press, 1987), chapter 5; Uriel Dann, *Studies in
     the History of Transjordan, 1920-1949: The Making of a State* (Boulder: Westview
     Press, 1984), pp. 83-84; Elizabeth Monroe, *Philby of Arabia* (London: Faber&Faber,
     1973), pp. 129-130. A welcome exception is: Toby Dodge, *An Arabian Prince, English
     Gentlemen and the Tribes East to the River Jordan: Abdullah and the Creation and
     Consolidation of the Transjordanian State* (London: SOAS, 1994).

2 Khayr al-Din Zirikli, ʿAman fi ʿAmman [Two Years in Amman] (Cairo: Al-Matbaʿa
   al-ʿArabiyya, 1925), p. 13.

3 Resume of Salt and Amman reports from 23.10.20 to 3.11.20, RG-2/50a, Israel State
   Archives (ISA); Munib al-Madi and Sulayman Musa, Taʾrikh al-Urdunn fil-Qarn
   al-ʿIshrin, 1900-1959 [The History of Jordan in the Twentieth Century, 1900-1959]
   2nd edn. (Amman: Maktabat al-Muhtasib, 1988), p. 133.

4 Wilson, King Abdullah, p. 226n; Extracts from Peake's report, 14 January 1921,
   FO141/440, National Archives, London (NA); Sulayman Musa, Imarat Sharq
   al-Urdunn: Nashaʾtuha wa-Tatawwuruha fi Rubʿ Qarn, 1921-1946 [The Emirate of
   Transjordan: Its Growth and Development in a Quarter of a Century, 1921-1946]
   (Amman: Lajnat Taʾrikh al-Urdunn, 1990), pp. 79n, 93.

5 Samuel to Curzon, 20 December 1920, FO141/440; Samuel to Churchill, 3 March
   1921and report on the Political Situation in Palestine and Trans-Jordania, February
   1921, CO733/1 NA; Sulayman Musa, Wujuh wa-Malamih: Sura Shakhsiyya li-baʿd Rijal
   al-Siyasa wal-Qalam [Prominent Personalities: Personal Portraits of some of the Men of
   Politics and the Pen] (Amman: Wizarat al-Thaqafa wal-Shabab, 1980), pp. 27-30.

6 Revised record of conversation between Monckton and Alsberg, September 1968,
   Monckton papers, St Antony's College, Oxford; Saʿid al-Mufti, "Saʿid al-Mufti
   Yatadhakkaru" [Saʿid al-Mufti Remembers], Al-Dustur (Amman), 22 February 1976;
   Samuel to Curzon, 20 December 1920, FO141/440; Samuel to Churchill, 3 March
   1921, CO733/1; Musa, Imara, pp. 85-86; Aaron S. Klieman, Foundations of British
   Policy in the Arab World: The Cairo Conference of 1921 (Baltimore and London: The
   Johns Hopkins Press, 1970), pp. 75-76.

7 Report written by L. L. Bright, 13 March 1921, Somerset papers, St Antony's College;
   Musa, Imara, p. 95; Alec Seath Kirkbride, A Crackle of Thorns (London: John Murray,
   1956), pp. 26-27.

8 On the Cairo Conference: Klieman, Foundations, pp. 105-138; Wilson, King Abdullah,
   pp. 51-53.

9 The most recent example is Joseph A. Massad, Colonial Effects: The Making of National
   Identity in Jordan (NY: Columbia University Press, 2001), p. 27.

10 ʿUthman Qasim to Shakir bin Zayd, 23 August 1922 (courtesy of Sulayman Musa).

11 For the Ottoman relations with the Transjordanian tribes: Eugene L. Rogan, Frontiers of
   the State in the Late Ottoman Empire: Transjordan, 1850-1921 (Cambridge: Cambridge
   University Press, 1999); Norman N. Lewis, Nomads and Settlers in Syria and Jordan,
   1800-1980 (Cambridge: Cambridge University Press, 1987); Raouf Saʿd Abujaber,
   Pioneers over Jordan: The Frontier of Settlement in Transjordan, 1850-1914 (London: I.B.
   Tauris, 1989); Mustafa Hamarneh, "Social and Economic Transformation of Trans-
   Jordan, 1921- 1946" (Ph.D., Georgetown University, 1985); Nawfan Raja
   al-Hamud al-Sawariyya, ʿAmman wa-Jiwaruha khilal al-fatra 1864-1921 [Amman and
   its Surroundings, 1864-1921] (Amman: Bank al-Aʿmal, 1996).

12 Samuel to Churchill, 21 April 1921, FO371/6372 NA; Deeds to Samuel, 2 July 1921,
   CO733/4; Extracts from Lawrence in: Samuel to Churchill, 10 April 1921, CO733/2.

13 Deeds to Samuel, 2 July 1921, CO733/4; Situation in Trans-Jordania, August 1921,
   FO141/440; Abramson, Report no. 8, 1 October 1921, CO733/6. On the household
   army see: Philip Robins, "The Consolidation of the Hashemite Power in Jordan, 1921-
   1946" (Ph.D., University of Exeter, 1988), pp. 184-185.

14 Philip S. Khoury, "The Tribal Shaykh, French Tribal Policy, and the Nationalist
   Movement in Syria between Two World Wars," Middle East Studies 18 (1982), p. 184.

15 Al-Sharq al-ʿArabi [The Arab East] (Amman), 12 May 1924; Wilson, King Abdullah,
   p. 77. Abdullah gave a car and a chauffeur to Mithqal, Haditha al-Khuraysha from the
   Bani Sakhr and Rufayfan al-Majali from Karak. He allowed Mithqal to reclaim 10,000
   dunum of land which had been confiscated by the Ottomans, thus making him the
   biggest landowner in the country. Plots of land were also given to Rufayfan, Husayn

al-Tarawna and other shaykhs from Karak. Thomas, Trans-Jordan, 30 September 1923, CO733/67. Haditha al-Khuraysha registered the land in al-Muwaqqar under his name. Haditha to the Prime Minister, 9 May 1939, file *Shakawi al-ʿAshaʾir* [The Tribes' Complaints], the Prime Ministry files, National Library, Amman; Abujaber, *Pioneers*, p. 303n.

16   Numerous examples in *Al-Sharq al-ʿArabi* during the years 1923-1926.

17   Wilson, *King Abdullah*, pp. 61-62.

18   Mendel Cohen, *Be-Hatsar ha-Melekh ʿAbdullah* [At King Abdullah's Court] (Tel Aviv: ʿAm ʿOved, 1980), pp. 23, 25. Emphasis added.

19   Somerset to Father 8 May & 20 June 1921, Somerset papers; Kirkbride, *A Crackle*; Kamal Salibi, *The Modern History of Jordan* (London: I.B. Tauris, 1993), p. 100; Suleiman Mousa, "King Abdullah: A Centennial Salute," in idem, *Cameos: Jordan and Arab Nationalism* (Amman: Ministry of Culture, 1997), p. 134; ʿArif al-ʿArif diary, 19 June 1926, al-ʿArif papers, St. Antony's College; Bulus Salman, *Khamsa Aʿwam fi Sharqi al-Urdunn* [Five Years in Transjordan] 2nd edn. (Amman: Al-Dar al-Ahliyya, 1989), pp. 13-14.

20   Transjordan was declared an Emirate in May 1923. For the sake of convenience, the term is used here to depict the political arrangement since Abdullah assumed power in 1921.

21   Reports no. 1 & 2 from Chief British Representative Trans-Jordania, 21 April & 15 May 1921, CO733/3; Report no. 8, 1 October 1921, CO733/6; ʿAwda Qasus, *Mudhakkirat* [Memoirs, unpublished typescript], p. 141.

22   Samuel to Churchill, 30 April 1921 and Churchill to Samuel, 1 May 1921, CO733/2.

23   Report no. 5 from Chief British Representative, Trans-Jordania, 1 July 1921, CO733/4; Abujaber, *Pioneers*, p. 76.

24   Report no. 8 from Chief British Representative, Trans-Jordania 1 October 1921, CO733/6; Yusuf Salim al-Shuwayhat al-ʿUzayzat, *Al-ʿUzayzat fi Madaba* [The ʿUzayzat in Madaba, n.d., n.p], p. 128.

25   Report no. 4, 5 June 1921, CO733/3 and report no. 7, 1 September 1921, CO733/6.

26   For a critical account of Abdullah's conduct see: Robins, "The Consolidation," pp. 128-133.

27   Ibid., p. 187; Wilson, *King Abdullah*, p. 62; Dodge, *Arabian Prince*, pp. 29-32; Major C. S. Jarvis, *Arab Command: The Biography of Lieutenant Colonel F. W. Peake Pasha* (London: Hutchinson, 1942), p.114; Deeds to Samuel, 2 July 1921, CO733/4.

28   The following account is based on: Abramon, Report no. 4, 5 June, 1921, CO733/3 and report no. 5, 1 July 1921, CO733/4; Musa, *Imara*, pp. 120-122; Jarvis, *Arab Command*, p. 75; F. G. Peake, "Trans-Jordan," *Journal of the Royal Central Asian Society* 23 (1939), p. 384; Interview with ʿAbdullah Kulayb al-Shurayda, *Al-Dustur*, 6 May 1987; Saʿd Abu Diyya, *Safahat Matwiyya min Taʾrikh al-Urdunn* [Folded Pages from the History of Jordan] ([Amman]: Dar Al-Bashir, 1998), p. 216; Testimony of Najib Shurayda, Kulayb's nephew, in ʿAmir Jadallah Musa, "Al-ʿAlaqat al-Urdunniyya - al-Suʿudiyya ma bayna 1921-1928" [Jordanian-Saudi Relations, 1921-1928] (B.A. dissertation, University of Jordan, 1977), p. 10; Salih Mustafa Yusuf al-Tall, *Mudhakkirat* [Memoirs, unpublished MS], p. 15.

29   Jarvis, *Arab Command*, pp. 77, 87-88.

30   Abramson to Samuel, 9 June 1921, CO733/3.

31   Wilson, *King Abdullah*, pp. 64-65.

32   For a useful account of the social and cultural gap between the Arab nationalists and the local population see: Robins, "The Consolidation," p. 187. Also: Qasus, *Mudhakkirat*, pp. 140, 143-144; Jarvis, *Arab Command*, pp. 77, 114; Hamarneh, "Social and Economic," pp. 126-127.

33   Peake to Somerset, 21 November 1921, Somerset papers.

34   Deeds to Samuel, 2 July 1921, CO733/4.

35 Situation in Trans-Jordania, August 1921, FO141/440; Abramson, report no. 7, 1 September 1921, CO733/6.
36 Situation in Trans-Jordania, August 1921, FO141/440.
37 Abramson, Report no. 6, 1 August 1921, CO733/5.
38 Deeds to Samuel, 2 July 1921, CO733/4; Somerset to Father, 8 May & 20 June 1921, Somerset papers.
39 Wilson, *King Abdullah*, pp. 63-64.
40 Dann, *Studies*, p. 44; Jarvis, *Arab Command*, pp. 85-86, 89.
41 Qasus, *Mudhakkirat*, pp. 140-141; Peter Gubser, *Politics and Change in Al-Karak, Jordan* (London: Oxford University Press, 1973), pp. 93, 99-101; Philby, Trans-Jordan situation report no.1, 1 April 1922, CO733/21 and no. 2, 1 July 1922, CO733/23.
42 Peake to Philby, report for 2 October 1922-18 January 1921, CO733/42.
43 Philby, Trans-Jordan situation report, no.1, 1 April 1922, CO733/21; Samuel to Churchill, 19 July 1922, CO733/23.
44 *Al-Sharq al-cArabi*, 31 March 1924.
45 Peake to Philby, 19 January 1923 and Philby to Samuel, 4 February 1923, CO733/42.
46 Macan Abu Nowar, *The History of the Hashemite Kingdom of Jordan: Vol. I: The Creation and Development of Transjordan, 1920-29* (Oxford: Ithaca Press, 1989), p. 77.
47 Qasus, *Mudhakkirat*, p. 142.
48 Abu Nowar, *The History*, pp. 92-93.
49 Thomas, Trans-Jordan, 30 September 1923, CO733/67.
50 Philby, Trans-Jordan situation report, no.1, 1 April 1922, CO733/21.
51 Philby, Trans-Jordan situation report, no. 2, 1 July 1922, CO733/23.
52 Thomas, Trans-Jordan, 30 September 1923, CO733/67.
53 Jarvis, *Arab Command*, p. 114; Monthly report on Transjordan, December 1923, FO371/10106.
54 Monthly report on Trans-Jordan, October 1923, CO733/51.
55 Monthly report on Transjordan, December 1923, FO371/10106.
56 Zirikli, *cAman*, p. 192; Jarvis, *Arab Command*, p. 101; Musa, *Imara*, 147-148; Jadallah Musa, "Al-cAlaqat," pp. 11-14.
57 *Report by his Britannic Majesty's Government on the Administration under Mandate of Palestine and Transjordan for the year 1924*, p. 69.
58 Jadallah Musa, "Al-cAlaqat," pp. 168-170; *Al-Sharq al-cArabi*, 18 August 1924.
59 H. St. John Philby, *Stepping Stones* [unpublished MS], pp. 130-133, 141, Philby papers, St Antony's College. Also: Peake, draft of autobiography, pp. 79-80, Peake papers, Imperial War Museum.
60 Acting High Commissioner to Secretary of State, 1 August 1923, CO733/48; *Al-Sharq al-cArabi*, 25 August 1924.
61 Thomas, Trans-Jordan, 30 September 1923, CO733/67.
62 This point is made in Abu Diyya, *Safahat*, p. 373; The narrative here is based on Sulayman Musa, "Harakat al-Balqa' - Aylul 1923" [The Balqa' Movement - September 1923], *Al-Ra'y* (Amman), 4,5, 6 October 1997 unless indicated otherwise. For a detailed study of the revolt see: Yoav Alon, "The Balqa' Revolt: Tribes and Early State-Building in Transjordan," *Die Welt Des Islams* 46 (2006), pp. 7-42.
63 Jarvis, *Arab Command*, p. 107; Monroe, *Philby*, p. 130; P. J. Vatikiotis, *Politics and the Military in Jordan: A Study of the Arab Legion, 1921-1957* (London: Frank Cass, 1967), p. 66; Samuel to Colonial Secretary, 18 July 1924, RG-100/649/11 ISA.
64 Monthly report on Trans-Jordan, October 1923, CO733/51.
65 *Al-Sharq al-cArabi*, 28 January & 11 February 1924, reproduced in Muhammad Yunis al-cAbbadi, *Al-Rihla al-Mulukiyya al-Hashimiyya* [The Hashemite Regal Journey] (Amman: Wizarat al-Thakafa, 1997), pp. 68, 70; Philby, *Stepping Stones*, p. 148; Qasus, *Mudhakkirat*, pp. 190-191; Wilson, *King Abdullah*, p. 78.

66 H. Na'man, *Abdullah Amir 'Ever ha-Yarden* [Abdullah the Prince of Transjordan]
    (Jerusalem: Qiryat Sefer, 1942), p. 52. Also: Peake "Trans-Jordan," p. 388; Musa, *Imara*,
    p. 162; Max Adrian Simon Oppenheim, *Die Beduinen* (Leipzig: Otto Harrassowitz,
    1943), vol. II, pp. 215, 221, 225-226; *Al-Sharq al-'Arabi*, 20 October 1924.

67 Andrew Shryock and Sally Howell, "'Ever a Guest in our House': The Amir Abdullah,
    Shaykh Majid al-Adwan and the Practice of Jordanian House Politics, Remembered
    by Umm Sultan, the Widow of Majid," *International Journal of Middle East Studies*
    33 (2001), pp. 247-269. For examples of such occasions: *Filastin* (Jaffa), 24 August
    1933, reproduced in Zuhayr Ghanayim, *Al-Khabar al-Hashimi fi Jaridat Filastin* [The
    Hashemite News in the Newspaper *Filastin*] (Amman: Al-Bank al-Ahali al-Urdunni,
    1997), p. 312 and *Al-Urdunn* (Amman), 21 August 1935. On Sultan's wealth: Eliyahu
    Epstein, "*Be-Artsot Hamizrah*" [In the Orient Countries], *Yarhon Ahdut ha-'Avoda* 13
    (1931), p. 469.

68 Monthly report on Trans-Jordan, October 1923, CO733/51; Salih Kni'an al-Fayiz,
    son of shaykh Za'al al-Fayiz, claims to have possessed a receipt for the payment of taxes
    collected from his father in 1923. Interview: Manja, Jordan, 31 July, 1998.

69 Jarvis, *Arab Command*, p. 107; Peake "Trans-Jordan," p. 388; Thomas, Trans-Jordan, 30
    September 1923, CO733/67.

70 Dann, *Studies*, pp. 83-84; Monroe, *Philby*, pp. 129-130.

71 Wilson, *King Abdullah*, pp. 76-77.

72 Samuel to Duke, 5 October 1923 and Philby to Samuel, 17 October 1923, CO733/52;
    Thomas, Trans-Jordan, 30 September 1923, CO733/67.

73 Wilson, *King Abdullah*, p. 77.

74 Monthly report on Transjordan, December 1923, FO371/10106.

75 Samuel to Devonshire, 7 December 1923, CO733/51. Good summery of British
    reservations: Thomas, Trans-Jordan, 30 September 1923, CO733/67.

76 Thomas, Monthly report on Trans-Jordan, October 1923, CO733/51; Monthly
    report on Trans-Jordan, December 1923, FO371/10106; Peake to Cox, 11 May 1924,
    CO733/68.

77 Dann, *Studies*, p. 83.

78 Samuel to Thomas, 30 May 1924, CO733/68; Peake to Cox, 11 May 1924, CO733/
    68; Monthly report on Trans-Jordan, 1-31 July 1924, CO733/72; Secretary of State to
    the Officer Administering the Government of Palestine, 28 August 1924, CO733/72.

79 Thomas, Trans-Jordan, 30 September 1923, CO733/67.

80 Cox to Chief Secretary, 20 August 1924, CO733/72.

81 Cox, Report on Trans-Jordan, 1 September - 31 October 1924, CO733/75.

82 Ibid.

83 Abdullah bin al-Husayn, *Mudhakkirati* [My Memoirs] (Jerusalem: Bayt al-Quds, 1945),
    p. 219.

84 Dodge, *Arabian Prince*, p. 7.

Chapter Three

1 Mary C. Wilson, *King Abdullah, Britain and the Making of Jordan* (Cambridge:
   Cambridge University Press, 1987), p .94.

2 Ibid.; Uriel Dann, *Studies in the History of Transjordan, 1920-1949: The Making of a
   State* (Boulder: Westview Press, 1984), p. 7.

3 Situation report for 1.1-3.1.3.28, CO831/1/2, National Archives, London (NA).

4 Ma'an Abu Nowar, *The History of the Hashemite Kingdom of Jordan: Vol. II: The
   Development of Trans-Jordan, 1929-1939* (Amman: Al-Ra'y, 1997), pp. 62-63.

5 Bernard Wasserstein, *The British in Palestine: The Mandatory Government and the Arab-
   Jewish Conflict, 1917-1929* (London: Royal Historical Society, 1978), p. 246.

6   Anthony Kirk-Greene, *Britain's Imperial Administrators, 1858-1966* (London:
     Macmillan Press, 2000), pp. 65-66; Robert Tignor, *Modernization and British Colonial
     Rule in Egypt, 1882-1914* (Princeton: Princeton University Press, 1966), p. 104.
7   Heather J. Sharkey, *Living with Colonialism: Nationalism and Culture in the Anglo-
     Egyptian Sudan* (Berkeley: California University Press, 2003), pp. 71, 169n.
8   Philip Khoury, *Syria and the French Mandate: The Politics of Arab Nationalism, 1920-
     1945* (Princeton: Princeton University Press, 1987), p. 77.
9   The French army numbered 15,000 troops and was assisted by the Syrian Legion,
     which by 1924 numbered 6,500 men commanded by 137 French and 48 local officers.
     Ibid., pp. 71, 79.
10   *Al-Sharq al-ʿArabi* [The Arab East] (Amman), 19 May & 23 June 1924.
11   *Report by his Britannic Majesty's Government on the Administration under Mandate of
     Palestine and Transjordan for the year 1926* [Hereafter: *Annual Report*], p. 66.
12   Dann, *Studies*, p. 9; Wilson, *King Abdullah*, pp. 86-87; P. J. Vatikiotis, *Politics and the
     Military in Jordan: A Study of the Arab Legion, 1921-1957* (London: Frank Cass, 1967),
     pp. 64-71.
13   Wilson, *King Abdullah*, p. 94; *Annual Report*, 1925, p. 62; *Annual Report*, 1926, pp. 72-
     73; *Annual Report*, 1927, pp. 79-80; *Annual Report*, 1928, pp. 108, 111; *Annual Report*,
     1929, p. 167; *Al-Sharq al-ʿArabi*, 8 September 1924.
14   Wilson gives the figure of 20,000 but stresses that it is too high (p. 94). Epstein
     estimated the population of Amman in 1931 as 12,000: Eliyahu Epstein, "Be-Artsot
     Hamizrah" [In the Orient Countries], *Yarhon Ahdut ha-ʿAvoda* 13 (1931), p. 118. Musa
     suggests 10,000: Sulayman Musa, *ʿAmman ʿAsimat al-Urdunn* [Amman the Capital of
     Jordan] (Amman: Manshurat li-Amanat al-ʿAsima, 1985), p. 84.
15   Wilson, *King Abdullah*, p. 94; Eugene L. Rogan, "The Making of a Capital: Amman,
     1918-1928," in Jean Hannoyer and Seteney Shami (eds.), *Amman: The City and its
     Society* (Beirut: Cermoc, 1996), p. 98.
16   *Al-Sharq al-ʿArabi*, 1 February 1928.
17   Report on Trans-Jordan, 1.1-25.2.25, CO733/91 NA; Report on Trans-Jordan, 1-
     31.7.25, CO733/96; Situation Report [for the last quarter of 1927], CO831/1/2; Peter
     Gubser, *Politics and Change in Al-Karak, Jordan* (London: Oxford University Press,
     1973), p. 21.
18   *Al-Sharq al-ʿArabi*, 20 October & 3 November 1924, 15 December 1926.
19   Ibid., 1 June 1927; Situation report for 1/4/27 to 30/6/27, FO371/12272 NA;
     Wauchope to Cunliffe-Lister, 24 May 1934, CO831/28/3.
20   *Al-Sharq al-ʿArabi*, 1 March 1926.
21   Peake, Situation report, 17 November 1929, CO831/5/9.
22   Correspondence between Assistant Governor of Maʿan and the prime ministry, 7-
     8 September 1926, reproduced in Muhammad ʿAdnan al-Bakhit (ed.), *Al-Wathaʾiq
     al-Hashimiyya, Awraq ʿAbdullah bin al-Husayn*, Vol. X: *Al-ʿAlaqat al-Urdunniyya-al-
     Suʿudiyya, 1925-1951* [The Hashemite Documents, the Papers of Abdullah bin al-
     Husayn: Jordanian-Saudi Relations, 1925-1951] (Amman: Jamiʿat Al al-Bayt, 1997),
     pt 2, pp. 99-101.
23   *Al-Sharq al-ʿArabi*, 1 April, 1 November & 1 September 1926.
24   Situation Report [for the last quarter of 1927], CO831/1/2.
25   *Al-Sharq al-ʿArabi*, 15 October 1927, 15 April 1928; *Annual Report*, 1925, p. 61. *Al-
     Jarida al-Rasmiyya li-Hukumat Sharq al-Urdunn* [The Transjordanian Government
     Official Gazette, hereafter *Al-Jarida al-Rasmiyya*], 16 October 1929; Cox to Luke, 28
     August 1930, CO831/7/8.
26   Major C. S. Jarvis, *Arab Command: The Biography of Lieutenant Colonel F. W. Peake
     Pasha* (London: Hutchinson, 1942), p. 67.
27   Gubser, *Politics and Change*, p. 73.

28 *Al-Sharq al-ʿArabi*, 29 September 1924.
29 Ibid., 4 August 1924.
30 Ibid., 20 April & 1 September 1925.
31 *Mudhakkirat al-Majlis al-Tashrīʿi* [Minutes of the Legislative Council, hereafter *al-Majlis al-Tashrīʿi*], 27 August 1931.
32 [Assistant Governor of Maʿan] to HQ-Amman, 7 September 1926, reproduced in al-Bakhit, *Al-Wathaʾiq*, vol. X, pt 2, pp. 99-101.
33 *Al-Majlis al-Tashrīʿi*, 27 August 1931; *Al-Jarida al-Rasmiyya*, 1 October 1931.
34 *Al-Sharq al-ʿArabi*, 15 June 1926, 15 December 1927, 15 February 1928; *Al-Jarida al-Rasmiyya*, 28 January 1929, 16 January 1932, 17 August 1940; Acting High Commissioner to Cunliffe-Lister, 10 March 1933, CO831/22/11.
35 Plumer to Amery, 14 December 1925, CO733/99; Plumer to Amery, 26 June 1928, CO831/3/5.
36 Report on Transjordan, 1/7/1925 to 31/7/1925, CO733/96; *Al-Sharq al-ʿArabi*, 31 March 1928; ʿArif al-ʿArif diary, 29 May 1927, 19 August 1928, al-ʿArif papers, St Antony's College, Oxford.
37 W. B. Seabrook, *Adventures in Arabia* (London: G.G Hurrap, 1928), pp. 132, 26.
38 Ludwig Ferdinand Clauss, *Als Beduine unter Beduinen* 3rd edn. (Freiburg: Verlag Herder, 1954), p. 107.
39 Yoav Alon, "The Last Grand *Shaykh*: Mithqal al-Fayiz, the State of Trans-Jordan and the Jewish Agency" (M.A., Tel Aviv University, 1999).
40 Cited in Maʿan Abu Nowar, *The History of the Hashemite Kingdom of Jordan: Vol. I: The Creation and Development of Transjordan, 1920-29* (Oxford: Ithaca Press, 1989), pp. 152, 160n.
41 Gubser, *Politics and Change*, pp. 21, 84, 102.
42 Ibid., p. 66.
43 *Al-Majlis al-Tashrīʿi*, 17 February 1937; *Al-Sharq al-ʿArabi*, 5 January 1925, 15 March 1926.
44 Muhammad ʿAli al-Sawirki al-Kurdi, *Taʾrikh al-Salt wal-Balqaʾ* [The History of al-Salt and the Balqaʾ] (Amman: Dar ʿAmmar, 1998), p. 163.
45 Sulayman Musa, *Imarat Sharq al-Urdunn: Nashaʾtuha wa-Tatawwuruha fi Rubʿ Qarn, 1921-1946* [The Emirate of Transjordan: Its Growth and Development in a Quarter of a Century, 1921-1946] (Amman: Lajnat Taʾrikh al-Urdunn, 1990), p. 241.
46 MacEwan to Chief Secretary, 30 June 1925, CO733/95; Report on Trans-Jordan, 1.5.25 to 1.7.25, CO733/96.
47 *Al-Sharq al-ʿArabi*, 1 September 1925; Plumer to Amery, 8 September 1925, CO733/97.
48 Plumer to Amery, 18 May 1926 and Situation report for period ending 31.5.26, CO733/114.
49 Wilson, *King Abdullah*, p. 108; Situation report on Trans-Jordan, 1.7.29-30.9.29, CO831/5/9; Sulayman Bashir, *Judhur al-Wisaya al-Urdunniyya* (The Roots of the Jordanian Trusteeship) (Jerusalem: n.p.; 1980).
50 Wilson, *King Abdullah*, pp. 97-98; *Al-Sharq al-ʿArabi*, 20 June 1928; *Al-Jarida al-Rasmiyya*, 28 January 1929; Musa, *Imara*, p. 203.
51 Joseph A. Massad, *Colonial Effects: The Making of National Identity in Jordan* (NY: Columbia University Press, 2001), pp. 59-60, 71.
52 Shakib Musa Abu Kush, *Al-Hayat al-Tashrīʿiyya fil-Urdunn, 1921-1947* [Legislative Life in Jordan, 1921-1947] (Al-Zarqaʾ: Al-Wikala al-ʿArabiyya, 1996), pp. 69, 82; Muhammad ʿAbd al-Qadir Khrisat, *Al-Urdunniyyun wal-Qadaya al-Wataniyya wal-Qawmiyya* [The Jordanians and National and pan-Arab Issues] (Amman: Al-Jamiʿa al-Urdunniyya, 1991), pp. 95-97, 213-215.
53 *Al-Sharq al-ʿArabi*, 15 October 1928; *Al-Jarida al-Rasmiyya*, 1 December 1931.
54 Department of Health, Annual Report, 1927, CO831/2/2.

55 *Al-Sharq al-ᶜArabi*, 1 March & 15 February 1926.

56 Ibid., 15 February 1928; Fredrick G. Peake, *A History of Jordan and its Tribes* (Coral Gables, Florida: University of Miami Press, 1958), p. 109.

57 *Al-Sharq al-ᶜArabi*, 1 March, 15 August & 15 September 1928.

58 Ibid., 15 April 1928.

59 Ibid., 3 September 1923.

60 Ibid., 17 November 1924; *Al-Jarida al-Rasmiyya*, 11 February 1929.

61 *Al-Sharq al-ᶜArabi*, 16 March 1925, 15 August & 15 November 1926.

62 Ibid., 1 March, 15 August, 15 September & 25 September 1928; Musa, *Imara*, p. 200; Abu Kush, *Al-Hayat al-Tashrīʿiyya*, pp. 69, 82; Khrisat, *Al-Urdunniyyun*, pp. 95-97, 213-215.

63 ᶜAwda Qasus, *Mudhakkirat* [Memoirs, unpublished typescript], pp. 170-171; Al-ᶜArif diary, 13 & 21 September 1928, al-ᶜArif papers; Musa, *Imara*, pp. 196-200.

64 Gubser, *Politics and Change*, p. 110.

65 *Al-Sharq al-ᶜArabi*, 15 July 1925.

66 Report on Trans-Jordan, 1.1-25.2.25, CO733/91; *Al-Sharq al-ᶜArabi*, 4 May 1925; Peake, situation report, 17 November 1929, CO831/5/9.

67 Cox to Chief Secretary, 3 September 1925 and Plumer to Amery, 8 September 1925, CO733/97; *Annual Report*, 1929, p. 163; *Al-Sharq al-ᶜArabi*, 15 March 1926; *Annual Report*, 1930, p. 218.

68 *Annual Report*, 1926, p. 70; Annual Report of the Department of Health, 1926, CO733/137/8; Annual Report of the Department of Health, 1927, CO831/2/2.

69 *Al-Jarida al-Rasmiyya*, 1 November 1929.

70 Plumer to Amery, 18 May 1926, CO733/114.

71 Report for 1/5/25-1/7/25, CO733/96; *Al-Sharq al-ᶜArabi*, 15 October 1925.

72 Wilson, *King Abdullah*, pp. 99-100; Riccardo Bocco and Tariq M. M. Tell, "*Pax Britannica* in the Steppe: British Policy and the Transjordanian Bedouin," in Eugene L. Rogan and Tariq Tell (eds.), *Village, Steppe and State: The Social Origins of Modern Jordan* (London: British Academic Press, 1994), p. 111; Idem, "Frontières, tribus et Etat(s) en Jordanie orientale à l'époque du Mandat," *Maghreb-Machrek* 147 (1995), pp. 26-47.

73 Minister of Justice to the Prime Minister, 21 August 1929, reproduced in al-Bakhit, *Al-Wathā'iq*, vol. X, pt 2, p. 159; The Hadda Agreement, Appendix to *Annual Report*, 1926, pp. 75-78.

74 Governor of ᶜAqaba to *Mutasarrif* of Maᶜan, 29 November 1928 and *Mutasarrif* of Maᶜan to the Prime Minister, 1 December 1928, reproduced in al-Bakhit, *Al-Wathā'iq*, vol. X, pt. 2, pp. 157-158. For an interesting discussion on the logic of pre-modern methods of measurement see: James C. Scott, *Seeing Like a State* (New Haven and London: Yale University Press, 1998), chapter 1.

75 The Hadda Agreement, Appendix to *Annual Report*, 1926, pp. 75-78.

76 *Al-Sharq al-ᶜArabi*, 1 May 1926.

77 Bocco and Tell, "*Pax Britannica*," p. 114.

78 Abu Nowar, *The History*, vol. I, pp. 173-175.

79 Situation report for period ending 30/6/26, CO733/129.

80 Plumer to Amery, 18 May 1926 and Situation report for period ending 31/5/26, CO733/114; Situation report for 1/4-31/6/28, CO831/1/2.

81 Extracts from Plumer to Shuckburgh, 20 January 1927 and Cox to Symes, 13 January 1927, CO733/133/8.

82 Situation report for period ending 31/5/26, CO733/114.

83 *Al-Sharq al-ᶜArabi*, 3 & 16 June 1924.

84 Ibid., 11 June 1926; Pulmer to Amery, 18 May 1926 and Situation report for period ending 31/5/26, CO733/114.

85 High Commissioner to British Consul in Jedda, 28 December 1926, CO733/133/8;

Situation reports for 1.1-31.3.28 and 1.4-30.6.28, CO831/1/2. For the tribal practice of partial payment see: Dale F. Eickelman, *The Middle East and Central Asia: An Anthropological Approach* 3rd edn. (Upper Saddle River (NJ): Prentice-Hall, 1998), pp. 131-132.

86   *Al-Sharq al-ʿArabi*, 15 September 1926; Cox to Chancellor, 15 June 1929, CO851/5/9; Munib al-Madi and Sulayman Musa, *Taʾrikh al-Urdunn fil-Qarn al-ʿIshrin, 1900-1959* [The History of Jordan in the Twentieth Century, 1900-1959] 2nd edn. (Amman: Maktabat al-Muhtasib, 1988), p. 368.

87   Cox to Plumer, 23 May 1928, CO831/3/1; Philip Robins, "The Consolidation of the Hashemite Power in Jordan, 1921-1946" (Ph.D., University of Exeter, 1988), p. 205.

88   Cox to Shuckburgh, 4 November 1928, CO831/3/1.

89   Plumer to Amery, 15 September 1927, CO733/133/8; MacDonnell to Passfield, 24 September 1930, CO831/9/2.

90   Abu Nowar, *The History*, vol. I, p. 152; *Al-Sharq al-ʿArabi*, 15 September 1925.

91   Report on Trans-Jordan for 1/5/25-1/7/25, CO733/96; *Al-Sharq al-ʿArabi*, 18 May & 15 June 1925.

92   ʿAbd al-Rahman al-Shahbandar, *Mudhakkirat al-Duktur ʿAbd al-Rahman al-Shahbandar* [Memoirs of Dr. ʿAbd al-Rahman al-Shahbandar] (Beirut: Dar al-Irshad, 1968), pp. 213-214.

93   Situation report for 1/4/27-30/6/27, FO371/12272.

94   Peake to Plumer, 1 November 1927, CO733/143/1.

95   Plumer to Amery, 18 November 1927, CO733/143/1; Plumer to Shuckburgh, 18 November & 1 December 1927, CO733/143/1.

96   Situation report for 1.4-30.6.28, CO831/1/2.

97   Cox to Plumer, 12 November 1928, CO831/1/1. On Whitehall's position see more correspondence in this file as well as in CO831/4/5.

98   Wilson, *King Abdullah*, pp. 100-101; Alec Seath Kirkbride, *A Crackle of Thorns* (London: John Murray, 1956), pp. 82-91; *Annual Report*, 1931, p. 207; *Al-Jarida al-Rasmiyya*, 16 August 1931.

99   Abu Nowar, *The History*, vol. I, pp. 193-194; Al-ʿArif diary, 25 & 31 July 1927, al-ʿArif papers; Glubb, An Annual report on the administration of the Shamiya desert and the defence of the Iraq frontiers lying therein, 1 May 1929-13 May 1930, CO730/168/8 NA (courtesy of Toby Dodge).

100   *Al-Jarida al-Rasmiyya*, 1 April 1929.

101   Agreement between Palestine and Transjordan, 22 June 1930, reproduced in: Muhammad Yunis al-ʿAbbadi, *Al-Amir Shakir bin Zayd: Siratuhu wa-Masiratuhu min khilal al-Wathaʾiq al-Taʾrikhiyya* [Emir Shakir bin Zayd: His life and Activities as Reflected in the Historical Documents] (Amman: Wizarat al-Thakafa, 1996), pp. 64-66, 73-76; Decision of the meeting between the Tribal Control Board and the Sinai authorities, ʿAqaba, 1 March 1931, reproduced in ibid., pp. 68-73; Jarvis, *Arab Command*, pp. 113-114.

102   Sami Zubaida, *Islam, the People and the State* 2nd edn. (London: I.B. Tauris, 1993), pp. 170, 149.

Chapter Four

1   Joseph Kostiner, *The Making of Saudi Arabia, 1916-1936: From Chieftaincy to Monarchical State* (NY and Oxford: Oxford University Press, 1993), chapter 2; Riccardo Bocco and Tariq M. M. Tell, "*Pax Britannica* in the Steppe: British Policy and the Transjordanian Bedouin," in Eugene L. Rogan and Tariq Tell (eds.), *Village, Steppe and State: The Social Origins of Modern Jordan* (London: British Academic Press, 1994), pp. 112-115.

2   Situation reports for 1.1-31.3.28, 1.4-30.6.28 and 1.7-30.9.28 CO831/1/2, National
     Archives, London (NA); Abdullah to Plumer, 16 February and 24 April 1928,
     reproduced in Muhammad ʿAdnan al-Bakhit (ed.), *Al-Wathaʾiq al-Hashimiyya, Awraq
     ʿAbdullah bin al-Husayn*, Vol. X: *Al-ʿAlaqat al-Urdunniyya-al-Suʿudiyya, 1925-1951*
     [The Hashemite Documents, the Papers of Abdullah bin al-Husayn: Jordanian-Saudi
     Relations, 1925-1951] (Amman: Jamiʿat Al al-Bayt, 1997), pt 1, pp. 273-285; Plumer
     to Amery, 16 May 1928, CO831/2/6; *Report by his Britannic Majesty's Government
     on the Administration under Mandate of Palestine and Transjordan for the year 1928*,
     [Hereafter: *Annual Report*], p. 95; Bocco and Tell, "*Pax Britannica*," pp. 115-116.
3   Kostiner, *The Making*, pp. 121-124, 127-129; Maureen Heaney Norton, "The Last
     Pasha: Sir John Glubb and the British Empire in the Middle East, 1920-1949" (Ph.D.,
     John Hopkins University, 1997), chapter 4.
4   Kirkbride, Report on visit to tribes East of the Hejaz Railway, 27 December 1928,
     CO831/5/1.
5   Chancellor to Amery, 5 February 1929, Chancellor papers, Rhodes House Library,
     Oxford.
6   Cox to Chancellor, 7 February 1929 and Kirkbride, Report on the punitive action against
     Fahed el Trad of the Gamaʾan section of the Zebn, 3 January 1929, CO831/5/1.
7   Chancellor to Amery, 31 May 1929, CO831/5/1; *Annual Report*, 1929, p. 167;
     Situation reports for 1.1-31.3.29 & 1.4-30.6.1929, CO831/5/9; Cox to Chancellor, 7
     February 1929, CO831/5/1.
8   Cox to Abdullah, 9 April 1929 cited in Sulayman Musa, *Imarat Sharq al-Urdunn:
     Nashaʾtuha wa-Tatawwuruha fi Rubʿ Qarn, 1921-1946* [The Emirate of Transjordan:
     Its Growth and Development in a Quarter of a Century, 1921-1946] (Amman: Lajnat
     Taʾrikh al-Urdunn, 1990), pp. 323-324; Cox to OC RAF Trans-Jordan and Palestine,
     21 May 1929, Situation report, 1.4-30.6.29 and Stafford to Cox, 28 May 1929,
     CO831/5/9; Chancellor to Amery, 31 May 1929, CO831/5/1.
9   Abdullah to Prime Minister, 10 March 1928, reproduced in Muhammad Yunis
     al-ʿAbbadi, *Al-Amir Shakir bin Zayd: Siratuhu wa-Masiratuhu min khilal al-Wathaʾiq al-
     Taʾrikhiyya* [Emir Shakir bin Zayd: His life and Activities as Reflected in the Historical
     Documents] (Amman: Wizarat al-Thakafa, 1996), p. 44.
10   Chancellor to Amery, 31 May 1929 and enclosure 1: Note of Conversation of High
     Commissioner with the Amir Abdullah on 14.4.29, CO831/5/1; Cox to Davis, 19
     August 1930, FO371/14459 NA.
11   Dowding, Report on the Raiding Situation on the Transjordan-Nejd Frontier, enclosed
     to Chancellor to Passfield, 25 January 1930, Chancellor papers.
12   Chancellor to Amery, 31 May 1929, CO831/5/1; Glubb, A monthly report on events
     in the deserts of Transjordan for the month of July 1932, Glubb papers [Hereafter,
     Glubb's report. Most of Glubb's reports are held at St Antony's College, Oxford. Reports
     held at the National Archives (NA) are indicated as such].
13   Bocco and Tell, "*Pax Britannica*," p. 117; Air Ministry to Under Secretary of State for
     the Colonies, 8 July 1929, CO831/5/1.
14   A/Officer Commanding the Arab Legion to Officers Commanding Districts, Raiding,
     19 June 1929 and Protocols of the first and second sessions of the TCB, 17 & 18 June
     1929, reproduced in Muhammad Yunis al-ʿAbbadi, *Al-Amir Shakir*, pp. 81-83, 48-53.
15   Stafford, Report on Beduin Control Board 1.1.30-30.6.30, FO371/14460; Extracts
     from Peake's report on 13 June 1930 as cited in Cox to Luke, 19 August 1930, FO371/
     14459; Stafford to the British Resident, 3 November 1930, FO371/14460; Joseph
     A. Massad, *Colonial Effects: The Making of National Identity in Jordan* (NY: Columbia
     University Press, 2001), pp. 56-57.
16   Stafford, Report on Beduin Control Board 1.1.30-30.6.30, FO371/14460; Fawwaz Abu
     Taya, "ʿAwda abu Taya: Hayatuhu – Dawafiʿuhu fil-Thawra al-ʿArabiyya, Atharuhu fil-

Thawra al-ᶜArabiyya" [The Life of ᶜAwda abu Taya: His Motives and Impact during the Arab Revolt] (B.A. dissertation, Al-Jamiᶜa al-Urdunniyya, 1970), pp. 42-46 (courtesy of Martin Housden).

17   Kirkbride to Chancellor, 13 August 1929 and Cox to Chancellor, 8 October 1929, CO831/7/8.

18   Dowding, Report on the Raiding Situation on the Transjordan-Nejd Frontier, enclosed to Chancellor to Passfield, 25 January 1930, Chancellor papers.

19   Chancellor to Passfield, 26 June 1930, FO371/14459.

20   Muhammad Yunis al-ᶜAbbadi, Al-Amir, p. 32 and Shakir and Peake to Abdullah, 14 January 1932, reproduced in ibid., pp. 101-102; Al-Jarida al-Rasmiyya li-Hukumat Sharq al-Urdunn [The Transjordanian Government Official Gazette, hereafter Al-Jarida al-Rasmiyya], 16 October 1929; Cox to Luke, 28 August 1930, CO831/7/8; Glubb's report, December 1934.

21   Cox to Chancellor, 8 October, 1929, CO831/7/8.

22   Kostiner, The Making, pp. 136, 154-155.

23   Bocco and Tell, "Pax Britannica," pp. 117-118.

24   Ibid., pp. 118-121.

25   Meeting of Situation Conference, 24 March 1930, Chancellor papers; Extracts from Chancellor to Shuckburgh, 11 April 1930, CO831/10/1; Cox to High Commissioner, 28 August 1930, CO831/7/8.

26   Chancellor to Passfield, 26 June 1930 and Record of conference held at the Colonial Office on the 26th August 1930, CO831/10/1.

27   Cox to Acting High Commissioner, 25 September 1930, CO831/7/8; MacDonnell to Abdullah and Abdullah to MacDonnell, 24 September 1930 and Abdullah to Cox, 7 October 1930, reproduced in al-Bakhit, Al-Watha'iq, vol. X, pt 1, pp. 394-400; Situation report, 1.10-31.12.30, CO831/14/12; Bocco and Tell, "Pax Britannica," p. 118.

28   Ibid., pp. 118-121; Kostiner, The Making, p. 154; Glubb, Note on the situation on the southern frontier of Trans-Jordan, (n.d.) [November-December 1930], CO831/11/1.

29   Glubb's reports, November 1932, January 1933; Kirkbride to Cox, Notes on inspection of Southern Trans-Jordan, 29.2.32 to 6.3.32, CO831/19/8.

30   Bocco and Tell, "Pax Britannica," p. 109; Cox to Wauchope, 19 July 1932, CO831/19/8.

31   Glubb's report, February 1932.

32   Glubb's reports, May & December 1933, August-December 1934, January 1935, January 1938. Eliyahu Epstein, "Be-Artsot Hamizrah" [In the Orient Countries], Yarhon Ahdut ha-ᶜAvoda 13 (1931), p. 472; Glubb, A note on the question of the Wadi Sirhan (n.d.), Glubb papers.

33   Glubb's reports, November 1932, July 1935; Epstein, "Be-Artsot Hamizrah," p. 473.

34   Glubb's report, November 1932.

35   Annual Report, 1929, p.138; Cox to Wauchope, 25 March 1932 and Treasury to CO, 25 May 1932, CO831/18/1.

36   Bocco and Tell, "Pax Britannica," p. 121.

37   Ludwig Ferdinand Clauss, Als Beduine unter Beduinen 3rd edn. (Freiburg: Verlag Herder, 1954), p. 90; Al-Jarida al-Rasmiyya, 1 February 1929; Glubb's report, June 1936, CO831/37/3; Glubb's reports January 1934, January 1935.

38   Glubb's reports, December 1933, August-October 1934; Bocco and Tell, "Pax Britannica," p. 121.

39   Glubb, A Note on the Situation on the Southern Frontier of Trans-Jordan (n.d.) [December 1930], CO831/11/1.

40   Peake to Cox, 24 December 1930 and Cox to Chancellor, 11 December 1930, CO831/11/1.

41   FO to Ryan, 13 February 1931, CO831/11/1.

42   Rendel (FO) to Blaxter (CO), 23 February 1931 and Burnett (Air Ministry) to Blaxter,

24 February 1931, CO831/11/1; Ryan to FO, 1 March 1931, CO831/11/2.

43 FO to Ryan, 13 February 1931, Rendel to Blaxter, 23 February 1931and Burnett to
    Blaxter, 24 February 1931, CO831/11/1; Ryan to FO, 1 & 3 March 1931, CO831/11/2.

44 Air Staff Memorandum on the situation on the Transjordan and Nejd frontier, 19
    March 1931, CO831/11/3; Government of India to Secretary of State for India, 9
    March 1931, CO831/11/2; Shuckburgh to Chancellor, 24 March 1931, Chancellor
    papers.

45 FO to Ryan, 7 March 1931, CO8311/2; Shuckburgh to Chancellor, 24 March 1931,
    Chancellor papers.

46 Ryan to FO, 31 March 1931 and more correspondence in CO831/11/3; Bocco and
    Tell, "*Pax Britannica*," p. 118; Record of an Interdepartmental Meeting held at the
    Foreign Office, 23 September 1931, CO831/11/5; John Bagot Glubb, *The Story of the
    Arab Legion* (London: Hodder&Stouhgton, 1948), pp. 206-211.

47 Burnett to Shuckburgh, 11 February 1931, CO831/11/1; Glubb to Peake, Situation on
    the Nejd Frontier (n.d.) [Around October-November 1931], CO831/13/3.

48 Glubb, *The Story*, pp. 97-101; Saᶜd Abu Diyya and ᶜAbd al-Majid Mahdi, *Al-Jaysh al-
    ᶜArabi wa-Diblumasiyyat al-Sahra* [The Arab Legion and Desert Diplomacy] (Amman:
    Mudiriyyat al-Matabiᶜ al-ᶜAskariyya, 1987), pp. 103-108; Norman N. Lewis, *Nomads
    and Settlers in Syria and Jordan, 1800-1980* (Cambridge: Cambridge University Press,
    1987), p. 133; Alec Seath Kirkbride, *A Crackle of Thorns* (London: John Murray, 1956),
    pp. 63-70.

49 Glubb, *The Story*, p. 103.

50 Glubb, Note on the action to be taken on Dr. MacLennan's report (n.d.) [1935],
    CO831/31/17.

51 Kirkbride, *A Crackle*, p. 68; Norton, "The Last Pasha," pp. 180-186; *Annual Report,*
    1932, p. 204; Glubb, *The Story*, pp. 106-112.

52 Enclosure, Hall to Parkinson, 1 December 1935, CO831/30/11; High Commissioner
    to Secretary of State for Colonies, 10 June 1931, CO831/14/7.

53 Glubb, *The Story*, p. 113.

54 Glubb's report, December 1930; Wauchope to Ormsby-Gore, 31 August 1936,
    CO831/39/14.

55 Glubb's report, December 1932; Glubb's report, May 1936, CO831/37/3.

56 For example: Glubb to Peake, 14 March 1933 and Glubb's report, January 1935, Glubb
    papers.

57 Glubb, Note on the objects and application of the Tribal Courts Law 1936, Glubb
    papers.

58 Glubb, *The Story*, pp. 176-178; Glubb's report, December 1934.

59 Glubb, Note on the objects and application of the Tribal Courts Law 1936, Glubb
    papers; On *qadi al-qilta*: Muhammad Abu Hassan, *Al-Qada' al-ᶜAsha'iri fil-Urdunn*
    [Tribal Law in Jordan] (Amman: Al al-Bayt, n.d), pp. 109-110.

60 *Annual Report*, 1936, pp. 320-321; Tribal Court Law, 1936, CO831/37/7.

61 Abu Hassan, *Al-Qada' al-ᶜAsha'iri*, p. 485.

62 On *rizqa*: Ibid., pp. 158-159; ᶜAwda Qasus, *Al-Qada' al-Badawi* [Bedouin Law]
    (Amman: n.p., 1936), pp. 25-28.

63 Abu Hassan, *Al-Qada' al-ᶜAsha'iri*, p. 297.

64 Ahmad ᶜUwaydi al-ᶜAbbadi has reproduced abundant correspondence between tribal
    judges and officers of the Arab Legion documenting cases tried by the new system in:
    Al-Jara'im al-Sughra ᶜind al-ᶜAsha'ir al-Urdunniyya [Minor Crimes among the Jordanian
    Tribes] (Amman: Dar al-Fikr, 1987).

65 Glubb's report, January 1938; Extracts from enclosure of High Commissioner to
    Secretary of State, 14 February 1938, CO831/47/2; Glubb's report, January 1940.

66 For one such case: Minister of Interior to Prime Minister, 25 March 1941, reproduced

in ʿAdnan al-Bakhit, (ed.), *Al-Wathaʾiq al-Hashimiyya, Awraq ʿAbdullah bin al-Husayn*, Vol. XVI: *Al-ʿAshaʾir al-Urdunniyya, 1921-1951* [The Hashemite Documents, the Papers of Abdullah bin al-Husayn: The Jordanian Tribes, 1921-1951] (Amman: Jamiʿat Al al-Bayt, 2001), pt 1, pp. 189-199.

67 Glubb, *The Story*, pp. 110-112; Glubb's report, April 1932. On *wisaqa* and *kafala:* Abu Hassan, *Al-Qadaʾ al-ʿAshaʾiri*, pp. 412-416, 239-240.

68 Glubb, *The Story*, pp. 109-110, 181; An example of such a case is reproduced in al-ʿAbbadi, *Al-Jaraʾim*, pp. 295-296.

69 Glubb, Note on the Proposed Future Strength of the Arab Legion, enclosed to McMichael to MacDonall, 20 January 1940, CO831/56/7.

70 Bocco and Tell and Abu Diyya and Mahdi represent two exceptions.

71 Roger Beaumont, *Sword of the Raj: The British Army in India, 1747-1947* (Indianapolis: The Bobbs-Merrill Company, 1977), pp. 140-141; Philip Mason, *The Men Who Ruled India* (London: Pan Books, 1985), pp. 267-272; Charles Chenevix Trench, *The Frontier Scouts* (London: Jonathan Cape, 1985), p. 12; Glubb's report, March 1935.

72 Bocco and Tell, "*Pax Britannica*," p. 122.

73 Glubb, *The Story*, p. 167.

74 Glubb's reports, November & December 1932, January 1933, January 1935; A. Konikoff, *Trans-Jordan: An Economic Survey* (Jerusalem: The Jewish Agency, 1943), p. 54; Wauchope to MacDonald, 20 July 1935, CO831/32/2.

75 Glubb to Peake, 22 December 1932, Glubb papers.

76 Norton, "The Last Pasha," pp. 198, 208-209; Bocco and Tell, "*Pax Britannica*," pp. 120-122; Massad, *Colonial Effects*, chapter 3.

77 Kathryn Tidrick, *Heart-beguiling Araby* (Cambridge: Cambridge University Press, 1981), pp. 194-195, 212-213.

78 Kostiner, *The Making*, pp. 158-163; Mary C. Wilson, *King Abdullah, Britain and the Making of Jordan* (Cambridge: Cambridge University Press, 1987), p. 101.

79 Abdullah to Cox, 29 June 1932, reproduced in al-Bakhit, *Al-Wathaʾiq*, vol. X, pt 1, pp. 79-80; Glubb, Memorandum on the Beni Atiya Situation and Cox to Young, 12 October 1932, CO831/17/11.

80 Cox to Young, 29 October 1932, CO831/17/11.

81 Note on the move into Saudi Arabia of certain sections of the Beni Atiya Tribe, January 1933, CO831/17/2.

82 Glubb's report, November 1932.

83 Glubb's report, July 1932; Peake to Cox, 9 September 1932, Glubb papers; Cox to Young, 12 October 1932, CO831/17/11; Wauchope to Cunliffe-Lister, 17 March 1933, CO831/22/2.

84 Cox to Peake, 13 December 1932, Glubb papers.

85 Political Situation, February 1933, CO831/23/11; *Mudhakkirat al-Majlis al-Tashrīʿi* [Minutes of the Legislative Council], 27 April 1933; *Al-Jarida al-Rasmiyya*, 16 April 1933.

86 Peake to Glubb, 30 May 1933, Glubb to Peake, 1 June 1933 and Glubb's report, December 1934, Glubb papers.

87 Minutes by Parkinson to Shuckburgh, 2 November 1932 and 27 January 1933, Cunliffe-Lister to Wauchope, 1 February 1933, Wauchope to Cunliffe-Lister, 17 March 1933, Minutes by Parkinson to Sir W. Wilson, 12 June 1933, CO831/22/2.

88 Glubb's reports, July - November 1933.

89 Glubb's report, July 1933.

90 Glubb's reports, June, July & September-October 1933; Peake to Cox, 31 March 1936, CO831/37/9; Kostiner, *The Making*, p. 166.

91 Glubb's report, December 1936.

92 Wauchope to Thomas, 10 February 1936, CO831/37/7; *Annual Report*, 1936, p. 320.

93   Ibid., pp. 320-322; Abu Hassan, *Al-Qada' al-ʿAsha'iri*, pp. 469-471, 475-479; Glubb's
     report, January 1940.
94   Glubb's reports, September 1939, July 1934.
95   Massad, *Colonial Effects*, pp. 59, 144, 148-162.
96   On being ridiculed by London for his sympathy towards the nomads, Glubb lamented:
     "For four years, I have appealed in vain for help for the bedouins of Transjordan. Indeed
     my reports have been sarcastically described as sentimental, exaggerated or overstated."
     Glubb's report, November 1934.

Chapter Five

1   Glubb, A monthly report on the administration of the desert, December 1939, Glubb
     papers [Hereafter, Glubb's report. Most of Glubb's reports are held at St Antony's College,
     Oxford. Reports held at the National Archives, London (NA) are indicated as such].
2   *Mudhakkirat al-Majlis al-Tashrīʿi* [Minutes of the Legislative Council, hereafter *al-Majlis
     al-Tashrīʿi*], 22 November 1931.
3   Alec and Alen Kirkbride, Note on inspection of the Ajloun District, 30 April 1932,
     CO831/19/8, NA.
4   Alen Kirkbride to Cox, 1 June 1934, CO831/27/8; Cohen to the Board, 11 February
     1934, S25/3515, Central Zionist Archives, Jerusalem [Hereafter: CZA].
5   *Report by his Britannic Majesty's Government on the Administration under Mandate of
     Palestine and Transjordan for the year 1929*, [Hereafter: *Annual Report*], p. 163; Alec and
     Alen Kirkbride to Cox, 3 July 1934, CO831/27/1; *Al-Sharq al-ʿArabi* [The Arab East]
     (Amman), 15 March 1926.
6   *Al-Majlis al-Tashrīʿi*, 22 November & 5 December 1931.
7   Ibid., 22 November 1931, 24 December 1932; Cox to Wauchope, 2 December 1932
     and Treasury to Colonial Office, 25 May 1932, CO831/18/1; Hall to Cunliffe-Lister,
     23 September 1933 and Treasury to Under-Secretary of State, 26 October 1933,
     CO831/22/4.
8   Cohen, Gad's information, 3.5.33, 4 May 1933, S25/4143 CZA.
9   For extensive discussion on the connection between the Jewish Agency and Abdullah
     and other Transjordanian notables: Sulayman Bashir, *Judhur al-Wisaya al-Urdunniyya*
     [The Roots of the Jordanian Trusteeship] (Jerusalem: n.p., 1980); Avi Shlaim, *Collusion
     across the Jordan* (Oxford: Oxford University Press, 1988); Joseph Nevo, *King Abdallah
     and Palestine: A Territorial Ambition* (Basingstoke: Macmillan, 1996); Yoav Gelber,
     Jewish-Transjordanian Relations, 1921-1948 (London: Frank Cass, 1997); Yoav Alon,
     "The Last Grand *Shaykh*: Mithqal al-Fayiz, the State of Trans-Jordan and the Jewish
     Agency" (M.A., Tel Aviv University, 1999).
10   Parkinson to Wauchope, 28 February 1933, CO831/34/6.
11   Cox to Wauchope, 7 April 1933, extracts from notes of discussion between the
     Secretary of State and the High Commissioner, 22 April 1933, Wauchope to Cunliffe-
     Lister, 19 August 1933, Cunliffe-Lister to Wauchope, 19 October 1933, CO831/24/6.
12   Wauchope to MacDonald, 13 June 1935, CO831/33/4; Smith to under-Secretary
     of State, 4 October & 9 November 1935, CO831/34/8; Vartan M. Amadouny,
     "Infrastructure Development under the British Mandate," in Eugene L. Rogan and
     Tariq Tell (eds.), *Village, Steppe and State: The Social Origins of Modern Jordan* (London:
     British Academic Press, 1994), pp. 135-139. Amadouny analyses these initiatives and
     their contribution to the economy.
13   Report on the political situation for December 1933, CO831/23/11; Wauchope to
     Cunliffe-Lister, 21 February, 12 March & 4 August 1934, Cox to Wauchope, 17 June
     1934, Secretary of State to the Officer Administrating the Government of Palestine, 13
     September 1934, CO831/27/8; Wauchope to Thomas, 24 January 1936, CO831/36/1;

MacMichael to MacDonald, 23 May 1938 and Secretary of State to High Commissioner, 5 July 1938, CO831/46/1; *Al-Jarida al-Rasmiyya li-Hukumat Sharq al-Urdunn* [The Transjordanian Government Official Gazette, hereafter *Al-Jarida al-Rasmiyya*], 19 April 1934; Muhammad al-Unsi to Cohen, 12 May 1934, S25/3515 CZA.

14 Alec and Alen Kirkbride to Cox, 3 July 1934, Hall to Cunliffe-Lister, 12 September 1934 and Secretary of State to High Commissioner, 19 February 1935, CO831/27/1; Wauchope to Cunliffe-lister, 26 January 1933, CO831/22/3.

15 *Al-Urdunn* (Amman), 22 September 1935.

16 Wauchope to Thomas and to Parkinson, 28 May 1936, High Commissioner to Secretary of State, 13 June 1936, CO831/36/1.

17 Treasury to under Secretary of State, 13 June 1936, Wauchope to Ormsby-Gore, 12 August 1936, Wauchope to Ormsby-Gore, 24 August 1936 and Treasury to under Secretary of State, 15 September 1936, CO831/36/1.

18 Glubb's reports, May & June 1936, CO831/37/3; Wauchope to Ormsby-Gore, 31 August 1936, CO831/39/14; Sason, Information of the Arab Bureau, 25 August 1936, S25/3240 CZA; Gelber, *Jewish-Transjordanian*, pp. 91-93.

19 Wauchope to Ormsby-Gore, 7 January 1938 and minutes, 25 June 1938, CO831/41/3; Minutes by Platt, 3 March 1939, CO831/54/3; High Commissioner to Secretary of State, 27 March 1939, CO831/53/7; High Commissioner to Secretary of State, 13 July 1940 and Treasury to under Secretary of State, 1 August 1940, CO831/55/6.

20 Political report for March 1938, CO831/46/6.

21 Situation reports for August, October & November 1941, CO831/58/2; Political reports for February to June 1942, CO831/58/3.

22 Situation reports for October & November 1941, CO831/58/2.

23 Situation report for October 1941, CO831/58/2; Riccardo Bocco and Tariq M. M. Tell, "*Pax Britannica* in the Steppe: British Policy and the Transjordanian Bedouin," in Rogan and Tell, *Village*, pp. 125-126; Political report for January 1944, CO831/60/2. On the resemblance between smuggling and raiding see: William Lancaster, *The Rwalla Today* (Cambridge: Cambridge University Press, 1981), p. 93; Political report for June 1942, CO831/58/3.

24 MacMichael to MacDonald, 2 August 1938, RG-2/412/T178/36, Israel State Archives, Jerusalem [Hereafter: ISA]; Dr. S. A. Jones, Nutrition of the Trans-Jordan Bedouin, appendix to Glubb's report, March 1940; Norman N. Lewis, *Nomads and Settlers in Syria and Jordan, 1800-1980* (Cambridge: Cambridge University Press, 1987), p. 136.

25 Maʿan Abu Nowar, *The History of the Hashemite Kingdom of Jordan: Vol. II: The Development of Trans-Jordan, 1929-1939* (Amman: Al-Raʾy, 1997), pp. 37-38; Sulayman Musa, *Imarat Sharq al-Urdunn: Nashaʾtuha wa-Tatawwuruha fi Rubʿ Qarn, 1921-1946* [The Emirate of Transjordan: Its Growth and Development in a Quarter of a Century, 1921-1946] (Amman: Lajnat Taʾrikh al-Urdunn, 1990), p. 212.

26 Glubb's report, October 1937.

27 *Al-Majlis al-Tashrïi*, 1 January 1931.

28 Musa, *Imara*, p. 215; Abu Nowar, *The History*, vol. II, pp. 61-62.

29 Kirkbride to High Commissioner, 29 July 1941, CO831/59/7; *Al-Jarida al-Rasmiyya*, 1 June 1943; *Al-Urdunn*, 11 July 1943.

30 *Al-Urdunn*, 23 July 1939; Political report, November 1939, CO831/51/8.

31 Michael J. Reimer, "Becoming Urban: Town Administrations in Transjordan," *International Journal of Middle East Studies* 37 (2005), p. 200.

32 Situation reports, May, June & October 1942, CO831/58/3; *Al-Urdunn*, 9 August 1942.

33 Petition to the High Commissioner (Arabic) and correspondence between Cox and Hall, 25 May-17 June 1935, RG-2/411/T/191/35 ISA; The Administrative Inspector to the Prime Minister, 6 April 1935, file 1/21/21, the Prime Ministry files, the National

Library, Amman; On reading petitions: Eugene L. Rogan, *Frontiers of the State in the Late Ottoman Empire: Transjordan, 1850-1921* (Cambridge: Cambridge University Press, 1999), p. 207. On Tafila's tribes: Ahmad ʿUwaydi al-ʿAbbadi, *Muqaddima li-Dirasat al-ʿAshaʾir al-Urdunniyya* [An Introduction to the Study of the Jordanian Tribes] 2nd edn. (Amman: Al-Dar al-ʿArabiyya lil-Nashr, 1985), pp. 139, 560-561.

34   Reimer, "Becoming Urban."

35   Situation reports, February & March 1941, CO831/58/2; Situation reports January, June & July 1942, CO831/58/3; High Commissioner to Secretary of State, 9 July 1942, CO831/59/16; *Al-Urdunn*, 18 February 1941.

36   Abundant documents on this matter have been reproduced in: Muhammad ʿAdnan al-Bakhit (ed.), *Al-Wathaʾiq al-Hashimiyya, Awraq ʿAbdullah bin al-Husayn, Vol. XVI: Al-ʿAshaʾir al-Urdunniyya, 1921-1951* [The Hashemite Documents, the Papers of Abdullah bin al-Husayn: The Jordanian Tribes, 1921-1951] (Amman: Jamiʿat Al al-Bayt, 2001), pt 1, pp. 122-284.

37   *Al-Jazira* (Amman), 28 December 1939.

38   Extract from Glubb's report for June 1936, CO831/39/9; MacMichael to MacDonald, 8 December 1938 and Arab Legion Establishment (11.1.39), enclosure to Chief Secretary to Andrews (CO), 24 January 1939, CO831/49/4; Glubb's report for August 1939; High Commissioner to Secretary of State, 27 March 1939, CO831/53/7.

39   MacMichael to Viscount Cranborne, 8 June 1942, CO831/59/5; Political report, July 1942, CO831/58/3; Musa, *Imara*, p. 348; P. J. Vatikiotis, *Politics and the Military in Jordan: A Study of the Arab Legion, 1921-1957* (London: Frank Cass, 1967), pp. 44-45.

40   Glubb's comments on the draft of Vatikiotis' *Politics and the Military in Jordan*, Vatikiotis papers, St Antony's College. Among the most prominent names to join the Legion were: Habis and ʿAtif Rufayfan al-Majali, Muhammad Musa al-Maʿayta, ʿAbdullah ʿAtallah al-Tarawna, Muhammad ʿAtallah al-Suhaymat (Karak), Muhammad Kulayb al-Shurayda (Kura), Tariq Salih al-ʿAwran, Shahir Mustafa al-Muhaysan (Tafila), Ahmad Muhammad al-Husayn, Anwar ʿAbdullah al-Daud (al-Salt), Radi Salim al-Hindawi (Nuʿayma), Nayif Minwar al-Hadid (Hadid tribes). The Arab Legion Officers List 1939, reproduced in Abu Nowar, *The History*, vol. II, pp. 311-312; *Al-Jarida al-Rasmiyya* between 1938-1945.

41   The employment of the Arab Legion in MacMichael to MacDonald, 20 January 1940, CO831/56/7.

42   Muhammad ʿAbd al-Qadir Khrisat, *Al-Urdunniyyun wal-Qadaya al-Wataniyya wal-Qawmiyya* [The Jordanians and National and pan-Arab Issues] (Amman: Al-Jamiʿa al-Urdunniyya, 1991), pp. 189, 193-198; Musa, *Imara*, pp. 341-343, 242-245; Political report, December 1938, CO831/46/6.

43   *Al-Raʾy* (Amman), 12 August 1994; Muhammad ʿAli al-Sawirki al-Kurdi, *Taʾrikh al-Salt wal-Balqaʾ* [The History of al-Salt and the Balqaʾ] (Amman: Dar ʿAmmar, 1998), pp. 95-102, 106, 109; Andrew Shryock, *Nationalism and the Genealogical Imagination: Oral History and Textual Authority in Tribal Jordan* (Berkeley: California University Press, 1997), p. 230.

44   Eliyahu Sason, Information of the Arab Bureau, 11 May & 14 June 1936, S25/3240; Cohen to Shertok and Ben Zvi, 18 May 1936, S25/3539 CZA; Glubb's report, June 1936, CO831/37/3.

45   Bocco and Tell, "*Pax Britannica*," p. 125.

46   Glubb's report, March 1940; Glubb's reports, May & June 1936, Cox to High Commissioner, 6 July 1936, attached to Glubb's report, June 1936, CO831/37/3; Cohen's report on his meeting with Unsi, 9 July 1936, S25/22233 CZA.

47   Glubb's report, July 1936, CO831/37/3; Sason, Conversation with Mithqal Pasha al-Fayiz, 27.10.36, S25/3491 CZA; Glubb's reports, March, June & August 1937, CO831/41/11.

48 Among the shaykhs who were detained, arrested or banished were: Salim and
    Muhammad abu al-Ghunaym (al-Ghunaymat), ᶜAbd al-Majid al-ᶜAdwan (ᶜAdwan),
    Rashid al-Khuzaᶜi (Furayhat, Jabal ᶜAjlun), Sulayman al-Sudi (al-Rusan), Salim
    al-Hindawi (Nuᶜayma village, ᶜAjlun), Muhammad al-Husayn (al-Salt, ᶜAwamla),
    Muhammad al-Salih (Ghazawiyya). Musa, *Imara*, pp. 242-245; Khrisat,
    Al-Urdunniyyun, pp. 193-195; Political report, December 1938, CO831/46/6.
49 Wauchope to Ormsby-Gore, 25 June, 1936, S25/22779 CZA.
50 Cox to Wauchope, 23 July 1936 and Wauchope to Cox, 25 July 1936, S25/22779
    CZA.
51 *Al-Majlis al-Tashrïi*, 26 February 1936; Abu Nowar (*The History*, vol. II, p. 209)
    reproduced this provision of the law.
52 *Al-Jarida al-Rasmiyya*, 1 March 1937; Situation reports, February & April 1937,
    CO831/42/1; Political report, December 1938, CO831/46/6; Political report, January
    1939, CO831/51/8.
53 Political situation, December 1937, CO831/41/8; Glubb's reports, October 1939,
    January 1940.
54 Draft of Traveling agreement between Trans-Jordan and Iraq, June 1933, CO831/25/12;
    Al-Jarida al-Rasmiyya, 16 August 1931, 17 September 1938; Political situation, January
    1936, CO831/37/1.
55 Political situation, May 1939, CO831/51/8; Bocco and Tell, "*Pax Britannica*," p. 119;
    Glubb's report, March 1940.
56 Political report, November 1939, CO831/51/8.
57 Glubb's reports, November 1938, June, August & September 1939; Political reports,
    July & November 1938, CO831/46/6; Situation report, August 1939, CO831/51/8;
    Political situation, June & July 1943, CO831/60/2; John Bagot Glubb, *The Story of the
    Arab Legion* (London: Hodder&Stouhgton, 1948), pp. 170-171.
58 Glubb's report, June 1939. Emphasis in original.
59 Glubb's report, December 1938; Glubb, *The Story*, pp. 170-171; Political report, July
    1938, CO831/46/6.
60 Glubb's report, September 1939.
61 Lewis, *Nomads and Settlers*, p. 135; Bocco and Tell, "*Pax Britannica*," p. 124; John
    Glubb, "The Economic Situation of the Transjordanian Tribes," *Journal of the Royal
    Central Asian Society* 25 (1938), p. 455; High Commissioner to Secretary of State, 14
    February 1941, CO831/58/11; Situation report, July 1941, CO831/58/2.
62 Political report, June 1945, CO831/60/3.
63 Michael Fischbach, "British Land Policy in Transjordan," in Rogan and Tell, *Village*,
    p. 93.
64 The following account draws on: Fischbach, "British Land Policy," pp. 80-107; Idem,
    "State, Society and Land in ᶜAjlun (Northern Transjordan), 1850-1950" (Ph.D.,
    Georgetown University, 1992); Idem, *State, Society and Land in Jordan* (Leiden: Brill,
    2000).
65 Fischbach, "British Land Policy," p. 93.
66 Ibid., p. 105.
67 Fischbach, *Land in Jordan*, pp. 99-104.
68 Ibid., pp. 92, 121-122, 175.
69 *Al-Jarida al-Rasmiyya*, 2 November 1935; *Al-Majlis al-Tashrïi*, 26 February 1936; Cases
    involving the Bani Hamida, ᶜAjarma and Madaba tribes during 1938-1944 in: File
    1/5/8 *Taswiyat al-Aradi wa-ᶜAlamat al-Misaha* [Land Settlement and the Demarcation
    Markers], Prime Ministry files, National Library, Amman; G. F. Walpole, "Land
    Problems in Transjordan," *Journal of the Royal Central Asian Society* 35 (1948), p. 62.
70 Mary C. Wilson, *King Abdullah, Britain and the Making of Jordan* (Cambridge:
    Cambridge University Press, 1987), p. 106.

71 Fischbach, "Land in ʿAjlun," p. 100; Idem, *Land in Jordan*, pp. 45-49; Rogan, *Frontiers*, pp. 85-94.

72 The Administrative Inspector to the PM, 6 April 1935, file 1/21/21, the Prime Ministry files.

73 Fischbach, *Land in Jordan*, pp. 69-70, 166; Joseph Merrill Hiatt, "Between Desert and Town: A Case Study of Encapsulation and Sedentarization among Jordanian Bedouin" (Ph.D., University of Philadelphia, 1981), p. 168; OC Muwaqqar post to OC Desert, 6 April 1939, file *Shakawi al-ʿAshaʾir* [The Tribes' Complaints], Prime Ministry files.

74 *Al-Jarida al-Rasmiyya*, 16 March 1939; Acting High Commissioner to the Colonial Secretary, 20 October 1934, CO831/27/2; Peake to Cox, 12 August 1938, Peake papers, Imperial War Museum; Glubb's report, April 1940, and Dr. S. A. Jones, Nutrition of the Trans-Jordan Bedouin, appendix to Glubb's report, March 1940; Fischbach "Land in ʿAjlun," p. 342.

75 Glubb, "The Economic," pp. 448-459; *Annual Report*, 1938, p. 319.

76 *Annual Report*, 1934, p. 361; *Annual Report*, 1935, p. 307; Glubb's reports, July 1934, August-October 1934; *Al-Jarida al-Rasmiyya*, 17 December 1938.

77 The Administrative Inspector to the PM, 6 April 1935, file 1/21/21, Prime Ministry files.

78 OC Maʿan to OC Desert Area, 5 January 1939, file *Shakawi al-ʿAshaʾir*, Prime Ministry files; Glubb's report, July 1935; Muhammad abu Taya to OC Maʿan, ʿAhid [al-Sukhun], 5 July 1939, reproduced in al-ʿAbbadi, *Muqaddima*, pp. 333-335.

79 Glubb's reports, September-October 1933, December 1934, January & February 1935; *Annual Report*, 1935, p. 307; Testimony of shaykh ʿAdub al-Zaban, *Al-Majlis al-Tashrīʿi*, 13 January 1946.

80 Lewis, *Nomads and Settlers*, pp. 141-143; Eliyahu Epstein, "The Bedouin of Transjordan: Their Social and Economic Problems," *Journal of the Royal Central Asian Society* 25 (1938), pp. 233; [Avira], At the house of Mithqal Fayiz Pasha, 15 June 1941, S25/3504 CZA; Dr. S. A. Jones, Nutrition of the Trans-Jordan Bedouin, appendix to Glubb's report, March 1940.

81 Correspondence in the file *Shakawi al-ʿAshaʾir*, Prime Ministry files; OC Desert Area to *Mutasarrif*ʿAjlun, 28 October 1945, reproduced in al-ʿAbbadi, *Muqaddima*, pp. 406-407.

82 *Annual Report*, 1936, p. 349; Glubb's report, June 1937, CO831/41/11;Glubb's report, January 1935.

83 *Annual Report*, 1938, p. 319.

84 Glubb's report, April 1940; Nuri to Mitchell and Mitchell to Nuri, 30 January 1940, in Dr. Ahmad ʿUwaydi al-ʿAbbadi's Collection of Jordanian Documents, Centre for Documents and Manuscripts, The University of Jordan.

85 Nasim Muhammad al-ʿAkash, *Al-ʿAshaʾir al-Urdunniyya fil-Madi wal-Hadir* [The Jordanian Tribes in the Past and Present] (Al-Zarqaʾ: Dar al-ʿAkash, 1997), vol. I, pp. 188, 202-203, 209; Al-ʿAbbadi, *Muqaddima*, pp. 409-411 and letter of 22 February 1943 addressed to OC Umm al-Qatin reproduced in ibid., p. 409.

86 Al-ʿAkash, *Al-ʿAshaʾir al-Urdunniyya*, vol. I, p. 209. The confusion seems to continue even today. In another book the Sharʿa of these two localities are regarded to be part of the Bani Sakhr. Miflih al-Nimr al-Fayiz, ʿAshaʾir Bani Sakhr: Taʾrikh wa-Mawaqif hata Sanat 1950 [The Bani Sakhr Tribes: History and Positions until 1950] (Amman: Matabiʿ al-Quwwat al-Musallaha, 1995), pp. 317-320. On becoming a shaykh see: Andrew Shryock, "The Rise of Nasir al-Nims: A Tribal Commentary on Being and Becoming a Shaykh," *Journal of Anthropological Research* 46 (1990), pp. 153-176.

87 Political reports, June & October 1938, CO831/4/6; Refael Tahon, Uri Brener and Yitzhak Avira, Review of the Ghazawiyya (Hebrew), Kibutz Maʿoz Hayim Archives.

88 Glubb's report, July 1935.

89 Correspondence in the file *Shakawi al-ᶜAsha'ir*, Prime Ministry files.
90 Hiatt, "Between Desert and Town," p. 168; Glubb's report, December 1938; Amadouny ("Infrastructure Development," p. 135) is mistaken in saying that water schemes financed by the CDF were designed to bring about sedentarisation.
91 Ibid.
92 Glubb's report, June 1937, CO831/41/11; Glubb's reports, September-December 1938, April 1940; *Annual Report*, 1936, p. 399; Minutes, 21 & 25 February 1941, RG-2/427/T/26/41 ISA.
93 These cases and additional disputes from 1938-1939 in file *Shakawi al-ᶜAsha'ir*, Prime Ministry files.
94 Telegram from 24 January 1939, file *Shakawi al-ᶜAsha'ir*, Prime Ministry files; ᶜUlyan Rizq al-Khawalda, *Al-Qawl al-Hasan fi Tahqiq Ansab Bani Hasan* [The Good Saying in the Inquiry into the Genealogy of the Bani Hasan] (no further details), pp. 233-234.
95 *Al-Jarida al-Rasmiyya*, 1 March 1936; Situation report, March 1940, CO831/55/8; Political report, May 1942, CO831/58/3; OC Desert Area to *Mutasarrif* ᶜAjlun, 28 October 1945, reproduced in al-ᶜAbbadi, *Muqaddima*, pp. 406-407; Record of agreement, 28 October 1944, reproduced in Ibid., pp. 373-374.
96 *Al-Majlis al-Tashrīᶜi*, 11 January 1931, 12 March 1936, 10 January 1946, 6 January 1947; Muhammad abu Taya to OC Maᶜan, ᶜAhid [al-Sukhun], 5 July 1939, reproduced in al-ᶜAbbadi, *Muqaddima*, pp. 333-335.
97 Various correspondence in file *Shakawi al-ᶜAsha'ir*, Prime Ministry files; OC al-Mafraq to OC Desert Area, 13 October 1945, reproduced in al-ᶜAbbadi, *Muqaddima*, p. 198.
98 Reproduced in Ahmad ᶜUwaydi al-ᶜAbbadi, *Al-Jara'im al-Sughra ᶜind al-ᶜAsha'ir al-Urdunniyya* [Minor Crimes among the Jordanian Tribes] (Amman: Dar al-Fikr, 1987), pp. 369-372.
99 Ibid., pp. 368-369.
100 Testimony of shaykh Mithqal al-Fayiz, 15 August 1953, reproduced in al-ᶜAbbadi, *Muqaddima*, pp. 292-293.
101 Amadouny, "Infrastructure Development," pp. 150-154; Musa, *Imara*, pp. 361-363; *Al-Urdunn*, 11 August 1940.
102 Glubb to Peake, 22 December 1932, Glubb papers; *Annual Report*, 1931, p. 185; *Annual Report*, 1935, p. 323; *Al-Jarida al-Rasmiyya*, 1 August 1931; Annual report of the Department of Health, 1933, CO831/32/1; Amadouny, "Infrastructure Development," pp. 152-153; Glubb's report, August-October 1934.
103 Amadouny, "Infrastructure Development," pp. 153-154; *Annual Report*, 1937, pp. 350, 363; *Annual Report*, 1938, p. 375. These figures reflect the number of cases which received treatment, and not necessarily the actual numbers of persons who reported to the clinics, as Amadouny states.
104 Glubb's report, January 1939.
105 *Al-Jazira*, 18 January 1939; *Al-Jarida al-Rasmiyya*, 16 July 1938; *Al-Urdunn*, 10 May 1940.
106 Glubb's reports, December 1932, August-October 1934, December 1933; Amadouny, "Infrastructure Development," pp. 155-156.
107 Eliyahu Eilat, *Shivat Tsiyon ve-ᶜArav* [The Return to Zion and Arabia] (Tel Aviv: Dvir, 1971), p. 13; [Avira], At the house of Mithqal Fayiz Pasha, 15 June 1941, S25/3504 CZA.
108 During an interview Salih Kniᶜan al-Fayiz, son of shaykh Zaᶜal, showed me his father's diary. Manja, Jordan, 31 July, 1998.
109 Glubb's reports, December 1932, September-October & December 1933, August-October 1934, December 1937, March 1938; Saᶜd Abu Diyya and ᶜAbd al-Majid Mahdi, *Al-Jaysh al-ᶜArabi wa-Diblumasiyyat al-Sahra* [The Arab Legion and Desert Diplomacy] (Amman: Mudiriyyat al-Matabiᶜ al-ᶜAskariyya, 1987), pp. 122, 130-135;

Annual Report, 1936, pp. 363, 349; *Annual Report*, 1937, p. 355; A. Konikoff, *Trans-Jordan: An Economic Survey* (Jerusalem: The Jewish Agency, 1943), p. 27.

110 Glubb, *The Story*, pp. 172-173; Glubb's reports, December 1937, March 1938, February 1939; *Al-Urdunn*, 22 March 1941.

111 Musa, *Imara*, pp. 349-357; Munib al-Madi and Sulayman Musa, *Ta'rikh al-Urdunn fil-Qarn al-ᶜIshrin, 1900-1959* [The History of Jordan in the Twentieth Century, 1900-1959] 2nd edn. (Amman: Maktabat al-Muhtasib, 1988), pp. 309-310; Maᶜan Abu Nowar, *The History of the Hashemite Kingdom of Jordan: Vol. I: The Creation and Development of Transjordan, 1920-29* (Oxford: Ithaca Press, 1989), pp. 224-225.

112 ᶜAbdullah Rashid, *Al-Katatib wa-Nuzumuha al-Taqlidiyya fi Madinat ᶜAmman, 1900-1958* [The *Katatib* in Amman and their Traditional Methods, 1900-1958] (Amman: Dar al-Yanabiᶜ, 1993), pp. 32, 59-60, 71-72.

113 Abu Nowar, *The History*, vol. II, pp. 253-257; Amadouny, "Infrastructure Development," p. 155.

114 *Al-Urdunn*, 26 December 1935; Political situation, October 1938, CO831/46/6; *Al-Jazira*, 18 December 1939.

115 Report by Muhammad al-Unsi, 12 December 1943, cited in Madi and Musa, *Ta'rikh*, p. 450.

116 *Al-Urdunn*, 8 October 1930.

117 Amadouny, "Infrastructure Development," pp. 155-156.

118 Musa, *Imara*, p. 356; *The Spectator* (London), 6 April 1937, cited in Amadouny, "Infrastructure Development," pp. 160-161.

119 Political report, October 1944, CO831/60/2; Abu Nowar, *The History*, vol. II, pp. 254-256.

120 Ibid., pp. 153-155.

121 Khrisat, *Al-Urdunniyyun*, pp. 183, 200; On Iraq: Elie Kedourie, *The Chatham House Version and other Middle Eastern Studies* (London: Weidenfeld and Nicolson, 1970), p. 275.

122 Abu Nowar, *The History*, vol. II, pp. 154-158.

123 Abdullah published poems and responded to the work of others in the two papers, *Al-Jazira* and *Al-Urdunn*. See also: Raslan Bani Yasin and Yusuf al-Rubaᶜi, *Al-Adab al-Urdunni al-Manshur fi Sahifat Al-Jazira al-Sadira fi ᶜAmman bi-Ta'rikh 1939-1954* [Jordanian Literature in the Pages of the Newspaper *Al-Jazira*, 1939-1954] (Irbid: Jamiᶜat al-Yarmuk, 1986).

124 Musa, *Imara*, p. 317.

125 Report by Lash (Glubb's assistant) for May 1937, CO831/41/11.

126 Political situation, September 1941, CO831/58/2; Kirkbride to MacMichael, 9 September 1941, CO831/58/2; Avira, The affair of negotiations to purchase a tractor in Transjordan, 4 October 1941, S25/3504; Dov, At Mithqal's house, 9 October 1941, S25/8005 CZA.

127 Glubb's report, August 1937, CO831/41/11; Glubb's report, March 1940.

128 Glubb's report, November 1937.

129 *Al-Urdunn*, 23 July 1939; *Al-Jarida al-Rasmiyya*, 1 August 1940.

130 Al-ᶜAbbadi, *Muqaddima*, p. 491.

131 Lewis, *Nomads and Settlers*, pp. 134-136; Tariq Tall, "The Politics of Rural Policy in East Jordan, 1920-1989," in Martha Mundy and Basim Musallam (eds.), *The Transformation of Nomadic Society in the Arab East* (Cambridge: Cambridge University Press, 2000), p. 93; Masᶜud Dhahir, *Al-Mashriq al-ᶜArabi al-Muᶜasir min al-Badawa ila al-Dawla al-Haditha* [The Modern Arab Mashriq from Pastoralism to the Modern State] (Beirut: Maᶜhad al-Inma' al-ᶜArabi, 1986), p. 259.

132 Al-ᶜAbbadi, *Muqaddima*, p. 758.

133 Glubb's report, March 1940.

134 Lewis, *Nomads and Settlers*, p. 143; *Al-Urdunn*, 12 March 1938.
135 Reimer, "Becoming Urban."
136 For example: *Al-Majlis al-Tashrïi*, 18 January 1931, 2 January 1935, 20 June 1936.
137 Emanuel Neuman to the members of the Zionist Executive, 23 February 1933, Z4/4118 CZA; Cohen, Report from the visit to Amman, 10 March 1933, S25/6313 CZA. On British reactions towards Jewish penetration into Transjordan: Gelber, *Jewish-Transjordanian*, pp. 38-42, 47-53, 67, 70.
138 Lewis, *Nomads and Settlers*, pp. 138-139; Acting High Commissioner to the Colonial Secretary, 20 October 1934 and the Colonial Secretary to the High Commissioner, 29 November 1934, CO831/27/2; Cox to High Commissioner, 6 July 1936, attached to Glubb's report, June 1936, CO831/37/3.
139 Glubb's report, February 1934; Peake to Cox, 23 March 1936, CO831/37/9.
140 Cohen, Visit in the house of M.U. in Shuna, 8 December 1937, S25/3491; Cohen, A letter from Trans-Jordan, 9 & 15 December 1937, S25/3539 CZA.
141 Bocco and Tell, "*Pax Britannica*," p. 119; Glubb's report, March 1940.
142 Avira, The affair of negotiations to purchase a tractor in Trans-Jordan, 4 October 1941, S25/3504 CZA; Hankin to JNF, 11 February 1944, KKL5/13672 CZA; Bocco and Tell, "*Pax Britannica*," p. 119.
143 Musa, *Imara*, p. 208; *Al-Jarida al-Rasmiyya*, 1 August, 1 July & 1 September 1946.
144 Cutting from the *Daily Telegraph*, 29 October 1941, CO831/59/11.
145 *Al-Urdunn*, 22 March, 8 April & 31 October 1936, 4 & 11 August 1940; Abdullah bin al-Husayn, *Al-Khayl al-Asa'il* [Pedigree Horses] 2nd edn. (Amman: Matbaʿat al-Tawfiq, 1983).
146 *Al-Urdunn*, 21 August 1935.
147 Ibid., 22 September 1940; On hospitality as a means to enhance political authority: Andrew Shryock and Sally Howell, "'Ever a Guest in our House': The Amir Abdullah, Shaykh Majid al-Adwan and the Practice of Jordanian House Politics, Remembered by Umm Sultan, the Widow of Majid," *International Journal of Middle East Studies* 33 (2001), pp. 247-269; Rogan, *Frontiers*, pp. 40-41.
148 *Al-Urdunn*, 8 April 1936, 17 November 1940; *Al-Jazira*, 21 November 1939, 11 January & 21 September 1940.
149 *Al-Urdunn*, 22 March 1936, 27 January 1941; *Al-Jazira*, 29 May 1940.
150 MacMichael to MacDonald, 21 February 1939, CO831/54/3.
151 High Commissioner to Secretary of State, 13 July 1940 and Treasury to under Secretary of State, 1 August 1940, CO831/55/6; Political report, June 1944, CO831/60/2.

Conclusion

1 Timothy Mitchell, *Colonizing Egypt* (NY: Cambridge University Press, 1988); Joseph A. Massad, *Colonial Effects: The Making of National Identity in Jordan* (NY: Columbia University Press, 2001).
2 Ronald Hyam, "The British Empire in the Edwardian Era," in Judith Brown and Wm. Roger Louis (eds.), *The Oxford History of the British Empire, Vol. IV: The Twentieth Century* (Oxford: Oxford University Press, 1999), pp. 47-63.
3 Hanna Batatu, *The Old Social Classes and the Revolutionary Movements of Iraq* (Princeton: Princeton University Press, 1978), chapter 6; Toby Dodge, *Inventing Iraq: The Failure of Nation Building and a History Denied* (NY: Columbia University Press, 2003); Yoav Alon, "The Tribal System in the Face of the State-Formation Process: Mandatory Transjordan, 1921-46," *International Journal of Middle East Studies* 37 (2005), pp. 221-222.
4 A similar situation was observed by Kostiner with regard to Saudi Arabia in the late 1930s. Joseph Kostiner, *The Making of Saudi Arabia, 1916-1936: From Chieftaincy to*

Monarchical State (NY and Oxford: Oxford University Press, 1993), pp. 190-191.

5   Toby Dodge, *An Arabian Prince, English Gentlemen and the Tribes East to the River Jordan: Abdullah and the Creation and Consolidation of the Transjordanian State* (London: SOAS, 1994), pp. 6-7, 9.

6   Sulayman Musa, *Ayam La Tunsa: Al-Urdunn fi Harb 1948* [Unforgettable Days: Jordan in the 1948 War] 2nd edn. (Amman: Matabi᷂ al-Quwwat al-Musallaha, 1998), pp. 50-51.

7   Shaul Mishal, *East Bank/West Bank: The Palestinians in Jordan, 1949-1967* (New Haven: Yale University Press, 1978).

8   Uriel Dann, *King Hussein and the Challenge of Arab Radicalism: Jordan, 1955-1967* (Oxford: Oxford University Press, 1989).

9   Ibid., p. 64; Lawrence Tal, *Politics, the Military and National Security in Jordan, 1955-1967* (Basingstoke: Palgrave Macmillan, 2002), p. 48; *Filastin* (Jerusalem), 28 July & 4 August 1957; John Slade-Baker diary, 23 April 1957, Slade-Baker Collection, St Antony's College, Oxford.

10 Asher Susser, *Both Banks of the Jordan: A Political Biography of Wasfi al-Tall* (Ilford: Frank Cass, 1994).

11 Andrew Shryock and Sally Howell, "'Ever a Guest in our House': The Amir Abdullah, Shaykh Majid al-Adwan and the Practice of Jordanian House Politics, Remembered by Umm Sultan, the Widow of Majid," *International Journal of Middle East Studies* 33 (2001), pp. 248, 266.

12 Andrew Shryock, *Nationalism and the Genealogical Imagination: Oral History and Textual Authority in Tribal Jordan* (Berkeley: California University Press, 1997).

13 Shryock, *Nationalism*, p. 70; Richard T. Antoun, "Civil Society, Tribal Process, and Change in Jordan: An Anthropological View," *International Journal of Middle East Studies* 32 (2000), pp. 441-463.

14 Linda L. Layne, *Home and Homeland: The Dialogics of Tribal and National Identities in Jordan* (Princeton: Princeton University Press, 1994).

15 *Jordan Times* (Amman), 13 & 19 June 2005, 12 October 2005, 13 March 2006.

16 Layne, *Home*, p. 138.

17 Ibid.

18 Massad, *Colonial Effects*, p. 71.

19 Ibid., pp. 71-73, 76-77, 250-251.

20 Recent example: ᷂Abd al-Salam al-Majali, *Rihlat al-᷂Umr: Min Bayt al-Shaᶜr ila Suddat al-Hukm* [A Life Journey: From the Tent to the Seat of Government] 2nd edn. (Beirut: Sharikat al-Matbuᶜat lil-Tawziᶜ wal-Nashr, 2004).

21 Benedict Anderson, *Imagined Communities: Reflections on the Rise and Spread of Nationalism* 2nd edn. (London: Verso, 1991).

BIBLIOGRAPHY

Archives and private papers

UK

National Archives, London (Formerly Public Records Office):
CO733 (Colonial Office, Palestine)
CO831 (Colonial Office, Transjordan)
FO141 (Foreign Office, Embassy and Consulates, Egypt)
FO371 (Foreign Office, Political)

Private Papers Collection, Middle East Centre, St Antony's College, Oxford:
ʿArif al-ʿArif
C. D. Brunton
J. B. Glubb
Jordan Collection
R. F. P. Monckton
H. St. John Philby
J. Slade-Baker
F. R. Somerset
P. J. Vatikiotis

Rhodes House Library, Oxford: J. Chancellor

Imperial War Museum, London: F. G. Peake

Jordan

The National Library, Amman:
Prime Ministry files
Al-Sharq al-ʿArabi [The Arab East] (Amman), 1923-1928
(renamed) *Al-Jarida al-Rasmiyya li-Hukumat Sharq al-Urdunn* [The Transjordanian
    Government Official Gazette], 1929-1946

Centre for Documents and Manuscripts, The University of Jordan:
Dr. Ahmad ʿUwaydi al-ʿAbbadi's Collection of Jordanian Documents

The Library, The Jordanian Parliament:
Mudhakkirat al-Majlis al-Tashriʿi [Minutes of the Legislative Council], 1929-1946

Israel

Central Zionist Archives, Jerusalem:
KKL5 (The Jewish National Fund)
S25 (The Jewish Agency's Political Department)
Z4 (Zionist Organisation, Central Office, London)

Israel State Archives, Jerusalem:
RG-2 (The Chief Secretary)
RG-100 (Herbert Samuel papers)

The Hagana Archives, Tel Aviv: Shneorson papers

Kibutz Ma'oz Hayim Archives: Scattered reports on the Arab tribes of the Bisan region

Newspapers

Al-Dustur (Amman)
Filastin (Jerusalem)
Al-Jazira (Amman)
Jordan Times (Amman)
Al-Ra'y (Amman)
Al-Urdunn (Haifa and later Amman)

Interviews

Dr. Ahmad 'Uwaydi al-'Abbadi, Wadi Sir, 24 May & 2 August 1998.
Dr. Haydar 'Abd al-Shafi (served in the Arab Legion), Kibutz Yad Mordechai, 9 August
    2003.
Dr. Muhammad Abu Hassan, Amman, 4 July 1998.
Muhammad Majid al-'Adwan, Amman, 29 April 1998.
Shaykh Nawwaf al-'Aytan, Rahhab (Mafraq), 19 June 1998.
Dr. Fares Dhaher Al-Faiz, Amman, 4, 5 & 20 July 1998.
'Akif al-Fayiz, Amman, 29 March 1998.
Salih Kni'an al-Fayiz, Manja, 31 July 1998.
Muslih Sa'd al-Halahla (an elder of the 'Ajarma), Umm al-Basatin, 27 July 1998.
Sulayman Musa, Amman, 4 & 28 June 1998.
Hamad Fadil al-Shahwan (son of shaykh Fadil of the 'Ajarma), Umm al-Basatin,
    27 July 1998.

Official publications

*Report by his Britannic Majesty's Government on the Administration under Mandate of Palestine
    and Transjordan* (1924-39). League of Nations. Geneva [Annual Reports].
A Handbook of Syria. Geographical Section of the Naval Intelligence Division, Naval Staff,
    Admiralty, [1920?].
Palestine and Transjordan. Admiralty War Staff, Naval Intelligence Division. London: HM
    Stationary Office, 1943.

Unpublished manuscripts

Philby, H. St. John. *Stepping Stones.*
Qasus, 'Awda. *Mudhakkirat* [Memoirs].
Al-Tall, Salih Mustafa Yusuf. *Mudhakkirat* [Memoirs].

Dissertations

Abu Taya, Fawwaz. "ʿAwda abu Taya: Hayatuhu – Dawafiʿuhu fil-Thawra al-ʿArabiyya, Atharuhu fil-Thawra al-ʿArabiyya" [The Life of ʿAwda abu Taya: His Motives and Impact during the Arab Revolt], B.A. dissertation, Al-Jamiʿa al-Urdunniyya, 1970.

Alon, Yoav. "The Last Grand *Shaykh*: Mithqal al-Fayiz, the State of Trans-Jordan and the Jewish Agency," M.A., Tel Aviv University, 1999.
——"State, Tribe and Mandate in Transjordan, 1918-1946," D.Phil, Oxford University, 2000.

Amadouny, Vartan Manoug. "The British Role in the Development of an Infrastructure in Transjordan during the Mandate Period, 1921-1946," Ph.D., University of Southampton, 1993.

Amawi, Abla Mohamed. "State and Class in Transjordan: A Study of State Autonomy," Ph.D., Georgetown University, 1992.

Fischbach, Michael Richard. "State, Society and Land in ʿAjlun (Northern Transjordan), 1850-1950," Ph.D., Georgetown University, 1992.

Hamarneh, Mustafa. "Social and Economic Transformation of Trans-Jordan, 1921- 1946," Ph.D., Georgetown University, 1985.

Hiatt, Joseph Merrill. "Between Desert and Town: A Case Study of Encapsulation and Sedentarization among Jordanian Bedouin," Ph.D., University of Philadelphia, 1981.

Musa, ʿAmir Jadallah. "Al-ʿAlaqat al-Urdunniyya - al-Suʿudiyya ma bayna 1921-1928" [Jordanian-Saudi Relations, 1921-1928], B.A. dissertation, University of Jordan, 1977.

Norton, Maureen Heaney. "The Last Pasha: Sir John Glubb and the British Empire in the Middle East, 1920-1949," Ph.D., John Hopkins University, 1997.

Owidi [al-ʿAbbadi], Ahmed Saleh Suleiman. "Bedouin Justice in Jordan: The Customary Legal System of the Tribes and its Integration into the Framework of State Policy from 1921 onwards," Ph.D., University of Cambridge, 1982.

Robins, Philip. "The Consolidation of the Hashemite Power in Jordan, 1921-1946," Ph.D., University of Exeter, 1988.

Published sources

Al-ʿAbbadi, Ahmad ʿUwaydi. *Muqaddima li-Dirasat al-ʿAshaʾir al*-Urdunniyya [An Introduction to the Study of the Jordanian Tribes]. 2nd Edn. Amman: Al-Dar al-ʿArabiyya lil-Nashr, 1985.
——*Fi Rubuʿ al-Urdunn* [Around Jordan]. 2 Vols. Amman: Dar al-Fikr, 1987.
——*Al-Jaraʾim al-Sughra ʿind al-ʿAshaʾir al-Urdunniyya* [Minor Crimes among the Jordanian Tribes]. Amman: Dar al-Fikr, 1987.
——*ʿAshaʾir al-Urdunn: Jawlat Maydaniyya wa-Tahlilat* [The Jordanian Tribes: Field Tours and Analysis]. Amman: Al-Ahliyya lil-Nashr wal-Tawziʿ, 2005.

Al-ʿAbbadi, Muhammad Yunis. *Al-Amir Shakir bin Zayd: Siratuhu wa-Masiratuhu min khilal al-Wathaʾiq al-Taʾrikhiyya* [Emir Shakir bin Zayd: His life and Activities as Reflected in the Historical Documents]. Amman: Wizarat al-Thakafa, 1996.
——*Al-Rihla al-Mulukiyya al-Hashimiyya* [The Hashemite Regal Journey]. Amman: Wizarat al-Thakafa, 1997.

Abu Diyya, Saʿd and ʿAbd al-Majid Mahdi. *Al-Jaysh al-ʿArabi wa-Diblumasiyyat al-Sahra* [The Arab Legion and Desert Diplomacy]. Amman: Mudiriyyat al-Matabiʿ al-ʿAskariyya, 1987.
——*Safahat Matwiyya min Taʾrikh al-Urdunn* [Folded Pages from the History of Jordan]. [Amman]: Dar Al-Bashir, 1998.

Abu Hassan, Muhammad. *Al-Qadaʾ al-ʿAshaʾiri fil-Urdunn* [Tribal Law in Jordan]. Amman: Al al-Bayt, n.d.

Abujaber, Raouf Saʿd. *Pioneers over Jordan: The Frontier of Settlement in Transjordan, 1850-*

1914. London: I.B. Tauris, 1989.

Abu Kush, Shakib Musa. *Al-Hayat al-Tashrīʿiyya fil-Urdunn, 1921-1947* [Legislative Life in Jordan, 1921-1947]. Al-Zarqaʾ: Al-Wikala al-ʿArabiyya, 1996.

Abu Nowar, Maʿan. *The History of the Hashemite Kingdom of Jordan: Volume I: The Creation and Development of Transjordan, 1920-29.* Oxford: Ithaca Press, 1989.

——*The History of the Hashemite Kingdom of Jordan: Volume II: The Development of Trans-Jordan, 1929-1939.* Amman: Al-Raʾy, 1997.

Abu al-Shaʿr, Hind. *Irbid wa-Jiwaruha, 1850-1928* [Irbid and its Surroundings, 1850-1928]. Amman: Jamiʿat Al al-Bayt, 1995.

Al-ʿAkash, Nasim Muhammad. *Al-ʿAshaʾir al-Urdunniyya fil-Madi wal-Hadir* [The Jordanian Tribes in the Past and Present]. 2 Vols. Al-Zarqaʾ: Dar al-ʿAkash, 1997.

Alon, Yoav. "Tribal Shaykhs and the Limits of British Imperial Rule in Transjordan, 1920-1946," *The Journal of Imperial and Commonwealth History* 32 (2004), pp. 69-92.

——"The Tribal System in the Face of the State-Formation Process: Mandatory Transjordan, 1921-46," *International Journal of Middle East Studies* 37 (2005), pp. 213-240.

——"The Balqaʾ Revolt: Tribes and Early State-Building in Transjordan," *Die Welt Des Islams* 46 (2006), pp. 7-42.

Al Rasheed, Madawi. *Politics in an Arabian Oasis: The Rashidi Tribal Dynasty.* London, I.B. Tauris, 1991.

Amadouny, Vartan M. "Infrastructure Development under the British Mandate," in Eugene L. Rogan and Tariq Tell. Eds. *Village, Steppe and State: The Social Origins of Modern Jordan.* London: British Academic Press, 1994, pp. 128-161.

Amawi, Abla M. "The Consolidation of the Merchant Class in Transjordan during the Second World War," in Eugene L. Rogan and Tariq Tell. Eds. *Village, Steppe and State: The Social Origins of Modern Jordan.* London: British Academic Press, 1994, pp. 162-186.

Anderson, Benedict. *Imagined Communities: Reflections on the Rise and Spread of Nationalism.* 2nd Edn. London: Verso, 1991.

Antoun, Richard T. "Civil Society, Tribal Process, and Change in Jordan: An Anthropological View," *International Journal of Middle East Studies* 32 (2000), pp. 441-463.

Ashton, Nigel J. "'A "Special Relationship" Sometimes in Spite of Ourselves:' Britain and Jordan, 1957-1973," *The Journal of Imperial and Commonwealth History* 33 (2005), pp. 221-244.

Ayubi, Nazih N. *Over-stating the Arab State: Politics and Society in the Middle East.* London: I.B. Tauris, 1995.

Al-Bakhit, Muhammad ʿAdnan. "Mudhakkirat al-Duktur Jamil Faʾiq al-Tutanji" [Memoirs of Dr. Jamil Faʾiq al-Tutanji], *Dirasat al-ʿUlum al-Tibbiyya* 12 (1985), pp. 16-19.

——Ed. *Al-Wathaʾiq al-Hashimiyya, Awraq ʿAbdullah bin al-Husayn, Volume X: Al-ʿAlaqat al-Urdunniyya-al-Suʿudiyya, 1925-1951* [The Hashemite Documents, the Papers of Abdullah bin al-Husayn: Jordanian-Saudi Relations]. 2 pts. Amman: Jamiʿat Al al-Bayt, 1997.

——Ed. *Al-Wathaʾiq al-Hashimiyya, Awraq ʿAbdullah bin al-Husayn, Volume XVI: Al-ʿAshaʾir al-Urdunniyya, 1921-1951* [The Hashemite Documents, the Papers of Abdullah bin al-Husayn: The Jordanian Tribes, 1921-1951]. 3 pts. Amman: Jamiʿat Al al-Bayt, 2001.

Bani Yasin, Raslan and Yusuf al-Rubaʿi. *Al-Adab al-Urdunni al-Manshur fi Sahifat Al-Jazira al-Sadira fi ʿAmman bi-Taʾrikh 1939-1954* [Jordanian Literature in the Pages of the Newspaper *Al-Jazira*, 1939-1954]. Irbid: Jamiʿat al-Yarmuk, 1986.

Baram, Amatzia. "Neo-Tribalism in Iraq: Saddam Hussein's Tribal Policies, 1991-6," *International Journal of Middle East Studies* 29 (1997), pp. 1-31.

Bashir, Sulayman. *Judhur al-Wisaya al-Urdunniyya* [The Roots of the Jordanian Trusteeship].

Jerusalem: n.p., 1980.

Batatu, Hanna. *The Old Social Classes and the Revolutionary Movements of Iraq.* Princeton: Princeton University Press, 1978.

Beaumont, Roger. *Sword of the Raj: The British Army in India, 1747-1947.* Indianapolis: The Bobbs-Merrill Company, 1977.

Ben-Dor, Gabriel. *State and Conflict in the Middle East.* Boulder: Westview Press, 1985.

Bocco, Riccardo and Tariq M. M. Tell. "*Pax Britannica* in the Steppe: British Policy and the Transjordanian Bedouin," in Eugene L. Rogan and Tariq Tell. Eds. *Village, Steppe and State: The Social Origins of Modern Jordan.* London: British Acadmic Press, 1994, pp. 108-127.

——"Frontières, tribus et Etat(s) en Jordanie orientale à l'époque du Mandat," *Maghreb-Machrek* 147 (1995), pp. 26-47.

Brown, Judith and Wm. Roger Louis. Eds. *The Oxford History of the British Empire, Volume IV: The Twentieth Century.* Oxford: Oxford University Press, 1999.

Cain P. J. and A. G. Hopkins. *British Imperialism: Volume II: Crisis and Deconstruction 1914-1990.* London: Longman, 1993.

Caton, Steven C. "Anthropological Theories of Tribe and State Formation in the Middle East: Ideology and the Semiotics of Power," in Philip S. Khoury and Joseph Kostiner. Eds. *Tribes and State Formation in the Middle East.* Los Angeles: I.B. Tauris, 1991, pp. 74-108.

Cell, John W. "Colonial Rule," in Judith Brown and Wm. Roger Louis. Eds. *The Oxford History of the British Empire, Volume IV: The Twentieth Century.* Oxford: Oxford University Press, 1999, pp. 237-243.

Chaudhry, Kiren Aziz. *The Price of Wealth: Economies and Institutions in the Middle East.* Ithaca and London: Cornell University Press, 1997.

Clauss, Ludwig Ferdinand. *Als Beduine unter Beduinen.* 3rd Rev. Edn. Freiburg: Verlag Herder, 1954.

Cohen, Mendel. *Be-Hatsar ha-Melekh ʿAbdullah* [At King Abdullah's Court]. Tel-Aviv: ʿAm ʿOved, 1980.

Dann, Uriel. *Studies in the History of Transjordan, 1920-1949: The Making of a State.* Boulder: Westview Press, 1984.

——*King Hussein and the Challenge of Arab Radicalism: Jordan, 1955-1967.* Oxford: Oxford University Press, 1989.

Dawn, Ernest C. *From Ottomanism to Arabism: Essays on the Origins of Arab Nationalism.* Urbana, IL: University of Illinois Press, 1978.

Dawud, Jurj Farid Tarif. *Al-Salt wa-Jiwaruha, 1864-1921* [Al-Salt and its Surroundings, 1864-1921]. Amman: Bank al-Aʿmal, 1994.

Dhahir, Masʿud. *Al-Mashriq al-ʿArabi al-Muʿasir min al-Badawa ila al-Dawla al-Haditha* [The Modern Arab Mashriq from Pastoralism to the Modern State]. Beirut: Maʿhad al-Inmaʾ al-ʿArabi, 1986.

Dodge, Toby. *An Arabian Prince, English Gentlemen and the Tribes East to the River Jordan: Abdullah and the Creation and Consolidation of the Transjordanian State.* London: SOAS, 1994.

——*Inventing Iraq: The Failure of Nation Building and a History Denied.* NY: Columbia University Press, 2003.

Dresch, Paul. *Tribes, Government and History in Yemen.* Oxford: Clarendon Press, 1989.

Eickelman, Dale F. *The Middle East and Central Asia: An Anthropological Approach* 3rd Edn. Upper Saddle River (NJ): Prentice-Hall, 1998.

Eilat, Eliyahu. *Shivat Tsiyon ve-ʿArav* [The Return to Zion and Arabia]. Tel-Aviv: Dvir, 1971.

Epstein [Eilat], Eliyahu. "Be-Artsot Hamizrah" [In the Orient Countries], *Yarhon Ahdut ha-ʿAvoda* 13 (1931), pp. 117-119, 467-474.

——"The Bedouin of Transjordan: Their Social and Economic Problems," *Journal of the*

Royal Central Asian Society 25 (1938), pp. 228-236.

Al-Fayiz, Miflih al-Nimr. *ʿAshaʾir Bani Sakhr: Taʾrikh wa-Mawaqif hata Sanat 1950* [The Bani Sakhr Tribes: History and Positions until 1950]. Amman: Matabiʿ al-Quwwat al-Musallaha, 1995.

Fischbach, Michael Richard. "British Land Policy in Transjordan," in Eugene L. Rogan and Tariq Tell. Eds. *Village, Steppe and State: The Social Origins of Modern Jordan*. London: British Academic Press, 1994, pp. 80-107.

——*State, Society and Land in Jordan*. Leiden: Brill, 2000.

Gelber, Yoav. *Jewish –Transjordanian Relations, 1921-1948*. London: Frank Cass, 1997.

Gelvin, James L. *Divided Loyalties: Nationalism and Mass Politics in Syria at the Close of Empire*. Berkeley: University of California Press, 1998.

Ghanayim, Zuhayr. *Al-Khabar al-Hashimi fi Jaridat Filastin* [The Hashemite News in the Newspaper *Filastin*]. Amman: Al-Bank al-Ahali al-Urdunni, 1997.

Glubb, John Bagot. "The Economic Situation of the Transjordanian Tribes," *Journal of the Royal Central Asian Society* 25 (1938), pp. 448-459.

——*The Story of the Arab Legion*. London: Hodder&Stoughton, 1948.

Gubser, Peter. *Politics and Change in Al-Karak, Jordan*. London: Oxford University Press, 1973.

Haghanduqa, Muhammad Khayr. *Mirza Basha Wasfi: Kitab Wathaʾiqi* [Mirza Pasha Wasfi: Documented Book]. Amman: Al-Jamʿiyya al-ʿIlmiyya al-Malakiyya, 1985.

Heussler, Robert. *Yesterday's Rulers: The Making of the British Colonial Service*. Syracuse: Syracuse University Press, 1963.

Bin al-Husayn, Abdullah. *Mudhakkirati* [My Memoirs]. Jerusalem: Bayt al-Quds, 1945.

——*Al-Athar al-Kamila lil-Malik ʿAbdullah bin al-Husayn* [The Complete Works of King Abdullah bin al-Husayn]. 2nd Edn. Beirut: Al-Dar al-Muttahida lil-Nashr, 1979.

——*Al-Khayl al-Asaʾil* [Pedigree Horses]. 2nd Edn. Amman: Matbaʿat al-Tawfiq, 1983.

Hyam, Ronald. "The British Empire in the Edwardian Era," in Judith Brown and Wm. Roger Louis. Eds. *The Oxford History of the British Empire, Volume IV: The Twentieth Century*. Oxford: Oxford University Press, 1999, pp. 47-63.

Jarvis, Major C. S. *Arab Command: The Biography of Lieutenant Colonel F. W. Peake Pasha*. London: Hutchinson, 1942.

Jureidini, Paul A. and R. D. McLaurin. *Jordan: The Impact of Social Change on the Role of the Tribes*. NY: Praeger Press, 1984.

Kedourie, Elie. *The Chatham House Version and other Middle Eastern Studies*. London: Weidenfeld and Nicolson, 1970.

Al-Khawalda, ʿUlyan Rizq. *Al-Qawl al-Hasan fi Tahqiq Ansab Bani Hasan* [The Good Saying in the Inquiry into the Genealogy of the Bani Hasan] (no further details).

Khoury, Philip S. "The Tribal Shaykh, French Tribal Policy, and the Nationalist Movement in Syria between Two World Wars," *Middle East Studies* 18 (1982), pp. 180-193.

——*Syria and the French Mandate: The Politics of Arab Nationalism, 1920-1945*. Princeton: Princeton University Press, 1987.

——and Joseph Kostiner. "Introduction: Tribes and the Complexities of State Formation in the Middle East," in Idem Eds. *Tribes and State Formation in the Middle East*. Los Angeles: I.B. Tauris, 1991, pp. 1-22.

Khrisat, Muhammad ʿAbd al-Qadir. *Al-Urdunniyyun wal-Qadaya al-Wataniyya wal-Qawmiyya* [The Jordanians and National and pan-Arab Issues] Amman: Al-Jamiʿa al-Urdunniyya, 1991.

Kirkbride, Alec Seath. *A Crackle of Thorns*. London: John Murray, 1956.

Kirk-Greene, Anthony. *Britain's Imperial Administrators, 1858-1966*. London: Macmillan Press, 2000.

Klieman, Aaron S. *Foundations of British Policy in the Arab World: The Cairo Conference of 1921*. Baltimore and London: The Johns Hopkins Press, 1970.

Konikoff, A. *Transjordan: An Economic Survey*. Jerusalem: The Jewish Agency, 1943.
Kostiner, Joseph. "The Hashemite 'Tribal Confederacy' of the Arab Revolt, 1916-1917," in
    E. Ingram. Ed. *National and International Politics in the Middle East: Essays in Honour of
    Elie Kedourie*. London: Frank Cass, 1986, pp. 126-143.
——*The Making of Saudi Arabia, 1916-1936: From Chieftaincy to Monarchical State*. NY
    and Oxford: Oxford University Press, 1993.
Al-Kurdi, Muhammad ʿAli al-Sawirki. *Taʾrikh al-Salt wal-Balqaʾ* [The History of al-Salt and
    the Balqaʾ]. Amman: Dar ʿAmmar, 1998.
Lancaster, William. *The Rwalla Today*. Cambridge: Cambridge University Press, 1981.
Layne, Linda L. *Home and Homeland: The Dialogics of Tribal and National Identities in
    Jordan*. Princeton: Princeton University Press, 1994.
Lewis, Norman. *Nomads and Settlers in Syria and Jordan, 1800-1980*. Cambridge:
    Cambridge University Press, 1987.
Lias, Godfrey. *Glubb's Legion*. London: Evans bros., 1956.
Louis, Wm. Roger. *The British Empire in the Middle East, 1945-1951: Arab Nationalism, the
    United States and Postwar Imperialism*. Oxford: Oxford University Press, 1984.
——"Introduction," in Robin W. Winks. Ed. *The Oxford History of the British Empire,
    Volume V: Historiography*. Oxford: Oxford University Press, 1999, pp. 1-42.
Luke, Sir Harry and Edward Keith-Roach. *The Handbook of Palestine and Transjordan*.
    London: Macmillan, 1934.
Lunt, James. *Glubb Pasha: A Biography*. London: Harvill Press, 1984.
Al-Madi, Munib and Sulayman Musa. *Taʾrikh al-Urdunn fil-Qarn al-ʿIshrin, 1900-1959* [The
    History of Jordan in the Twentieth Century, 1900-1959]. 2nd Edn. Amman: Maktabat
    al-Muhtasib, 1988.
Al-Majali, ʿAbd al-Salam. *Rihlat al-ʿUmr: Min Bayt al-Shaʿr ila Suddat al-Hukm* [A Life
    Journey: From the Tent to the Seat of Government]. 2nd Edn. Beirut: Sharikat al-
    Matbuʿat lil-Tawziʿ wal-Nashr, 2004.
Marx, Emanuel. "The Tribe as a Unit of Subsistence: Nomadic Pastoralism in the Middle
    East," *American Anthropologist* 79 (1977), pp. 343-363.
——"Economic Change among Pastoral Nomads in the Middle East," in Idem and A.
    Shmueli. Eds. *The Changing Bedouin*. New Brunswick, 1984, pp. 1-15.
Mason, Philip. *The Men Who Ruled India*. London: Pan Books, 1985.
Massad, Joseph A. *Colonial Effects: The Making of National Identity in Jordan*. NY: Columbia
    University Press, 2001.
Migdal, Joel S. *Strong Societies and Weak States: State-Society Relations and State Capabilities in
    the Third World*. Princeton: Princeton University Press, 1988.
Mishal, Shaul. *East Bank/West Bank: The Palestinians in Jordan, 1949-1967*. New Haven: Yale
    University Press, 1978.
Mitchell, Timothy. *Colonizing Egypt*. NY: Cambridge University Press, 1988.
——"The Limits of the State: Beyond Statist Approaches and their Critics," *American
    Political Science Review* 85 (1991), pp. 77-96.
Monroe, Elizabeth. *Philby of Arabia*. London: Faber&Faber, 1973.
Morris, J. *Farewell the Trumpets: An Imperial Retreat*. Harmondsworth: Penguin, 1978.
Al-Mufti, Saʿid. "Saʿid al-Mufti Yatadhakkaru" [Saʿid al-Mufti Remembers], 13 pts, *Al-
    Dustur* (Amman), 21 February – 22 May 1976.
Mundy, Martha. "Village Land and Individual Title: *Mushaʿ* and Ottoman Land Registration
    in the ʿAjlun District," in Eugene L. Rogan and Tariq Tell. Eds. *Village, Steppe and State:
    The Social Origins of Modern Jordan*. London: British Academic Press, 1994, pp. 58-79.
Musa, Sulayman. *Wujuh wa-Malamih: Sura Shakhsiyya li-baʿd Rijal al-Siyasa wal-Qalam*
    [Prominent Personalities: Personal Portraits of some of the Men of Politics and the Pen].
    Amman: Wizarat al-Thaqafa wal-Shabab, 1980.
——*ʿAmman ʿAsimat al-Urdunn* [Amman the Capital of Jordan]. Amman: Manshurat

li-Amanat al-ʿAsima, 1985.

——*Imarat Sharq al-Urdunn: Nashaʾtuha wa-Tatawwuruha fi Rubʿ Qarn, 1921-1946* [The Emirate of Transjordan: Its Growth and Development in a Quarter of a Century, 1921-1946]. Amman: Lajnat Taʾrikh al-Urdunn, 1990.

——*Min Taʾrikhina al-Hadith* [From our Recent History]. Amman: Lajnat Taʾrikh al-Urdunn, 1994.

——"King Abdullah: A Centennial Salute," in Idem. *Cameos: Jordan and Arab Nationalism*. Amman: Ministry of Culture, 1997, pp. 123-135.

—— "Harakat al-Balqaʾ - Aylul 1923" [The Balqaʾ Movement, September 1923], 3 pts. *Al-Raʾy* (Amman), 4,5, 6 October 1997.

——*Ayam La Tunsa: Al-Urdunn fi Harb 1948* [Unforgettable Days: Jordan in the 1948 War]. 2nd Edn. Amman: Matabiʿ al-Quwwat al-Musallaha, 1998.

Naʿman, H. *Abdullah Amir ʿEver ha-Yarden* [Abdullah the Prince of Transjordan]. Jerusalem: Qiryat Sefer, 1942.

Nevo, Joseph. *King Abdallah and Palestine: A Territorial Ambition*. Basingstoke: Macmillan, 1996.

Oppenheim, Max Adrian Simon. *Die Beduinen*. Volume II. Leipzig: Otto Harrassowitz, 1943.

Owen, Roger. *State, Power and Politics in the Making of the Middle East*. London: Routledge, 1992.

Peake, F. G. "Trans-Jordan," *Journal of the Royal Central Asian Society* 23 (1939), pp. 375-396.

——*A History of Jordan and its Tribes*. Coral Gables, Florida: University of Miami Press, 1958.

Qasus, ʿAwda. *Al-Qadaʾ al-Badawi* [Bedouin Law]. Amman: n.p., 1936.

Rashid, ʿAbdullah. *Al-Katatib wa-Nuzumuha al-Taqlidiyya fi Madinat ʿAmman, 1900-1958* [The *Katatib* in Amman and their Traditional Methods, 1900-1958]. Amman: Dar al-Yanabiʿ, 1993.

Reimer, Michael J. "Becoming Urban: Town Administration in Transjordan," *International Journal of Middle East Studies* 37 (2005), pp. 189-211.

Robins, Philip. *A History of Jordan*. Cambridge: Cambridge University Press, 2004.

Rogan, Eugene L. "Bringing the State Back: The Limits of Ottoman Rule in Jordan, 1840-1910," in Eugene L. Rogan and Tariq Tell. Eds. *Village, Steppe and State: The Social Origins of Modern Jordan*. London: British Academic Press, 1994, pp. 32-57.

——"The Making of a Capital: Amman, 1918-1928," in Jean Hannoyer and Seteney Shami. Eds. *Amman: The City and its Society*. Beirut: Cermoc, 1996, pp. 89-107.

——*Frontiers of the State in the Late Ottoman Empire: Transjordan, 1850-1921*. Cambridge: Cambridge University Press, 1999.

Royle, Trevor. *Glubb Pasha*. London: Little, Brown and Company, 1992.

Salibi, Kamal. *The Modern History of Jordan*. London: I.B. Tauris, 1993.

Salman, Bulus. *Khamsa Aʿwam fi Sharqi al-Urdunn* [Five Years in Transjordan] 2nd Edn. Amman: Al-Dar al-Ahliyya, 1989.

Al-Sawariyya, Nawfan Raja al-Hamud. *ʿAmman wa-Jiwaruha khilal al-fatra 1864-1921* [Amman and its Surroundings, 1864-1921]. Amman: Bank al-Aʿmal, 1996.

Scott, James C. *Seeing Like a State*. New Haven and London: Yale University Press, 1998.

Seabrook, W. B. *Adventures in Arabia*. London: G.G. Hurrap, 1928.

Al-Shahbandar, ʿAbd al-Rahman. *Mudhakkirat al-Duktur ʿAbd al-Rahman al-Shahbandar* [Memoirs of Dr. ʿAbd al-Rahman al-Shahbandar]. Beirut: Dar al-Irshad, 1968.

Sharkey, Heather J. *Living with Colonialism: Nationalism and Culture in the Anglo-Egyptian Sudan*. Berkeley: California University Press, 2003.

Shlaim, Avi. *Collusion across the Jordan*. Oxford: Oxford University Press, 1988.

Shryock, Andrew. "The Rise of Nasir al-Nims: A Tribal Commentary on Being and

Becoming a Shaykh," *Journal of Anthropological Research* 46 (1990), pp. 153-176.

——*Nationalism and the Genealogical Imagination: Oral History and Textual Authority in Tribal Jordan.* Berkeley: California University Press, 1997.

——and Sally Howell, "'Ever a Guest in our House': The Amir Abdullah, Shaykh Majid al-Adwan and the Practice of Jordanian House Politics, Remembered by Umm Sultan, the Widow of Majid," *International Journal of Middle East Studies* 33 (2001), pp. 247-269.

Shwadran, Benjamin. *Jordan: A State of Tension.* NY: Council for Middle Eastern Affairs, 1959.

Susser, Asher. *On Both Banks of the Jordan: A Political Biography of Wasfi al-Tall.* Ilford: Frank Cass, 1994.

Tal, Lawrence. *Politics, the Military and National Security in Jordan, 1955-1967.* Basingstoke: Palgrave Macmillan, 2002.

Tall, Tariq. "The Politics of Rural Policy in East Jordan, 1920-1989," in Martha Mundy and Basim Musallam. Eds. *The Transformation of Nomadic Society in the Arab East.* Cambridge: Cambridge University Press, 2000, pp. 90-98.

Tapper, Richard. "Anthropologists, Historians, and Tribespeople on Tribe and State Formation in the Middle East," in Philip S. Khoury and Joseph Kostiner. Eds. *Tribes and State Formation in the Middle East.* Los Angeles: I.B. Tauris, 1991, pp. 48-73.

——*Frontier Nomads of Iran: A Political and Social History of the Shahsevan.* Cambridge: Cambridge University Press, 1997.

Al-Tarawna, Muhammad Salim. *Ta'rikh Mintaqat al-Balqa' wa-Maʿan wal-Karak, 1864-1919* [The History of the Balqa', Maʿan and Karak Areas, 1864-1919]. Amman: Wizarat al-Thaqafa, 1992.

Teitelbaum, Joshua. *The Rise and Fall of the Hashemite Kingdom of Arabia.* London: Hurst, 2001.

Tidrick, Kathryn. *Heart-beguiling Araby.* Cambridge: Cambridge University Press, 1981.

——*Empire and the English Character.* London: I.B. Tauris, 1990.

Tignor, Robert. *Modernization and British Colonial Rule in Egypt, 1882-1914.* Princeton: Princeton University Press, 1966.

Trench, Charles Chenevix. *The Frontier Scouts.* London: Jonathan Cape, 1985.

ʿUbaydat, Mahmud. *Al-Urdunn fil-Ta'rikh* [Jordan in History]. Tarablus (Lubnan): Manshurat Jadwa Bres, 1992.

Al-ʿUzayzat, Yusuf Salim al-Shuwayhat. *Al-ʿUzayzat fi Madaba* [The ʿUzayzat in Madaba, n.d., n.p].

Vatikiotis, P. J. *Politics and the Military in Jordan: A Study of the Arab Legion, 1921-1957.* London: Frank Cass, 1967.

Walpole, G. F. "Land Problems in Transjordan," *Journal of the Royal Central Asian Society* 35 (1948), pp. 53-65.

Wasserstein, Bernard. *The British in Palestine: The Mandatory Government and the Arab-Jewish Conflict, 1917-1929.* London: Royal Historical Society, 1978.

Wilson, Mary C. *King Abdullah, Britain and the Making of Jordan.* Cambridge: Cambridge University Press, 1987.

Zirikli, Khayr al-Din. *ʿAman fi ʿAmman* [Two Years in Amman]. Cairo: Al-Matbaʿa al-ʿArabiyya, 1925.

Zubaida, Sami. *Islam, the People and the State.* 2nd Edn. London: I.B. Tauris, 1993.

INDEX